Hurricanes of 245 Squadron Aldergrove,
November 19 1940 (Via E.A. Cromie).

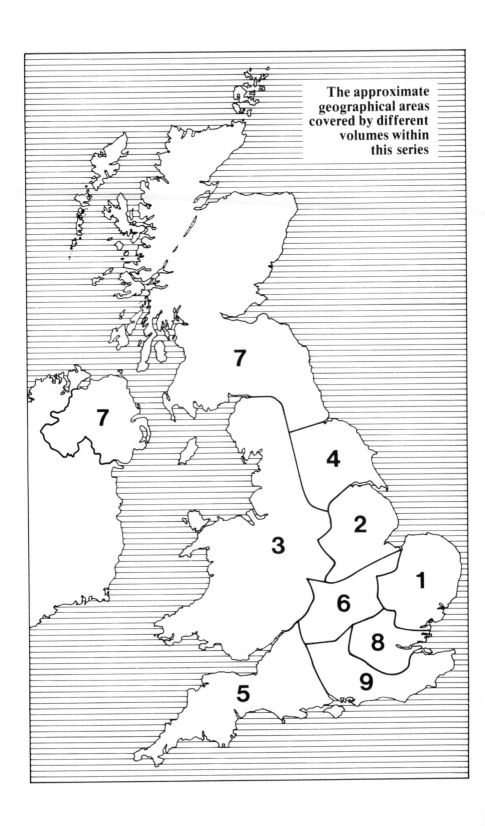

The approximate
geographical areas
covered by different
volumes within
this series

ACTION STATIONS

7. Military airfields of Scotland, the North-East and Northern Ireland

David J. Smith

 Patrick Stephens Limited

Title Page *Harvard and Dutch Navy sailors, Fearn March 1946* (Mrs E. Hall).

First published 1983
Second edition 1989

British Library Cataloguing in Publication Data

Smith, David J. (David John), *1943—*
    Action stations. — 2nd ed.
    7 : Military airfields of Scotland, the North-East
    and Northern Ireland.
    1. Great Britain. Great Britain. Royal Air Force.
    Aerodromes, history
    I. Title
    358.4'17'0941

    ISBN 1-85260-309-7

Patrick Stephens Limited is part of the Thorsons Publishing Group, Wellingborough, Northamptonshire, NN8 2RQ, England

Printed in Great Britain by Mackays of Letchworth, Hertfordshire

10 9 8 7 6 5 4 3 2

Contents

Introduction

At the beginning of the Second World War, Scotland saw a number of air war 'firsts' for this conflict—the first German bomber shot down, the first bombs on British soil, the first civilian killed by an enemy bomb, the first enemy capital ship sunk (by aircraft from an Orkney airfield)—the list goes on. The Battle of Orkney was fought and won long before the Battle of Britain began. The Luftwaffe never again attacked the Fleet Anchorage in Scapa Flow with any determination. North-east England, too, had its air battles in the early months and many a bomber was sent to destruction by the defending squadrons during the night blitzes on Tyneside and the Clyde.

Coastal Command units were in action from Scotland on the first day of the war and were to be so on the last. In the early days, the Hampdens and Beauforts harried German shipping, but it was the Beaufighters and Mosquitoes which created the greatest havoc in Scandinavian waters. With their formidable armament, it really was a case of 'the Wrath of the North' being returned from whence it came. Less dramatic, but just as effective, were the night sorties in the same area by Halifaxes late in the war, assisted by flares and radar.

From Northern Ireland the tide of the U-boat war was turned by the long-range Liberators and the flying boats. Scotland and the Province also fielded a host of support units without which the operational squadrons of the RAF could not function. They ranged from Air-Sea Rescue to Meteorological Reconnaissance Squadrons, and included flying training units from basic, to advanced to OTU (Operational Training Units), not forgetting all the specialised organisations like Flying Instructors Schools, Navigation and Air Gunners Schools and Coastal Command Development Units. The list is considerable and each unit played its part in ultimate victory.

Much of the material within these pages comes from official documents held by the Public Record Office and Royal Air Force Museum. For further information on the early days of aviation in Scotland and Ulster, the reader is recommended to sample John Corlett's book *Aviation in Ulster* and the Central Scotland Aviation Group's *Scotland Scanned*.

A book like this one cannot be written without a tremendous amount of help from friends and well-wishers, particularly Ernie Cromie of the Ulster Aviation Society who gave me a conducted tour of all the airfield sites in the Province and

Left *Avengers being unloaded from an escort carrier at Sydenham's wharf late in 1944. A variety of hangar types are discernible in the background* (Via M.J. Burrow).

provided other valuable assistance, including plans. Credit for supplying the information on First World War sites must go to Brian Martin and for the Scottish airfield plans to Aldon Ferguson. As with *Action Stations 3**, John Huggon came up with much background detail and photographs for his native Solway area and Roy Bonser gave unstinting aid as usual.

Thanks go to many others who helped in various ways, but particularly to: 655 Squadron, Army Air Corps, Captain John G. Smith, Chaz Bowyer, Dr A.A. Duncan, Chris Thomas, R.D. Cooling, Ray Sturtivant, Jack Harris, Frank Neal, Joe Relph, Arthur Stamper, Roelof de Laat, Peter H.T. Green, Harry Holmes, Alec Lumsden, V.L. Winterburn, M.J. Burrows, Chris Ashworth, Julian C. Temple, Jim Ferguson, H. Quinton, Dr J.E. Collins, and last, but not least, John Finch-Davies, who accompanied me on a marathon tour of Scottish airfields, and Geraldine Fox, who investigated RAF Morpeth on my behalf with all the enthusiasm that only she can muster!

David J. Smith
Bebington
November 1982

Military airfields of Wales and the North-West by David J. Smith (Patrick Stephens Ltd).

Glossary

AACU Anti-Aircraft Co-operation Unit
AAP Aircraft Acceptance Park
ADG Air Depot Group
ADGB Air Defence of Great Britain
AFSC Air Force Service Command (USAAF)
AFTS Advanced Flying Training School
AGS Air Gunnery School
AHU Aircraft Holding Unit
AMWD Air Ministry Works Department
ANS Air Navigation School
AONS Air Observer Navigation School
AOP Air Observation Post
AOS Air Observer School
APC Armament Practice Camp
A/S Anti-submarine
ASR Air-Sea Rescue
ASU Aircraft Storage Unit
ASV Air-to-Surface Vessel (Radar)
ATA Air Transport Auxiliary
ATC Air Training Corps
ATG Air Transport Group
ATS Armament Training Station
BABS Blind Approach Beam System
BAD Base Air Depot
BAT Flight Blind Approach Training Flight
BEA British European Airways
BEF British Expeditionary Force
BG Bomb Group (USAAF)
B&GS Bombing and Gunnery School
BTU Bombing Trials Unit
CANS Civil Air Navigation School
CCDU Coastal Command Development Unit
CCFIS Coastal Command Flying Instructors School
CCRC Combat Crew Replacement Centre
CGS Central Gunnery School
Circus Fighter-escorted daylight bombing attacks against short-range targets

CO Commanding Officer
CPF Coastal Patrol Flight
CTW Combat Training Wing
DI Daily Inspection
EFTS Elementary Flying Training School
EGS Elementary Gliding School
ELG Emergency Landing Ground
E&RFTS Elementary and Reserve Flying Training School
FAA Fleet Air Arm
FBFU Flying Boat Fitting Unit
FBSU Flying Boat Servicing Unit
FBTS Flying Boat Training Squadron
FIS Flying Instructors' School
FLS Fighter Leaders' School
FPP Ferry Pilots Pool
FRU Fleet Requirements Unit
FS Ferrying Squadron (USAAF)
FTS Flying Training School
FTU Ferry Training Unit
Gee Medium-range radio aid to navigation and target identification with ground transmitters and airborne receiver
GR General Reconnaissance
HFDF High Frequency Direction Finding
HQSFS Headquarters Service Ferry Squadron
HSL High Speed Launch
IFF Identification, Friend or Foe
LTU Loran Training Unit
MADDL Mirror Aerodrome Dummy Deck Landing
MAEE Marine Aircraft Experimental Establishment
MAP Ministry of Aircraft Production
MoA Ministry of Aviation
MU Maintenance Unit
(O)AFU (Observer) Advanced Flying Unit
OAPU Overseas Aircraft Preparation Unit

(O)FIS   (Operational) Flying Instructors School
ORB   Operations Record Book
OTU   Operational Training Unit
(P)AFU   (Pilot) Advanced Flying Unit
PRU   Photographic Reconnaissance Unit
PSP   Pierced Steel Plank
Q-Site   Decoy airfield
RAFNI   RAF in Northern Ireland
Ranger   Deep penetration flight to engage targets of opportunity
RFC   Royal Flying Corps
RFS   Refresher Flying School
RFU   Refresher Flying Unit
Rhubarb   Low level strike operation mounted in cloudy conditions against enemy fringe targets in occupied countries
RLG   Relief Landing Ground
RNAS   Royal Naval Air Station
Roadstead   Operations by fighters or bombers escorted by fighters to attack, by dive-bombing or at low level, ships either at sea or in harbour.
Rover   Armed reconnaissance against chance targets, usually shipping

RP   Rocket Projectile
RS   Reserve Squadron
SAL   Scottish Aviation Limited
SAR   Search and Rescue
Saracen Scheme   Plan under which each fighter OTU would be turned into an operational fighter squadron in the event of an invasion of this country
SBA   Standard Beam Approach
SFTS   Service Flying Training School
SLG   Satellite Landing Ground
SMT   Square Mesh Track
SOE   Special Operations Executive
SSS   Sub-Storage Site
TAG   Telegraphist Air Gunner
TBR   Torpedo Bomber Reconnaissance
TDS   Training Depot Station
TEU   Tactical Exercise Unit
TRS   Torpedo Refresher School
TS   Training Squadron
TT   Target Towing
TTU   Torpedo Training Unit
TWU   Tactical Weapons Unit
USAAF   United States Army Air Force
X-Raid   Approaching unidentified aircraft.

Origins

Scotland's first aviator was John Damien who leapt from the wall of Stirling Castle in 1507 with a pair of wings strapped to his arms. He was lucky to suffer nothing worse than a broken thigh and his excuse for the failure was that hens' feathers had been used in making the wings instead of eagles' feathers and hens were farmyard birds and not the soaring type. He did not, however, try it a second time!

Moving on a couple of centuries to 1784, it was a Scotsman, James Tytler, who became the first man to make a balloon ascent from British soil. It was one of the hot air variety, with a stove weighing 300 lb to provide the necessary heat, but was so uncontrollable when tried out at Edinburgh that Tytler abandoned his experiments.

The well-known Italian balloonist, Lunardi, was more successful later in 1784. He made a number of ascents in Scotland, culminating in a flight of 110 miles from Glasgow to Selkirk. After these pioneers there were very few other balloon flights in Scotland because of generally poor weather and the fact that it is impossible to go far from anywhere without landing in the sea.

In 1895/96 the English aviator, Percy Pilcher, made a number of pioneering glider flights from Wallacetown Ferry, near Cardross in Dunbartonshire. Powered flight was Pilcher's ultimate goal but his work was tragically cut short by a fatal crash after he had returned to England.

Scotland joined in the enthusiasm for aviation which spread across Europe in the late 1900s when it was realised that aeroplanes were a practical proposition. This interest resulted in the formation of the Scottish Aeronautical Society and flying meetings organised by this body at Lanark in 1910 and Scotstoun in 1914 drew large crowds. Two flying schools were formed in 1911 at Lanark Racecourse and Barrhead but both were short-lived.

In 1913, Scotland's first military airfield was prepared at Montrose and in the same year a naval seaplane base was set up at Cromarty. A second seaplane base was established at Dundee in April 1914. These three sites were swelled to a total of over 30 stations by the time the war ended, serving airships and kite balloons for observation, as well as sea- and landplanes. Scottish factories built over 2,000 aircraft under sub-contract, including the DH 9, BE 2C, FE 2b and Avro 504K.

The inter-war period was marked by drastic cuts in RAF strength and most of the wartime airfields closed. The swing to civil operations was slow at first in Scotland until Captain E.E. Fresson came on the scene in 1929. He started off as a 'barnstormer' giving air displays and joy rides all over Scotland, and it was not long before he realised the potential for air services to link the islands with the mainland.

While Fresson formed Highland Airways in 1933 to link Inverness with Orkney and Shetland, John Sword started Midland and Scottish Air Ferries Ltd the same year and spread out a network from Renfrew to the Western Isles. Overtaken by competition and financial difficulties, Midland and Scottish ceased operations in September 1934 having pioneered a number of routes which were flown subsequently by other companies such as Northern and Scottish Airways Ltd.

Some early flights with helicopters were made in Scotland in the 30s. The Glasgow firm of G. & J. Weir Ltd decided to set up an autogyro department to construct machines based on the Cierva patents. With the experience gained from building several autogyro models, the company turned its attention to helicopter design in 1937. The Weir W.5 was first flown at Dalrymple, Ayrshire on June 7 1938 and had the distinction of being the first helicopter to fly in Britain.

The results of many W.5 test flights led to the larger and more ambitious W.6 which flew in 1939. Two passengers were carried on its second flight, a remarkable achievement for its time. Unfortunately at this point development had to be discontinued because of heavy demands on the company's production capacity. Had the war not intervened, Britain might have led the world in the helicopter field.

Civil aviation in Scotland, as everywhere else in Britain, died suddenly the day war was declared. After a few weeks, during which the government formed the National Air Communications organisation, it was resurrected to operate a limited number of routes for official and military business and the carriage of vital supplies and mail. The NAC was replaced by the Associated Airways Joint Committee in June 1940 which grouped all the airlines (except Allied Airways, which had a separate contract in Scotland) into one unit.

In September 1939, Scotland had about 11 active military airfields; at the war's end there were 95. Long before the air battles in the South of England, the Battle of Orkney had been fought and won over the Fleet Anchorage in Scapa Flow. At one time Scapa had more barrage balloons than London. Judging by the complexity of the defences in the north, the military authorities must have considered invasion from this direction a distinct possibility. On March 8 1940 some bombs on the island of Hoy caused the first fatal casualties amongst British civilians.

The history of Scotland's airfields is linked inextricably with the development of both Coastal Command and the Fleet Air Arm, because it was from here and Northern Ireland that the U-boat war was fought and naval airmen were trained. Bomber Command made relatively few sorties from Scotland, mainly against *Tirpitz*, but their advanced bases were given longer runways, more dispersals and better facilities. The destruction of the *Tirpitz* was so important because she was a menace to British carriers, which could not be risked on prolonged operations at sea. Although she rarely left port, her value lay in continuing as a 'fleet in being'. After many attempts she was finally sunk by Lancasters from Scotland in November 1944.

Scottish airfields housed many of the training units so essential to wartime. There were also several flying boat bases and Prestwick became the main terminal for Trans-Atlantic aircraft deliveries. Most of the aerodromes hastily built at great expense were rapidly closed when the war ended. Some, however, were turned into regional airports, one of the few social benefits of the conflict.

Ulster's aviation history goes back as far as May 1824 with its first recorded balloon ascent. An engineer, Harry Ferguson, made the first heavier-than-air flights in the Province from Magilligan Strand. There was also Miss Lilian Bland, who built a biplane called the *May-Fly* to her own design, and flew it briefly in September 1910. For test runs, the 20 hp engine was fed with petrol from a whiskey bottle, through a borrowed ear trumpet. The noise she described as being 'like a cat fight on a very enlarged scale!'

There is no record of airfields anywhere in Ireland before 1917, when an increase in the RFC training programme required many new aerodromes. Sholto Douglas, a young pilot later to become Marshal of the Royal Air Force, was given the job of selecting eight sites in Ireland on which training schools could be established. The specification was simple—grass fields which would give good runs of about 500 to 600 yds in any direction. He set off in the early summer of 1917 in a BE 2C and picked such places as Collinstown (now Dublin Airport), Baldonnel and Aldergrove. Others included The Curragh, Fermoy and Gormanston.

There is some evidence to suggest that these and five more airfields scattered around Ireland had a secondary purpose of controlling the political situation there at that time. They were all very near the town from which they took their name and also came under 6th Brigade which was responsible for Home Defence.

Between the wars, Ulster saw visits by Amelia Earhart on a flight from Newfoundland in 1932, and by 24 Italian flying boats in 1933. Led by General Balbo, they moored in Lough Foyle during a flight from Rome to New York. Short and Harland Ltd were formed in 1936 and began to build the Bombay transport and Hereford bomber under sub-contract, pending the construction of their own designs.

There were still only three airfields in the Province when the war began— Aldergrove, Sydenham and Newtownards. The choice of sites was a routine duty of a branch of the Air Ministry founded in 1923 and known as the Airfields Board. In 1940, owing to Coastal Command's needs, the board was compelled to pay more than usual attention to Northern Ireland. Agents combed the Province for possible sites but it was not always rewarding. 'In County Armagh it has been found impossible to secure any suitable site . . . Several suggested sites in County Fermanagh are to be the subject of examination. County Tyrone is hilly and the outlook for the finding of a possible airfield site in that country is by no means promising.'

Despite the unsuitable terrain, damp climate and boggy soil, the board chose and approved seven new sites—Long Kesh, Maghaberry, Nutt's Corner, Ballykelly, Eglinton, Ballyhalbert and Kirkistown. In addition, SLGs (Satellite Landing Grounds) at St Angelo, Maydown, Langford Lodge, Ballywalter and Dundrum were found. Such was the shortage of sites that the first three were turned into full aerodromes.

Aldergrove, Limavady, Castle Archdale, Nutt's Corner and Ballykelly became Coastal Command's main operating bases until the end of the war, and their aircraft sank 29 U-boats. The VIIIth Air Force Composite Command formed in September 1942 to administer USAAF units expected to be based in

Ulster. Eventually most of the theatre training for newly arrived American combat crews was done here and the Base Air Depot at Langford Lodge helped support the VIIIth and IXth Air Forces on the mainland.

Few of Ulster's airfields remained open for long after the war and there are now only five active sites out of the one-time total of 26.

North-east England was notable in the First World War for the number of its landing grounds for Home Defence squadrons protecting the Tyneside industrial areas. They were usually just fields with rudimentary facilities, and flares to guide in the aircraft. Between the wars, a few permanent fighter stations were built and a string of training fields was constructed once the war started. With the exception of Newcastle and Sunderland Airports, they have all reverted to farmland with occasional use by private aircraft.

The air war and Anglo-Irish relations

To reach a better understanding of the conduct of air operations from Ulster in the Second World War, it is necessary to examine contemporary relations between Britain and Eire. During the First World War, Queenstown and Berehaven in the south of Ireland had been vital naval bases for convoy protection, and if the war had lasted much longer, airship and flying boat patrols would have begun from the new stations being built in 1918. The original Anglo-Irish Treaty of 1921 provided that, until such time as the Irish Free State could undertake her own defence, the responsibility would lie with His Majesty's Forces with access rights to specific harbours and other facilities. This meant of course that Irish neutrality was effectively disallowed.

Despite Winston Churchill's protests, the Anglo-Irish Agreement of 1938 relinquished the right to use the ports, a short-term political expediency. In September 1939 Eire declared her neutrality, mainly, it was said, as a protest at the partition of Ulster. The Irish ports thus became constitutionally out of the reach of the Admiralty. However, as the Germans overran more and more of Continental Europe, Prime Minister de Valera notified Churchill in May 1940 that Eire would fight if attacked by Germany and would, furthermore, call in Britain's help the moment it was needed. Churchill was sceptical about Eire's limited resources and divided internal sympathies. The bait of an early end to Partition, the one thing Eire really wanted, was held out in vague terms, if she would make common cause with Britain. De Valera, however, well aware of Churchill's traditional protective attitude to the Ulster Loyalists, did not trust him and ignored these overtures.

Contingency plans were drawn up by the Air Ministry on the assumption that Eire's neutrality was likely to be a short-lived affair. It was intended, therefore, when Eire had decided to join with Britain and political considerations permitted, to establish two fighter sector stations in that country for the defence of shipping and naval bases. Several squadrons, including 17 and 257, were earmarked to go to Eire, although they were not actually told this at the time. By December 1940 the planners envisaged an Irish Fighter Group composed of eight sectors covering the whole island. It was proposed that each sector station should be provided with facilities to accommodate up to three squadrons. Any reinforcements of permanent squadrons for Eire would be taken from British sectors in the first instance. Dowding had already said that these plans were based on false assumptions about the current and future allegiance of the Irish Government and people and he was proved right.

Meanwhile, in August 1940, temporary plans had been drawn up for use if the Germans invaded Eire. The two Battle squadrons at Sydenham (88 and 226) would move south and operate from Collinstown near Dublin, a Lysander squadron would go to The Curragh, and Baldonnel would be occupied by three Hurricane squadrons. However, the Commander-in-Chief of the German Navy, Admiral Raeder, had presented Hitler with his detailed findings on a possible invasion of Eire. These were not favourable because the cloud and fog prevalent there (Raeder's words) would make air cover unreliable. Thus it was at the beginning of 1941 that Britain and Germany, independently of each other, decided to respect Irish neutrality.

This did not, however, prevent Britain from requesting, and surprisingly being granted, the use of an access corridor over a strip of Eire territory between the Lough Erne flying boat base and the west coast, thus avoiding a long detour. The conditions were that the flight over Eire be at 'a good height' and that the arrangements be kept as secret as possible. The first British aircraft to use the corridor were Stranraers on February 6 1941. In August the permission was extended to include landplanes of the following types: Whitley, Wellington, Hudson, Blenheim, Beaufighter and Liberator. For rescue purposes the Eire authorities allowed a civilian-crewed trawler, the *Robert H. Hastie*, to operate from Killybegs.

This was the beginning of a pattern of co-operation with Britain which was far more friendly than strict neutrality should have allowed. British airmen landing in the south were allowed to slip back over the border, while Germans were interned. Irishmen were encouraged to enrol in the British forces and over 50,000 of them served during the war. Thousands more, of course, helped build the airfields on the mainland. When Belfast was heavily bombed in April and May 1941 de Valera sent firefighters to help. Dublin itself was bombed in error by the Luftwaffe on several occasions, a number of fatal casualties being sustained on May 30 1941.

During the 'Emergency', as the Second World War was referred to in Eire, 163 Allied and German aircraft are recorded as having crashed or force-landed in the Republic. All intrusions into Irish airspace were plotted in Central Control at Clondalkin near Dublin. In an attempt to persuade would-be violators to turn around, the Irish would broadcast the position, course and identification of intruders on a wide variety of radio frequencies. Unfortunately, this move more often than not brought swarms of British fighters into Irish airspace in search of prey! As a further reminder the word 'EIRE' was picked out in huge white letters at strategic points on the coastline!

Some of the strays were repaired and put into service with the Irish Air Corps, while many British aircraft were sent by road to the border and quietly handed back to the RAF. Later in the war, RAF salvage units were allowed free access to the Republic to retrieve crashed aircraft. Reversing the flow, an Irish pilot stole a Walrus amphibian and flew it to South Wales. After many adventures it now rests in the Fleet Air Arm Museum at Yeovilton! On another occasion, two RAF airmen under arrest and with no flying experience stole a Beaufighter, intending to fly it to Eire. Inevitably they crashed on take-off and were lucky to survive for the court martial.

The USA had not yet entered the war, but by April 1941 Roosevelt was authorising funds to construct bases in Scotland and Northern Ireland, believing that involvement was inevitable. In the autumn of 1941, Churchill asked the American President if he would station Air Corps units and an Armoured Division in Ulster to release British forces for duty elsewhere. Roosevelt made no promises at first but Pearl Harbour intervened and the first US troops landed in Belfast in January 1942 to be housed in camps already built under conditions of great secrecy.

Long before then, the Admiralty had written off the possibility of using the Eire ports and all convoys after July 1940 were routed round the north of Ireland. Cover was provided by air and naval bases in Ulster, which developed slowly as new airfields and long-range aircraft like the Liberator and Catalina entered service. When the USA entered the war it was expected that American fighters based at Ballyhalbert, Eglinton and Kirkistown would take over the entire air defence of Northern Ireland, a scheme known as *Shadow 82* to understudy 82 Group Fighter Command.

Although squadrons of the 52nd and 82nd Fighter Groups were stationed at Eglinton and Maydown for a short period, they soon went to North Africa and it was eventually decided to employ the Ulster bases for USAAF training and support and to leave defence with the RAF. Abandoned in May 1944 was a contingency plan to base 800 B-29s in Northern Ireland. It was really a fall-back scheme in case the airfields in England were threatened. Plans to extend many runways to the necessary 9,000 ft were shelved.

Thus it was that Ulster's airfields, badly sited and temporary as most of them were, played a vital role in winning the Battle of the Atlantic and in supporting the American bomber offensive. Without them it would have been almost impossible to bridge from Scotland and Wales the so-called Atlantic Gap.

Airfield defence

The events of 1940 and the sudden threat of invasion made airfields a prime target. The Air Staff calculated that fewer than 5,000 parachutists, temporarily paralysing the air defences by attacking seven vital aerodromes in south-east England, might pave the way for bomber raids and troop carrier landings in overwhelming force.

The RAF Regiment had yet to be formed, so ground defence was in the hands of Army detachments. Since there were so few firearms available, the RAF ground personnel equipped themselves with all sorts of improvised weapons. Churchill himself said in June 1940: 'Every man in RAF uniform ought to be armed with something—a rifle, a tommy-gun, a pistol, a pike or mace, and everyone, without exception, should do at least one hour's drill and practice every day. Each airman should have his place in the defence scheme. It must be understood by all ranks that they are expected to fight and die in the defence of their airfields. Every building which fits in with the scheme of defence should be prepared so that each has to be conquered one by one by the enemy's parachute or glider troops. In two or three hours the army will arrive . . . Every airfield should be a stronghold of fighting air-ground men and not the abode of uniformed civilians in the prime of life protected by detachments of soldiers.'

The *Pandah* Scheme enabled an airfield under attack to radio for help to a central control using a coded call sign. Details to be passed were approximate enemy strength, type, ie, infantry armoured cars or tanks or parachutists, and direction of approach. Army units could then be rushed to the scene.

With the German occupation of Norway, the Scottish airfields suddenly became vulnerable too. At Montrose in June 1940, for example, nine pillboxes were hastily built at strategic points on the perimeter, each designed to accommodate ten rifle men and one Lewis gunner. In addition, nine smaller machine-gun posts were constructed from which fire could be brought to bear on the landing ground. Fifty airmen were selected as 'para-shots'—marksmen who could pick off the descending parachutists.

The expected invasion never came, but by the beginning of 1941 most airfields were ringed with concrete defence posts, many of them of the familiar hexagonal design. At RAF Oakington, a pillbox with a mushroom-shaped head was developed, known as the Oakington Type Mk I. There was also a Mk 2 version and a number can still be seen around the country.

By April 1941, airfield defence was highly organised to cover three directions—upward, outward and inward. It consisted of small groups of posts, each group forming a locality. Dummy strong points were mixed with the real ones and the whole perimeter was strung with coils of barbed wire.

The scale of defences depended on an airfield's strategic importance. All stations, RLGs (Relief Landing Grounds) and satellites within 20 miles of selected ports were considered to be in Class 1 and were to be provided with pillboxes around the perimeter not less than half a mile apart and designed to overlook the airfield. A second series of pillboxes was sited to cover the approaches and dispersal points, making maximum use of natural cover for concealment. Rifle pits were to be sited around hangars and station buildings. At certain aerodromes these pits were developed into the elaborate Seagull Trench, a flattened W-shaped construction resembling, from above, a head-on view of a bird in flight. Light anti-aircraft weapons, mainly Bofors guns, were manned by RAF Regiment crews.

At Class 2 aerodromes, ie, those not strategically placed but having a responsibility to repel sea-borne attacks with bombers and fighters, there was a 25 per cent reduction in pillboxes for inward defence. For Class 3 aerodromes, a single ring of pillboxes with all-round fire capability was considered sufficient, but at some only barbed wire was provided.

The Pickett Hamilton retractable fort was a promising idea inspired in 1940 but failing to live up to expectations. By June 1941, a total of 170 had been installed at 59 airfields including Wick, Castletown, Evanton, Lossiemouth, Kinloss, Dalcross and Skeabrae. Further south, Peterhead, Dyce, Leuchars,

Left *Unusual multiple pillbox at Eglinton*

Right *Rudimentary pillbox on perimeter of Skeabrae* (J.C. Temple).

Perth and Drem also had them. By the time it was realised that they were virtually useless, 335 had been installed throughout Britain (and in many cases are probably still there).

The forts were placed on the landing area flush with the ground and able to bear a weight of 6–7 tons if an aircraft taxied over them. In the event of an attack they could be raised 3 ft above the ground by compressed air in about 15 seconds. Other versions were raised hydraulically or by counterbalance. Each was manned by two airmen with machine-guns who would keep watch through a manhole and only raise the fort when an attack was imminent.

This was all very well in theory but it would have been difficult to man the forts until our own flying operations had ceased and the crews would then have had to carry ammunition across an open space with no cover. The other major problem was water seepage and at many airfields they had to be pumped out continuously. Bomber Command considered them completely useless by 1942 and recommended that they not be installed at any more of its stations.

Defence was co-ordinated by a Battle HQ which, after some development, was standardised as the 11008/41 design for operational airfields and the smaller building for training fields (3329/41). There was, however, no hard and fast rule on this, as some satellites like Findo Gask had a 11008/41 type. They were not included in the original plans for a new airfield but sited by the local defence authorities with due regard for terrain and camouflage, usually being placed in a hedgeline for concealment.

The 11008/41 design was dominated by a 6 ft observation post 3 ft above the ground with an all-round view through a horizontal slot. The rest of the building was usually underground. How far depended on sub-surface water, and, if it projected very much, earth banks were provided. Its dimensions were approximately 21 ft by 8 ft with office, sleeping accommodation and a latrine, reached by a stairway. There was also an escape hatch to the rear of the observation position. The smaller type of building was entered only by a hatch and ladder, the small rooms being entirely underground. Because of their reinforced concrete construction, many of these Battle HQs have survived and quite dramatic they look, sometimes overgrown and staring out of a thicket. To explore them a torch is essential; not all are gutted, the one at Crosby-on-Eden, for example, has a white-painted ceiling with a compass rose marked out on it.

Mobile defence was furnished by a number of improvised vehicles. For instance, in June 1940, RAF Shawbury had a Morris six-wheel lorry on which were mounted two dustbin turrets with machine-guns on Scarff ring mountings. It was kept near the watch office and could be used instantly against enemy troop landings. Armoured cars known as Armadillos and armed with a 1½ lb gun and machine guns were hastily issued to aerodromes.

Air raid shelters of numerous types were provided, normally for small numbers of personnel, and were sited closely adjacent to the buildings they served. At the outbreak of war, they consisted mainly of locally constructed covered slit trenches, but they were soon superseded by pre-cast concrete shelters of the Stanton type each holding 25 or 50 men. Special types of sleeping shelter, each housing 18 or 33 men, heated and ventilated, were provided at aircraft dispersal points on fighter stations for the use of pilots at readiness. In the technical building areas, in order that taking shelter could be deferred until the last minute, and to avoid wasting time in shelters, traversed blast walls were built above ground, over which airmen could jump and shelter in a crouched position. Each shelter of this type gave protection for 10, 20 or 50 men depending on its size.

Stemming from the widespread fear that if war came gas would be used extensively, plans for decontamination centres were drawn up in 1937. In the event of such an attack on an aerodrome, the personnel would don their gas masks, but this would not protect them from the secondary effects of blistering gases. The decontamination centre was equipped with showers so that any toxic material could be washed off the skin, and contaminated clothing would be pushed through slots in the walls. A store of fresh clothing was kept in the centre and the airmen could thus be back on duty with little delay.

The block was fitted with comprehensive gas filtration and air ventilation, a pair of tall chimneys drawing fresh air from above the gas layer. The threat of air raids had so diminished by the end of 1943 that late war airfields were no longer provided with decontamination blocks.

Camouflage was a passive defence during airfield construction, hedges, ditches, trees and other natural features being retained as far as possible. Paths were provided in the most economical manner with local materials where possible. They were to be inconspicuous in colour and closely followed the lines of natural features such as hedges. If there were no hedges, long straight paths were to be avoided. When operational, the landing grounds were criss-crossed with painted hedges and tarmac runways were given a disruptive camouflage scheme to break up the outline. There were, too, the decoy airfield sites described elsewhere in these volumes.

The ultimate method of denying the airfield to the enemy was demolition. If the Germans had invaded, grass airfields would have been ploughed up systematically, marked runways being left until the last aircraft had taken off. Certain aerodromes in southern England were mined in 1940 and later in the war many runways were built with cavities so that Canadian pipe mines could be inserted underneath. This was to be confined to airfields within ten miles of the south coast between the Wash and Lands End, Scatsta being the only Scottish airfield so treated.

By April 1944, the threat from the enemy was so small that Churchill observed: 'I do not think we can afford to continue to maintain a special body of troops purely for the defence of aerodromes. The RAF Regiment was established at a time when invasion of this country was likely and when our life depended upon the security of our fighter aerodromes. Since then it has been reduced but the time has now come to consider whether the greater part of it should not be taken to reinforce the field formations of the army. I consider that at least 25,000 men should be transferred. (Two thousand went to the Guards in June 1944.) They would be much better employed there than loafing around over-crowded airfields warding off dangers which have ceased to threaten.'

Though they were never to be used in anger, most of the fixed defences still exist. The brick and reinforced concrete construction made them harder to demolish than huts and control towers and as they are usually in inconspicuous places they have generally been left alone or sealed to prevent access.

Landing grounds, airship stations and marine bases not covered in main text

Exact map references have been given where known. In come cases it has proved impossible to pinpoint the location exactly. This list is *not* exhaustive.

Alloa, Central. British Caudron Co flight testing *circa* 1917.

Alnwick, Northumbria. *See Stamford.*

Askernish, Western isles. *31/728240.* Northern & Scottish Airways 1934–39. Believed RAF ELG 1939–45.

Athlone, Eire. *Just NE of the town.* First World War LG.

Auldbar, Grampian. *54/57-76-.* RNAS balloons and airships, satellite of Montrose.

Baldonnel (Casement), Eire. Opened in 1918 as 23 TDS for day bomber training. This unit disbanded in 1919 but aerodrome continued to be used by various squadrons and is today the main base of the Irish Air Corps.

Ballyliffin, N Ireland. Sub-station of Luce Bay for airships.

Balta Sound, Shetland. An advanced mooring-out base for the seaplanes from Catfirth. Auxiliary Battalion, Royal Marines built a seaplane slipway here in April 1940.

Beacon Hill, Northumberland. *81/145917.* LG for 36 Squadron from October 1916 to May 1917.

Benton, Northumberland. *88/275695.* LG for 36 Squadron from June 1917 until end of 1918.

Berneray, Western Isles. *18/901809.* RAF ELG 1939–45.

Bishopton, Durham. *93/358208.* LG for 36 Squadron from October 1916 to end of 1918.

Blaris (Lisburn), N Ireland. LG used by Battles, etc, ATC Gliding School from *circa* September 1943.

Brims Mains, Highland. *11/044698.* ELG for Castletown-based fighters 1940–45. Possibly also a decoy airfield.

Carlingnose, Firth of Forth. A seaplane station was in use here in 1912.

Cairncross, Borders. *67/90-63-.* *8 miles NW of Berwick.* LG for 77 Squadron from October 1917 until end of 1918.

Carmunnock, Strathclyde. Aircraft built by Weir Ltd at Cathcart were flown from a field here until Renfrew opened in 1918.

Casement, Eire. *See Baldonnel.*

Castlebar, Eire. *Just NE of town.* First World War LG.

Catfirth, Orkney. *3/448537.* Opened in 1918 as a seaplane station for 300 Flight.

Catley Hill, Durham. *93/355338.* LG for 36 Squadron from October 1916 (when it was called Trimdon) until end of 1918.

Cleadon, Tyne and Wear. *88/399635.* LG for 36 Squadron from October 1916 to August 1917.

Collinstown, Eire. Opened in 1918 when 24 TDS formed here in May from 24 TS and 59 TS for day bomber training. No 24 TDS disbanded in 1919 but aerodrome remained in use and is today Dublin Airport.

Colinton, Lothian. *66/21-68-.* LG for 77 Squadron in 1916.

Currock Hill, Durham. *88/105595.* LG for 36 Squadron October 1916–April 1917.

Dungavel, Strathclyde. *71/65-37-.* Private aircraft flew from here in '30s, RAF ELG 1939–45, RAFVR Gliding School *circa* 1948/9.

Easington, Durham. *88/405425.* LG for 36 Squadron from October 1916 until end of 1918.

East Fingask, Grampian. *38/780275.* RAF dispersal satellite for Dyce.

Elford, Northumbria. *See Seahouses.*

Fair Isle, Shetland. *4/198697.* Highland Airways 1939–46. RAF ELG.

Fort George, Highland. *27/761566.* Seaplane station opened in 1913, in use until 1916.

Gifford, Lothian. *66/552695.* LG for 77 Squadron in 1918. Originally known as Townhead.

Glimerton, Lothian. *66/296677.* LG for 77 Squadron from late in 1916 until end of 1918.

Gormanston, Eire. Opened in 1918 when 22 TDS formed here in August from 26 TS and 69 TS for day bomber training. No 22 TDS disbanded in 1919 but aerodrome continued in use and is today an Irish Air Corps base.

Hoperigg Mains, Lothian. *66/44-73-.* LG for 77 Squadron 1916/17.

Horsegate, Northumberland. *88/125595.* LG for 36 Squadron in 1917/18.

Houton Bay, Orkney. *6/30704.* Seaplane station from 1917. Units based in October 1918 were 306, 307 and 430 Flights.

Kilconquhar, Fife. *59/48-02-.* LG for 77 Squadron in 1918.

Killeagh, Eire. An airship patrol station was under construction here at the end of the First World War.

Kincairn, Central. *Near Stirling.* LG for 77 Squadron in 1916/17.

Lambton Park, Tyne and Wear. ATC Gliding School *circa* 1944.

Larne, N Ireland. Airship sub-station 1916–18.

Lisburn, N Ireland. *See Blaris.*

Longhorsley, Northumberland. *88/161926.* LG for 36 Squadron from early 1917 until end of 1918.

Lough Foyle, N Ireland. US Navy seaplane station in 1918.

Malahide, Eire. *5 miles NE of Dublin.* Sub-station of the airship patrol station on Anglesey.

New Haggerston, Northumberland. *75/022425.* LG for 77 Squadron from 1916 until end of war. In 1918 it was used also by 526 Flight of 256 Squadron on coastal patrol duties.

Omagh, N Ireland. *Just NW of the town.* First World War LG.

Oranmore, Eire. *5 miles E of Galway.* First World War LG.

Peterhead, Grampian. *30/128445.* A seaplane repair and store base was opened here in 1918.

Ponteland, Northumberland. *87/145725.* LG for 36 Squadron from 1916 until end of war.

Queenstown, Eire. US Navy seaplane station in 1918.

Rennington, Northumberland. *81/213195.* LG for 36 Squadron from 1916 until end of war.

Rosyth, Fife. *65/110818.* Seaplane base and repair depot in 1917/18.

Scapa Flow, Orkney. *6/443087.* Seaplane base opened in August 1914. In 1918 a Fleet Aircraft Repair Base and Stores Depot.

Seahouses (Elford), Northumbria. *75/190203.* LG for 77 Squadron from 1916 until end of war. In 1918 also used by 526 and 527 Flights of 256 Squadron for coastal patrol duties.

Skateraw, Lothian. *67/73-75-.* LG for 77 Squadron in 1917/18.

Snelsetter/Hoy, Orkney. *7/320887.* RAF ELG 1939–45.

Snipe House, Northumberland. *81/16-08-.* LG for 36 Squadron in 1917/18.

Sollas, Western Isles. *18/810750.* RAF ELG 1939–45.

South Belton, Lothian. *67/654773.* LG for 77 Squadron from late in 1916 to end of war.

South Kilduff, Fife. *3 miles W of Kinross.* LG for 77 Squadron from 1916 to 1918.

South Shields, Tyne and Wear. *88/370680.* A seaplane repair depot opened here in 1917 and continued in use until end of war.

Spennymoor, Durham. *93/240325. 6 miles S of Durham.* LG for 36 Squadron from 1916 to 1918.

Stamford (Alnwick), Northumbria. *75/229203.* LG for 36 Squadron in 1916.

Stenness, Orkney. *10 miles W of Kirkwall.* Seaplane station for 309, 310 and 311 Flights in 1918.

Strathbeg, Grampian. *30/083577.* Seaplane station opened here in 1916 and was the base of 400 Flight of 249 Squadron in 1918.

Tallaght, Eire. *7 miles SW of Dublin.* Opened in 1918 when 25 TDS formed here in August. Unit disbanded in 1919 but there was continued use by various squadrons.

The Curragh, Eire. *5 miles E of Kildare.* A portion of the Military Camp was used from December 1917 when 19 TS moved here from Hounslow. Irish Flying Instructors School in 1918. Training ceased in 1919 but the aerodrome remained active.

Tynehead, Lothian. *73/39-59-.* LG for 77 Squadron in 1917/18.

Tynemouth, Tyne and Wear. *88/358709.* LG for 36 Squadron from late 1916 to end of war. In 1918 also a coastal patrol base for 507 and 508 Flights of 252 Squadron.

Wexford, Eire. *1 mile N of town.* US Navy seaplane base was opened here in 1918.

Whiddy Island, Eire. *In Bantry Bay.* US Navy seaplane station in 1918.

Whitley Bay, Tyne and Wear. A naval aerodrome was opened here early in 1915 and remained in use in 1916.

Whiteburn, Borders. *15 miles NW of Berwick.* Opened in 1916 as a flight station for 'C' Flight of 77 Squadron. In August 1917 it housed 'B' Flight and in 1918 'A' Flight.

Key to airfield numbers on following pages

No	Name	No	Name
1	Abbotsinch	69	Kirkpatrick
2	Acklington	70	Kirkton
3	Aldergrove	71	Kirkwall
4	Alness	72	Lanford Lodge
5	Annan	73	Largs
6	Arbroath	74	Leanach
7	Ashington	75	Lennoxlove
8	Ayr	76	Leuchars
9	Ayr (racecourse)	77	Limavady
10	Balado Bridge	78	Loch Doon
11	Ballyhalbert	79	Long Kesh
12	Ballykelly	80	Longman (Inverness)
13	Ballywalter	81	Longside
14	Banff	82	Lossiemouth
15	Benbecula	83	Low Eldrig
16	Bishops Court	84	Macmerry
17	Black Isle	85	Macrihanish
18	Boa Island	86	Maghaberry
19	Boulmer	87	Maydown
20	Bowmore	88	Methven
21	Brackla	89	Milfield
22	Brunton	90	Millisle
23	Buddon	91	Milltown
24	Buttergask	92	Montrose
25	Campbeltown	93	Morpeth
26	Castle Archdale (Lough Erne)	94	Mullaghmore
27	Castle Kennedy	95	Murlough
28	Castletown	96	Newcastle (Gosforth)
29	Charterhall	97	Newtownards
30	Cluntoe	98	Nutt's Corner
31	Connel	99	Oban
32	Crail	100	Ouston
33	Cramlington	101	Perth
34	Dalcross	102	Peterhead
35	Dallachy	103	Port Ellen
36	Donibristle	104	Prestwick
37	Dornoch	105	Rattray (Crimond)
38	Dounreay	106	Renfrew
39	Drem	107	St Angelo
40	Dumfries	108	Sandy Bay (Lough Neagh)
41	Dundee (Stannergate)	109	Scatsta
42	Dundonald	110	Skeabrae
43	Dunino	111	Skitten
44	Dyce	112	Smoo Groo
45	East Fortune	113	Stirling (Raploch)
46	East Haven	114	Stornoway
47	Edzell	115	Stracathro
48	Eglinton	116	Stravithie
49	Elgin	117	Sullom Voe
50	Errol	118	Sumburgh
51	Eshott	119	Sydenham
52	Evanton	120	Tain
53	Fearn	121	Tealing
54	Findo Gask	122	Tiree
55	Fordoun	123	Toome
56	Forres	124	Turnberry
57	Fraserburgh	125	Turnhouse
58	Grangemouth	126	Twatt
59	Greencastle	127	Usworth
60	Greenock	128	West Freugh
61	Hatston	129	Whitefield
62	Helensburgh	130	Wick
63	Kidsdale (Burrow Head)	131	Wig Bay
64	Killadeas	132	Wigtown
65	Kinloss	133	Winfield
66	Kinnell	134	Winterseugh
67	Kirkistown	135	Woodhaven
68	Kirknewton	136	Woolsington

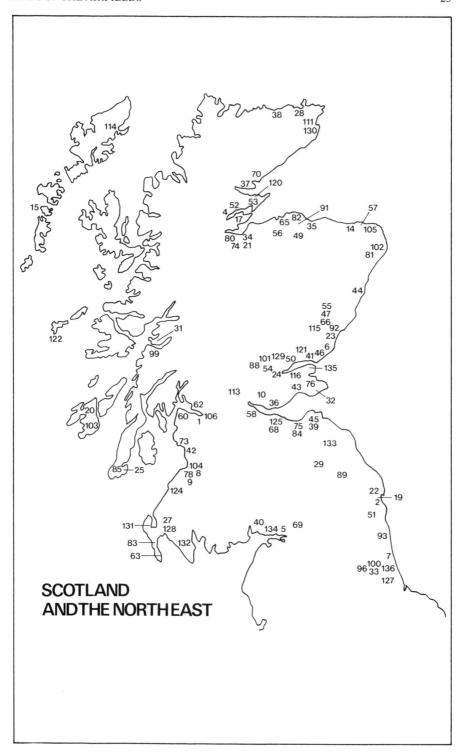

SCOTLAND
AND THE NORTH EAST

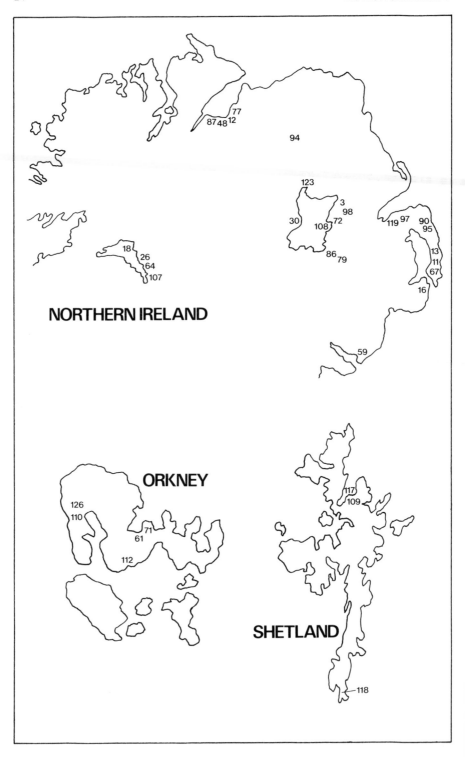

NORTHERN IRELAND

ORKNEY

SHETLAND

The airfields

Abbotsinch, Strathclyde

64/NS475667. *5 miles W of Glasgow City Centre off M8*

Glasgow's fine airport shows its RAF and naval past by the continued existence of a few wartime buildings. The airport opened in 1932, but an RAF Station HQ was not formed until July 1 1936 under 6 Auxiliary Group, Bomber Command, by which time 602 Squadron, there since 1933, had re-equipped with Hinds. Other Hind squadrons at Abbotsinch between July and November 1936 were 21 and 34.

No 16 Reconnaissance Group, Coastal Command, took over the station on January 1 1937, 269 Squadron being posted in from Bircham Newton with Ansons for inshore patrols. No 602 Squadron remained here and both squadrons, in company with 603 Squadron, made a mass flypast over Ibrox Stadium on the official opening of the Empire Exhibition by His Majesty the King on May 2 1938.

On October 9 1939, just over a month after the war had started, 2 Coastal Patrol Flight was formed to operate in the Clyde area with Tiger Moths. The aircraft were continually grounded by fog, however, and no submarines were ever reported. At the same time 602 Squadron, by now flying Spitfires, was sent to Grangemouth. The first of several naval units arrived on December 12 1939 in the shape of 816 and 818 Squadrons with Swordfish from HMS *Furious.*

A unit which was to be based here for several years was formed in March 1940—the Torpedo Training Unit. It was equipped initially with Swordfish and Shark aircraft and trained both RAF and naval crews but standardised on the Beaufort when the Navy built up its own training organisation.

Parallel activities during this period included a visit by General Sikorski, GOC the Polish Army, to inspect 309 Squadron which had formed on October 8 1940 for Army co-operation and was to move to Renfrew on November 6. There was also the arrival of a detachment of the Merchant Ship Fighter Unit with Hurricanes for initial operations from CAM ships, and a parachute display by a Whitley on July 17 1941. The latter developed into a drama when one of the parachutists became entangled with the aircraft. The pilot landed as slowly as possible and the man was lucky to escape injury. In September, two US Navy personnel were attached to the TTU to gain an insight into its workings.

Abbotsinch was also used for aircraft storage, some 126 being dispersed on the field in October 1941, including 49 Hurricanes and 30 Blenheims. Bothas from the factory at Dumbarton were test-flown and also lodging on the station from late January 1942 was 1441 Combined Operations Development Flight which formed here under 17 Group with two Ansons, two Lysanders and a Tiger Moth. From these small beginnings sprang 516 Squadron at Dundonald (*qv*).

The skills of torpedo dropping were taught over the Firth of Clyde and there were favourable comparisons with the Navy's own training unit at Crail. With more and more aircraft passing through, chiefly Bostons, Bothas and Martlets, a less congested airfield was required. On February 9 1942 an opening-up party was sent to Turnberry, preceding the move of part of the TTU to this new base.

Some unusual American aircraft were to be seen at Abbotsinch, such as a few

Kingfishers in May 1942, many Airacobras in October and the first USAAF P-38s which were in transit to England. Another rare bird was Fokker F. XXII *HM149* which joined the Station Flight on September 30 1942. The increased wear and tear necessitated the layering of a 1,450 yd Sommerfeld Track runway in February 1942.

The airfield was handed over entirely to the Royal Navy on August 11 1943, to whom the Maintenance Yard had been known as HMS *Sanderling* since as long ago as June 1940. Maintenance Command was allowed to retain the use of two of the hangars for the storage of packed aircraft, and Lockheeds from nearby Renfrew did some of their assembly and modification work while runways were being built at Renfrew. Scottish Airways also used Abbotsinch during this period. No 1680 (Western Isles) Communications Flight was based there, and later moved to Prestwick.

No 730 Communications Squadron formed on April 17 1944, leaving for Ayr the following month. Two Seafire Squadrons, 802 and 804, were present in July and August 1945 and February 1947 respectively. There was also a Sea Otter Unit, 1702 Squadron, in September 1945.

After the war, Abbotsinch was the home of 1830 and 1843 Squadrons with Fireflies, 1834 with Sea Balliols and the Aircraft Holding Unit, which was responsible for the storage and scrapping of hundreds of surplus naval aircraft. In 1959/60, for example, over 400 could be seen parked all over the airfield. The types included Sea Hawks, Sea Venoms, Avengers and Skyraiders. The AHU also prepared current naval types, such as the Sea Vixen, for service.

In the mid-50s, it was decided that pre-delivery and post-overhaul flying required specially trained pilots, so the Maintenance Test Pilots School was formed at Abbotsinch. Other lodgers were 633 Gliding School which formed in March 1960, and 1962 Flight of 666 Squadron equipped with Austers from circa 1953. There was also 602 Squadron with Spitfires and, from 1950 until disbandment in 1957, Vampires.

The Navy left in October 1963, the airfield then being prepared for use as Glasgow's airport. It took over from over-crowded Renfrew on May 2 1966 and is now used by many major airlines. The past is not quite forgotten, however, as the badge and bell of the former RNAS now hang in the aptly named 'Sanderling Bar' in the terminal building. There are, too, a couple of naval type hangars still in use.

Acklington, Northumberland

81/NU230010. 3 miles NE of Felton on B6345

On August 16 1940, believing that all our fighter squadrons had been committed to the struggle in the south, the Luftwaffe sent about 100 bombers with an escort of 40 Bf 110s against Tyneside. Unfortunately for them, several Hurricane and Spitfire squadrons had been withdrawn from the battle to rest in and simultaneously guard the north.

The pilots protested that they were not at all tired and then this unexpected consolation came on the scene. Nearly 30 enemy aircraft were shot down, many by Acklington-based aircraft, for a British loss of two pilots injured. Never again was a daylight raid attempted outside the range of the best fighter protection and henceforth everywhere north of the Wash was safe by day.

Acklington, the north-east's main fighter base, was built on the site of a First World War landing ground known as Southfields, used by 77 Squadron. It had opened in 1938 for 7 Armament Training School which was renamed 2 Air Observers School on November 15 1938. As soon as the war began, the school moved to Warmwell, Dorset and the airfield was transferred to Fighter Command initially as a satellite to Usworth.

No 607 Squadron moved in on October 9 1939 with Gladiators but left to join the Air Component of the BEF (British Expeditionary Force) the following month. Hurricanes of 111 Squadron spent November 1939 at Acklington, leaving for Drem on December 7. Another Gladiator squadron, 152, re-formed on October 1 1939, becoming operational in November but beginning to convert to Spitfires in January 1940.

No 43 Squadron had been flying Spitfires from here since November 1939, and on January 30 1940, Flight Lieutenant C.B. Hull and Sergeant F. Carey shot down a He 111 in the sea off Coquet Island. On February 3, three of 152 Squadron's pilots destroyed another Heinkel. Between them, the two squadrons shot down three more aircraft before 43 went to Wick in February and 152 to Warmwell in July.

Acklington in August 1968 (J. Huggon).

Other fighter squadrons based at Acklington during 1940 were 72 from March to August and 79 in July/August. Both claimed several enemy bombers and were thus well blooded by the time both units moved to Biggin Hill and the Battle of Britain. Withdrawn from Biggin for a rest at the end of August was 32 Squadron which stayed until December 1940. No 72 Squadron returned to the north-east in mid-December 1940, leaving for Gravesend in July 1941. Also forming part of the Tyneside defences in December 1940 and January 1941 were the Hurricanes of 258 Squadron.

No 315, a new Polish squadron, formed

Acklington 1981 (F. Neal).

here on January 21 1941 with Hurricanes, but it was not yet operational when it moved to Speke in mid-March. Another Polish Hurricane squadron, 317, formed on February 22. Taking only a month to become operational, it began convoy patrols and moved to Ouston at the end of April 1941.

Heavy night attacks on the north-east brought a detachment of 141 Squadron from Ayr on May 1 1941. The Defiants shot down several raiders before being withdrawn in August as enemy activity died down.

The Canadians' first night fighter squadron, 406, formed at Acklington on May 10 1941 with Merlin-Beaufighters. Whilst working-up, one of the crews claimed the first victory during a raid on Newcastle on the night of September 1. Further successes followed during the full

moon period each month and by the end of the year the squadron could claim five destroyed and four damaged. No 406 left for Ayr in January 1942.

On October 4 1941, 43 Squadron had returned from Drem, its Hurricanes seeing some action before going to Tangmere in June 1942. In contrast, 74 Squadron's Spitfires flew only uneventful patrols between July and October 1941.

No 141 Squadron, which had by now converted to Beaufighters, was already operating on detachment at Acklington when the whole squadron moved there at the end of January 1942. An occasional victory was scored before the unit moved to Tangmere in June.

A detachment of Spitfires from 167 Squadron kept up the convoy escort in the early summer of 1942 before the airfield was occupied by 1 Squadron Typhoons. This squadron had been withdrawn from the south coast in July 1942 to convert from Hurricanes to the new type. There were many teething troubles, but despite these two pilots managed to shoot down an Me 210 on September 6 1942. The Typhoons moved to the south in February 1943.

Beaufighters of 219 Squadron arrived in June 1942, stayed until October 21 1942 and transferred to Scorton. Detachments of Beaufighters of 410 Squadron were also on the station for various periods in 1942 until the entire squadron was posted in October, by which time Mosquitoes were beginning to replace the Beaufighters. The squadron's first kill after months of fruitless patrols came on January 21 1943 when a Do 217 was sent down near Hartlepool. In February the squadron moved to Coleby Grange in Lincolnshire.

The Turbinlite Havoc which illuminated its prey with a searchlight for an attack by an accompanying Hurricane was a promising idea which was not very successful in practice. No 1460 Flight formed at Acklington in December 1941, became 539 Squadron on September 2 1942 and disbanded on January 25 1943. Only nine operational sorties were flown in all, none being successful, and improved radar in the Beaufighter rendered the whole idea obsolete.

No 409 Squadron took over responsibility for the night defence of Newcastle in February 1943 but the enemy was now showing little interest in the area so detachments were sent to fly Rangers from Coltishall and Middle Wallop to relieve the boredom.

On June 10 1943, the main party of the USAAF's 416th Night Fighter Squadron reached Acklington by rail from Cranfield, the Beaufighters being flown in over the next two days. After a period of working-up during which a pilot was killed in a crash at Warkworth, the air echelon of 11 Beaufighters took off for Portreath on August 4 en route for Algiers.

In July 1943 a Soviet military mission visited the station to observe our methods of fighter interception at night. As a measure of mutual distrust they were not shown the advanced type of AI radar coming into service and doubts were expressed at letting them see too much at the GCI station!

Day fighter squadrons on the airfield in 1943 included 198 with Typhoons in February/March, 350 with Spitfires from March until June and again in July and August, 349 from August to October and 130 from November until early in the New Year.

The diversion of several heavy bombers from operations on December 1 1943 brought tragedy to the district. Stirling *EH880* belonging to 75 Squadron, Mepal, crashed into a farmhouse on the approach, killing five children and all of the crew except the mid-upper gunner. Similar diversions on January 3 1944 brought in 17 Lancasters without incidents.

In December 1943, 25 Squadron arrived at Acklington to re-equip with the latest night fighter Mosquito, the NF XVII. Five Wellingtons of the 'Wellington Conversion Unit' were attached to the squadron for affiliation duties. When operational in February 1944, 25 Squadron left for Coltishall.

Day fighter patrols at this time were in the hands of 316 Squadron which had been there since September 1943. Its Spitfires moved to Woodvale in February 1944. No 409 Squadron was still at Acklington with Beaufighters, beginning conversion to Mosquitoes in February 1944 and leaving for West Malling in May. A couple of Typhoon squadrons, 56 and 266, made short detachments in February and March 1944 for exercises which included rocket firing. Other squadrons there for brief periods in the first part of 1944 were 164 to convert from Hurricanes to Typhoons in March, 222 with Spitfires, and 322 in March/April to convert from Mk V Spitfires to Mk XIVs in preparation for the Invasion.

A detachment of Typhoons from 3 Tactical Exercise Unit at Honiley spent a fortnight at Acklington in June 1944, after which the airfield was withdrawn from service for reconstruction. This failed to stop the odd emergency landing, including Westland Welkin *DX289* from Wittering with engine failure.

More dramatic was the arrival of three Mustangs from the 4th Fighter Group at Debden on August 8 1944. Two of them were escorting home a Major who had been badly shot up escorting a Beaufighter attack on a convoy off South Norway. Severely wounded, he managed to land safety. The same day a Fortress landed from Glatton to collect the crew of another Fort which had ditched off Blyth.

Fourteen Corsairs from Eglinton stayed for two days in December 1944 to take part in an Army exercise but apart from some Lancaster diversions there was little flying until 59 OTU re-formed here in February 26 1945 with Typhoons. The unit was short-lived however and disbanded on June 6 1945.

Acklington was now designated a forward airfield in the Newcastle Sector with one day and one night fighter squadron. No 19 Squadron's Mustangs were here between May and August 1945 and 219 with Mosquitoes from August 1945 until April 1946. The first of Acklington's many jets were operated by 263 Squadron which re-formed here on August 19 1945 with Meteor F3s but left for Church Fenton in September.

In May 1946, 2 Armament Practice Station was transferred from Spilsby, later becoming known as the Fighter Armaments Trials School. Various aircraft were used for target towing and before the unit disbanded many fighter squadrons had been detached for firing practice.

Acklington became a first-line fighter station once more in 1957, housing 29 Squadron (Meteor/Javelin) from January 1957 until July 1958 and 66 Squadron (Hunter) from February 1957 to September 1960

Reversion to a training role came on August 4 1961 when 6 FTS arrived from Ternhill with Provosts, later to be replaced by Jet Provosts. The school disbanded in June 1968 and the airfield was transferred to 38 Group for 18 Squadron Wessex operations until 1969.

From 1957, search and rescue was provided by Whirlwind detachments from various squadrons, 202 Squadron 'B'

Flight being the final flying unit at Acklington before it moved to Boulmer in 1972. The station was then put on Care and Maintenance. The main site is now a prison and the runways have been almost entirely obliterated by open-cast mining.

Aldergrove, Antrim

14/J150800. 4 miles S of Antrim on A50

The oldest airfield in the Province, and now the largest and most important, Aldergrove was opened early in 1918 as 16 AAP. It was intended that HP V1500 bombers built by Harland and Wolff would be test flown from here but teething troubles caused delays and only a handful were completed. The site had been selected by Sholto Douglas, who later became Marshal of the Royal Air Force, during a tour of Ireland in 1917 to look for suitable areas for development.

Aldergrove closed in December 1919 but was retained by the RAF and reactivated annually for exercises. From June to September 1922, 2 Squadron was based to counter possible trouble in Ulster and a detachment of its Bristol F 2bs was retained until February of the following year.

No 502 Squadron was formed at Aldergrove on May 15 1925 as a night bomber unit equipped successively with Vimys, Hyderabads and Virginias. In October 1935 it became a day bomber unit operating first Wallaces and then Hinds. No 9 Squadron's Virginias came over from Andover in January 1936, the unit then re-equipped with Heyfords and returned to England in October.

In March 1936, 2 Armament Training Camp (later Armament Training Station) formed, and many first-line squadrons and FTS detachments subsequently spent time here. A unit which in various forms was destined to have a long-term association with Aldergrove, the Met Flight, started operations in October 1936 with Bulldogs.

No 2 ATS (Armament Training Station) combined with 1 ATS on April 17 1939 to become 3 AOS (Air Observer School) which in turn was renamed 3 B&GS (Bombing and Gunnery School) on November 1 1939. A variety of obsolete types, including Heyfords, was flown until the school disbanded on July 11 1940, naval personnel being trained there too.

Such was the lack of defences that when the threat of invasion first developed, the

service authorities in Northern Ireland had recognised that they could, if necessary, improvise from the B&GS an emergency force of one fighter squadron and two light bomber squadrons of Battles and one composite reconnaissance squadron of Swordfish and Sharks. Another stopgap unit, 4 CPF, formed on December 1 1939, but its Tiger Moths flew to Hooton Park via Squires Gate five days later.

A naval unit, 774 Squadron, arrived in November 1939 for armament training with Rocs, Skuas, Swordfish and Sharks but transferred to Evanton in July 1940. No 416 Flight, already at Aldergrove, was formed into 231 Squadron on July 1. Its Lysanders exercised with the Army and patrolled the border with the Republic, but moved to Newtownards on July 15.

No 23 MU's personnel began to arrive at Aldergrove in November 1939, the first aircraft for storage, a Short-built Bombay, being delivered on December 6.

During its first year, the MU specialised in preparing Wellingtons, Hampdens and Blenheims for service.

For the air defence of Belfast and convoy patrols, 245 Squadron's Hurricanes arrived from Turnhouse on July 20 1940, a Fighter Sector HQ being set up at the same time. There were numerous scrambles against shipping raiders but no contacts were made and it was not until February 4 1941 that the first enemy aircraft was sighted. Even then, the pursuing fighters were unable to climb fast enough to intercept it.

Detachments of several Coastal Command squadrons operated in 1940, including Blenheims of 236 and 254 Squadrons, Hudsons of 224 and 233 and Whitleys of 102 Squadron on loan from Bomber Command. The whole of 233 Squadron moved in from Leuchars in December 1940 and flew anti-submarine patrols before leaving for St Eval in August 1941.

Left *Aldergrove on a pre-war Empire Air Day* (Via E.A. Cromie).

Below left *Liberator IIIs of 120 Squadron Aldergrove. Note control tower under construction* (Imperial War Museum).

Right *Roc of B&GS Aldergrove attacks Shark* (Via E.A. Cromie).

Below right *Aldergrove on January 5 1942* (Via E.A. Cromie).

History was made on November 11 when the first transatlantic delivery flight arrived, composed of seven Hudsons from Botwood in Newfoundland. The leader was D.C.T. Bennett of later Pathfinder fame and the crossing was completed in about 9½ hours. They took off for Speke the next day.

A new squadron, No 272, formed on November 19 1940, from two Flights of 235 and 236 Squadrons equipped with Blenheims. Shipping escort patrols began the following day and continued until the unit moved to Chivenor the following April.

Meanwhile 502 Squadron was flying Ansons in all weathers, covering the North-West Approaches, the pilots leaning out the mixture to coax a few extra miles of range out of their obsolete machines. Evidence of the U-boats' depradations was everywhere—floating wreckage, and great patches of oil and lifeboats, many of them upturned or empty. Submarines were spotted now and then but it needed a direct hit from the Ansons' small bombs to make any impression on them so they could only be forced to dive.

In August 1940, a flight of five Whitleys equipped with the new ASV radar was allocated to 502 Squadron. Before the 502 Squadron Special Flight, as it was known, tested the apparatus under operational conditions, the entire squadron moved to Limavady in January 1941 having by now converted totally to Whitleys.

The first air raid on the Belfast area came on the night of August 7/8 1940. No 245 Squadron made single aircraft patrols and in the course of one of them, Squadron Leader J.W.C. Simpson DFC destroyed an He 111 over Downpatrick. Belfast's final raid came on May 5/6 1941 and Squadron Leader Simpson again shot down an enemy bomber, his 12th victory.

Beaufighters of 252 Squadron were there in April 1941 flying convoy patrols, but most of the aircraft were sent to Malta early in May. The few remaining operated from Ulster until mid-June 1941. No 254 Squadron, whose Beaufighters had come from Sumburgh at the end of May, took over the shipping escorts until December when it left for Dyce. No 143 Squadron had given up its Beaufighters at Sumburgh and reverted to a training role with Blenheim IVs, later going to Limavady in April 1942.

The Fighter Sector HQ was transferred to Ballyhalbert on June 28 1941 and on July 15 when 245 Squadron left, Aldergrove was allocated to Coastal Command.

Anson N5213 of 502 Squadron Aldergrove over Lough Neagh (Via A. Stamper).

The fighters had gone but a 233 Squadron Hudson made up for it by shooting down a Condor which was attacking a convoy on July 23.

Runway construction began in September 1941, but the airfield remained operational. No 206 Squadron's Hudsons

Anson of 502 Squadron being loaded with 100 lb anti-submarine bomb (Via A. Stamper).

Rearming a No 245 Squadron Hurricane at Aldergrove, November 18 1940 (Via E.A. Cromie).

had arrived from St Eval the previous month and were soon busy on convoy protection. In January and February 1942, U-boat sightings were frequent but attacks were inconclusive even though the Hudson crews believed they had scored hits.

At the end of April 1942, 311 Squadron moved in from Norfolk with Wellingtons, flying its first patrol from the new base on May 22. The stay was brief however, as the unit went on to Talbenny in mid-June to make room for 9 OTU which formed at Aldergrove on June 7. No 206 Squadron moved to Benbecula on June 30 and the station was left temporarily in a training capacity, 1 Armament Practice Camp also being a long-term lodger.

After the OTU was sent to Crosby on September 9, the main activity centred around 23 MU which was still handling mainly Wellingtons and Hampdens, and 1402 Met Flight. The flight was a direct descendent of the pre-war unit known originally as Station Flight Aldergrove, then 402 Flight and finally 1402 Met Flight from January 15 1941. Bulldogs, Gauntlets and Gladiators were operated successively for height climbs. An amalgamation with 1402 Met Flight came in March 1942. The latter had been using Blenheims for met reconnaissance on the Atlantic *Bismuth* sorties until it was allocated some Hudsons for greater range. The work was deceptively routine but vital to the planning of bombing operations, as most of Britain's future weather brews

out to the north-west.

The station became fully operational again on the arrival of the Liberators of 120 and the Fortresses of 220 Squadron on February 14 1943. The Fortresses moved to Benbecula the following month but not before one of them had depth-charged a U-boat and possibly sunk it. On March 11, *B* of 120 Squadron on a convoy patrol encountered a fully surfaced U-boat but it dived and escaped. A second submarine was sighted but the Liberator was unable to reach it in time to make an attack. It was third time lucky however when another was straddled with depth charges and a 3-mile oil streak developed. Yet another sub was forced to crash-dive but there was no armament left to attack it. This was, without a doubt, an eventful sortie for a Coastal Command aircraft.

No 86 Squadron arrived at Aldergrove in March 1943 with more Liberators, as the anti-U-boat war began to swing in favour of the Allies. The submariners' morale must have been shaken badly by the presence of more and more of these big aircraft far out over the ocean. Even a brief spell on the surface could attract attention and many submarines must have gone down without trace, even though the aircrews were unable to confirm this. No 120 Squadron claimed several destroyed in the opening months of 1943 before it moved to Iceland in April.

The replacement Liberator squadron early in May was No 59 from Thorney Island. Its crews soon joined the fray over the Atlantic but a new U-boat tactic soon became apparent—fighting back on the surface with multiple cannon and machine-guns. No 86 Squadron suffered a fatal casualty on June 12 1943 and other aircraft were to sustain damage in subsequent actions. Many more submarines were attacked but as usual sinking was never confirmed.

The Met Flight's Gladiators were gradually replaced by Hurricanes in 1944 but the last biplanes were not relinquished until February 1945, by which time the unit was based at Ballykelly.

No 23 MU retained a major responsibility for Wellingtons but many other types passed through its hands, one of the most unusual being the Corsair. Preparation work on this fighter began in June 1944, 98 being flown in. By the end of August 136 Corsair IIIs were held. In January 1945 the most common aircraft on the unit were Ansons, Oxfords, Corsairs and Stirlings.

Another support unit was 1674 HCU which formed at Aldergrove on October 10 1943 to take over Fortress training from 1 OTU, Liberators being operated too. It moved to Longtown on October 19 but returned on February 1 1944. The Liberators and Halifaxes stayed until August 1945 when they left for Milltown and disbandment.

After the war, 518 Squadron (ex Tiree) began met flights from Aldergrove in September 1945 with Halifaxes, being renumbered 202 Squadron on October 1 1946. Hastings replaced the Halifaxes in October 1950 and five nine-hour trips were made every week until disbandment on July 31 1964. From March 1948 to August 1951 another met squadron, No 224, also flew Halifaxes from Aldergrove.

No 502 Squadron returned to its birthplace in July 1946, flying, successively, the Mosquito, Spitfire and Vampire, until going the way of all the auxiliary squadrons in March 1957. Another familiar squadron, No 120, came back in April 1952 to operate Shackletons, returning to Kinloss seven years later.

On May 12 1960, a Flight of Sycamore helicopters of 228 Squadron became 118 Squadron at Aldergrove, disbanding on August 31 1962.

Nutt's Corner having reached the limits of possible expansion, Aldergrove became, on September 26 1963, Belfast Airport once more. This time there was no improvisation with wartime buildings, a modern terminal had been built. No 23 MU kept up the RAF presence until disbanding in 1978 and the airport now handles over one million passengers a year.

Alness (Invergordon), Highland

21/NH655675. 1 mile S of Alness, just off A9

Alness is the sole wartime flying boat base still used by the RAF, but of course only marine craft can be seen here now, and that from a distance, as it is not very accessible. The former decontamination centre is close to Alness town and a few other dispersed buildings also survive, along with the concrete floors of dozens of Nissen huts.

The station, which dates back to the pre-war period, was known first as Invergordon, but, in its early days, it is doubtful if it was anything more than a mooring area with a slipway for beaching the aircraft. Although flying boats had called here on many previous occasions, its first recorded squadrons were 201 from Calshot, whose Londons stayed for a week in October 1938. At the same time the Singapores and Stranraers of 209 Squadron were detached here from Felixstowe along with 228's Stranraers for patrols out towards Norway.

A month before the war began, 240 Squadron arrived from Calshot with Londons, moving to Sullom Voe on November 4 1939 and returning for two months in the spring of 1940. Between October 23 and November 6 1939, a detachment of Sunderlands of 210 Squadron operated from here to cover the exits from the North Sea. The aircraft returned towards the end of November and stayed until May 21 1940. No 201 Squadron came back in November 1940 and was beginning to re-equip with Sunderlands when it left for Sullom Voe on May 26 1940.

In June 1941, 4 (C) OTU was moved from Stranraer to Invergordon, with the officers' mess set up at Dalmore House, Alness. The OTU was flying a mixed bunch of marine aircraft including Lerwicks and Sunderlands. One of the Lerwicks reported sighting a U-boat in the Moray Firth on May 3 1941 but on investigation it proved to be a known wreck which was still giving off oil streaks.

The OTU was training ten crews on each course by October 1941, and in February of the following year it was decided to split the unit into two. Initial training of pilots on flying boats was to be concentrated at Stranraer and operational training confined to Invergordon, using Sunderlands, Catalinas and any miscellaneous types such as Singapores

'Fine pitch, rich mixture, flaps going out'. Approaching to touch down at Alness 1945. View from starboard galley hatch of 4 OTU Sunderland (R. Codd, via Chaz Bowyer).

and Stranraers which could be useful for observer instruction.

A melancholy incident occurred on August 25 1942 when the Duke of Kent left Invergordon for Iceland in a Sunderland of 228 Squadron. Inexplicably, the aircraft crashed into high ground near Dunbeath in Caithness and all on board were killed. A memorial marks the spot.

Sunderland I P9606 ZM-R of 201 Squadron Invergordon 1940 (Via R.C.B. Ashworth).

The summer of 1942 saw an increased output of trained aircrew, averaging 22 crews per month, but further expansion was hindered by the small number of Sunderlands and Catalinas available. More problems were caused by the withdrawal of the older types from service. All the Singapores and Stranraers had gone by October and the Londons were being flown away to Saunders Roe at Cowes for breaking up.

In November 1942, Sunderland serviceability on the station was considered to be appalling. Only four of the 16 on establishment were flyable owing to shortage of spares and lack of NCO fitters. The new Nissen-hutted camp at Dalmore was also making very slow progress owing to scarcity of labour.

As the difficulties were gradually

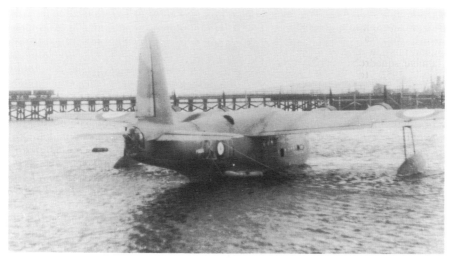

overcome, the OTU became an efficient unit, streamlining the training of crews for Coastal Command. The station itself officially became known as RAF Alness on February 10 1943.

Accidents in training on the big boats were frequent, many being minor collisions whilst manoeuvring on the waters of the Cromarty Firth. Some, however, were catastrophic, like the Sunderland which crashed and exploded on the railway line two miles north-east of Invergordon after engine failure on take off. There were no survivors from this one, nor from Sunderland *DP178* which disappeared without trace on a night flight in good weather on March 14 1945.

Operation *Uplift* took place in October 1944, being the flying of 'time-expired' personnel from Iceland and the ferrying out of replacements. The operation took three weeks using nine Sunderlands of 4 OTU and six from 201 Squadron. A total of 1,115 passengers was carried from Reykjavik to Alness and 593 made the outward trip.

No 4 OTU went on flying after the war ended and in June 1946 the CO visited Killadeas in Northern Ireland to investigate the possibility of moving to that station. It was, however, found unsuitable and the unit transferred to Pembroke Dock on August 15 1946. Thereafter, Alness was used by RAF Sunderlands spasmodically until the type was retired.

Annan, Dumfries and Galloway

85/NY215700. 3 miles NE of Annan on B722

Annan was an unhappy choice for an airfield site, particularly one at which fighter pilots were trained. One pilot described it as 'several dozen Nissen and wooden huts dumped down on a Scottish hilltop and linked by muddy tracks'.

In this unlikely spot a highly professional flying school was forged and the pupils worked long hours and flew in the foulest weather. In one memorable extract from the station's records: 'April 30 1944—the weather—not suitable for publication—no flying whatsoever. It is better to draw a blanket over the whole day as everyone is hopping mad. The gentlemen who selected the site for the aerodrome must find their ears burning today!' A further entry reads 'another misty morning of the type that long-haired poets are apt to rave over and long-haired instructors curse.'

The main party of 55 OTU moved into Annan from Usworth on April 28 1942. The aircraft used were mainly Hurricanes and from May 13 the unit commenced to share the satellite airfield at Longtown with 59 OTU, 'C' and 'D' Flights being

Hurricane AG162 of 55 OTU flying from Annan (Imperial War Museum).

Swordfish NF399 of Arbroath Station Flight 1948 (R.C. Sturtivant collection).

detached there with senior pupils for advanced training.

No 107 Squadron operated 16 Bostons from Annan between August 4 and 10 1942 in support of an exercise. At the same time, quite a number of American pilots were passing through the OTU, most of them being transferred to the USAAF on completion of their courses.

The long-suffering people of Cumberland were subjected to dummy *Rhubarbs*, the Solway Firth serving as the English Channel and the countryside on the other side as France. Anything and everything remotely considered a military target was subjected to cine-gun assault at zero feet. The Isle of Man, too, served as a useful lesson in low-level navigation. A coastline from wave-top height is almost invisible until the last moment, and in a few weeks pinpoint accuracy would be essential to ensure hitting the enemy coast between, instead of on top of, German AA batteries.

Martinets replaced the Lysanders for target-towing in mid-1943 and by November the unit had on strength 80 Hurricanes, 18 Masters, two Typhoons, five Martinets and a few communications aircraft. It was re-formed into 4 TEU on January 26 1944 comprising 'A' 'B' and 'C' Squadrons, 'B' Squadron being detached to the satellite at Great Orton which had replaced Longtown back in October 1943.

The unit was redesignated yet again as 3 TEU on March 28 1944 and 'A' Squadron

specialised in air gunnery, rocket firing, dive-bombing and tactical bombing in formation, 'B' Squadron in Typhoon conversion and 'C' Squadron in tactical bomber formation, convoy attacks and low-level cross-countries. The Typhoon conversion squadron moved to Honiley on May 10 1944 and the rest of the TEU was transferred to Aston Down, 45 aircraft flying out on July 17. Annan was then taken over by 14 MU Carlisle for storage.

After the war, the nuclear power station known as Chapelcross was built on one end of a runway and housing was sited on the old dispersals. One of the original three 'T1' hangars still remains but the only aircraft to land here now is the occasional helicopter.

Arbroath, Tayside

54/NO620435. 2 miles NW of Arbroath on A933

During the war years, Arbroath must have been one of the Navy's busiest stations. Unfortunately, in three cases out of four, one took off and landed over graveyards, which was not very inspiring!

Planned as an observer training school, it was built in 1939/40 and commissioned as HMS *Condor* on June 19 1940, a decoy site being established at Kelly Moor. The first recorded unit was a deck landing school, 767 Squadron, which stayed until April 1943, when nearby East Haven became available. This task was shared with 768 Squadron from December 1940 until June 1942.

The chief observer units at Arbroath were 751, 753 and 754 Squadrons, the first came from Ford and the others from Lee-on-Solent in September 1940. They flew a variety of aircraft, including Swordfish, Albacores, Walrus and Sharks. No 751 left in April 1944 and 754 disbanded in March of that year but 753 lasted as long as October 1945, when it moved to Rattray.

Two more observer training squadrons, 740 and 741, formed on May 4 and March 1, respectively. The chief aircraft on strength was the Swordfish. No 740 soon disbanded in September 1943 and 741 in March 1945.

Other lodgers were 763 Squadron with Swordfish and Albacores, from October 1940 until February 1941 when it left for Worthy Down, and 758 for TAG training from October 1940 until disbanding in February 1941. There was also a long-standing unit for radar instruction, 783 Squadron, which formed here on January 9 1941, not leaving for Lee until May 1947. A succession of types was operated, including Walrus, Swordfish, Anson, Fire-fly, Avenger and Barracuda. It might have been one of the latter which glided down a street in Arbroath after its pilot had baled out and came to rest suspended between two houses. (The scrape marks were still visible until recently.)

In support of all these second line units was 791 Squadron, which formed on October 15 1940 for target-towing, disbanding in December 1944. A further specialised unit was 778 Squadron which conducted service trials on many different types of naval aircraft. It arrived from Lee in July 1940, moved to Crail in March 1943 and returned at the end of August 1944. It finally left for Gosport in August 1945.

From 1945, *Condor* was an air engineer school until it closed in September 1970. No 772 Squadron came from Anthorn in December 1946 with Sea Otters, Fireflies, Ansons and other aircraft, disbanding in October 1948. Other FAA squadrons included 801 with Sea Hornets in 1948.

The airfield became the home of 45 Commando, Royal Marines, in 1970 but 662 Gliding School has continued to glide from there. Military helicopters are frequent visitors, Montforterbeek Flight of Gazelles being based on the airfield.

Because of the surrounding trees, it is difficult to see much of the aerodrome today. Visible are three 'T2's in a block and a large hangar like the one at Crail.

Ashington, Northumberland
81/NZ240890. 1 mile NW of Ashington on unclassified road off A197

Ashington opened in 1916 for 'C' Flight of 36 (HD) Squadron equipped chiefly with BE 2s and FE 2bs. In 1917 'C' Flight moved to Seaton Carew and was replaced by 'B' Flight.

In November 1918 the whole squadron moved to Ashington and disbanded here in June 1919. During 1918, 525 Flight of 256 Squadron used the aerodrome for coastal patrols with DH 6s.

Ayr, Strathclyde
70/NS355245. Just E of town

Ayr was an important fighter station for the defence of central Scotland and later an Armament Practice Camp where many squadrons brushed up on their gunnery and ground attack prior to going into action. It suffered, however, from being overshadowed by its near neighbour Prestwick. Since the war, the now disused aerodrome has been partly absorbed by Prestwick's new subsidiary runway.

Prior to April 7 1941, when the new airfield opened, fighter operations in this area were carried out by aircraft based at Prestwick as part of the Turnhouse Sector. RAF Ayr had been under construction since the autumn of 1940 and was said at the time to be the first of a new type of wartime station on which the keynote was dispersal. As usual it was still unfinished when first occupied. The future grass areas were still ploughed up and uneven, turf was being laid along the edges of the three runways and a line of electricity cables across the field was removed just in time for the official opening when a flight of 602 Squadron began flying Spitfires from here.

Difficulties were experienced, however, as no light or power was available and all fuel had to be brought over from Prestwick. The rest of 602 Squadron transferred from Prestwick on April 15 and flew uneventful convoy patrols until July when they flew south to join the Kenley Wing.

If enemy activity by day was sparse, the nights brought prey for 141 Squadron which had moved in on April 29 1941. Its Defiant crews claimed eight kills whilst flying from Ayr and Acklington during the heavy May blitz on Glasgow and Tyneside. The bulk of the squadron remained at Ayr, and on May 5 partici-

Beaufighter IIF of 406 Squadron in an Ayr blast pen 1942 with NAAFI van (F.A. Whitehead via R.C.B. Ashworth).

pated in a 'Fighter Night' over Glasgow. Sergeant Lawrence found a He 111 and set it on fire but had to break off since he was out of ammunition. The Heinkel reached the outskirts of Newcastle before crashing. Two nights later a Ju 88 was shot down near Lennoxtown and a He 111 was attacked over Ayrshire and was believed to have crashed in the sea. Another Defiant squadron, the Canadian 410, formed here on June 30 1941 and moved to Drem in August.

No 141 Squadron converted to Beaufighters and flew them operationally from August 1941 onwards but there were no more successes until after it moved to Acklington on June 29 1942. No 406 Squadron was also here with Merlin-engined Beaufighters from January–June 1942. No 312 Squadron was here between August 19 1941 and January 1 1942, non-operational whilst converting from Hurricanes to Spitfires. Another Spitfire squadron, 340, was based from December 29 to April 1 1942 but saw no action. Part of the squadron was to be detached here again in the second half of 1943. On April 6 1942, 165 Squadron re-formed at Ayr with Spitfires and became operational on May 1 for air defence patrols. The Squadron left for Gravesend in August 1942.

Other Spitfire squadrons there for varying periods in 1942 were 72 in August and September, 232 in May and June and 222 from October until March of the following year. Strangers to this Fighter Command station were a flight of 18 Squadron's Blenheims, there for five days in May 1942, 241 Squadron, an Army

Co-operation unit which operated Mustangs, which came from Bottisham in May 1942 but left for overseas in November, and a flight of Austers of 651 Squadron, there in August 1942. Eighteen Spitfires of 558 Squadron, the emergency squadron available under 58 OTU Grangemouth, were detached in October 1942.

The proximity of Prestwick meant that Ayr attracted a few strays, some in error, others by design. Among the first visitors were two Fortress Is for the RAF, which arrived on April 14 1941. Airacobras were seen on October 20 1942 and around this time many P-38 Lightnings were passing through, having flown the Atlantic via Greenland and Iceland. Operational diversions included six Halifaxes returning from Dusseldorf on August 1 1942 and 12 Lancasters after an attack on St Nazaire on March 23 1943.

Owing to a crashed aircraft blocking the runways at Prestwick, on September 13 1943 two Liberators and a C-53 landed, and two days later a B-17 diverted in because of severe cross-winds at Prestwick. Return Ferry Liberators often used Ayr, and on August 14 1941 *AM260* had crashed disastrously on take-off killing all 22 on board.

The New Zealand 488 Squadron had arrived here from Church Fenton in September 1942 with Beaufighters but saw no action, and conversion to Mosquitos began on July 30 1943 when the first aircraft was delivered. The squadron left for Drem the following month. Other residents were the Austers of 652 Squadron from Methven, which arrived on July 3 1943 staying until November, 835 Squadron with Swordfish and Sea Hurricanes, there from July to November

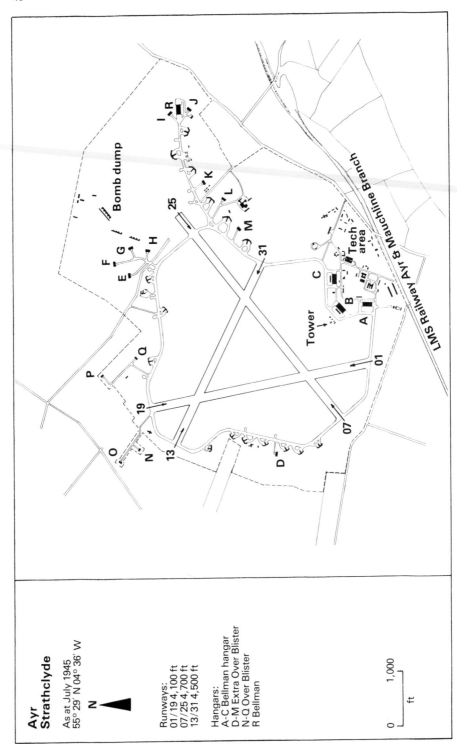

Ayr
Strathclyde

As at July 1945
55° 29′ N 04° 36′ W

N

Runways:
01/19 4,100 ft
07/25 4,700 ft
13/31 4,500 ft

Hangars:
A-C Bellman hangar
D-M Extra Over Blister
N-Q Over Blister
R Bellman

0   1,000
L_____|
        ft

1943, the USAAF's 415th Night Fighter Squadron with Beaufighters, there from April to June 1943 and 278 Squadron with Ansons and Spitfires in residence from February to April 1944. No 169 Squadron re-formed at Ayr on October 1 1943 with a few Mosquitos and a Beaufighter to begin training with *Gee*, leaving for Little Snoring in December for intruder operations.

No 1490 Flight provided target-towing facilities from October 1942 for the many local squadrons using Lysanders and Masters. In October 1943, this unit became 14 APC (Armament Practice Camp). A string of squadrons passed through in 1944 on short detachments to the APC, including 438, 439, 440 and 486 with Typhoons and 313, 322 and 611 with Spitfires.

On July 2 1944, part of 772 Squadron, consisting of seven Blenheims, five Swordfish, four Martinets and two Fulmers flew in from Macrihanish. This heralded the transfer of Ayr from ADGB 13 Group to the Admiralty, on loan, on September 16 1944, when it was named HMS *Wagtail*. No 14 APC now closed and the airfield began to house squadrons disembarked from carriers in the Clyde. The former included 1843 with Corsairs, there between August and October 1944, 1770 with Fireflies, 882 with Wildcats and Fireflies, there in May and June 1945, 846 with Avengers there at the same time and 802 with Seafires there from September 1945 until April 1946. Also, a small land-plane detachment of MAEE Helensburgh transferred here from Prestwick in September 1944.

A gaggle of Spitfires of 58 OTU sit at Balado Bridge, 1942 (R.E.G. Sheward via C.H. Thomas).

The airfield closed in 1946 but the site was used from 1951 until 1957 as a storage annexe for USAF units at Prestwick. There are no buildings left on it now but it once had three Bellmans and 17 Blisters dispersed around the perimeter.

Ayr (racecourse), Strathclyde

70/NS350220. Just E of town

No 1 School of Aerial Fighting formed here in September 1917 with Camels, DH 2s and other types. It became 1 School of Aerial Fighting and Gunnery on May 10 1918 and moved to Turnberry the same day. The North Western Area Flying Instructors School formed here on July 1 1918, mainly flying the Bristol Fighter, until it moved to Redcar in 1919.

Balado Bridge, Tayside

58/NO095035. 2 miles W of Milnathort on A91

Opened on March 20 1942 as a satellite to Grangemouth, it was hoped that its weather record would prove better than that of the parent and thus increase the amount of flying hours available for training. All 58 OTU's advanced flying was to be done from the satellite, the first batch of pupils arriving on March 23. It was soon to be designated the Advanced Training Centre, unofficially 'Synthetic City' from the number of ground training aids in use.

From April 1942, the OTU's air-firing squadron, previously stationed half at Grangemouth and half at Macmerry, moved to Balado. Beginning at the end of May, in co-operation with 13 Group, senior pupil pilots from Balado were sent to Dyce to get a taste of flying under active service conditions.

The airfield itself was gradually improved as the mud dried out and the grass grew beside the two runways. (Three had been planned but only the tiny stub of the third was laid, similar to what happened at Charterhall.) Some of the living sites, however, did not have water laid on for many months and only four Blister hangars were provided. The aerodrome is also recorded as having a combined 'B1' and Super Robin hangar, an unlikely alliance which perhaps dated from later in the war.

Simulated night flying started from Balado on August 5 1942, the pilots wearing special goggles to reproduce dark conditions. The runway-in-use was marked by eight sodium flares.

No 58 OTU became 2 Tactical Exercise Unit on October 17 1943 and its Spitfires and Hurricanes continued to use Balado until the unit closed in June 1944. The airfield was then transferred on loan to the War Department on November 3 1944.

Spitfire P7739 of 58 OTU at Balado 1942 (R.E.G. Sheward via C.H. Thomas).

After the war it became an aircraft graveyard when McDonnell Aircraft of nearby Milnathort broke up many hundreds of surplus FAA aircraft. The work reached a peak in 1946/47, but even as late as February 1952 there were many airframes still to be seen in various stages of dismemberment. The most numerous were Harvards but there were also Fulmars, Fireflies, Martinets, Barracudas, Expeditors and a rare Fairchild Cornell FT673. Three Expeditors were all that remained in 1955.

The most interesting relic present in March 1952 was not naval at all, being a Vultee BT-13A with the American civil

Expeditor HD763 derelict at Balado, August 1956. Compare same aircraft in section on Fearn (P. Quaile).

Photo of Wrens at Ballyhalbert marking the hits on a target drogue in 1945. Seafire IIIs of 718 Squadron in background (E. Jackson via M.J. Burrows).

registration *NX54084*. This was the aircraft in which Mrs Morrow-Tait finished her round-the-world flight in 1950, having crashed her Proctor *G-AJMH Thursday's Child* in Alaska! There were also some gliders and light aircraft based at Balado from 1946 up to the time it was closed for flying in 1957 and all operations transferred to a new site at Portmoak. It is now a radio station with aerials inside 'golf-ball' housings.

Ballyhalbert, Down

21/J635635. At Ballyhalbert, off A2.

Starting life as a key fighter station in the

The same area as pictured above in 1983 (E.A. Cromie).

defence of Belfast and now in retirement as a caravan site, Ballyhalbert saw many squadrons come and go and its runways and dispersals are still in good condition even though blocked by trailers.

It was completed in mid-1941 as a Sector Station with a satellite at Kirkistown. Originally administered by 13 Group when it opened on June 28 1941, it came under the new 82 Group on September 25 of that year. There were three tarmac runways, two Bellman hangars and eventually six Blisters, and a decoy site was operated at Keaney. The first operational unit was 245 Squadron whose Hurricanes flew air defence and convoy patrols from July 14 until they moved to England on September 1 1941.

No 504 Squadron brought its Hurricanes in on October 26 1941, (damaging seven of them in a strong cross-wind), but soon converted to Spitfires. Occasional enemy reconnaissance aircraft over Northern Ireland were pursued to the

limit of the Spitfires' fuel, some being damaged and one forced down. There was a steady drain of pilots owing to accidents, several being caused by the airfield's poor weather records. A scramble in bad visibility on February 9 1942 resulted in one Spitfire putting down in a ploughed field near West Freugh, another was homed with 6 gallons of petrol left and another disappeared without trace. The unfortunate pilot, Sergeant Cannon, was eventually washed up in a dinghy on the Mull of Galloway, having died of exposure.

A night fighter squadron, No 25, with Beaufighters, was posted here on January 24 1942 and stayed until May 16. The day defence role passed to 501 Squadron on October 19 1942 and its Spitfires stayed until April 30 1943. The USAAF's 5th Fighter Squadron was detached there from Eglinton in the autumn of 1942 with Spitfires and 1493 Gunnery Flight was also in residence. There were some FAA squadrons here for brief periods, including 887 and 888.

Complaints about hasty and inadequate construction were common on wartime airfields but Ballyhalbert seems to have had more than its fair share of trouble. In January 1943 all the brick buildings were in a deplorable state and after heavy rain most of them were streaming with water coming in through the walls. On at least one occasion the CO called for a Court of Inquiry.

No 130 Squadron took over on April 30 1943 with Spitfires, moving to Honiley on July 5. Two weeks later Mustang 1s appeared, operated by a detachment of 26

Squadron and sharing the station with 315 Squadron's Spitfires which moved to Heston to join 2nd TAF on November 13 1943. More Spitfires arrived in the hands of 303 Squadron until this unit also joined 2nd TAF at the end of April 1944. Night defence was not overlooked either, this being the responsibility of a detachment of 125 Squadron's Beaufighters, which were there from November 1943 until March 1944.

The Kirkistown satellite was lost in March 1944, being transferred to RAFNI for administration, but this did not stop Ballyhalbert from accommodating a number of Royal Navy Squadrons in the opening months of 1944. On February 5, No 24 Fighter Wing, consisting of 887 and 897 Squadrons, flew in from Burscough, leaving in April for Culmhead, Devon. A detachment of Fulmars of 784 Squadron was here for a short time, as were the Hellcats of 1840 Squadron. The latter practised high- and low-level attacks on gun positions in the Belfast area and made interceptions and dummy attacks on small formations of Liberators from Cluntoe.

Ballyhalbert was not destined to become an RNAS until April 1945, but nevertheless it was occupied almost solely by naval squadrons from August 1944. On August 5, No 3 Naval Wing—808 and 805 Squadrons—equipped with Seafires, arrived from Lee-on-Solent and a detachment of two Martinets from 725 Squadron at Eglinton was sent to provide target towing facilities for them. Other

The 518/40 type watch tower at Bally-halbert (E.A. Cromie).

squadrons included 812 and 1846 for varying periods.

One of the last RAF units there, 1494 TT Flight, departed for North Weald in March 1945 and Ballyhalbert was transferred on loan to the Admiralty on April 24, although 1402 Met Flight, which had been there since late in November 1944, remained on a lodger basis under Coastal Command. The station was commissioned as HMS *Corncrake* on July 17 1945. No 718 Squadron with Seafires, Corsairs and Harvards arrived from Henstridge in August only to disband in November. The airfield was in naval parlance 'paid off' on November 13 1945 and transferred to Coastal Command on January 15 1946.

Ballykelly, Londonderry

4/C630240. 2 miles W of Limavady on A2

Unlike its near neighbour, Limavady, Ballykelly was kept open after the war and remained an RAF station until 1971. No doubt the proximity of the hills to Limavady was unacceptable in peacetime but they were also close to Ballykelly and the Shackleton crews called the highest 'Ben Twitch' because it always lurked there unseen in bad weather.

In mid-1940 the Airfields Board chose and approved a new site at Ballykelly, a contract was let and on June 1 1941 the RAF opening up party arrived to take over the partly finished aerodrome. Air Vice Marshal Carr, AOC RAFNI, landed

the first aircraft on the north/south runway on June 21, followed soon afterwards by the CO of Limavady in a Hudson.

Pending the allocation of operational aircraft, the airfield was not used very much, although a Hudson from Newfoundland crash-landed on August 25. The first week in December 1941, Coastal Command Development Unit was transferred from Carew Cheriton in South Wales. The unit flew several types, including the Hudson and Whitley, and more details of its work can be found in *Action Stations 3*.

CCDU was displaced to Tain on June 18 1942 to make way for 220 Squadron's Fortresses from Nutt's Corner two days later. Long-range convoy escort was their main duty, at least one Fort being out each day, and ASR sorties were also flown as required.

More American machines arrived on the station on July 21 1942 in the shape of the Liberators of 120 Squadron from Nutt's Corner. They had been using Ballykelly occasionally since the beginning of the year but the whole squadron was to be based here now, apart from detachments to Iceland. Routine patrols were flown, some Liberators refuelling at Predannack in Cornwall on the way home.

On August 16 there was a notable success when *F-AM917*, piloted by Squadron Leader T.M. Bulloch, was escorting a convoy. A U-boat was sighted and depth-charged and, although it submerged, wreckage came to the surface and it was thought to have been sunk.

There was a little-known attachment of

Above *Ballykelly 1982 showing frying pan, diamond hardstandings and V-Bomber ORPs.*

Below *Ballykelly BABS (Blind Approach Beam System) 1944.*

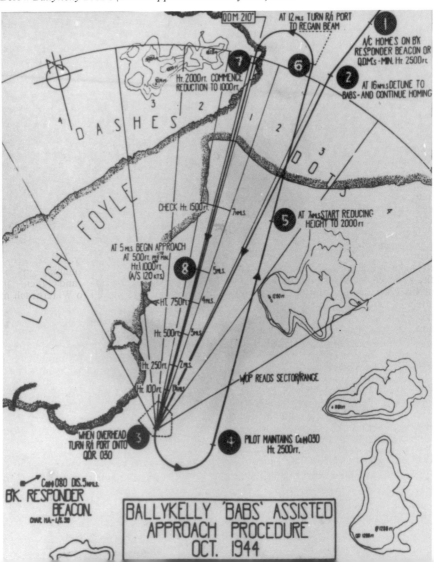

Fortress N5116N *of Chicago Tribune at Ballykelly, 1948.*

the US Navy's VP-73 Squadron there from October 27 1942 with Cansos. The next day, four Marauders staged through from Iceland. No 120 Squadron moved to Aldergrove on February 14 1943 and there was a gap in operational flying while many Royal Navy units disembarked temporarily from carriers. They included 811 with Swordfish and Wildcats in April, 836 with Swordfish, 892 with Wildcats, and 819 with Swordfish the same month. Swordfish squadrons 833, 834, 835 and 837 were all there briefly in May.

The Liberators of 86 Squadron arrived from Aldergrove on September 3 1943 for anti-submarine patrols, remaining here until March 1944 when they moved to Iceland. No 120 Squadron returned to Ballykelly from Iceland in March 1944, wasting no time in getting back into action. The same month Flight Lieutenant Kerrigan attacked a U-boat, but return fire knocked out an engine and killed one of his crew. Despite this, he found and attacked two more submarines, two more crew members being mortally wounded and a second engine lost. They were lucky to reach Skitten for a forced-landing.

Despite regular patrols, few submarines were sighted during the closing months of the war and the squadron disbanded at Ballykelly on June 4 1945. It was then Coastal Command's top-scoring squadron with 16 confirmed U-boat sinkings to its credit.

No 59 Squadron had been transferred over from Aldergrove in mid-September 1943, flying Liberators on anti-submarine patrols. U-boat encounters were many and a typical one on January 13 1944 involved Flying Officer Loney and crew. A submarine was sighted on the surface and a run-in made out of the sun. The Liberator dropped to 50 ft in the face of intense flak and six depth charges were released. Two more were dropped, and the conning tower was raked with machine gun fire. Two minutes later, the submarine dived stern upwards, leaving no debris, destruction being assessed as probable.

As a contribution to the success of the Normandy Invasion, the squadron made many sorties off the French coast under 19 Group control, covering the flanks. After June 20 the Liberators retired to their more usual hunting ground off the west coast of Ireland. Sadly, three aircraft were lost with no survivors in accidents during June.

In the autumn of 1944, some of the Liberators were fitted with cine cameras to film their attacks, but the level of sightings decreased sharply. The squadron took a hand in the rounding up of surrendering U-boats and then in September 1945 moved to Waterbeach in Cambridgeshire.

Disbanding at Ballykelly on October 24 1945 was 281, an ASR squadron with Sea Otters and Wellington XIVs. They had moved from Limavady in August when the latter closed. Ballykelly itself went to Care and Maintenance late in 1945, until the Joint Anti-Submarine School formed in 1947, flying Lancasters, Neptunes and Shackletons until at least 1963.

Operational squadrons were back once more in 1952, when 269 Squadron re-formed here on March 10 1952 with Shackletons. No 240 Squadron moved in from St Eval in June 1952 with more

Shackletons. No 269 was renumbered 210 Squadron on December 1 1958 and a month earlier 240 had become 203 Squadron. Both continued to fly maritime patrols until 203 left for Malta in February 1969 and 210 went to the Persian Gulf in November 1970.

No 203 Squadron re-formed at Ballykelly with Shackletons on January 1 1954 and flew the type until ceasing operations at the end of March 1971. The station has been occupied subsequently by the Army, who call it appropriately 'Shackleton Barracks'.

In its heyday Ballykelly was ideal for Liberators, being built with two of the 2,000 yd runways thought essential for this heavy aircraft. Hangarage was five 'T2's, three of them being extra long with 23 bays. Some were displaced when the huge Ballykelly Cantilever hangar was built to house Shackletons. Its vast interior now shelters Lynx and Gazelle helicopters of 655 Squadron. There is also an Admiralty 'S' shed and a Super Robin of twice the normal length.

A unique feature of Ballykelly was that when one of the runways was lengthened during the war it crossed a railway line. This necessitated a direct link between Flying Control and a local signal box.

Ballywalter, Down

15/J630675. 2½ miles S of Ballywalter on both sides of A2

Known officially as 16 SLG, this site was one of several prepared for 23 MU Aldergrove during the early months of 1941. It did not look a very promising choice when the first test landing was made by an Anson on April 25 1941. It was found that owing to the peculiar behaviour of the wind blowing across the landing strip an extension of about 250 yds was essential before operational types could be landed with any degree of safety.

Some more land was requisitioned and the SLG opened on June 1. Wellingtons were among the aircraft stored here but it was not used much at first, the total of its aircraft in the first nine months being 55 inward and 35 out. It was in full use for the latter part of the war, however, until it closed on March 14 1945.

Today it is easy to see where the landing strips were aligned. A tractor shed and pillbox remain and a gap in a stone wall through which aircraft were once towed into adjacent woodland has been filled with concrete blocks.

Standard tractor shed at Ballywalter SLG (E.A. Cromie).

Banff, Grampian

29/NJ620645. 6 miles W of Banff on B9139

One of the finest wartime airfield photographs was taken from the control tower at Banff early in May 1945. It reeks of atmosphere, with a line of Mosquitoes, heavy with rockets and fuel tanks, threading their way along the perimeter track to the end of the runway. Other Mosquitoes sit on their dispersals, the Station Flight Proctor looking out of place amongst all these warplanes. Bringing a touch of home to this bleak spot, the members of the fire crew have decorated their hut with a little white-stoned garden.

From the same tower today the contrast is absolute. The hangars are gone, the concrete is overgrown, the fire station no more. One somehow hopes to find a white-painted stone in the grass but there is nothing. Only the hills remain, silent, unchanged, the Banff Strike Wing but a millisecond in their long memory.

Banff, known locally as Boyndie, was built for Coastal Command during 1942, originally as a two-squadron General Reconnaissance station with a satellite at Dallachy. Because of the need for advanced bases in north-east Scotland, facilities were offered for up to 24 Bomber Command aircraft, although it was noted at the time that 3 OTU would be based there when the station opened and that the congestion might be unacceptable.

Plans changed however, and 3 OTU moved its HQ from Cranwell to Haverfordwest in South Wales. Banff was then transferred to the control of 21 Group Flying Training Command on April 5 1943 and the newly completed airfield was opened on April 21.

Towards the end of May, 14 (P)AFU Oxfords were ferried up from Ossington in Nottinghamshire. The unit was a very large one and had three BAT Flights affiliated to it; No 1512 at Banff itself, No 1542 at the Dallachy satellite and No 1518 detached at Edzell. Fraserburgh was also employed as a satellite. An enormous amount of flying was accomplished as the AFU got into its stride again despite the usual difficulties with problems like incomplete accommodation. The total flying hours completed in September were 12,009 by day and 2,691 by night.

While all this twin-engined pilot training was going on, there was the occasional unusual visitor. In August, for example, two Horsas stayed for ten days in connection with Operation *Tyndall*. On February 12 1944 a BOAC Lodestar on the Stockholm–Leuchars run diverted in.

In July 1944, the U-boats were withdrawing from the Bay of Biscay ports for bases in Germany and Scandinavia and it was decided to transfer the bulk of the 19 Group squadrons from south-west England to Scottish aerodromes to counter the threat from this new direction. Banff and Dallachy were expected to house four Wellington squadrons and plans were made to remove 14 (P)AFU at any time after September 1 1944 on receipt of 14 days' notice from Coastal Command. This timetable was accelerated and on August 10, the (P)AFU was

Below *Laden with rockets and long range tanks, Mosquitoes thread their way to the runway, Banff May 1945* (Via Chaz Bowyer), and **bottom** *desolation—the same scene in 1981.*

Top *Loading rockets on a Strike Wing Mosquito at Banff 1945* (Charles E. Brown).
Above *Red-spinnered Mosquito runs up on dispersal at Banff* (RAF Museum).

informed that it was to disband on August 31 rather than move to Haverfordwest as. had been suggested.

There was now a surplus of trained pilots and the (P)AFU could look back on a 12-month period during which its output was 1,516 pupils and a total of 113,896 flying hours. For the remaining 2½ months the astonishing figure of 620 pilots and 35,516 flying hours was achieved as the unit strove to complete the syllabus for as many pilots as possible.

The operational aircraft which replaced the Oxfords early in September were not Wellingtons, however, but a mixed Strike

Wing consisting of the Beaufighters of 144 and 404 Squadrons and the Mosquitoes of 235 Squadron. There was also a Mosquito Strike Wing comprising 248 and 333 (Norwegian) Squadron. The Beaufighter units moved to Dallachy in October 1944 and Banff was left to specialise in Mosquitoes, 143 Squadron joining the wing from Strubby on October 23 and converting from Beaufighters to Mosquitoes almost immediately.

Group Captain Max Aitken led the Strike Wing and at one time his six squadron commanders were made up of an Englishman, an Australian, a new

Zealander, a Norwegian, a Frenchman and an Irishman. Such was the severity of the losses that four of these commanding officers were killed on operations.

The first armed recce of the Norwegian coast came on September 14, when 44 aircraft took off, comprising 29 Mosquitoes and 19 Beaufighters. Four motor vessels sailing north and protected by two escorts were attacked and hits claimed on all of them. More *Rovers* took place at regular intervals, the basic plan being that the Mosquitoes would cover the torpedo-carrying Beaufighters against enemy fighters and smother flak ships, and 333 Squadron's experienced Norwegian pilots, often with local knowledge, would act as pathfinders to locate pinpoint targets in misty fiords.

The Mosquitoes used rocket projectiles for the first time from Banff on October 26 and could now bring the equivalent of a broadside from a cruiser against enemy shipping. Some of the Mosquitoes, the Mk XVIII, were armed with a six-pounder gun. Air opposition was absent at first but on December 7 1944 the strike Mosquitoes came face-to-face with fighters for the first time. Twenty-five from Banff with 40 Beaufighters of the Dallachy Wing, protected by 315 Squadron's Mustangs from Peterhead, were engaged by about a score of Bf 109s and Fw 190s. In the ensuing battle 315 Squadron claimed four 109s and two 190s collided. Two Mosquitoes, a Beaufighter and a Mustang failed to return.

Although the enemy was suffering badly from the incessant attacks which often struck right into his harbours, there was a steady toll of missing aircraft with little hope of further news from their crews. Strike Wing casualties were heavier than in any other flying done by the RAF in the last six months of the war.

Surviving a ditching for very long this far north in wintertime was impossible and an ASR detachment of 279 Squadron Warwicks loaded with survival gear would fly out to meet the returning aircraft and escort any crippled ones. On January 15 1945, six Mosquitoes were lost through intense flak and enemy fighter action, after two large merchant ships had been blown up in Leirvik Harbour.

If the activities of other RAF squadrons decreased as the war neared its end, that of the Coastal Strike units tended to accelerate. Most German shipping was by now of necessity concentrated between Denmark and Norway and some dramatic

actions took place in which ships were literally blasted apart by rockets. On April 9, 37 Mosquitoes of 143, 235 and 248 Squadrons sank three U-boats. Another highlight for Banff's Mosquitoes came on April 21 after a chance encounter with 18 Junkers torpedo bombers, which were heading for Scotland to harry shipping in a belated attempt to mete out some retribution. Some 45 Mosquitoes fell on them and nine Ju 88s and 188s were shot down.

Aircraft from Banff took part in the final shipping strike of the war, on May 4 1945, when small convoys were attacked in Kiel Bay. One Mosquito came back with part of a mast and a German ensign embedded in the nose!

Whereas VE-Day brought an end to operations for many of the Allied Air Forces, Coastal Command continued operating. There was fear of enemy submarines disregarding or being unaware that hostilities had ended. Thus the Mosquitoes flew convoy escort sorties until May 21 and searched for survivors from lost aircraft. Typically, Max Aitken, who had flown on the very first day of the war in Europe, saw to it that he also flew on the last. The final hours before VE-Day saw him out across the North Sea on patrol as far as Northern Denmark.

On June 1 1945, 143 Squadron was renumbered 14 Squadron, retaining its Mosquitoes until disbandment on March 31 1946. No 333 Squadron went to Norway in June and 235 and 248 Squadrons disbanded at Banff in mid-July 1945. No 489 Squadron repositioned from Dallachy on June 16 1945. No 404 Squadron, which had come from Dallachy to convert to the Mosquito in

Banff tower 1981.

March 1945, disbanded at Banff on May 25.

The airfield closed in the middle of 1946 and later became a target for simulated bombing by Lossiemouth units. It was reopened by the Banff Flying Club in 1976, the old tower being renovated and a runway cleared, but development plans seem to have been shelved.

Benbecula, Western Isles

22/NF785560. At Bailivanish on B892

The dominant factor at Benbecula was the almost constant wind and indifferent weather. Not for nothing did the CFI of a certain OTU threaten his pupils with a posting to Benbecula 'to pilot a balloon' if they broke the rules!

The wartime airfield grew out of a pre-war grass aerodrome used by Scottish Airways and known as Balivanich. Although the process of opening up had begun in August 1941, the station was very slow in becoming operational and there were few movements until well into the following year. The first night landing occurred on May 23, when an air ambulance ferried a serious case to the mainland. Being one of the few airfields on the Western Isles, Benbecula made a useful ELG and a *Darkie* watch for lost or crippled aircraft was maintained from 1942 onwards. The first to find a haven was Wellington *C* of 7 OTU on June 27 and later in the year Boston *BZ230* landed direct from Newfoundland.

On June 30 1942, 206 Squadron formed here with Hudsons for anti-submarine sweeps, the first being made by four aircraft the following day. Several U-boats were attacked during subsequent months but with no definite result. The squadron gradually re-equipped with Fortresses and on November 25 1942 one of these dropped seven depth charges on a submerged submarine. Although oil was seen rising to the surface the kill remained unconfirmed.

The first definite victory by a Benbecula-based aircraft took place on January 15 1943, when a Fortress captained by Flying Officer Clark sent a U-boat to the bottom. The squadron spent many hours ecorting convoys, rounding up stragglers and searching for lifeboats. Often all they achieved was a brief glimpse of oil streaks and wreckage swallowed up in rain and fog. Occasionally they were successful, one instance being when a Fortress directed a Corvette to the SS *Cornwall* which was derelict after an attack.

A second Fortress squadron, No 220, arrived from Aldergrove on March 13 1943. The soul-destroying flights over empty grey sea were enlivened from time to time by encounters with U-boats. On August 3, *F* of 220 Squadron sighted one fully surfaced already being attacked by a Catalina. The Fortress stood off and covered the flying boat's run-in with its mid-upper and beam guns. The Catalina's depth charges failed to release, the submarine was lost in rain and visual contact was not regained. The patrol was continued and they later sighted what was thought to be a periscope. Depth charges were dropped but the target turned out to be a dead whale. These poor creatures were often the innocent victims of the Battle of the Atlantic because of their vague resemblance to underwater craft.

Fortress FL459 of 220 Squadron on bleak Benbecula 1943 (Imperial War Museum).

On June 11 1943 Fortress *R* of 206 Squadron flown by Wing Commander R.B. Thomson, DSO, made a successful attack which sank the *U-417*. The aircraft, however, was crippled by return fire and had to ditch. An SOS message brought would-be rescuers to the scene, the first, a US Navy Catalina from Iceland, being wrecked by the heavy seas and her crew had to take to their dinghy. The Fortress crew was eventually rescued by a Catalina of 190 Squadron.

The long-range squadrons, 206 and 220, left for the Azores early in October 1943 leaving Benbecula non-operational until September 21 1944 when the Wellington XIVs of 179 and 304 Squadrons moved in from Chivenor. The airfield had, in the meantime, been considered as an Atlantic Ferry staging post but was never officially recognised as such. Two Swordfish squadrons, 838 and 842, operated under Coastal Command from Benbecula in the autumn of 1944 for short-range patrols.

The enemy's increased use of *Schnorkel* made U-boat tracking very difficult and during the whole of October, 304 Squadron made over 80 sorties without a single sighting. Leigh Light tactics involved a high standard of instrument flying. The pilot had to make the run-in on instruments towards a radar contact and not allow himself to be distracted when the light was switched on. Only after the target had been illuminated could he glance outside the cockpit and make a definite changeover to visual flying. As soon as the target disappeared an equally definite change had to be made back to instrument flying. Considering that the run-in was made at 50 to 100 ft, often against heavy flak, this was one of the most dangerous tasks for an aircrew.

However, at Benbecula the Wellingtons' sorties were so abortive that a detachment of six was sent to Limavady at the end of January 1945. The squadron left for Cornwall in March, 179 Squadron having already gone to Chivenor towards the end of October 1944. No 36 Squadron was the replacement, but their move involved the loss of one Wellington without trace after the weather suddenly closed in at Benbecula. After this sad beginning the Squadron soon settled down to Hebridean conditions and in the words of the squadron diary: 'Learned to walk at the correct angle in the continuous gale and not to expect more than the occasional glimpse of the sun'.

In April, after the snow clearance and runway de-icing party had been in action for several days, some of the squadron members who still had desert sand in their boots considered volunteering for a warmer climate. The squadron carried out its last operational sortie on June 1 1945 and disbanded on the same day. The station went to Care and Maintenance in January 1946 and thereafter was used by BEA services.

The three runways at Benbecula used a method of construction known as 'sand carpet', which consisted of bitumen laid directly over compacted sand, resulting in a flexible surface. Although the land was not really suitable for airfield construction the strategic demands of the Battle of the Atlantic overruled this. Its exposed position only 16 ft above mean sea level subjected it to almost continuous high winds and ten special hangars were built known as '½T2's. They were supposed to offer less side area to the gales, but nevertheless doors were sometimes blown on to the aircraft inside. In 1949 Royal Dutch Airlines (KLM) acquired two of the hangars from Benbecula and re-erected them as one large building on the southern corner of Schiphol Airport. It was named *Hebrides* and was capable of taking three DC-6s. Perhaps it is still there.

In recent years the South Uist Rocket Range and RAF air defence radar unit have attracted trooping and supply flights. Indeed, when the range was being built Benbecula was returned to the RAF during 1957/8.

Bishops Court, Down

21/J580425. 4 miles NE of Ardglass off A2

One of the few wartime airfields still active in Northern Ireland, it was built quite late in the war, originally as a USAAF CCRC, and not opened until April 1 1943. The first aerial visitors were Ansons *EF358* from Jurby and *EF980* from Dumfries on April 16. Fairchild UC-61 *43-14422* of the USAAF called on June 11, an aircraft which seems to have been a common visitor at many Irish airfields around this time.

No 7 Air Observers School had formed on a 'paper date' of March 17 1943 but its first intake of trainees did not arrive at Bishops Court until July 31. At the same time, the first pupils were posted in for 12 AGS, a new unit which formed here on

August 1 1943 with the usual Ansons and Martinet target tugs.

The aerodrome attracted many stragglers, such as a Wellington on December 19 1943 which had been airborne for nine hours, most of the time over Eire. One of the AOS' own Ansons got lost whilst night flying and landed at Baldonnel near Dublin. After a night's hospitality the crew members were allowed to take off for their base.

During June 1943, the station was used as a diversion for Coastal Command Liberators, the 2,000 yd runway being much longer than usual for a training field. Two arrived at dusk one day for refuelling and took off at dawn the next day on patrol. Another Liberator landed

Bishops Court under construction on January 10 1943 (Via E.A. Cromie).

during the night but the ground handling of the aircraft was difficult because of the large quantities of petrol they required from small bowsers.

The early summer weather was so poor in 1944 that the AOS (since February 2 1944, renamed 7 (O)AFU) often put 40 aircraft up at night in July to get the training programme back on schedule. The AGS was having its troubles too; an

ATC cadets with Anson at Bishops Court 16 July 1946 (Via E.A. Cromie).

engineer was sent from the Bristol Aeroplane Company to investigate the continued low standard of serviceability of the Martinets' engines.

An organisation was set up to deal with the diversion of operational Coastal Command aircraft during September 1944, and, in spite of limited refuelling facilities and problems with accommodation, the station was proud that the aircraft were sent out on time in every case. Refuelling parties worked throughout the night but the airmen concerned definitely felt that they were doing something important for the war effort. Training was almost as important but there was no glamour attached to it and little excitement, such as the night when a Liberator accidentally dropped a depth charge on the tarmac whilst taxi-ing. Thankfully it did not go off and an armament party came from Ballykelly next morning to deal with it.

No 12 AGS closed down on May 26 1945, having trained 47 courses of air gunners, the personnel of the uncompleted 48th course being sent to RAF Barrow to complete their instruction. The (O)AFU became 7 ANS on May 31 and was redesignated 2 ANS on June 4 1947. By now flying Wellingtons, it moved to Middleton St George on October 1 1947.

The airfield was reduced to Care and Maintenance in January 1948 but was reactivated in 1952 and 3 ANS formed on March 3 with Ansons and Varsities. This unit disbanded on April 14 1954. Around 1955, the airfield was considered as a base for all-weather fighters and Operational Readiness Platforms were built at each end of the 06/24 runway, but no squadrons were ever sent there.

Being very exposed to the elements, Bishops Court had no less than 35 Enlarged Over Blister hangars by December 1944, as well as four 'T2's and full Mk II Drem lighting. Today, all the hangars have gone but the tower still stands and one of the runways is kept serviceable for occasional liaison flights to the adjacent radar site.

Black Isle, Highland

27/NH715605. 2 miles N of Rosemarkie off B9160

Sometimes referred to as Fortrose, after the nearest town where the personnel were billeted, 42 SLG had its first trial on August 12 1941 when an Anson was landed here. The official opening date was August 22, when it was affiliated to 46 MU, Lossiemouth. The consulting engineers, as with all SLGs in Britain, were Messrs Rendall, Palmer and Tritton.

The Beaufighter was the most numerous type stored here, but the greasy surface of the strip after rain caused difficulty with these heavy aircraft. On November 10 1942, Beaufighter *EL445* skidded and hit *EL533*, resulting in damage to both. A Halifax made a successful test landing in August 1942 but it was never found necessary to disperse four-engined types here.

The SLG acquired a Super Robin hangar from Lossiemouth in March 1944 and it was found to be just big enough to house one Beaufighter and two Defiants. The requirement for camouflage was no longer so important in the summer of 1944, and Black Isle, originally intended for the storage of 50–60 aircraft, found itself holding up to 117.

As soon as the European war ended, storage gave way to the breaking up of surplus Beaufighters, a working party from the Bristol Aeroplane Co being attached to 46 MU and its SLGs for the purpose. By the end of September 1945, the only aircraft left at Black Isle were two Warwicks in poor condition. After some remedial work they were flown out early in October, the SLG closing soon afterwards. The land is now a Forestry Commission nursery but several buildings survive.

Boa Island, Fermanagh

17/H115635. 5 miles W of Kesh on A47

Pronounced 'Bo' and sometimes known as Rock Bay, this satellite to Killadeas was used by 131 OTU from May 31 1944. Catalinas and Sunderlands flew from here until March 1945. A few buildings and the slipway can still be seen today.

Bogs O'Mayne, Grampian

See Elgin

Boulmer, Northumberland

81/NU255135. 2 miles E of Lesbury on unclassified road

This was the rather obscure satellite of Eshott and it is thus ironic that it is still in active use by the RAF long after the grass grew in the cracked runways of the parent station.

Eshott was occupied by 57 OTU for Spitfire training in mid-November 1942 and there was a rush to finish Boulmer so that the OTU's Advanced Training Squadron could move here. The target opening date of March 1 was met and the first Spitfires landed on that day. The OTU's Flight of Masters for conversion work on to single-seat fighters operated occasionally from Boulmer to relieve congestion at Eshott.

No 59 OTU at Milfield also employed Boulmer as a satellite for its Hurricanes in 1943/44 and another lodger unit was the 9 Group Battle School. This taught airfield defence to ground personnel and was here until well into 1944.

The intensive Spitfire flying resulted in the usual run of training accidents. The proximity of the sea enabled one pilot to ditch successfully after engine failure in the circuit when he was ill-placed to avoid houses on the shore.

No 57 OTU fell victim to the contraction of the RAF after VE-Day and disbanded on June 6 1945. Boulmer was then reduced to Care and Maintenance as a satellite of Acklington, although a Proctor did make a precautionary landing in bad weather on October 29 1945.

In the '60s the airfield was used as an RLG by 6 FTS Acklington and also lodged an SAR Flight of Whirlwinds. Today it has Sea Kings. An RAF air traffic control unit, Border Radar, has also been there for many years.

Bowmore, Strathclyde

60/NR311601. Alongside Bowmore town.

Bowmore was never much more than a satellite to Oban and other marine bases. It possessed no hangarage or slipway but there were three dispersed sleeping sites and one communal site. A small bomb dump was situated just to the south-west of the town. There had, incidentally, been a pre-war land aerodrome at Bowmore

connected to Renfrew by aircraft of Midland and Scottish Air Ferries.

On September 21 1940, 'G' Flight was formed at Bowmore to operate the three Short S.26 flying boats built for BOAC as their G-Class. The base was used also by the Oban squadrons as an unofficial satellite. For example, on March 28 1941 Sunderland *R* of 201 Squadron flying from there had a brief battle with a Condor and a Ju 88 attacking a merchant ship. The Condor was engaged head-on and hits were claimed, the Sunderland remaining undamaged.

Meanwhile, the 'G-boats' had been fitted with gun turrets and bomb racks, the first operational patrol being carried out by *Golden Fleece* on December 15 1940. *Golden Hind* became operational on February 2 1941 and on March 13 the flight became 119 Squadron and was joined by *Golden Horn* on April 10. The C-Class boats *Clio* and *Cordelia* were also used, but were withdrawn for transport duties soon after the squadron moved to Pembroke Dock on August 4 1941.

The next squadron to fly anti-submarine patrols from here was 246 with Sunderlands. It actually formed on September 1 1942 but did not become operational until December 12. It disbanded on April 30 1943 and the aircraft were distributed amongst other units.

A detachment of 422 Squadron arrived from Oban in May 1943 and its Canadian airmen wasted no time in setting up a softball diamond. Sunderland *S* of 422 Squadron had to ditch out in the Atlantic on September 10 after being badly damaged in an attack on a U-boat but most of the crew members were picked up by the Royal Navy.

At the end of September it was be-

Sunderlands and G-Boat at Bowmore (Imperial War Museum).

coming increasingly evident that the running of an operational squadron at Bowmore would be very difficult during the coming winter months. A severe gale in the unsheltered mooring area would be disastrous and this, combined with the lack of a slipway and other maintenance facilities, resulted in the squadron moving to Castle Archdale at the beginning of November 1943.

Since about February 1943, Catalinas of 131 OTU Killadeas had been using Bowmore for alighting practice, even after the station closed down on January 15 1944. The marine craft section was retained on stand-by, however, for re-fuelling and flare-path duties for 131 OTU and any other diverted or transit aircraft.

One January night in 1944, a diverted Sunderland belonging to 422 Squadron sank in a gale whilst riding at anchor in Loch Indaal. Four of the crew were on board at the time and three of them managed to launch à dinghy. The second pilot was not able to reach it and was eventually rescued from the tailplane none the worse for his experience. The flying-boat base finally closed in July 1945 and peace returned to Loch Indaal.

Brackla, Highland

27/NH855520. 4 miles SW of Nairn on B9090

Many airmen remember Brackla with a shudder, for after it became an Aircrew Allocation Centre late in 1944, scores were posted here direct from a tour of duty in the tropics. One ex-Catalina Flight Engineer arrived from Ceylon in January 1945 and found a Nissen hut in the Scottish winter unbearable even with six blankets!

The airfield started life, however, as an RLG for 2 AGS at Dalcross, opening in July 1941. It proved particularly useful the following winter when the parent station became somewhat the worse for wear and a drying-out period was needed. The RLG was extended in April 1942, having also housed a Conversion Flight of Whitleys from 19 OTU since January 7 1942.

No 2 AGS was still permitted to land at Brackla but used Leanach in preference, until asked by the MAP to go elsewhere. They began flying from Brackla again on December 5 1943, but it was made clear that, although the domestic buildings were occupied temporarily by soldiers, the airfield belonged to Bomber Command as second satellite to Kinloss.

Since 19 OTU was not actually using Brackla during this period, another lodger, 19 (P)AFU, employed it as an RLG for its Oxfords from December 3 1943 until disbandment on February 25 1944. It had by now acquired wire mesh runways and four 'T2' hangars, none of which survives today. The OTU gave up Brackla on April 27 1944 and it was later used by 14 (P)AFU at Banff as an RLG from June 17 until September 1944.

The following month, four officers of 45 MU Kinloss inspected Brackla with a view to using it for the breaking down of Halifax aircraft and found it eminently suitable. They did not take it over, however, until February 7 1945 as 102 SSS. The first of 130 Halifaxes was ferried in on February 20 for long-term storage and eventual scrapping. The site is believed to have been active until late in 1946 and there is not much left to see apart from the usual collection of huts.

Brunton, Northumberland

75/NU205255. At Tughall off B1339

With a decoy site at Elford, Brunton was occupied first by part of 59 OTU on August 4 1942, when 17 Hurricanes flew in from Longtown. The unit began to receive Typhoons in May of the following year for conversion flying but Hurricanes were still the main equipment. Under the *Saracen* Scheme 559 Squadron is recorded as being at Brunton in March 1943, but moved to Milfield in May.

By June 1943, 59 OTU had become the specialised Typhoon OTU, but, the supply of aircraft being limited, most of the training course continued to be done on Hurricanes until matters improved. Brunton's runways and perimeter track were by now showing signs of wear and an extensive reconstruction programme was started in the summer of 1943, carefully planned to keep disruption of flying to a minimum.

No 59 OTU disbanded in January 1944 to become the FLS with effect from the 26th of that month. Although Brunton was still nominally a satellite of Milfield, it seems to have been used very little by the FLS, apart from being a convenient target for small practice bombs. Refuelling and rearming exercises by the FLS were also carried out at intervals in 1944.

The FLS moved to Wittering on December 27 1944 and 56 OTU began to

use Brunton in January 1945 for the final
phase of its training syllabus. All aircraft
were withdrawn from the satellite on May
21 1945 and it was then closed.

On October 28 1948, a Mosquito from
Acklington crash-landed at Brunton and
in recent years light aircraft have been
flown from here. The site is also currently
used for free-fall parachuting.

A little-known fact is the presence of an
airship sub-station at Chathill, one mile
north-west of Brunton. It came under the
control of East Fortune and opened in
1918.

Buddon, Tayside

54/NO53-31- 1 mile NE of Monifieth off
A930*

On May 1 and 2 1966, 600 troops were
landed at the Army training area at
Buddon from the assault ship HMS
Fearless as part of a combined operation.
They were supported by two Wessex helicopters operating from the ship's flight
deck and spent two weeks building a 5,000
ft airstrip, complete with emergency bulk
fuel installations. On May 13, a Beverley
of 47 Squadron made several landings and
take-offs from the packed sand surface.
This was the first time that a temporary
airfield project of this magnitude had
been attempted in Britain. The strip
continued to be used until 1976 by Beaver
aircraft liaising with the adjacent Army
camp.

**At the time of writing the complete map refer-
ence is not available.*

*Brunton 1981. Note symmetrical pattern
of runways and perimeter track* (F. Neal).

Burrow Head (Kidsdale), Dumfries and Galloway

See Kidsdale

Buttergask, Tayside

*53/NO205335. 2 miles S of Burrelton on
unclassified road off A94*

Although only a large field, this aerodrome saw thousands of movements by
trainee pilots 'circuit bashing' in Tiger
Moths. It was taken into use as an RLG
by 11 EFTS at Perth some time in 1941
and was still in use as late as November 8
1945 when a Tiger Moth crashed whilst
practising forced-landings here. Whether
it was used continuously between these
dates is not recorded in the EFTS diary.

Campbeltown, Strathclyde

*68/NR680205. 2½ miles W of Campbel-
town on B843*

One pilot described Campbeltown thus:
'The field really was quite primitive.
Ground-to-air signals were still in the
stone age and there was only one small
hangar, supplemented by a Bessonneau
with a tendency to fly off on its own. The
control tower consisted of Mr McGeachy,
the Scottish Airways agent, a stove, ample
supplies of tea, and a telephone. During
night flying one of the observers was laid
on with an Aldis lamp . . . .. It was an

unmistakeable Admiralty selection, between two sharp ranges of hills and up and down in all directions like the ocean wave in six cross-winds!'

It was also 90 miles from a railway, so that spare engines had to come by sea. Despite these drawbacks, the Royal Navy requisitioned the aerodrome on February 12 1940 and shared it with Scottish Airways who had been flying through here since 1934, linking Kintyre with Glasgow.

Swordfish and Albacores were the most common naval types to be seen, there being little room for anything faster. Nos 816 and 818 Squadrons operated Swordfish in February/March 1940 and later in the year 828 arrived from St Merryn with Albacores for a period of working-up. Target-towing was provided by 772 Squadron with Swordfish and other types from July 1940 to July 1941.

The station was commissioned on April 1 1941 as HMS *Landrail*, later becoming *Landrail II* when nearby Macrihanish opened as parent station. Lysanders of an RAF unit, 614 Squadron, stayed for a few days in May 1941 for combined exercises. Other based squadrons included 832 with Albacores from May 29 to August 1941, and 810 with Swordfish between February 26 and March 9 1942. More of the ageing biplanes were flown by 766 Squadron from February to July 1943.

The build-up of Macrihanish from 1941 soon eclipsed Campbeltown, although the latter's personnel were able to live at the larger aerodrome. By 1943, Campbeltown's role was to absorb the overflow from the parent-housing, for example, the aircraft of squadrons on shore leave.

Those other than biplanes had to be landed at Macrihanish and towed or taxied along the road to the satellite. The fact that the circuits of the two airfields overlapped also precluded any development at Campbeltown and it closed in mid-1945.

Castle Archdale (Lough Erne), Co Fermanagh
17/H175585. 4 miles W of Irvinestown off B82

On the morning of May 26 1941, a chance encounter by Catalina Z of 209 Squadron sealed the fate of the battleship *Bismarck*. The ship had evaded British pursuit on her maiden raid against Allied merchant shipping but the sighting report ensured that her sinking of HMS *Hood* would soon be avenged. The Catalina's captain was Flying Officer Dennis Briggs but it was actually the American co-pilot, Ensign Leonard B. Smith, who spotted the vessel. Since America was still neutral, the presence of a number of US Navy pilots gaining operational experience with Coastal Command and passing on their knowledge of the Catalina, was a strict secret, so Smith's part in it was never made public.

The flying boat base from which the Catalinas ranged out over the ocean had opened early in February 1941 as RAF Castle Archdale but was renamed RAF Lough Erne on Air Ministry orders on February 18. (The title was to revert to

Catalina over Enniskillen June 5 1943 (Via Ian Henderson).

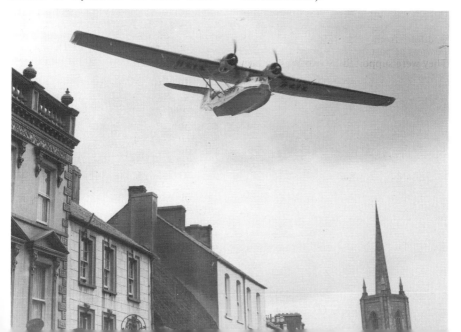

Top *Cluttered maintenance area at Castle Archdale 1944* (P.H.T. Green collection).

Above *Close-up of the same area* (Via Chaz Bowyer).

Below *Sunderlands at Castle Archdale* (Public Archives of Canada).

Castle Archdale in January 1943.) It was anticipated that 240 Squadron, then at nearby Killadeas, would operate from there but in the event it did not move in entirely until August 1941. In the meantime its Stranraers flew ocean patrols from the Lough.

Towards the end of March 1941, 209 Squadron brought its Lerwicks from Stranraer. The type was not a success and they were soon replaced by Catalinas, one of which sank an Italian submarine on May 16. It was shadowing a convoy and the escorting corvettes confirmed the kill.

No 209 Squadron moved to Iceland in August 1941, its place being taken by the Catalinas of 240 Squadron from nearby Killadeas on August 25. This unit was posted to the Far East at the end of March 1942.

No 201 Squadron's Sunderlands arrived from Sullom Voe on September 30 1941 to fly Atlantic patrols. It was monotonous work made hazardous by the severe winter of 1941/42 and it was not until April 1942 that a U-boat was attacked. The squadron's first confirmed submarine sinking took place on May 31 1943, when Flight Lieutenant Hall and crew encountered the *U-440*. To help bottle up the Channel for D-Day, 201 Squadron moved to Pembroke Dock in April 1944.

Lough Erne was considered to be almost the ideal stretch of water for flying boat operations and it was envisaged that in the event of Foynes in the Republic being denied to Allied aircraft, the Clipper services would use it as a terminal. Fortunately this never happened, but occasional civil boats alighted on the Lough, including a Pan Am Clipper which took Queen Wilhelmina of the Netherlands and her party to New York on June 17 1942. The Queen returned *en route* for London the following summer.

No 119 Squadron began to re-form here as an operational unit with its Catalinas beginning to arrive during May 1942. After a period of working up it moved to Pembroke Dock on September 6 1942. Three days later, 302 FTU formed at Castle Archdale to train crews for ferrying flying boats overseas. It left for Stranraer on December 1 1942. From Oban came 228 Squadron on December 11, equipped with Sunderlands and staying up to May 4 1943, little action being seen.

Two Canadian squadrons, 422 and 423, then came on the scene. No 422 had formed on April 2 1942 at Lough Erne and worked-up on Lerwicks. This type was not to be used operationally and the unit re-equipped with Catalinas in August and moved to Oban in November 1942. After it returned to Castle Archdale in November 1943, operations were begun in the Western Approaches with Sunderlands.

Flight Lieutenant W.Y. Martin's crew seemed to have all the luck, as on December 27 1943 they attacked a blockade-running enemy merchant vessel, sustaining damage themselves. The same crew mauled a U-boat so severely on March 10 1944 that the crew abandoned it. This was the last attack made by the squadron before it moved to Pembroke Dock in November 1944.

For about three years, beginning in November 1942, 423 Squadron made its

Flying boat dock at Castle Archdale believed to have been built for Shetlands (E.A. Cromie).

home in Northern Ireland, flying Sunderlands off the Lough and sometimes detaching them to Pembroke Dock. Many subs were attacked, several being confirmed destroyed, including *U-456* which was shared between Flight Lieutenant Musgrave and two destroyers. In September 1944 the unit flew no less than 100 operational sorties. Its last U-boat fight occurred as late as May 4 1945.

Sunderland F-423 Squadron made the last operational flight from Castle Archdale on May 13 1945, an uneventful patrol to the south-west of Ireland. No 423 joined Transport Command in August and moved to Bassingbourn to re-equip with Liberators. On June 27 1945, 202 Squadron disbanded. It had been flying night Leigh Light patrols with Sunderlands from Archdale since September 1944 but had made few attacks.

Lough Erne was, and still is, a remote and extremely beautiful part of Ulster. Entertainment was basic but one Catalina pilot who diverted in on a ferry flight was surprised to find a Palm Court style quartet playing in the officers' mess. McKenna's Bar and Ma Bothwell's Dining Room in Irvinestown were popular rendezvous and an opportunity to escape from what the Canadians knew as 'Skonk Hollow' after the L'il Abner cartoon.

Flying Control was carried out from the operations room up to late in 1943, when it was transferred to a control room overlooking the Lough. A control pinnace was permanently on the water in radio contact with the shore.

For night flying the take-off path was delineated by three small lights on anchored floats which could be changed. Compared to the elabroate lighting of the Drem Mk II system, it was very rudimentary and once the third light was passed during take off there was nothing on which to keep straight. A fully-laden boat might need a run of up to three minutes and thus quite a long part of the take-off run was in darkness. The Lough was buoyed for day and night flying, but pilots were required to 'know' the areas which were safe, as they were not, of course, defined in the manner of runways on land.

In the great freeze-up of January 1945, the Lough had 5 in of ice on it and many aircraft had hulls damaged by the squeezing effect. Ice-breaking patrols were made by marine craft, but they had to give up in the end and it was then possible to walk out to the aircraft, some of which were

half a mile offshore.

After the war, 230 Squadron was here with Sunderlands from April to September 1 1946. In 1945, a large dock was built, supposedly for the Short Shetland (a type which never reached production), although there is only circumstantial evidence to support this.

The entire vast complex of the base has now been cleared, but the numerous hardstandings and hut bases make an excellent caravan park. The operations block has been converted into a tourist centre and is scarcely recognisable. In retrospect, Lough Erne must have been one of the most picturesque places in the British Isles from which to fight a war.

Castle Kennedy, Dumfries and Galloway

82/NX120595. 3 miles ESE of Stranraer on A75

Opened in 1941 under 25 (Armament) Group, Castle Kennedy was first occupied by the CGS from July 3, although most of the flying was done from nearby West Freugh because of waterlogging. No 10 AGS formed on July 24 1941 with Defiants and Lysanders. The unit moved to Barrow on December 16 1941, the CGS having already moved out earlier during the month.

The airfield was then closed for the construction of two concrete runways and 3 AGS reformed here on April 20 1942. By now, three Callender-Hamilton hangars had been erected and the living quarters and instructional sites had been completed in the grounds of Loch Inch Castle.

The AGS was moved to Mona in Anglesey on December 19 1942 to make room for 2 TTU, a new organisation forming under 17 Group, with Beaufighters and Beauforts. No 2 TTU was absorbed by 1 TTU on September 29 1943 and the airfield was allocated to Flying Training Command on October 25. It had been offered to the Navy earlier in the year to meet one of their requirements but this was not acted upon.

No 3 AGS returned to its old home in November 1943, bringing Ansons and Martinets. Luce Bay was the air-to-air firing area, a typical course having about 90 pupils. The duration depended on suitable flying weather, but was usually about seven weeks, during which each gunner did 16 hours in the air but many more on

Callender-Hamilton hangar at Castle Kennedy (J. Huggon).

the ground learning how to manipulate a power turret.

Its routine but vital job done, the school disbanded on June 21 1945, the airfield then passing to 41 Group Maintenance Command. No 57 MU Wig Bay then used it as a service manned Sub-Storage Site, No 104. The first aircraft, 15 Wellingtons, were flown in towards the end of June although the main type stored was the Mosquito, some 40 being in hangars on the station in October 1945. The aerodrome was by now closed for flying but available in emergency.

In 1955 it was reopened for car ferry flights by Bristol 170s of Silver City Airways. A Newtownards service was flown until 1957, after which the airfield was used occasionally by light aircraft. The three hangars are still to be seen but the nine Blisters are long gone.

Castletown, Highland

12/ND215670. 1½ miles SE of Castletown on B876

This is an airfield whose remoteness belies its one-time strategic importance in the defence of Scapa Flow and Northern Scotland. Situated in rolling country close to the sea, it is a pleasant if breezy place in summer but one shudders to think how bleak it could be in winter, with icy gales sweeping in from the north and waves crashing against the towering Dunnet Head.

It opened as a satellite to Wick in May 1940 and received 504 Squadron's Hurricanes from that station on June 21. The squadron was resting after the hard

fighting in France, and, after an uneventful stay, left for the south and the Battle of Britain on September 1. The next day, 3 Squadron's Hurricanes took over, but only stayed for a fortnight, being replaced by 232 Squadron from Sumburgh. The Fulmers of 808 Squadron had already arrived on September 9 from St Merryn in Cornwall and stayed until October 2.

With this force, Castletown prepared for the invasion, which was thought imminent at several points around the British mainland. A scheme for counterattacking should the airfield fall into enemy hands had been devised, but it was thought likely that a landing on Dunnet Head would prove very unhealthy for the Germans. The main reason was 'Big Bertha', a 4.7 in gun, formerly naval but now in the hands of the RAF.

Nothing happened, however, and on October 2 the Fulmars left for Donibristle, with 232 Squadron going to Skitten on October 13. No 3 Squadron from Dyce relieved them, staying until January 7 1941.

Some light relief came in October 1940, when a high-ranking officer visited the camp and was taken to inspect the new cookhouse. Unfortunately, an overnight gale had blown off most of the roof, but his sense of humour proved equal to the occasion!

On November 25 1940, three Hurricanes of 3 Squadron challenged a Whitley near Wick which did not respond and tried to reach cloud cover. Knowing that the Luftwaffe was supposed to be using a captured Whitley for meteorological purposes, they opened fire. The aircraft crash-landed at Wick with an engine burning and no injuries to the crew, which was fortunate, as it had come from Kinloss!

No 1 Canadian Squadron became operational at Castletown at dawn on December 12 1940, already having over 70 confirmed kills to its credit during the fighting over the Home Counties. They were unlucky up here, however, being robbed of an almost certain victory over a Ju 88 on Christmas Day when Martlets from Skeabrae intervened. In January, they chased another Ju 88, but it vanished into dense cloud.

Squadron followed squadron in rapid succession at Castletown for air defence patrols over Scapa. Some of the moves were complicated; for example on January 7 1941, 3 Squadron left for Skeabrae. Two Harrows carried ground crews and stores and on the return journey air-lifted those of 804 Squadron from Skeabrae to Skitten. No 260 Squadron then moved from Skitten, thus completing a triangular move. One wonders why it was all necessary but no doubt it was part of a grand plan.

Later in January a raging blizzard covered the North with a deep layer of snow but the problem was overcome at Castletown by rolling the runways until the snow became packed. Aircraft then continued to operate normally, the rations were dropped on home-made parachutes from a Hurricane to an RAF detachment at Sango who were cut off by the snow. RAF Skitten, too, was supplied with provisions and a Harrow was sent to Inverness to collect a supply of fresh beef.

No 260 Squadron went to Skitten on February 10 and a few days later Castletown lost its popular CO when Wing Commander D.F.W. Atcherley was posted to command 25 Squadron at Martlesham. No 3 Squadron was now

Butts at Castletown.

responsible for Scapa defence, supported by 213 Squadron also equipped with Hurricanes. There was a further reshuffle in April 1941, when 17 Squadron was withdrawn from Martlesham to Castletown for a rest, to be replaced at the former by 3 Squadron.

In May, Spitfires began to arrive for 124 Squadron which re-formed here on May 10. It became operational in June, flying coastal and convoy patrols and acting also as a post-OTU to introduce pilots to operational flying and then post them to units in the South.

No 124 itself went to Biggin Hill in November 1941. Blenheims of 404 Squadron flew in on June 20 from Thorney Island but moved to Skitten on July 4. No 607's Hurricanes were thus displaced from Skitten and arrived over Castletown in a most impressive squadron formation. Further ceremony was provided in August when Marshal of the RAF, Lord Trenchard, inspected this lonely outpost. Castletown fighters also provided an escort when HM the King flew from Inverness in a Hudson to inspect the Fleet at Scapa. Escorted by 36 fighters, his aircraft flew over Castletown en route to Hatston.

Other based squadrons in 1941 included the Norwegian-manned 331 in August/September and 54 from November until June the following year. No 167 arrived from Acklington on June 1 1942 and one of its aircraft almost shot down a Ju 88 in August but lost it in the mist after a three-second burst. This squadron was posted to Ludham in Norfolk in October 1942 to relieve 610 Squadron, which took over at

Castletown until January 1943, when it went to Westhampnett. Defensive patrols were undertaken by 131 Squadron's Spitfires which stayed until June 1943.

A new ASR Squadron, 282, formed here on January 1 1943, at first with Walruses, but these were supplemented by Ansons in March. In November it took over 281 Squadron's detachments at Drem and Ayr and operated around the Scottish coasts until it merged with 281 Squadron on January 31 1944. A detachment of 278 ASR Squadron was also here from February 10 until April 22 1944.

On June 26 1943, 14 Harrows flew in the ground staff of 310 Squadron from Exeter, those of 131 Squadron embarking for the return trip. No 310 had a few high-altitude Spitfires for attacking enemy reconnaissance machines over the Orkneys and moved to Sumburgh on July 19 1943.

No 504 Squadron was here in April 1944 and on April 22 two Spitfires on a dusk patrol east of the Orkneys shot down the first aircraft claimed by Castletown units for several years. The Ju 188 was sent into the sea near the Pentland Skerries with Flying Officer Waslyk and Sergeant Thorne sharing the victory.

On April 30 1944, a Spitfire Vc of 504 Squadron was the last operational aircraft to leave Castletown. It was a pity that there were no fighters at readiness on May 18 when two Ju 188s flew in from the north-west at zero feet and disappeared inland without a shot being fired.

There were a few unusual visitors in June 1944 in connection with the unexpected arrival of a transatlantic Liberator on the obstructed airfield at Dounreay. Dakota KG615 collected the crew from Castletown and a couple of B-17s flew in spares and a ferry crew to retrieve the Liberator.

Very little happened after this, although another B-17 (43-39303) landed on February 20 1945, lost on a flight from Greenland. One of the last aerial visitors was a Hoverfly helicopter from Twatt on March 24 1945 which left for Dounreay. The Navy showed a brief interest in Castletown until the availability of Lossiemouth filled its requirements in the north of Scotland.

Today it is difficult to imagine that this collection of decaying huts and overgrown concrete was such a busy place. The former decontamination centre is full of cow manure, the Bellman and 'T3' hangars are long dismantled and the watch tower demolished. Light aircraft have been flown in recent years but the runways are in very poor condition.

Charterhall, Borders

74/NT765465. 3 miles NE of Greenlaw on B6460

Just after midnight on January 8 1943, Blenheim *BA194* crashed near Duns in Berwickshire killing the pilot Richard Hillary and his navigator Walter Fison. This was not an uncommon event at this night fighter training station known grimly as 'Slaughter Hall' because of its high accident rate, but Hillary was the author of *The Last Enemy*, a book which has become a classic of aviation literature. Badly burned in the Battle of Britain, Hillary wanted to get back onto operations and chose night fighters. Orbiting a flashing beacon at night he probably suffered vertigo and spiralled into the ground.

The airfield from which he flew was built on the site of a former First World War landing ground known as Eccles Tofts which had been used by 77 Squadron in 1916 and late 1917. Squadron Leader Lewis Brandon in his book *Night Flyer* described it as: 'The most dispersed station I ever saw. Everything was miles from anywhere else and tons of leather must have been wasted in the interminable tramping from one place to another.'

On February 16 1942, a Defiant, lost and short of fuel on a flight from Desford to Kirkbride, became the unfinished airfield's first visitor. Attempting to avoid obstructions, the pilot swung the aircraft too sharply and the undercarriage collapsed.

The first RAF contingent—two officers and 31 men—arrived in April 1942 to prepare the new station for 54 OTU due to move in from Church Fenton in a month's time. Work was being pushed on to complete the runways, but many important buildings, like the watch office, ops room and PBX were still under construction, and it was estimated that 500 of the OTU's airmen would have to live under canvas for the time being. A hangar was promised by May 1, but this was an idle boast on the part of the contractor.

The first echelon of 54 OTU duly marched in on May 2, the aircraft, which consisted mainly of Blenheims and Defiants, landing during the next few days. The OTU found the airfield to be in a very incomplete state with sections of unsurfaced perimeter track, open manholes and 22 of the 32 hardstandings still unfinished. Nevertheless, day flying commenced on May 13 and by night on May 19, despite the Drem lighting system being minus its outer circle.

The Blenheims were slowly replaced by Beaufighter IIs, there being 17 on strength by the end of May. Somewhat underpowered for its heavy weight compared with the Hercules Mk 1, the Mk 2 had the reputation of being a killer at first. In experienced hands it gave little trouble, but pupil pilots often lost control on one engine or failed to master its tendency to swing viciously on take off. One Beaufighter at Charterhall swung and hit a Blister hangar and a parked Beaufort, but its great strength ensured that the crew were able to walk away.

In July 1942, 54 OTU was rearranged, training being divided between a Conversion Squadron using Oxfords and Blenheims, and an Intermediate Squadron with Blenheims and Beaufighters. On completion of the two stages, pilots passed to the Advanced Squadron at the Winfield satellite for AI training.

On May 1 1944, Charterhall became partly operational at night, a Beaufighter being scrambled after a hostile aircraft reported over Turnhouse. The enemy aircraft was too low to be picked up by GCI and was soon lost. Other interceptions were attempted on subsequent nights but were also unsuccessful. It was, however, a morale boosting exercise for instructors and advanced pupils alike.

Charterhall 1981 (F. Neal).

The station and its satellite received the first of many heavy bomber diversions in the early hours of May 28 1944, when ten Lancasters landed from operations over Germany. Seven more Lancasters landed from French targets on June 8. The best night, however, was to be February 17 1945 when 26 Halifaxes from 6 Group put down at Charterhall after attacking targets in the Ruhr.

The OTU's average strength in January 1945 was 20 Beaufighter IIs, 49 Beaufighter VIs and 19 Mosquitoes. Almost all the Beaufighters were replaced by Mosquitoes in April and May 1945.

Moving on to July 1945, a detached flight of 770 Squadron came here for radar trials on Mosquito XXVs. The OTU contracted a little with the end of the European war and the Winfield satellite was closed on May 31.

No 54 OTU moved to East Moor in Yorkshire on November 1 1945 and a month later the airfield was occupied by 130 Squadron with Spitfires. This unit left for Acklington on January 24 1946. Another Spitfire squadron was here for three weeks in January 1946, No 165 returning from Norway after air defence duties. It moved on to Duxford on January 18. No 303 Squadron enjoyed a temporary stay with Mustangs for an air-to-ground firing course between March 6 and March 23 1946 and became the last flying unit here.

Of the original three 'T1' hangars and one Bellman hangar, two of the former can be seen. The eight Blisters around the perimeter are all gone now and the 518/40 watch tower has been demolished.

Cluntoe, Tyrone
14/H945755. 4 miles E of Coagh off B161
Every Eighth Air Force enthusiast has heard of bases like Bassingbourn,

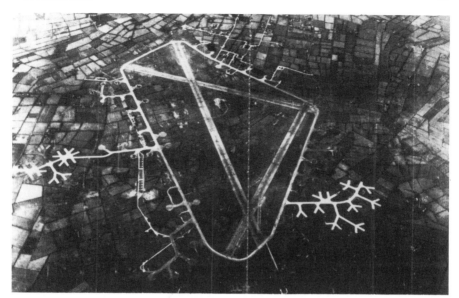

Cluntoe with new multiple hardstandings yet to be camouflaged.

Duxford and Polebrook but few have heard of Cluntoe and still fewer can point it out on a map. Nevertheless, it was one of several support airfields in Northern Ireland which had a direct influence on the Eighth's performance in action.

Cluntoe was originally planned for use as a bomber OTU, and construction was started by civilian contractors in December 1940. Subsequently, it was found that the RAF had enough aerodromes in Northern Ireland to meet current requirements, and building work proceeded at a slow pace. It was July 20 1942 before RAF personnel actually moved in and even then they were only a Care and Maintenance party. They also carried out anti-sabotage patrols as this area was, and of course still is, politically sensitive.

Built to the usual three-runway pattern, Cluntoe was located close to the south-west shore of Lough Neagh, about 30 miles west of Belfast. The dispersed living quarters were situated on rising ground to the west. Several working farms remained amongst the military activity throughout the war, despite official misgivings about security. The station was provided with a standard OTU site equipped with a variety of synthetic training devices which were to be adapted to USAAF procedures.

The setting-up of the Eighth Air Force in England soon revealed a problem; many of the American crews had done all their training in the clear skies of the south-western United States and were totally unprepared for the sort of weather they would encounter in Britain and Northern Europe. Also, they were unfamiliar with RAF Flying Control procedures and all the other details of flying in a war zone.

The answer was in some ways similar to the RAF's Operational Training Unit system and it was known as a Combat Crew Replacement Centre (CCRC). Bovingdon in Hertfordshire became the base of the first one, and a second was to be established at nearby Cheddington. A number of aerodromes in Northern Ireland were also earmarked as bases, but only a handful were ever occupied by the USAAF. For example, Bishops Court was built for a CCRC but was used instead by an RAF Air Observer School.

The CCRC was slow to get under way, however, and Cluntoe was not taken over by 8th Composite Command as Station 238 until August 30 1943. In the meantime, it had opened as an emergency landing ground from October 13 1942, the runway having been cleared of anti-invasion obstructions. During the long opening-up period, the first USAAF movements were two Piper Cubs which landed on February 4 1943 for a tour of the station. On March 25, a Beaufort, coded *45* of 5 OTU, made a precautionary landing, short of fuel, in bad weather. The pilot found the runway by mistaking garbage fires for beacons! The following day Gladiator *N5576* of 1402 Flight, Aldergrove arrived as visibility over base was zero. Other visitors included UC-61A Forwarders *43-14422* and *43-14489* and B-17F *41-24480*. On August 21 a B-17 force-landed with engine trouble after a flight from Newfoundland.

On July 1 1943, a UC-75, serial number *430*, arrived from Greencastle with Brigadier-General Hill and several other high-ranking officers for a tour of inspection. The main purpose of the visit was to obtain suggested sites for a maximum of 100 additional hardstandings so that heavy bombers ferried in from the States could be held, pending allocation to combat units. This was possibly due to excessive demands on parking space at the Base Air Depot at Burtonwood. The parking areas were laid down within a few months and included one of the rare star-shaped dispersals officially known as 'multiple standings'. Hawarden airfield, for instance, had one for use by No 48 MU.

No 4 CCRC was established at Cluntoe in November 1943 and between November 21 and February 20 1944, 57 B-17 crews passed through the school. During the same period, 45 pilots of the 311th Ferrying Squadron were instructed in UK flying procedures and 103 radio operators received special radio and navigational training. Late in February 1944, the training of B-24 crews began. Aircrew assigned to the CCRC received group instruction as crews, and specialised instruction in their respective fields. For example, gunners practised firing on targets towed by A-35 Vengeances, from a line of gun turrets along the shore of Lough Neagh.

On March 7 1944, the unit was re-designated No 2 CCRC, but its mission remained the same, with the addition of high-altitude bombing and tactics in the ETO. Gunners were to be trained separately at Greencastle. During June 1944, 328 crews passed through Cluntoe and all were convinced of the value of the short course. In the words of the CCRC's historical officer: 'This is a crossroads where returning veterans of 30 missions meet the fresh combat crews from the States. For veterans, this period of instruction is an interlude on the journey back home. For new crews, this is the last stop, a crowded ten days of final instruc-

tion before assignment to a combat group.'

The training routine continued mostly without incident, but on March 2 1944, a B-24 crashed in the Antim Hills. Private William H. Payne, the right waist-gunner, was awarded the Soldier's Medal for dragging seven men clear of the burning wreck but, sadly, only two survived. Less serious were several accidents caused by collapsing undercarriage legs on A-35s, for example *FD135* on June 3 1944. The RAF was only too happy to palm off excess stocks of this mediocre machine on the USAAF, and replacements soon arrived, retaining their British serials. As well as the B-24s and A-35s an AT-6 Harvard and a Cub were on strength with the CCRC.

Training began to run down in August 1944, during which month only 210 crews went through, and the CCRC finally closed down early in November. On November 8 1944, Cluntoe was transferred from the control of the USAAF to that of HQ RAF Northern Ireland. The RAF was not impressed with the aerodrome's position and presumably this was the reason for its lack of future use. The records state that all rations had to be collected twice weekly from Portadown, 60 miles return, and milk daily from Cookstown, 22 miles return. The latter was the nearest railhead and bus stop for all movements of personnel and stores.

One of the last aircraft movements was Anson *R9760*, coded *G2*, of 10 (O)AFU, Dumfries, which force-landed due to technical trouble on January 11, 1945. Cluntoe closed down at the end of June 1945 and for many years afterwards the 'T2' hangars were used for the storage of grain.

The expansion of RAF training during the Korean War resulted in the refurbishing of Cluntoe for 2 FTS which re-formed here in February 1953 with Prentices and Harvards. Its function was to carry out all-through training from *ab initio* up to 'wings' standard. The school moved to Hullavington in Wiltshire in May 1954 and re-equipped with Provosts. In February 1955, Cluntoe is recorded as being a 'station in reserve' for the Royal Navy, but it saw no further use.

Cluntoe today is an incredible mixture of dereliction, modern housing and light industry all cheek-by-jowl. Although the hangars are gone, the tower survives, along with such buildings as a bombing

trainer. The runways are in good
condition, fringed by houses for which
planning permission seems unnecessary in
Ulster!

Connel, Strathclyde

*49/NM905350. Near Connel Bridge on
A828*

Connel's curious configuration of two
intersecting runways only 12 degrees
different in direction was dictated by its
cramped position on the narrow coastal
strip north of Oban. High ground up to
1,000 ft only one mile to the north and
north-north-east did not help either.

The airfield fulfilled two functions; one
as a landplane annexe to the nearby Oban
flying boat base, the other as an ELG in
an area almost devoid of aerodromes
because of its unsuitable terrain. It was
also employed occasionally as an
advanced base for exercises in the area by
516 Squadron from Dundonald.

On January 18 1944, it was taken over
by 244 MU as an air ammunition park
under 42 Group, Maintenance Command
and was closed for flying on February 21
1944. This did not, however, prevent a
USAAF Liberator, *41-28772 en route*
from Iceland to Prestwick, making a precautionary landing on March 18 and
running off the end of the runway. It was
soon repaired and flown on to its original
destination.

In April 1944, arrangements were made
to house up to 200 aircrew from 302 FTU
on the station, owing to the acute shortage
of accommodation at Oban. The airfield
was reopened as an ELG in August 1944,
being taken over again by Oban under
Care and Maintenance when 244 MU
moved to Cottam in Yorkshire at the end
of that month.

Aircraft in distress were frequent
visitors, such as an Anson from Jurby on
February 7 1945 with its port engine out of
action. Weather diversion involved many
Ansons from the Observer Schools in the
Irish Sea area, but a lost USAAF B-17 on
March 20 1945 was unusual. Connel
remained an ELG until the end of 1945
and one of the last recorded movements
was by Wellington *HD212* to and from
Thornaby on October 16 1945.

In 1967, the site was purchased by Oban
Council for development, a service linking
Glasgow with Oban and Mull being
inaugurated on September 1 by Loganair.
This schedule was not destined to last,

however, but the airfield remained open,
later being run by Strathclyde Regional
Council as Oban/North Connel. Light
aircraft fly from here and glider launching
was begun in 1981.

The wartime buildings, including the
two 'T3' hangars, have all been cleared,
but concrete bases remain. It is doubtful if
there was ever a proper watch office and
unfortunately no original works plans
have survived.

Crail, Fife

*59/NO625085. 1 mile NNE of Crail on
coast*

One of the best preserved abandoned airfields in Scotland lies quite close to the
attractive little fishing village of Crail. It
was built in 1918 by the firm of Laing,
who employed 300 tradesmen on the job
and a total workforce several times as
large. No less than 100 horse-drawn
vehicles were used to haul the materials.

When the new aerodrome opened in
July 1918, 27 TDS formed, using such
aircraft as the RE 8, FE 2b and Avro 504K
for fighter reconnaissance. The American
120th Aero Squadron had a detachment at
Crail in August 1918 and between March
and June 1919, 104 Squadron is recorded
as being here, although this was probably
in cadre form only, pending disbandment.

The airfield closed in 1919 and lay
dormant until work commenced on re-
building it as a Royal Naval Air Station in
September 1939. It became HMS *Jackdaw*
on October 1 1940 with a decoy site at
Boghall. Its main role was to be TBR
training, and 785 Squadron formed here
on November 7 1940 with Swordfish and
Albacores, using the Firth of Forth for
practice torpedo dropping. Two weeks
later 786 Squadron was formed, also for
torpedo training with the same types.
Both units later progressed to the
Barracuda and Avenger.

An FRU, 770 Squadron, came from
Donibristle in June 1941 and stayed until
the end of January 1944, when it moved
to the satellite at Dunino. Another
specialised squadron at Crail was 778, the
Carrier Trials Unit, which arrived from
Arbroath in March 1943 and flew most
naval types before returning to Arbroath
on August 30 1944.

Many first-line squadrons passed
through at different times, including 823,
which re-formed here on November 1
1941; 832 with Albacores in October/

November 1942; 817, which formed in March 1941 and left in July; and 820 working up on Albacores in October 1943.

No 711 Squadron re-formed for torpedo training on September 12 1944, with Barracudas and Avengers, disbanding in December 1945. No 786 Squadron disbanded in December 1945 and 785 followed in February 1946. No 747 Squadron brought its Barracudas from Ronaldsway in November 1945, only to disband the following month. Crail's last flying unit was 780 Squadron, which came for instrument training from Hinstock in December 1946 and went on to Donibristle at the end of March 1947.

Throughout the war, the airfield was used as a diversion by Leuchars aircraft,

particularly Hampdens in 1942. It became HMS *Bruce* in 1947, and was a foreign language school, using the domestic site for accommodation. In 1952, men of the Black Watch were billeted here pending shipment to Korea. Between March 1953 and February 1958, St Andrews UAS flew Chipmunks from Crail to reduce congestion in the circuit at Leuchars. A civil Auster flew from the airfield in 1966/67 and the site is now used for go-cart racing.

Today, the five Bellman hangars have gone, leaving only their concrete floors and the earth blast walls so often built on wartime naval airfields. A large gable-roofed hangar, rather like a 'VR' Type, still stands alongside a unique building which defies identification. Both have

Left *Avenger FN795 at Crail with Bellman hangars in background* (Imperial War Museum).

Below left *Barracuda at Crail* (R.C. Sturtivant collection).

Right *Waving off a Barracuda of 785 Squadron at Crail March 28 1945* (J.A. Howell).

Below *Barracuda II of 711 Squadron out from Crail* (R.C. Sturtivant collection).

thick steel doors and have been used for sugar beet storage, although they are now empty. There is no sign of any surviving buildings from the First World War.

The control tower is the three-storey naval type, but much more substantially constructed. The balconies are protected by concrete parapets, perhaps against the winter gales in these parts, but also because of the airfield's vulnerable position on the coast and the danger from low-flying raiders.

Another interesting building is the Torpedo Trainer, which has a huge concrete bowl inside, with painted clouds and a horizon line. There is also a seat suspended in the middle, from which the pupil practised visual acquisition of the target after breaking cloud had been simulated by means of lights and other devices. This is worthy of the FAA Museum but moving it would be difficult and costly.

The four runways are still in good condition and one has the number painted on in naval style—12 in a circle. The winds were sometimes so strong that a Swordfish would have to land with plenty of power on so as to maintain forward speed over the ground!

A colleague of mine, who was a Catalina ferry pilot, recalls alighting on the Forth after being diverted from Largs because of bad weather. A flight of Spitfires led them to a spot just off Crail, and when the flying boat was down, the control tower flashed a series of instructions in the high speed morse beloved of the Royal Navy!

Top *Crail tower 1981.*

Above *Torpedo Trainer building, Crail.*

Below *The unusual main hangar at Crail with hangar bases and earth traverses in fore-ground.*

This was incomprehensible to the RAF crew, who never did find out what was required of them. A launch then appeared and led them round the coast to Woodhaven.

Cramlington, Northumberland

88/NZ243775. 1 mile W of Cramlington on A1172

Now an industrial estate, Cramlington opened early in 1916, and 36 (HD) Squadron formed here in February. In December, this unit moved to Seaton Carew, but the aerodrome continued to be used as a night landing ground for home defence until the end of the war.

No 47 Reserve Squadron formed here in November 1916, but moved later in the same month to Waddington. Nos 52 and 61 Reserve Squadrons formed in January and May 1917 respectively, but both left within a few days. In December 1917, 75 Training Squadron came from Waddington with DH 4s and DH 9s, being renumbered 52 Training Depot Station the following July for day bomber training. It disbanded in 1919.

Close to the aerodrome, and also known as Cramlington, an airship station opened in 1918.

The airfield was re-opened for civil use in the '20s, but closed when the war began and did not survive afterwards.

Crimond (Rattray), Grampian

See Rattray

Dalcross, Highland

27/NH775520. 8 miles NE of Inverness between B9039 and A96

Immediately before the war, Longman aerodrome needed expansion, but land purchase was likely to be expensive. Captain Fresson of Scottish Airways found an ideal alternative location at Dalcross, and, when war broke out, suggested it to an Air Ministry survey party who were looking for airfield sites in this area.

He warned them, however, that tarmac runways would be essential, as the ground became very boggy in winter. This advice was ignored and it was prepared with the usual grass surface. Aircraft first flew from here in the winter of 1940, but the mud was soon impassable and the airfield closed for runway construction.

The uncompleted station was reopened by an advance party on June 15 1941 to prepare for occupation by 2 Air Gunners School, which formed here on July 10. To remedy the lack of trained drogue operators for the target-towing aircraft, 30 airmen were sent to Evanton for a short course of instruction. During August, the airfield was used by Whitleys of 19 OTU to fulfil their night flying programme, and, in the autumn of 1941, some Oxfords were detached from 11 SFTS at Shawbury while runways were built there.

Air gunner training began on August 16 1941, using Defiants and Lysanders. An RLG at Brackla was available, and was used extensively during the following winter, owing to flooding at Dalcross. By

Handley Page W.8 over Cramlington (Via F. Neal).

April 1942, Martinets had entirely superseded the Lysanders for target-towing and three training turrets were placed on the ground for practice in following aircraft circling the aerodrome. The Defiants were slowly replaced by the much more suitable Anson.

A detached flight of 2 FIS Montrose had been at Dalcross since April 1942, mainly flying Oxfords, but on October 20 1942, it was re-formed into the nucleus of 19 (P)AFU. The first intake of pilots, numbering 23, soon arrived. They started ground instruction and began flying Oxfords on October 27, alongside the last few instructors from the FIS courses. Accommodation proved inadequate for the AFU, consisting of four Nissen huts one mile round the aerodrome perimeter from the main site. An issue of 50 ladies' bicycles, as there was a shortage of the men's variety, helped the airmen get from their dispersed domestic site two miles to the west, but gave rise to some ribald comments.

December saw the first output of pupils to OTUs, but also the unit's first fatal flying accident, when Oxford *BG240* crashed near Cawdor whilst practising single-engined flying. Because of the distance from the nearest available BAT Flight it was agreed with 21 Group that for the time being the pupils should be trained in general reconnaissance for Coastal Command. This obviated the necessity for Beam Approach courses, pending the opening of a BAT Flight affiliated to the unit.

Other difficulties in 1943 were brought about by the lack of RLGs. Local arrangements were made with Kinloss and Lossiemouth for the use of Forres and Elgin by

'VR' hangar at Dalcross packed with Oxfords of 8 AFTS, September 1952 (R. Hendry).

limited numbers of aircraft. After protracted negotiations with the MAP, permission was given also to use the SLG at Leanach. It was brought into service on June 6 1943, for the sole purpose of simulated night flying using sodium flares, specially lit instruments and blue goggles worn by the pilot. This was particularly important because of the few hours of darkness in the northern summer for real night flying.

The AFU was given two days' notice that Elgin would not be available after July 31 1943 and the possibility of finding alternative accommodation seemed unlikely. Some frantic enquiries resulted in the offer of Tain for up to seven aircraft at a time, thus stabilising the position once more.

From August 31 1943, the AFU course was extended to eight weeks, and in October to 12. Forres RLG was barred to the Oxfords from November 20 because of flooding and Leanach too had to be given up around this time. This situation was unlikely to improve, so Kinloss offered the use of its satellite at Brackla, AFU flying beginning there on December 3.

Yet another hindrance was caused by large-scale invasion exercises on the south shore of the Moray Firth. This forced the closure of the AFU's low-flying area because of artillery practice. The unit ORB noted: 'When aircraft appear, the nearest warship's signal lamps start working overtime. If any of the local

Lysander of 2 AGS Dalcross (Via V.L. Winterburn).

inhabitants read the Morse Code they would doubtless be most surprised by some of the warnings couched in the language of the sea rather than diplomacy!'

Flying Training Command's New Year greeting for 19 (P)AFU was for the unit to expect disbandment on February 25 1944. Flying duly ceased on February 12 and all aircraft and pupils were transferred to 21 (P)AFU at Tatenhill in Staffordshire along with the majority of the instructors. The aircraft completed the long flight without incident, the only casualty on the move being the cockpit training fuselage on a Queen Mary trailer, damaged in a collision with an Army lorry 20 miles south of Dalcross.

Three first-line squadrons stayed for short periods in 1943. They were 88 Squadron with Bostons, which came on July 14 for an exercise, and a detachment of 63 Squadron's Mustangs, there from June 6 to June 14. At the end of December, 'B' Flight of 652 Squadron based Austers for combined operations training in the area. In May 1944, the aerodrome was made available for 19 OTU, so that unit could maintain its night flying programme during the few hours of darkness available.

Moving back to 2 AGS, this unit had taken part in a scheme to train former WAAF balloon operators as flight mechanics during 1943, and operated a miniature 'School of Technical Training' at Dalcross.

In December 1944, the AGS converted from Ansons to Wellingtons, the Martinet being retained for target-towing, and also received a few Spitfires, whose greater relative speed made cine-gun training more realistic.

Field Marshal Montgomery landed at Dalcross on May 9 1944 and other unusual visitors that year included nine Halifaxes of 102 Squadron on December 13, diverting after operations, and, on December 26, 15 more Halifaxes, this time from 424 Squadron.

Unlike most AGSs which disbanded at the end of hostilities in Europe, 2 AGS lasted until November 24 1945. In January 1946, 122 Squadron brought its Spitfires here from Wick. It was renumbered 41 Squadron on April 1 and moved to Wittering on April 15 1946.

Dalcross from an Anson 1944 (Via V.L. Winterburn).

Dalcross was by now the HQ of 13 Group, and its Communications Flight aircraft were kept here, although from 1947 it was operated by the MOA as Inverness Airport. From May 1951 until 1953, 8 AFTS was based with Oxfords, reflecting the demand for pilots during the RAF's Korean War expansion. Scheduled services by BEA continued alongside the RAF activity.

The airport was closed for almost all of 1974, airline services being transferred to Kinloss while the 06/24 runway was lengthened and strengthened to permit the operation of BAC 111s. Today the large 'VR' hangars are long dismantled, but the two wartime Bellmans and many 'temporary' buildings are still in use. Three roofless Blister hangars can be seen, and many local fences are made of Sommerfeld track and its steel pickets.

Dallachy, Grampian

28/NJ365635. 2 miles N of Fochabers on B9104

The Dallachy Strike Wing was never as well known as the other Coastal wings operating from Banff, North Coates and Langham, but in its short period of existence it saw as much action as any. Consisting of 144, 404, 405 and 489 Squadrons, its Beaufighters ranged up and down the rugged coast of Norway. The tactical sequence was the cannon attack on the escort, the rocket attack and finally the torpedo launch at the main target. Losses from these operations were high, with a steady drain on crews from accurate flak and the German fighters which sometimes made an appearance.

The Dallachy Wing was to remember February 9 1945 as 'Black Friday' because on this date no less than nine Beaufighters (six from 404) and an escorting Mustang failed to return. The target was reported by reconnaissance as a destroyer with escorts. A total of 31 Beaufighters took off from Dallachy and rendezvoused with 12 Mustangs, two ASR Warwicks following to locate any casualties.

The Banff Wing also took part in the strike as a separate formation, being intercepted by Fw 190s and losing one Mosquito, but not before they had severely mauled the attackers. Braving heavy flak from the ships and shore batteries, the Beaufighters blew up the destroyer and badly damaged a minesweeper and other craft. One aircraft had to force-land back at Dallachy with a 2 ft square hole in the tailplane and most of its companions had lesser damage. The next morning, 17 Beaufighters flew out in line abreast along the return track searching for survivors of ditchings, but found nothing.

On April 8 1945, 24 Beaufighters, accompanied by 14 Mustangs and the usual pair of Warwicks to patrol the home-bound leg, made a supremely difficult sortie against ships in a steep-sided fjord. Six were moored right against the cliffs at each end of the fjord and a steep dive was necessary to hit them. Two aircraft were lost during the attack and three others suffered hits.

The strike photographs in the Dallachy squadrons' ORBs show many scenes of Norwegian tranquility—fir trees, neat little houses, patches of snow, still water in tiny harbours; the only anomaly is a

Dallachy tower.

vessel in the foreground smothered in cannon and rocket fire. Today the airfield from which this destruction took wing is a peaceful sight itself and it is difficult to visualise the activity here in that last bitter winter of the war.

It has now been cleared almost entirely of its original buildings. The former technical site with its 'T2' hangar has been levelled and is now a wilderness of gorse bushes. The watch tower still stands with the faded yellow letters '23' painted on to denote the runway-in-use. (The other three directions would have been displayed on boards slotted over it as required, a difficult task in a high wind, and, with the sort of gusts you get in these parts, involuntary hang-gliding was a distinct possibility!)

Typical of mid-war airfields, Dallachy has 35 diamond hardstandings and a single frying pan. There was also a second 'T2', and three double Blisters around the perimeter track, all of which have gone now. The old operations block can be seen near a modern bungalow beside the approach road on the south side of the aerodrome. Although Dallachy is a recognised gliding site, there was no sign of activity when we visited it, only waving corn and skylarks. Almost unimaginable is the sight of rocket-laden Beaufighters waddling to the take-off point and then forming up over the field before disappearing to the north-east, some never to return.

The airfield was built for Coastal Command in 1942 and early 1943, the lie of the land dictating only two runways instead of the usual three. Bomber Command was interested in it as an advanced base but was warned by Coastal that it was intended to move 3 OTU from South Wales to Banff and Dallachy and the resultant congestion might prove unacceptable. The runways were, in any case, too short for heavy bombers, and the plan was dropped.

In 1942, the Navy had an urgent requirement for an aerodrome at which to establish an observer school. As naval airfields were already overcrowded the Air Ministry was approached and offered Dallachy as a temporary solution for three months after its scheduled completion date of March 31 1943. The Admiralty in the meantime would have to build its own new base and move there, or alternatively build a new station for the RAF out of its own funds and return Dallachy permanently.

The Navy was not happy about Dallachy as it had only two runways and the inevitable cross-winds would make intensive flying training very difficult, particularly with types like the Swordfish and Martlet. It was also in the middle of one of the most aircraft-congested areas of Britain and close to several firing ranges. The Navy thus decided to find its own airfield site and for the moment expand the existing observer training programme at Arbroath. The only naval unit which ever flew from Dallachy was 838 Squadron with Swordfish under Coastal Command control for most of October 1944.

The transfer of 3 OTU did not occur, and the airfield was lent to Flying Training Command for 14 (P)AFU, which brought its Oxfords north from Ossington to Banff late in May 1943. Separate day and night flights were set up at Dallachy after flying began here on June 25. As described in the section on Banff, the AFU flew an enormous number of hours, a goodly proportion of them from the satellite. One of the unit's affiliated BAT Flights, No 1542, formed here on June 8 1943.

In July 1944, with the U-boats withdrawing from the threatened Bay of Biscay ports, Coastal Command prepared to switch the bulk of its forces from the south-west to north-east Scotland. Banff and Dallachy were earmarked for Wellington squadrons and Flying Training Command was informed that it must vacate these stations at two weeks' notice. Since there was a surplus of trained pilots, it was decided that 14 (P)AFU would be one of those to disband, which it duly did on August 31 1944 along with its BAT Flights.

It was not Wellingtons which arrived, however, but Beaufighters. The Royal New Zealand Air Force squadron, 489, had moved from Leuchars to Langham in Norfolk in April 1944 to attack shipping from the Dutch and Belgian ports. By October it seemed evident that Norwegian coastal traffic was more worthy of the squadron's attention, so it switched to Dallachy at the same time as did the other units which were to form the wing.

A detachment of 524 Squadron's Wellingtons from Langham joined the wing for a time for a trial known as Operation *Ashfield*. The radar-equipped 'Wimpeys' were supposed to locate enemy shipping at night and lay a Drem system of flame floats on the sea so the strike aircraft could assemble for an attack. The experiment was unsuccessful, however, and the Wellingtons soon returned to Norfolk, it being felt that individual *Rovers* would be more fruitful.

No 144 Squadron gave up its torpedo role in January 1945 for that of flak suppression in support of the Strike Wing, remaining as such until the war ended. Both 144 and 455 Squadrons disbanded on May 25 1945, but 489 moved to Banff on June 16 to convert to Mosquitoes. No 404 had already gone to Banff in March 1945.

The Army took over the site on November 24 1945 and it became a Territorial training centre until 1958. Lossiemouth units also employed it for simulated bombing.

Donibristle, Fife

66/NT160840. 2 miles E of Rosyth on A92

Having one of the most pleasant and sheltered situations of all Scottish airfields, Donibristle's survival from 1917 until 1959, when bigger and better airfields had closed in 1945, was due mainly to its convenient location. Opened early in 1917 as a landing ground for 77 Squadron, it was handed over to the RNAS in August 1917 to become a 'ship's aeroplane base'. Aircraft could be repaired or stored, access from the Firth of Forth being facilitated by a railway and lane to the water's edge. It was also a Salvage Park and had an added responsibility for Turnhouse aircraft.

After the Armistice, the station, which by now was administered by the RAF, became a Fleet Aircraft Repair Depot. Its main work consisted of overhauling aeroplanes for aircraft carriers and for RAF Leuchars but it also rebuilt DH 9As as three-seater fleet spotters and scrapped surplus engines and airframes from all over Scotland.

Torpedo development trials formed part of its duties too, and when the General Strike of 1921 broke out, Donibristle assisted the civil authorities with aerodrome handling parties at Renfrew and Newcastle.

In 1921 the station was reduced to a Care and Maintenance basis, but reopened in 1925, principally as a shore base for disembarked carrier units. On October 1 1928, the Coastal Defence Torpedo Flight was redesignated 36 Squadron at Donibristle and subsequently took part in many exercises with naval

vessels from Rosyth. Its Hawker Horsleys were taken to Singapore in the autumn of 1930.

No 100 was another shore-based torpedo squadron equipped with Horsleys. It arrived here from Bicester on May 1 1934 and soon perfected the new techniques of torpedo delivery in the sheltered waters of the Forth. The squadron was re-equipped with Vildebeestes and sent out to Singapore in December 1933 to be replaced at Donibristle by 22 Squadron, which re-formed here on May 1 1934 with Vildebeestes. The following year, the squadron was posted to Malta to stand by during the Abyssinian Crisis, returning to Scotland in August 1936 whence its 'B' Flight was expanded into 42 Squadron at Donibristle on December 14 1936.

In 1939, the airfield was controlled by 17 Group Coastal Command, but, with the establishment of the FAA as a separate service, it was handed back to its former owners and became HMS *Merlin* on May 24 1939.

Being close to the naval dockyard at Rosyth, its facilities were expanded into a major aircraft repair yard. Initially, the yard was manned by a composite group of Navy, RAF and civilian staff. No RAF personnel remained at the end of 1940, and, by 1944, civilian staff totalled 200 and servicemen and women about 1,000.

The station continued to act as a shore base for carrier squadrons and naval first- and second-line units were resident for varying periods. Re-equipping with Skuas, 801 Squadron embarked in HMS *Courageous*, leaving its Sea Gladiators to form 769 Squadron here for deck landing training.

Other squadron movements included 802, which reformed with Martlets on November 1 1940 and worked up on the new type before joining HMS *Audacity* on September 13 1941, and 803, which exchanged its Skuas for Fulmars and flew out to HMS *Formidable* in November 1940.

Amidst all the transients, a new second-line unit formed in December 1940. This was 782 Squadron, which was destined to serve here in a communications role until disbanding in July 1953. Many Dominies were operated throughout its career, supplemented during the war by Sparrows (transport Harrows), Oxfords, Beech Travellers and Stinson Reliants.

Deck landing training was the duty of 768 Squadron, which formed at the end of

1940 with Swordfish, subsequently flying Albacores and transferring in 1943 to Macrihanish.

1941 saw the formation of three front-line squadrons, 800 and 884 with Fulmars and 882 with Wildcats. The last two went to Turnhouse for operations under RAF Fighter Command. The following year, squadrons passing through included 808 and 886 with Fulmars, 893 with Fulmars and Wildcats, 819 with Swordfish and 822's Albacores from Crail.

Another new squadron, 860, formed at Donibristle on June 15 1943, was composed mainly of Dutch nationals who had served with the Royal Netherlands Naval Air Service before escaping to the UK. Their Swordfish moved to Dunino in October.

No 827 Squadrom arrived on April 6 1944 with 12 Barracudas; embarking on *Furious* two weeks later. The station's final first-line unit was 813 Squadron, whose Swordfish left on April 26 1944. After this the only new wartime squadron here was 739, a Blind Approach Development Unit, which moved in from Worthy Down in October 1944 with Ansons and Oxfords, only to be disbanded in March 1945.

Meanwhile, the Air Yard had made an outstanding contribution to the support of the Navy's flying units. Almost all naval types were handled at first, but by 1944 the yard was specialising in the repair and inspection of the Grumman Avenger torpedo bomber and Wildcat fighter. The total of aircraft repaired, inspected and reconditioned reached over 7,000 at the

Donibristle in the '20s (Via R. Bonser).

end of the war, and a notice to this effect could still be seen on a hangar after the unit's closure in 1959.

The derequisition of many of Donibristle's workshops restricted operations for a while and the Air Ministry was asked to release Warton in Lancashire as a replacement Air Yard. This was not to be, however.

Soon after the war, 'Doni-bee' was reduced to 782 Squadron and a Station Flight, but in March 1947 they were joined by 780 Squadron, an AFU with Oxfords and Ansons which stayed until May 21 1947. Carrier aircraft, mainly Sea Furies and Fireflies, still disembarked here, but the little airfield was incapable of accepting the new generation of jet air-craft soon to come into service. The last Squadron to be commissioned here was 800 with Seafires in April 1949.

Other activities included a year's residence in 1952 by the Fireflies of 1830 Squadron, displaced from Abbotsinch whilst this base was reconstructed, and the disbandment of 782 Squadron. The Squadron's Dominies stayed, however, to be flown by Airwork pilots as the Northern Communications Squadron.

Airwork now took over the running of the airfield, although the Air Yard was not affected and continued to overhaul such types as the Seafire, Firebrand, Harvard and Sea Fury. In the mid-'50s more modern aircraft like the Gannet and the Skyraider and the Dragonfly and Whirlwind helicopters joined the inventory.

Defence economies resulted in FAA operations being concentrated at fewer shore establishments. Donibristle was one

of those for the axe and its work was gradually transferred to Belfast and Fleetlands in Surrey. By April 1959 the process was complete and the last aircraft to leave the Yard, Skyraider *WT950*, was delivered to the AHU at Abbotsinch.

The airfield site is now divided between an industrial estate, where the Air Yard once stood, and a housing estate on the south side, on the site of the control tower and other hangars. Surprisingly, out of the collection of Bellmans, 'VR's and other types, not one hangar has survived. Some 20s style barrack blocks are still in use as offices, but of the flying field and its two short runways, only a few stretches of tarmac remain, still pathetically showing traces of the dotted white centre line markings.

Dornoch, Highland

21/NH800885. ½ mile S of Dornoch

An unlikely place for an SLG, Dornoch was probably chosen because of the dearth of suitable level areas in this part of Scotland. It was actually sited on a golf course close to the sea shore, preparation cost about £38,000 and effective camouflage was virtually impossible. The Royal Golf Hotel in the attractive little town was taken over to provide billets for the airmen when the SLG, No 40, opened on August 8 1941.

Spitfires, Havocs and Whitleys were among the aircraft types stored here by 45 MU Kinloss. In September 1941, 41 Group Maintenance Command decided to offer the 46 MU SLG at Leanach to Flying Training Command and replace it with Dornoch. The latter was taken over by 46 MU on September 9 1943, who mainly used it for Beaufighter storage. There were 90 aircraft here in April 1944 and in July 108.

When the MU acquired Elgin as 105 SS the role of its SLGs was reversed, with aircraft being prepared for service instead of storage. The last took off on September 27 1945, and the final load of scrap from broken up machines was sent away in time for the closure date of September 30.

The strip was re-established in 1967. Loganair Services to Inverness and Wick were operated in 1972 but proved uneconomic. It is still used occasionally by light aircraft and there is no sign of any wartime buildings apart from a rather odd tin shed near the caravan site.

Dounreay, Highland

12/NC995675. 7 miles W of Thurso on A836

Although started as early as 1942, Dounreay could hardly be called an action station as nobody seemed to want it. It only found its true role after the war, as we shall see.

In December 1942, the new airfield, intended for Coastal Command when completed, was inspected as a possible advanced base for bombing raids against Norwegian targets. The comments were not encouraging, it being noted that the aerodrome would be unsuitable for the operation of heavy bombers because neither of the two runways was aligned with the prevailing wind. The approaches, too, were poor because of the surrounding hills.

In January 1943, Coastal Command stated that it did not intend to occupy Dounreay because of a shortage of manpower and was prepared to offer its sole use to Bomber Command. Reading between the lines, it is fairly obvious that Coastal was anxious to keep bomber squadrons away from its more suitable but congested airfields on the north-east coast.

Another inspection was made in February when the runways were found to be nearly complete but with no facilities available. The officer reported: 'This aerodrome is on the extreme north coast of Scotland and is unsheltered from very strong gales, low cloud and very heavy rain, making it unfit for use consistently when the weather at Skitten about 30 miles away is fit. The prevailing wind is down the short runway which ends at the edge of a cliff and would require extending.'

When more or less complete in April 1944, the station was occupied by a Care and Maintenance party and the runways obstructed, a procedure which caused some grief to a USAAF Liberator off course on a flight from Labrador to Nutts Corner on June 3 1944. Coast crawling and hoping to find somewhere to land, the crew probably spotted Dounreay with some relief. Collision with obstacles caused some damage and parts were brought in via RAF Castletown in a B-17 to effect repairs. The Liberator was flown out successfully on June 12 and peace descended once again.

The Navy began to show an interest in Dounreay when an airfield with an adjacent Class B Repair Yard was required near Scapa Flow for disembarked squadrons. Hatston was the eventual choice for the Yard and Dounreay was transferred to the Navy on May 15 1944, intended to be HMS *Tern II* but never commissioned. It was transferred to the charge of Flag Officer Carrier Training on August 1 1945 but was still on Care and Maintenance in January 1949 and passed to the Air Ministry on October 1 1954.

The site was selected for the development of a nuclear power station, construction being started in 1954. Apart from the fact that it was still Government-owned, it also met several other requirements. A very remote site was essential in view of the experimental nature of the station and the coastal position offered the plentiful water supply essential for this work. The airfield provided a level site and a ready-made airstrip for communications, although at first, support aircraft landed at Wick.

The first visitor seems to have been Beagle 206 *G-ATYD* on July 7 1967. One runway (the north-east to south-west strip) was retained, the research station having been built on the northern half of the airfield. The wartime control tower has now been modernised with a modern glasshouse on top.

The well known fast-breeder reactor is here and also HMS *Vulcan*, a nuclear propulsion test and training establishment and submarine development centre. All in all, it is a far cry from the derelict huts which still exist south of the perimeter road on the old domestic site.

Drem, Lothian

66/NT860810. 2 miles S of Dirleton on B1345

A date which will always be prominent in RAF history is October 16 1939. On that day He 111s attacked warships anchored near the Forth Bridge and Spitfires shot down two of them. They were the first enemy aircraft brought down over Britain since the First World War, one being credited to 603 Squadron from Turnhouse and the other to 602 from Drem.

One of the fighter bases, Drem, had begun as a home defence landing ground for 77 Squadron in 1916/17 known as West Fenton. The site was later developed into a proper aerodrome for 2 TDS which formed here on April 15 1918 with such types as the Pup, Camel and SE 5a. The TDS disbanded in 1919, by which time the

airfield had been renamed Gullane. The American 41st Aero-Squadron was also here from April to August 1918 when its Spads and Camels departed to France.

The airfield remained unused until September 1933, when it was employed as a fuelling point by the Harts of 602 and 603 Squadrons during a coast defence exercise. Deserted once again, it was eventually rebuilt for flying training and 13 FTS formed here early in 1939 with Oxfords, Harts and Audax.

When the war began, Drem was well-positioned for the day fighter defence of the Scottish Lowlands, and thus, on October 17 1939, received the Spitfires of 609 Squadron from Acklington. No 13 FTS was disbanded on October 27 and the station was transferred officially to Fighter Command four days later. In the meantime 72 and 602 Squadrons had arrived with more Spitfires.

One of the first actions from Drem was a tragic mistake when two Hampdens of 44 Squadron were shot down over the Forth on December 21, one crew-member being killed. The following day a section of 602 Squadron engaged two He 111s east of the Isle of May and shot one of them down. Almost daily scrambles were made to investigate *Bogies* but it was not until February 22 1940 that another He 111 was brought down to crash land at Coldingham. Five days later, 609 Squadron dispatched a Heinkel into the sea off Dunbar.

No 72 Squadron had returned to Leconfield on January 12 and a Hurricane squadron, 111, came from Dyce on December 12 and moved to Wick at the end of February, later to return for a month in the autumn. The Blenheim night fighters of 29 Squadron from Debden spent five weeks here in April/May 1940, but saw no action. (The squadron was to be here again in the spring of 1944 whilst converting from Mosquito XIIs to XIIIs.)

August 1940 saw 602 Squadron move south to Westhampnett, 609 having already gone to Northolt in May. Five more Hurricane squadrons, 145, 232, 245, 263 and 605 were here for short periods in 1940 and the Defiants of 141 Squadron stayed for just over a week in October.

Bad weather after operations over Germany brought 11 Whitleys of 4 Group into Drem on February 12 1941. A continuous rotation of fighter units from the south arrived for rest periods on mostly unsuccessful convoy patrols. They

included 611 with Spitfires from Horn-church in November, leaving for Kenley in June. Other Spitfire units spending much shorter periods here in 1941 were 64, 123 and 340, the latter coming back again in mid-1943.

One pilot wrote: 'This seems to be a quiet spot with plenty of grouse shooting and fishing. Food is the best I have yet met in the Air Force. Given good weather and a few Huns it would be perfect.' Local families, hearing that a 'war-torn squadron' had come to recuperate, clamoured to give them hospitality, but were surprised to find their guests were hardly the hysterical wrecks they had been led to believe!

A night-fighter squadron, 600, was based there temporarily in March 1941, equipped with Beaufighters and a few Blenheims. It was one of the latter which scored a victory over Clydeside. No 43 Squadron, here from March to October 1941, also saw some action with its Hurricanes. No 410 Squadron stayed from August 1941 to June of the following year converting from Defiants to Beau-fighters in May but having no combats.

The Q-site at Whitekirk had attracted many enemy bombs, but on August 12 1942 a Ju 88 dropped bombs on the correct target, damaging the control building and four Spitfires, but fortunately

Whirlwind of 263 Squadron after re-equipping in July 1940 in log dispersal at Drem (J. Munro).

not causing any casualties.

The Australian 453 Squadron re-formed at Drem on June 18 1942, with Spitfires, becoming operational for convoy protection on July 10. It left for Hornchurch in September 1942, to be replaced by 222 Squadron. Whirlwinds returned briefly to local skies during August 1942 in the form of 137 Squadron, although there had been detachments of this unit based here before. A new Typhoon Squadron, 197, formed on November 21 1942, becoming operational in February 1943 for east coast patrols. It moved to Tangmere at the end of March to intercept low level raiders.

Although there were still some day fighters here in 1943, including 130 and 65, the station began to be associated mainly with night-fighter units. On June 16 1943, a Mosquito of 605 Squadron used the aerodrome as a forward base for an intruder patrol over Denmark in which an enemy aircraft, believed to be an He 177, was destroyed.

As enemy activity was increasing slightly in the area, 488 Squadron, previously at

Drem 1942 (RAF Museum).

Ayr and converting from Beaufighters to Mosquitoes, arrived in August 1943. However, no prey presented itself and the unit left for Bradwell Bay in September. No 96 Squadron was the replacement armed with Mosquitoes and Beaufighters but again there were no combats and they moved to West Malling in November. A Polish Squadron, 307, was next in line at Drem, its Mosquitoes flying in from Predannack. Only its Sumburgh detachment had any success and the squadron moved to Coleby Grange at the beginning of March 1944.

A Royal Navy Squadron, 784, had lodged at Drem since October 18 1942, as a night fighter school, flying Fulmars and Ansons at first but later Fireflies, Hellcats and Harvards. An associated ground radar site was situated on a headland at Cockburnspath.

A Fleet Requirements Unit, 770 Squadron, was also based there from July 16 1944 operating the usual assortment of second-line types until it disbanded on October 1 1945. A second night fighter school, 722 Squadron, re-formed here on May 15 1945 but became part of 784 in November.

Returning to 1943, another lodger unit formed on July 5. This was 1692 Radio Development Flight equipped with two Beaufighter VIs and five Defiants. Some Mitchells of 226 Squadron were detached here from Swanton Morley in July for fighter affiliation exercises. No 186 Squadron re-formed at Drem on April 27 as a fighter-bomber unit but did not receive its Hurricane aircraft until August, by which time its personnel had moved to Ayr. ASR cover was provided in October and November by 281 Squadron.

Squadrons here for air defence duties in 1944 included 91, with Spitfires, in March/April, and 309, with Hurricanes and Mustangs, from April to November. A detachment of 278 ASR Squadron was based between February 1 and April 22 flying Ansons, Spitfires and a Walrus.

A summary of notable happenings in 1944 would also include the crash of a USAAF Fortress just after take-off on February 4. There were no survivors from the 306th BG crew and RAF passengers. An Anson dropped food to the lighthouse keepers at St Abbs Head, cut off by snow in March. USAAF ground units arrived in April for an unspecified purpose and in June 12 Seafires of 880 and 881 Squadrons stayed for a few days whilst the carrier *Furious* was undergoing repair.

No 340 was one of the last fighter units detailed here—between December 1944 and January 1945—and on April 21 1945 Drem was taken over by the Royal Navy and commissioned as HMS *Nighthawk* on June 21.

On May 11 1955, Spitfires of 603 Squadron intercepted three Ju 52s known to be flying from Stavanger and escorted them into Drem. In direct contrast to the events of October 1939 they were carrying surrender delegates of the German armed forces.

After the night fighter school moved to Dale on February 1 1946, the airfield reverted officially to RAF control on March 15, but there is no record of any further use.

It remained a grass field throughout its life and hangarage consisted of three Bellmans and 12 Blisters. It is now used by a government civil engineering department for testing bridge sections.

Drem gave its name to the standard lighting system later adopted by the RAF. The glare of the exhaust from a Spitfire made night landings extremely difficult but one of the pilots here in the early days successfully experimented with a circle of glim lamps positioned on the normal curving approach for the type.

Dumfries, Dumfries and Galloway

84/NX000790 3 miles NE of Dumfries on A701

The airfield was planned before the war as an Aircraft Storage Unit and eventually expanded to a considerable size, gaining two tarmac runways in the process. The original 'E' 'L' and 'J' Type hangars are still used for storage and the three-storey

Dumfries tower with faded 'Flying Control' inscription (J. Huggon).

control tower is now the focus of the Dumfries and Galloway Aviation Museum, which displays, amongst others, a Super Sabre, a Meteor and a Vampire.

Although 18 MU formed here on June 17 1940, the runways were obstructed for the first few weeks pending the arrival of the ground defence personnel. Warmwell in Dorset, the home of 10 B&GS was becoming uncomfortably hot for training aircraft and was also needed for fighter squadrons, so the school was evacuated to Dumfries in mid-July. The accommodation was found to be completed but various 'details' like cooking stoves and piped water had yet to be provided so the whole camp was billeted out in the town for a week.

The station was transferred from 41 to 25 Group with the MU as lodger, and flying training began on July 22. Harrows, Battles, Fairey Seals and Henleys were amongst the types operated. The airfield surface soon began to show signs of wear and the Air Ministry was asked to build hard runways. In the meantime an auxiliary landing ground near Annan (Winterseugh) was to be used as much as possible and a tent erected there for lectures in the event of bad weather.

The MU, meanwhile, was getting into its stride, with many aircraft flown in for storage or preparation. A total of 141 were on the station in August 1940, including Battles, Wellingtons, Beauforts, Hurricanes and Oxfords. Some Robin hangars were requested to house the smaller types. Norwegian troops were helping to guard the dispersals and this is probably why King Haakon and Crown Prince Olav of Norway inspected the unit on August 29.

The Harrows were replaced by the slightly more modern Whitley in October 1940. Enemy aircraft were often over at night on their way to and from Glasgow and occasionally got mixed up with returning Whitleys but fortunately there were no incidents.

The B&GS was redesignated 10 AOS on September 13 1941 and at the same time the maintenance of the station was taken over by a civilian contractor, Scottish Aviation Limited. At the beginning of October, all the Whitleys were exchanged for Bothas with 10 AGS at Evanton. The AOS became 10 (O)AFU on April 25 1942. Five airmen were detached to other units to take part in the Thousand Bomber raid on Cologne in May 1942.

No 11 Service Ferry Flight was at

Dumfries for about three months in 1941, but was disbanded on July 1 and was absorbed into HQ SFS at Kemble. The MU's main aircraft type was by now the Wellington but others like the Whirlwind, Dominie and Blenheim were being handled also. Typhoons began to arrive in 1942.

In the early hours of March 25 1943, a single Do 217 strafed the airfield beacon site, but fortunately no one was hit. The bomber crashed soon afterwards into a hill near the coast. Another encounter with an enemy aircraft came on November 29, when a Czech pilot from the AFU, which by now was flying Ansons, nearly collided with a 'Bv 140 seaplane' over the Solway. There was no such type as a Bv 140 but it is an interesting story anyway!

The AFU continued to turn out air crew for the OTUs with a steady drain of aircraft in accidents. The worst night in its history was August 9 1943, when three Ansons crashed in the Lakeland hills, having, it is believed, been blown off course by strong northerly winds.

No 658 Squadron's Austers arrived on March 21 1944 for liaison work at the Langholm Ranges. They were not the first AOP Squadron to be based here temporarily for exercises, 651 being present in August 1942, and 652 for the first two months of 1943.

As an indication of flying activity in 1945, 17 Ansons airborne on training details were diverted on February 3 when the Dumfries lighting failed completely. No 10 (O)AFU became 10 ANS on July 24 1945, but moved to Chipping Warden in Northamptonshire the following month to leave the airfield free for aircraft storage.

No 18 MU, in summarising its wartime achievements, estimated that it had prepared and dispatched a total of 4,688 aircraft. Dumfries was taken over by 41 Group on August 21 1945 and the east/west runway closed to enable more aircraft to be parked on the perimeter track as they were flown in from the SLGs for disposal. The total stock of aircraft at the end of August reached 663. No 215 MU, a packing depot, had operated alongside 18 MU for some time, but was disbanded on September 25 1945. Other maintenance work during the war had embraced Typhoon test flying by Scottish Aviation and modifications to American aircraft for the FAA by Blackburn Aircraft.

No 18 MU closed in 1957, the site being

developed into an industrial estate from 1959. There was an RAF Regiment Training School in the 50s and gliding was done by the RAFVR until 1957. The Dumfries and District Gliding Club used the airfield for many years, until it became unsatisfactory because of encroaching buildings, and powered aircraft also landed from time to time.

Dundee (Stannergate), Tayside

54/NO433307. 2 miles E of Dundee on A930

A seaplane station was opened here in 1914 for the RNAS, the location sometimes being referred to as Stannergate.

In 1918 the units based were 401 Flight of 249 Squadron with Short 184s and Felixstowe flying boats, and 318 and 319 Flights of 257 Squadron with Fairey Babies and Felixstowe F 2As. Pending completion of the depot at Brough near Hull, Dundee acted as an Acceptance Depot for seaplanes in 1918. It probably closed in October 1919 after 249 Squadron disbanded, 257 having already stood down at the end of June.

One notable character at RNAS Dundee, Major C. Draper, used to amuse himself by flying seaplanes backwards and forwards through all 29 of the Tay Bridge's arches! In 1953 the very same gentleman shocked the Establishment by flying an Auster Autocrat under 16 Thames bridges between Blackfriars and Kensington!

The station was reopened in 1940 as a

Dundee 1918 (Via Chaz Bowyer).

satellite to Arbroath, being commissioned on July 15 as HMS *Condor II*. Prior to this, 751 Squadron kept a Walrus and Shark detachment here for observer training. No 703 Squadron with Vought Kingfishers moved to Dundee when operational, and disembarked here when her aircraft were in UK waters.

The 751 detachment remained until May 1944, when the squadron disbanded, and the base closed the following month.

Dundonald, Strathclyde

70/NS360355. 4 miles NE of Troon off A759

Dundonald was a small grass airfield whose size and primitive facilities belied its vital role in the success of the amphibious landings in Normandy and elsewhere. It started life as an RLG for 12 EFTS at Prestwick in March 1940 and was probably used until the School disbanded in March 1941.

No 516 Squadron began to form here on April 28 1943, from a nucleus provided by 1446 Combined Operations Flight, which had disbanded the day before. The aircraft establishment consisted of eight Mustangs, eight Hurricanes, two Blenheims, two Lysanders, two Ansons and a Proctor. No time was lost, as on the same day Mustangs and Hurricanes took part in a forward control demonstration with the Combined Signal School, in

Top *Blenheim of 516 Squadron off Ayrshire coast* (R.D. Cooling).

Above *'A' Flight personnel of 516 Squadron with Blenheim IV at Dundonald* (R.D. Cooling).

Below *Hurricane II of 516 Squadron off the Isle of Arran* (R.D. Cooling).

One of No 516 Squadron's Lysanders (R.D. Cooling).

which they were vectored on to a formation of Spitfires of 64 Squadron. Other sorties supported a Commando exercise and 'attacked' landing craft.

Sorties were flown almost daily when weather permitted, many of the exercises being highly elaborate and carefully controlled because both troops and aircraft often used live ammunition, including 25-pounder guns and 3 in mortars on the ground. On May 2 1943, for example, at Inverary, Mustangs and Hurricanes strafed the beach during the assault whilst Ansons and Lysanders laid a smoke screen. Still in May, 63 Squadron was detached to Dundonald and performed tactical reconnaissance during its stay.

The constant wear on the Sommerfeld Track runways rendered the airfield unserviceable early in June and the Royal Engineers had to make hasty repairs. No 516 Squadron, by now reorganised into 'A' Flight fighters and 'B' Flight for the remainder, was inspected ceremonially on June 15 by Lord Louis Mountbatten, Chief of Combined Operations.

In July, another form of exercise joined the Squadron's repertoire, when one aircraft was dispatched to locate and shadow a force of landing craft at sea. On receipt of the pilot's report by R/T, two Mustangs were sent out to intercept and attack, mainly for the benefit of naval AA personnel.

Many hitherto quiet places on the west coast and islands, like Ardrossan and Brodick, were the scenes of realistic assault landings with ultra-low flying. Birds were a constant hazard, many aircraft being damaged by hitting flocks of seagulls. A fatal accident occurred when a Hurricane struck the ramp extension of a landing craft and crashed into the sea off Troon. Similarly, a Blenheim hit the mast of another, ripping open its fuselage and carrying away the tail wheel. The ageing aircraft was declared a write-off when it got back to Dundonald.

Taking realism to the ultimate degree, on August 19 1943, two Blenheims dropped sticks of 100 lb white phosphorus bombs near troops at Blind Mans Bay while Lysanders laid smoke inland and Mustangs shot up the beach with live ammunition.

The autumn of 1943 saw the reconstruction of the main runway at Dundonald, the squadron moving to Ayr on October 13 and doing all flying from there until the job was finished six months later. The squadron's broadly defined role made it the reluctant recipient of many extraneous duties such as vertical photography for camouflage checks, trials with captured German radio equipment and air experience in the Ansons for ATC cadets.

The airfield was host to a B-17 on December 17, unable to land at Prestwick after a transatlantic trip. Detachments from other squadrons were based here for short periods, such as a Beaufighter from 409 Squadron, to take part in calibration exercises with fighter direction tenders in February 1944. At the end of that month, nine Mustangs of 414 Squadron arrived and other squadrons were subsequently based for varying periods on bombardment spotting and other courses. They included FAA Seafire squadrons such as 808 and 885.

Sleuth Exercises formed part of 516 Squadron's duties from April 1944. They consisted of shadowing Royal Navy carriers off the Isle of Man with Blenheims, which were in turn intercepted by FAA fighters. Another B-17 landed on October 21 1944, having flown from Newfoundland and mistaken Dundonald for Prestwick!

Its job done, 516 disbanded on September 2 1944 and the station was placed on Care and Maintenance. The aim was to keep it in good working order in case it should be required subsequently for other purposes and in the meantime as an ELG. Apart from a brief flurry of activity in the middle of December, when 97 Italian POWs were at large in the district and guards were trebled, very little happened until February 14 1945, when an Avenger on its way from Lee-on-Solent to Renfrew made an emergency landing in bad weather, when it was almost out of fuel.

The Royal Navy used the airfield in March for testing a target glider. It was towed into the air by a Martinet and cast off over Troon Bay. On April 11, Norseman *44-70268* from Steeple Morden landed due to a battery fault and on May 24 Beaufort *ML791* called in from Nutt's Corner.

The Army's 22nd Beach Signals Unit was allowed to use the station as a lodger from May 28 and various other organisations inspected the airfield for possible uses. These ranged from naval explosives storage to a Ministry of Works depot. A US Army Colonel even visited under the impression that his unit was to take over. A USAAF C-47 called in connection with this on June 3 1945 but nothing came of it and the War Department took control.

Probably the last aircraft movement was Dominie *X7407* which made several local flights on July 23. Four days later the signals square and wind socks were removed and on August 1 1945 the airfield officially closed, although the site was retained by the Army and is now farmland, having been derequisitioned in 1952.

As a footnote, there is a report of another landing strip at nearby Barassie, which was visited by a USAAF Spitfire and a Harvard on July 8 1944. The Spitfire undershot and crashed, its pilot being unhurt.

Dunino, Fife

59/NO565115. 1 mile W of Kingsbarns off unclassified road

Being far from level, Dunino is a very unlikely looking airfield which has totally returned to agriculture. It was all grass, with the customary tarmac perimeter track, which has broken up so badly that

it is now, literally, a farm track. A cracked approach road leads to a cluster of dilapidated buildings used by farmers and augmented by some modern structures. A solitary Admiralty 'S' shed and three Blisters, one roofless, betray the long-deserted airfield's mixed RAF/RN ancestry.

It is possible, with permission, to drive partly round the airfield, but the last half mile to the watch tower is best done on foot. The tower is an unusual one with a D/F aerial still in place on the roof. Not far away a gun post dominates the airfield from a hillock on the boundary.

Dunino's first recorded use was by a detachment of 'B' Flight 614 Squadron during April 1941 and 309 Squadron began to move from Renfrew on May 8 1941. The pilots were mainly Polish and the aircraft were Lysanders. Personnel lived under canvas at first, the aircraft being picketed in the open and a nearby house was requisitioned as the officers' mess. The Lysanders were detached all over Scotland to take part in exercises with the Army, and on November 25 1942, 309 Squadron moved its HQ to Findo Gask.

This allowed the Royal Navy, who had requested the use of Dunino and other aerodromes the previous summer to ease overcrowding, to take it over on December 15 1942 as HMS *Jackdaw II*.

Dunino tower with D/F aerial still in place.

Although one of the conditions of the transfer was that the RAF might still have use of it if necessary, the station was expanded to accommodate three Squadrons with TBR facilities.

Three squadrons known to have been here were 825 with Swordfish from February 3 to March 9 1943, 827 with Barracudas between April 24 and August 12 1943 and 813 with Swordfish from December 13 1943 to January 20 1944.

The second-line squadrons based there were 737 with Walruses, which formed in February 1943 and disbanded the following September, and 770, an FRU which came from Crail on January 29 1944 and left for Drem on July 16 1944. The airfield was also used for the storage of reserve aircraft, many Barracudas being present in 1945.

Because of its undulating surface, Dunino was deemed unsuitable for post-war retention and was eventually paid off in 1946, although the site was retained by the Navy until 1957. Possibly it had Square Mesh Track runways at one time, as there are sections of this material made into fences.

Dyce, Grampian

38/NJ880215. 6 miles NW of Aberdeen on A947

On May 9 1943, three Spitfires of 165 Squadron intercepted a Ju 88 crossing the coast about 15 miles north of Aberdeen. Normally the outcome would have been inevitable, but this time the enemy aircraft lowered its wheels and fired flares. It would appear that the fighters had, in any case, been briefed not to attack and they escorted the Ju 88 into Dyce. It belonged to 10/NJG3 at Kristiansand and was equipped with the latest FuG *Lichtenstein* BC night fighter radar. It was said that the pilot was a British

The defecting Ju 88 at Dyce with Mosquito in background (Imperial War Museum).

agent and that the whole thing had been prearranged. The Junkers was hidden in a Blister hangar and flown to the RAE at Farnborough on May 14 in company with a Beaufighter.

A more straightforward defection occurred on December 26 1944, when a Bf 109G of 7/JG77 flew across from Norway and landed at Dyce. Unfortunately it overturned at the end of the landing run but the pilot was extricated unhurt.

Dyce's history was not usually so dramatic, dating back to early 1930 when National Flying Services Ltd, as part of its grandiose scheme to establish a chain of 1,000 aerodromes throughout Britain, suggested a 130-acre site at Dyce for development as Aberdeen Airport. Despite a tempting offer, the local council had little faith in the venture. Highland Airways had started an Aberdeen–Wick–Orkney service in May 1933 using Dragons. A field near Seaton was used, alongside Aberdeen promenade, but was closed on May 22 1935, the whole operation being moved to Kintore on the A96 about 12 miles north-west of the city.

Mr E.L. Gandar-Dower took it upon himself to set up an airport at Dyce, which opened officially on July 4 1934 with the customary air display, three Hawker Nimrods providing the only military presence. Gandar-Dower's Aberdeen Airways operated a Short Scion and several Dragons on services linking Dyce with Wick, Thurso and Orkney. The name of the company was changed to Allied Airways in 1937, by which time the routes had been extended to include Shetland and Edinburgh. A very ambitious five times weekly service to Norway (Stavanger) was started in July 1937 with a DH 86B Express.

The image shows a group of RAF pilots posed in front of an aircraft, with handwritten name labels: F/O COVERLEY, F/O WEBB, F/O JACK, W/C McINTOSH, F/O GRANT, F/O McKELLAR, F/O FERGUSON, F/O RITCHIE (back row); F/L URIE, F/L ROBINSON, F/L FARQUHAR, F/L JOHNSTONE, F/L (seated row).

602 Squadron pilots at Dyce, March 1940 (RAF Museum).

No 612 Squadron formed here on June 1 1937 as an army co-operation unit of the Auxiliary Air Force, receiving Hectors later that year. It was transferred to a general reconnaissance role with Ansons in July 1939, although some Hectors were retained until November. Coastal patrols were begun when war was declared and Dyce became an RAF station on October 16 1939. The same day, 612 Squadron flew its first convoy escort—to Bergen-bound shipping.

In December 1939, an unlikely unit formed in Dyce—No 1 Coastal Patrol Flight—flying unarmed Tiger Moths. Coastal Command knew that the mere sight and sound of any aircraft would send a U-boat submerging immediately to a depth at which its vital periscope was useless. These so-called 'Scarecrow Patrols' carried a signal pistol and the only survival gear in the event of a ditching was an inflated car inner tube and two carrier pigeons.

Very few U-boats were actually sighted, but the deterrent value was incalculable. On January 25 1940, two of 1 CPF's Tigers were instrumental in the destruction of an enemy submarine. Flight Lieutenant Hoyle and Pilot Officer Child sighted a line of oil on the surface advancing steadily at about four knots and attracted the attention of a passing destroyer. Depth charges were dropped and the U-boat was confirmed as sunk. All the CPFs were disbanded in May 1940, when more suitable armed types were becoming available.

Runways were built in the spring of 1940, the original bomb dump being demolished to allow expansion of the landing ground. Other improvements included the erection of four Bellman

hangars to which were added later in the war 14 Blisters and two 'twin T3's. Three Pickett-Hamilton retractable forts were installed and a Q-site laid out at Harestone Moss.

Part of 603 Squadron was here from January 17 until April 14 1940 with Spitfires, 602 Squadron then taking over for the air defence of the Aberdeen area until May 28 1940, when it returned to Drem. The next fighter squadron was 145 with Hurricanes, which arrived from Drem on August 31 and stayed until October 9, when it left for Tangmere. In August, a detachment of Defiants from 141 Squadron flew some unsuccessful night fighter patrols from Dyce.

No 111 Squadron's Hurricanes were transferred from Drem on October 12 1940. The usual sector patrols were flown with the occasional inconclusive scramble until the squadron went south to North Weald on July 20 1941. Its place was taken by the Czech 310 Squadron from Martlesham Heath towards the end of July 1941. The Hurricanes flew day and night patrols, but the only result was a Blenheim attacked in error and slightly damaged. The unit was also converting to Spitfires, which it eventually took to Perranporth in Cornwall just before Christmas 1941.

The early war years also saw Coastal Command strike squadrons operating from Dyce. The first was 248 with Blenheims from May to July, when it moved to Sumburgh. The squadron was here again between January and June 1941 and February to May 1942. No 254

Squadron brought its Blenheim IVs from Sumburgh in July 1940, returning there on January 7 1941. No 235 Squadron flew operations along the Norwegian coast between June 1941 and March 1942 with Blenheims until it re-equipped with Beaufighters in December 1941. From July to September 1941, 143 Squadron's Blenheims flew convoy patrols from Dyce.

The final operational units based here before the station reverted to a training role were detachments of 416 Squadron with Spitfires, which were here from November 1941 up to June 1942 and again in July and August and 410 Squadron's Beaufighters, here in the late summer of 1942. On August 29 1942, a flight of six Fulmars of 887 Squadron arrived from St Merryn for a short stay. Coastal Command was represented by 404 Squadron from September 1942, converting from Blenheims to Beaufighters for North Sea patrols before moving to Chivenor in January 1943.

In July 1942, Dyce was earmarked as the advanced base for 44 Squadron's Lancasters, should they be required for Norwegian operations. Facilities for possible USAAF detachments were also to be provided. However, after investigation in October 1942, it was considered that the airfield would never be suitable for heavy bombers, owing to poor approaches, and Banff, still unfinished, was suggested as an alternative.

The Air Ministry planners decided that Dyce's defects would have to be accepted only if operational necessity warranted it. They stated at the time: 'With the exception of those to the north and south-east, the approaches to this aerodrome are particularly bad. Aircraft approaching in either of these two directions would still be faced with a serious obstruction at the far end of the runway in the event of overshooting. It is therefore considered that the aerodrome is unsuitable for extension to Bomber Command operational requirements. This is more on account of the obstructions formed by the surrounding high ground than the actual difficulties of extending the runways themselves. It is also considered that the existing runways are adequate for fighter or fighter-bomber aircraft and no extension could be usefully made.'

The next phase of the airfield's history began on March 1 1943, when 8 OTU moved from the cramped aerodrome and

quarters at Fraserburgh. This unit was responsible for training photographic reconnaissance pilots, being equipped mainly with Spitfires plus a few Mosquitoes. At the time of the move, other lodgers on the station included 1509 BAT Flight which had been flying Oxfords from here since May 1942 and a Calibration Flight of Blenheims belonging to 71 Signals Wing. (No 1509 BAT Flight was to disband on August 14 1944.)

Swedish Airlines (ABA) continued to fly DC-3 services between Stockholm and Dyce. These diplomatic courier flights had started on February 16 1942, the aircraft being painted in the 'neutral' overall orange. One DC-3 was shot up by German fighters in June 1942, despite care usually being taken to cross the Skaggerak under cover of darkness. On the night of August 27/28 1943, SE-BAF left Dyce and disappeared en route. It was later presumed to have been shot down and on October 22 SE-BAG was attacked just off the Swedish coast and forced down in the water.

Later on, safe conduct for the flights was negotiated with the Germans. The aircraft were equipped with rows of lights which were to be kept illuminated throughout the flight. The Dyce ground-crew nicknamed them 'Flying Christmas Trees'. The flights continued under these rules between January and May 1944 until being broken off owing to the British diplomatic blockade.

In August 1943, 8 OTU was reorganised with one Flight of 37 Spitfires, supported by seven Masters for the training of single-engine pilots and a flight of 25 Mosquitoes and two Ansons for twin-engine training. The pilots ranged all over Britain on high-level photo practice, sometimes going as far as East Anglia and the Home Counties. the Home Counties.

In August 1944, Coastal Command authorised a limited number of operational flights over Norway by 8 OTU, the first taking place on September 19. Recces of areas like Christiansand and Bergen were carried out, refuelling stops being made at Sumburgh if necessary. Four operational sorties were made in September, three by advanced pupils and the fourth by an instructor. Unfortunately, persistent bad weather over the targets prevented the missions from being entirely successful.

At the same time, professionals, in the form of a detachment of 540 Squadron, were flying from Dyce, completing some 26 sorties in November alone. The most outstanding occurred on November 12, when a Mosquito photographed the *Tirpitz*, capsized in Tromso Fjord less than two hours after the Lancaster attack.

The OTU moved to Haverfordwest on January 12 1945, and Dyce was temporarily quiet again. The Admiralty was looking for a base for a new fighter school and suggested East Fortune, Chaterhall or Milfield. The Air Ministry was only able to offer Dyce, however, but the Navy turned it down as unsuitable.

The end of the war in Europe brought a rash of fighter squadrons for short periods on the way to postings in Norway. The Norwegian 331 and 332 were the first in April 1945, taking their Spitfires on to Stavanger in May. Towards the end of May, 129 Squadron flew its Mustangs up from Bentwaters to convert to Spitfires and left for Sumburgh three weeks later. No 165 Squadron also exchanged Mustangs for Spitfires at Dyce in June before moving to Norway. More Spitfires from 130 Squadron were here in June and 234 Squadron came from Peterhead on July 3, its Mustangs setting course for Bentwaters about three weeks later.

No 122 Squadron stayed at Dyce from July to October 1945, when its Spitfires moved to Wick. There was then a gradual transition back to civil use, military interest being maintained by the Tiger Moths and later Chipmunks of Aberdeen UAS and the Spitfires and Harvards of 612 Squadron, which re-formed on May 10 1946. No 612 converted to Vampires in July 1951, moved to Edzell in October and returned to Dyce in November 1952,

The R34 memorial at East Fortune.

finally disbanding with all the other Auxiliary units in March 1957.

For many years, the airport was a quiet backwater, but oil changed that overnight. In the past decade it has become the largest and busiest heliport in Europe. Many new buildings have been erected, but some wartime structures have been retained. The small tower has been replaced by a temple-style building known as a 'Ziggurat'.

East Fortune, Lothian

66/NT555785. 3 miles NE of Haddington on B1377

East Fortune's chief historical interest was that from here, in July 1919, the airship R.34 lifted off on what was to be the first east-west crossing of the Atlantic. The R.34 reached a point near New York 108 hours later, having achieved the first non-stop flight between Britain and the USA. The return trip was made to Pulham in Norfolk, the airship flying back to East Fortune in August 1919. However, it was not to be here for very long, as the airfield was put up for disposal and closed on February 5 1920.

It had been commissioned as an RNAS site on August 23 1916, but had already been in use since late in the previous year as a sub-station of Dundee. The airfield's strategic position at the mouth of the Firth of Forth made it ideal for coastal patrols, and in the first half of 1916 Avro 504s flew from here. They were housed originally in a hired marquee, but high winds forced a move to outbuildings adjoining the large house which served as officers' quarters.

The development of a network of airship patrols resulted in its expansion into a major base, and proper hangarage was erected. When the station was commissioned, the first of five non-rigid airships of the Coastal Class arrived. In July 1917, the North Sea Class blimps appeared, serving until after the Armistice and supplemented by some smaller craft. To protect the Battle Cruiser Squadron and its escorts based at Rosyth, patrols over the approaches to the Forth and Tay were reinforced by flying boats based at Dundee.

A rigid airship was first seen here in August 1917, when R.9 made a short visit and was housed in a new airship shed. The R.24 was East Fortune's first rigid on strength, having arrived on October 28

DH 9 H4275 *at East Fortune* (P.H.T. Green collection).

1917 from Beardmore's at Inchinnan. The R.29 followed from Howden in Yorkshire on June 29 1918.

East Fortune became an RAF station on April 1 1918 and began to figure in plans for a torpedo attack on the German High Seas Fleet in its ports. A large programme of torpedo bomber training was begun and 201 Training Squadron was set up to provide training facilities with Cuckoos. The Fleet and Torpedo Pilot Finishing School was also formed but became 208 TDS before moving to Leuchars the following month.

On October 19 1918, 185 Squadron formed at East Fortune with more Cuckoos for service in HMS *Argus*, but the Armistice forestalled the plans and it disbanded on April 14 1919. No 1 Torpedo Training School, which had been set up here in 1918 and became 201 TS in August 1918, was redesignated the

R.29 at East Fortune (H.A. Vasse, P.H.T. Green collection).

Torpedo Training School in 1919 and disbanded in 1920.

The domestic site on the north side of the airfield became a sanatorium, but when the Second World War broke out, East Fortune was requisitioned as a satellite of nearby Drem in June 1940. It was a full year, however, before any flying units came, in the form of 60 OTU from Leconfield on June 4 1941. This was a night fighter unit equipped with Defiants and some Blenheims, Masters and Oxfords.

In October 1941, it was redesignated a twin-engined night fighter OTU and was re-equipped with Beaufighters and Blenheims. Coastal Command Beaufighter crews began to train here from June 1942 and on November 24 1942, 60 OTU became 132 OTU in 17 Group Coastal Command. The new role of the station was now strike training with Beaufighters, Beauforts, Blenheims and Mosquitoes.

The OTU received some of the new Buckmasters in 1945, but, by the end of that year, Mosquito VIs formed the main equipment, some 33 being on strength. No 132 OTU disbanded on May 15 1946 and the airfield was transferred to Fighter Command on September 30 but soon closed.

Barracuda P9678 *of 768 Squadron flying out of East Haven* (FAA Museum).

Allocated to the USAF in 1950, but not used, it was sold off by the Air Ministry in February 1960 and employed as Edinburgh Airport in 1961 while Turnhouse was closed for runway work.

The Scottish Museum of Flight has had its home here for many years and displays an interesting collection of historic aircraft, several with Scottish connections. The original Callender-Hamilton hangars are still in use and the former Battle HQ can be seen by a strip of woods on the western perimeter.

East Haven, Tayside

54/NO595375. 4 miles SW of Arbroath off A92

'I found myself standing at the end of a runway on the windy coast of Angus, waving a pair of oversized yellow ping-pong bats at a succession of passing Stringbags.' This was how one pilot, temporarily turned Deck Landing Officer, succinctly described what went on at East Haven.

The air station was commissioned as HMS *Peewit* on May 1 1943, accommodation having been increased during construction to house up to four squadrons and ease the serious overcrowding at Arbroath. No 796 Squadron, the Deck Landing Training School, moved here from Arbroath on November 7 1943 and operated a variety of naval types, including the Sea Hurricane and Barracuda, until it moved to Rattray on August 2 1945.

The ground, or, more accurately, ship side of the operation was taught by 731 Squadron, formed here specifically for

the training of Deck Landing Control Officers on December 5 1943. This Squadron flew all manner of naval machines, ranging from the obsolescent, like the Sea Hurricane and the Fulmar, to first-line types such as the Seafire and Firefly. It finally disbanded in November 1945.

The station's last inhabitant was an Operational Flying School, 767 Squadron, recorded as being here until July 1946 with Barracudas, Ansons and Fireflies. Here also from 1943 until disbandment in April 1946 was 768 Squadron, which flew Barracudas, Swordfish and Martlets. The airfield closed in August 1946, having also housed a school of aircraft handling and a fire-fighting school.

East Haven in the '80s is a disappointing sight to the airfield enthusiast, having been cleared of almost all its buildings. Amongst the handful remaining are three 'S' hangars in the south-east corner, now inherited by the farms on whose land they had been built. There is a lot of Square Mesh Track in use as fencing in the vicinity, probably once employed for dispersal areas, as the field was built with four tarmac runways. A piece of SMT has even been fashioned into an attractive little archway in a cottage garden!

Sections of the runways are still in reasonable condition, and parachute dropping was regularly done from here. One of the runways bears traces of white lines across it, marking the limits of a dummy deck.

Edzell, Tayside

45/NO630690. At Bridgend 2 miles NW of A94

Slightly to the north of the Second World War site was a First World War field, which opened in 1918; 26 Training Depot Station forming here on July 15 for single-seat fighter training, mainly with SE 5As, until disbanding in 1919. It was also the probable site of an AA landing ground in the 30s, the exact location varying from year to year with crop rotation!

No 44 MU formed at Edzell on August 1 1940, the landing area already being in use by 8 SFTS Montrose as an RLG. The buildings, however, were still incomplete and essential services like electricity and sewerage were yet to be laid on. The first aircraft for attention, a Hurricane, arrived on August 13 and was housed in an unfinished 'K' Type hangar. No 41 Group Maintenance Command ordered 44 MU to prepare as many Hurricanes as possible to replace losses in the fighting over Southern England, but the actual number was low at first owing to the lack of facilities.

Mr C.H. Brown, then an LAC Airframe Fitter (Rigger) at 44 MU, arriving at Edzell early in 1941, recalls: 'For about six weeks we never had a kite sent over to us for daily inspection or repair. All we did was sweep and sweep the hangar floor with a two foot broom to remove the cement dust, and some occasional PT. When eventually we had a Hurricane sent over to us for a DI there was a queue of fitters to get the job. That winter I remember spending hours clearing the runways and aeroplane wings of snow. The snow was hedge-high and we lost two airmen trying to get from one side of the airfield to the other. A search party was sent out and when they were found one was taken to hospital with frostbite and exhaustion.'

The random way in which death could strike without warning is illustrated by Mr. Brown's experience. He had been detailed to do a DI on Whitley *BD686*, but, as there was no immediate hurry, had gone off to collect his issue of 'winter woollies'. 'When I returned, to my astonishment, the kite was taxi-ing off with my pal Angus (Armourer) taking my place. In those days it was normal practice for the Engine Fitter and Rigger to go with the aircraft on test flights if, of course, it was not a single-seater. The Whitley crashed in Edzell woods on take-off with no survivors. So by the grace of God I was not my turn to cop it. It was a sad day at the funeral—I was one of the pall bearers. However, the Fates were determined that I should "get it", as within weeks I was run over by an Oxford

while pushing it up the hill into the hangar and spent two months in Stracathro Hospital.'

With invasion thought to be imminent in 1940, improvised defences were provided at all RAF stations. At Edzell, Black Watch detachments occupied strong points around the airfield and manned a searchlight continuously at night in case of glider landing. Three Armadillo armoured cars were allocated, one with a 1½ lb COW gun, although no ammunition was available! By the end of September, two 4.5 in howitzers were positioned on the hills to the north of the aerodrome, typical of the unsuitable and cumbersome artillery defending many of the vulnerable Scottish airfields at that time.

During October 1940, Oxfords, Wellingtons and Proctors began to fly in, many of the Proctors being dispersed to Perth to make more room for operational types at Edzell. More hangarage, including two 'K' Types and one 'L' Type, was brought into use in January 1941, but without heating and lighting at first. Part of a hangar was loaned to Messrs Cunliffe Owen in February for the assembly and repair of Hudsons, an activity which was to keep them busy here until the end of the war.

On February 12, the roof of a new 'L' Type hangar partially collapsed during the operation of covering it with earth for camouflage and protection against incendiary bombs. Two Proctors inside were completely buried.

Hampdens and Ansons were among the types handled in April 1941 and SLGs at Stravithie and Methven were taken into use to spread the MU's ever-increasing workload and storage requirements. The first of two runways was completed in April 1942, and in June, Fighter Command declared its intention of using the airfield as a temporary base for operational squadrons if necessary.

Included in the aircraft being handled by the MU in 1942 were Albemarles, Beauforts, Defiants and Hurricanes. At the end of September, 348 aircraft were held at Edzell and its SLGs, the accommodation of wooden aircraft having reached saturation point, despite the erection of 14 Robin hangars.

No 8 SFTS ceased to use Edzell as an RLG when the school disbanded on March 25 1942. No 2 FIS, which had re-formed at Montrose in January 1942, then employed Edzell as an RLG again and

Wildcat of unknown unit at Eglinton 1944 (Via M.J. Burrow).

some Blister hangars were put up for its Oxfords and Masters. A Beam Approach system was installed in 1943 for the use of 1518 BAT Flight which moved in from Scampton on June 14. Its Oxfords, which were affiliated to 14 PAFU at Banff, stayed until disbandment on August 20 1944. It had been planned to form 1543 BAT Flight here in June 1943 but this was cancelled.

In the middle of 1944, the MU was dealing with Beauforts, Defiants, Horsas, Magisters and Mosquitoes. The long awaited north-east/south-west runway was finally finished in July and the same month Beaufighter Xs made an appearance. At the end of July 1945 the total stock of aircraft was 819, many of them Mosquitoes and all waiting for disposal. Well into 1946, the number of aircraft held rarely fell below this figure, as the might of the wartime RAF was scrapped here and at every other ASU in Britain.

No 44 MU continued to be active after the war, with Dakotas and many other types passing through. No 612 Squadron flew Vampires from here, starting in October 1951 and returning to Dyce on November 12 1952. No 662 Gliding School then operated here until 1957.

Edzell is now occupied by the American National Security Agency for long-range electronic surveillance, the station being administered by the US Navy. The runways are covered with aerials but most of the wartime MU hangars still exist, although closer inspection is not recommended.

Eglinton, Londonderry

7/C540220. 1 mile NE of Eglinton off A2

Generally thought of as a naval station, Eglinton was actually built for the RAF and thus had only three runways instead of the conventional four. Its control tower also was an RAF type and its original hangars were 12 Blisters, ten 'S' sheds being added later when the Royal Navy was in occupation. Planned as a Coastal Command base under 15 Group, it became instead a day fighter base for the defence of Londonderry, which, by virtue of its position, had suddenly become one of Britain's most vital ports.

An HQ staff was in residence from April 1941, but the runways were still not finished and the first and only Coastal aircraft to arrive consisted of a detachment of ten Hudsons of 53 Squadron during August 1941. Pending the arrival of Eglinton's own aircraft, Hurricanes from 504 Squadron Ballyhalbert were detached here in September to escort convoys passing through the sector. This job was taken over by 133 (the third Eagle Squadron) on October 8 1941, a foretaste of the American units to come.

Several scrambles were ordered after

Batsman gives the 'Cut' signal to a Hellcat at Eglinton 1944 (Via E.A. Cromie).

Above *Hellcats in a wet Blister hangar at Eglinton 1944* (Via M.J. Burrow).

Right *Fromson hangar which could also be employed as shooting butts, Eglinton. The aircraft's tailwheel would be drawn up the ramp in foreground to align the guns.*

Ju 88s, on shipping recce, but bad weather prevented contact. The proximity of the border was another hazard, one pilot baling out of his Spitfire in November and being interned. On another occasion, Spitfires intercepted a presumed enemy aircraft over Eire territory, but broke off promptly when it turned out to belong the the Irish Air Corps! No 133 Squadron was sent to Kirton-in-Lindsey on January 2 1942 to be replaced by 134 Squadron, with Spitfires and a few Hurricanes. It was joined by 152 Squadron from Coltishall in January also with Spitfires.

On April 23 1942, four US Navy Vindicator aircraft called in via Crail in Scotland, and a few days later a Hudson landed from Newfoundland short of fuel. It turned out that this aircraft had force-landed in Donegal, but had been allowed to proceed by the Irish authorities. A B-17 from Newfoundland came in on May 8, and on May 13 a Wellington and two Hurricanes arrived from Boscombe Down for a few days of secret firing trials against targets in Strangford Lough.

No 134 Squadron had departed late in March, but the pilots of 152 Squadron were still here in July to greet new arrivals from the USA in the shape of the 52nd Fighter Group, which soon received a full compliment of Spitfires. The Americans were not impressed with the Irish weather, a few days' rain bringing the remark 'No wonder Ireland is so green,it never has a chance to get any other way'. Bearing in mind that this was July, the station ORB records 'An American pilot asked "When do you get summer?" He was informed that the summer of 1942 occurred here between 1400 and 1900 hours on May 31!'

The Group's 2nd Fighter Squadron was detached to the nearby satellite at Maydown on August 7, and, on the following day, part of 152 Squadron and the 5th FS, comprising a total of 16 Spitfires, escorted a convoy. This was the 52nd FG's first operational duty since its arrival in Britain. The 5th FS became operational at sunrise on August 11, releasing 152 Squadron for air firing and other training, although it was available in emergency. Having passed on the benefit of its experience to the Americans, 152 left for Angle on August 16.

Two sections of the 5th FS were scrambled on August 23 against a hostile reported over Eire, but 504 Squadron's Hurricanes got there first and shot it down. After a couple of weeks of routine convoy escort, the 52nd FG left for Goxhill via Ouston, their Spitfires now proudly painted with USAAF stars.

No 41 Squadron spent some time here in September, as did 11 Mustangs of 4 Squadron for an Army exercise. The advance party of the USAAF's 82nd FG arrived from England on October 4 1942, the personnel of its 97th FS being established at Maydown. Mrs Roosevelt, wife of the President, visited the Group on November 10, just before their P-38 aircraft began to be delivered from Speke, Burtonwood and Abbotsinch.

A few Spitfires were also available for familiarisation, and both types were flown extensively from Eglinton and Maydown. Some long practice escort missions with B-17s were flown by the Lightnings. At the end of December, a total of 43 Lightnings left for St Eval on their way to join the 12th Air Force in North Africa.

Maydown was closed on January 4 for expansion, and the six men who operated the decoy 'Q'-site, which also served Ballykelly, were withdrawn. A detachment from 501 Squadron Ballyhalbert was on hand for air defence, but its duties usually involved shepherding lost aircraft.

One such on January 24 was a Fortress from Marrakesh which was escorted into Eglinton. One night a Hudson from Iceland was well off course for Prestwick, the pilot having mistaken the west coast of Ireland for the West of Scotland until the lights of towns were seen. When very short of fuel, they spotted Eglinton's aerodrome lighting and made a safe landing.

On May 1 1943, Eglinton and its satellite were loaned to the Royal Navy, the RAF establishment being reduced to the minimum required to maintain fighter lodger units. At the end of the month, three Ansons were detached from 275 Squadron Valley for close-in ASR searches and later a Walrus was made available as well, the detachment staying until April 1944. Many searches were made for missing aircrew, some successful, others fruitless, such as when a UC-78 Bobcat aircraft carrying the Commander of the US Navy base at Londonderry (Commodore James A. Logan) from Eglinton to Hendon was believed down in the Irish Sea, but was eventually discovered wrecked on a mountain with no survivors.

The station's first Royal Navy aircraft after it commissioned as HMS *Gannet* on May 15 were the Swordfish of 835 and 837 Squadrons from Ballykelly on May 30 1943, but the main use thereafter was for the formation and working-up of naval

Left *518/40 type tower at Eglinton.*

Below *Eglinton May 1958 with Gannets and Skyraiders* (FAA Museum).

fighter units. As a back-up, 725 Squadron was formed here on August 27 1943 for target towing and other duties with Rocs, Skuas and Martinets, staying until September 24 1945.

Several Corsair squadrons were here in 1945, including 1835 which re-formed on April 21 1945. No 1837 also re-formed on July 1 1945, moving to Nutt's Corner on July 31. Two Hellcat units, 891 and 892 Squadrons formed here on June 1 1945, 892 leaving on July 6 and 891 during August. The hulks of two Eglinton Corsairs can still be seen lying in the mud of Lough Foyle where they ditched so long ago.

Training at Eglinton diversified somewhat after the war ended, 794 Squadron, a fighter school, arrived from St Merryn in August 1945 with Corsairs and Fireflies. Anti-submarine training was given by 744 Squadron from November 29 1945, with Barracudas and Ansons. This unit was destined to be here until 1953. Strike training was the duty of 719 Squadron, from May 1946, with Barracudas and Fireflies. Other miscellaneous units based during this period included a detachment of 758 Squadron from Hinstock, 718 Squadron, which held Seafire conversion courses until disbandment in March 1947 and 795 Squadron, which provided refresher flying on Fireflies.

Sea Furies and Fireflies of 805 and 816 Squadron worked-up in 1948, prior to transfer to the Royal Australian Navy for that service's first carrier, HMAS *Sydney*. Similarly, the new air arm of the German Federal Navy had one of its first squadrons commissioned at Eglinton in May 1958. This was a Gannet unit for anti-submarine duties, all training having been done in Northern Ireland under the wing of the Royal Navy.

Many other squadrons were based here for varying periods in the 50s, including 815 with Barracudas and then Avengers, and 737 and 812 with Fireflies. The Royal Navy left in April 1959, but part of the aerodrome only was reactivated in 1960 as HMS *Sea Eagle* for helicopters, closing again in September 1966. Londonderry City Council then reopened the airfield for civil use, but services by Emerald Airways were short-lived. Since then, private flying has gone on from here on a limited scale, the Eglinton Flying Club being the main user. Light industry has taken over some of the wartime buildings. The airfield shows evidence of its RAF/Navy ancestry in the variety of its hangars. There are a number of Blisters, Pentads and 'S' sheds, and a Fromson which houses a Piper Cherokee. Some of the original fighter pens have been cleared, others are in reasonable condition. The tower is a 518/40 type, modified by the Navy and there are some interesting non-standard air raid shelters and defence positions nearby.

Elgin, Grampian

28/NJ200600. 3 miles SW of Elgin on B9010

This wartime satellite to Lossiemouth, sometimes referred to as Bogs O'Mayne, is now farmland again. Having been laid out early in the war, it had no runways, but otherwise possessed all the facilities and dispersed sites of similar later stations in other parts of Britain. Twenty circular hardstandings were spaced around the perimeter, some leading off the taxi track, others being merely circles on the grass. The watch office was of the 13079/41 type common to bomber OTU satellites, but there is no trace of it now.

It stood close to the few surviving buildings on the road running down the western side. One of these is the Flight Office and across the road opposite some new bunglows is a fine memorial to 20 OTU incorporating the unit's badge. There was once a 'B1' and 'T2' hangar and seven Blisters, but all have been taken away. The dispersed living sites, too, are almost all demolished.

The airfield was obstructed by the Royal Engineers as soon as it was completed at the beginning of June 1940. As 20 OTU expanded, it was cleared and became available for use on June 30. The parent station at Lossiemouth being somewhat congested, 57 Squadron's Blenheims were moved to the satellite to continue anti-shipping operations over the North Sea until they left for Wyton on November 1 1940. There is evidence too that 21 Squadron's Blenheims and a 614 Squadron Lysander detachment used Elgin in 1940.

The Hurricanes of 232 Squadron were here for defensive duties from December 4 1940 until moving to Montrose at the end of April 1941. A second fighter squadron, 17, brought its Hurricanes from Castletown on July 29, staying until September 16 1941, when it left for Tain.

No 20 OTU's Wellingtons were of

course constant users, and in June 1941, a sodium flarepath was installed for simulated night-flying to augment the few hours of darkness in the northern summer. The demands of training crews for the night bomber force took a steady toll of aircraft. In one dramatic accident on August 6 1942, a Wellington almost reached Elgin with its port wing on fire, but the weakened structure collapsed just short of the boundary and only one of the crew survived.

In May 1943, Oxfords of 19 (P)AFU began to use Elgin under a local arrangement, but, owing to the OTU's requirements, this lasted only until July. Wear and tear on the grass late in 1944 was remedied temporarily, but by the following January the airfield was again unusable and the detached Whitleys were evacuated to Lossiemouth. An Airfield Construction Squadron laid Bar and Rod Track and the satellite was returned to service on March 20 1945. Almost three months later, on June 24, it went to Care and Maintenance as 20 OTU began to wind down.

On July 28 1945, Elgin was taken over by 46 MU as 105 Sub Storage Site to specialise in the storage of Lancasters and Harvards. When the Royal Navy acquired Lossiemouth in July 1946, 46 MU remained there, slowly disposing of its stock of aircraft either by flying out or scrapping them. No 105 SSS came under the control of 45 MU at Kinloss on January 1 1947 and probably closed not long afterwards.

Errol, Tayside

59/NO270240. 2 miles NE of Errol on B958

Errol's 'claim to fame' was its use by Russian crews to train on the Albemarle. For this purpose, 305 FTU formed here on January 1 1943 within 44 Group, the FTU designation being a convenient cover for the unusual activity. The first group of trainees, comprising three pilots and three flight engineers, arrived on January 11, via BOAC at Prestwick, and began flying on January 25. By May 2 1943, 20 crews had been trained and had ferried their aircraft to Russia.

Continuation training for Soviet crews was undertaken by 305 FTU until April 18 1944, the unit disbanding at the end of the month. Limited Mosquito instruction was given also, *DK296* a Mk IV, for example, leaving on delivery in April 1944.

A well-appointed airfield with three runways, six 'T1' hangars (only one survives) and 13 Blisters, Errol opened on August 1 1942 with the move of 9 (P)AFU from Hullavington in Wiltshire. No 21 Advanced Flying Course was posted in on August 9, with a total of 37 pilots (nine of them New Zealanders).

Training was devoted to naval pilots, although this was ostensibly an RAF unit. Masters and Hurricanes were the main equipment, Swordfish and Albacores being added later. Three Walruses were loaned early in 1943, but despite protests that at least one should be retained for rescue work in the River Tay, they were allotted away in April.

The same month a Wing Commander from Flying Training Command made a visit to discuss the formation of a BAT Flight at Errol. At that time, owing to the Russian commitment, lack of accommodation and shortage of mechanics, it was considered impracticable. When facilities eventually improved, 1544 BATF formed here on January 25 1944, flying Oxfords until disbandment on August 30 1944. The flight was attached to 14 (P)AFU, then at Banff.

Two Barracudas were allocated to 9 (P)AFU in May 1943 for conversion purposes and on August 6 two Whitleys arrived from Kirkbride towing gliders in connection with Operation *Tyndall*.

Errol was the base for another operation in March 1944, involving the packing and air-dropping of supplies sufficient for 5,000 infantry for 12 hours. Six Dakotas of 271 Squadron were used.

A satellite at Findo Gask had been provided in July 1943, but was closed during the winter months for improvements. It reopened in March 1944, the (P)AFU then being split into 1 Group Fighter Training ('A' & 'B' Flights) which stayed at Errol and 2 Group TBR Training ('C' & 'D' Flights) at Findo.

By 1944, Tealing, with its two tarmac runways, was redundant, and, after the usual negotiations, was transferred to 9 (P)AFU as a satellite in place of Findo, with effect from September 9. The Masters were now being replaced by Harvard IIs and had gone entirely before October was out, a most popular move it was thought!

No 9 (P)AFU disbanded on June 21 1945, 64 pupils being posted to 5 (P)AFU at Tern Hill in Shropshire. Errol was then placed on a Care and Maintenance under the parentage of Montrose, one of its last

Above *Harvard FE756 'T 44' of 9 (P)AFU low-flying out of Errol April 1945* (Via M.J. Burrow).

Below *12779/41 type tower crumbles at Errol.*

movements being probably a Wellington from Dalcross with engine trouble in August 1945. No 260 MU used the hangars for equipment storage from July 1945 until disbanding in June 1948.

In 1947, the Minister of Civil Aviation issued a preliminary list of airfields which were to be acquired and operated by the Ministry in accordance with the White Paper on British air services, published in December 1945. One of them was Errol, but nothing came of this. However, in 1967 it was suggested that Errol be reopened to replace Dundee Riverside Park, which was susceptible to flooding, but a local action committee was formed to combat non-agricultural development.

Riverside, an entirely post-war airfield, has since acquired a hard runway, and Errol lies forgotten. Its tower survives, as do many of the huts near the road. It is interesting to reflect that long before it became a proper airfield, the site was used in the 1900s by Preston Watson for the first trials of powered aircraft in Scotland.

Eshott, Northumberland

81/NZ185985. 1 mile S of Felton on A1

Built in the mid-war period, this airfield was never intended to be anything other than temporary. The accommodation consisted entirely of nissen huts, the hangarage being a single 'T3' and eight Blisters.

No 57 OTU had been displaced somewhat hurriedly from Hawarden in mid-November 1942 to make way for an Army Co-operation OTU and arrived at Eshott to find it still unfinished. This was a not uncommon state of affairs in wartime and Spitfire training was resumed almost immediately. To save taxying time, Sommerfeld Tracking 'short cuts' were laid on the airfield connecting the perimeter track to the runways and the special Spitfire curved approach pattern was incorporated into the Drem lighting system.

With the impending closure of the OTUs at Milfield and Annan, the unit was informed in January 1944 that it would be required to increase pilot output. Pupils from most of the Allied nations passed through and it was an unlucky Norwegian who was killed in a mid-air collision over the airfield on April 12 1944 with a USAAF Thunderbolt attached to the FLS at neighbouring Milfield. Throughout 1943 and 1944 the OTU was averaging two fatal casualties per month, a terrible figure, but one considered acceptable to

Eshott 1981.

meet the demands of the training programme.

After raids on northern Germany on December 31 1944, no less than 26 Liberators were landed successfully at Eshott after being observed orbiting and homed by *Darkie*.

Training was suspended on May 15 1945, the pupils being sent elsewhere and the OTU disbanded on June 6. The final flying units here consisted of detachments of 288, 289 and 291 Squadrons with an assortment of Oxfords and other types.

Most of Eshott's buildings have now been cleared, including the 12779/41 watch office and the three 'T1's. The north-east/south-west runway is remarkably long for a fighter training station; perhaps the airfield was planned for something bigger?

Evanton, Highland

21/NH625665. 1 mile NE of Evanton on A9

A thriving industrial estate has ensured the preservation of this atmospheric old airfield. Rather like Donibristle, its hangars and technical site are on a higher level than the landing ground and one wonders how aircraft were towed or taxied up the sharp inclines. The mixture of RAF and RN use is obvious from the assortment of hangars, 'F' and 'S' Types, Bellmans and a 'B1'. There is an intriguing pillbox near the shore with a dummy pitched roof on top to make it look like an innocent dispersal hut from a distance.

On August 16 1937, 8 Armament Training Camp opened here under HQ Training Command, taking over the buildings known previously as Novar Camp, which had been administered by Coastal Command. The small airfield had been used by the FAA for disembarked units from carriers at the Fleet Anchorage, Invergordon. This task continued, 800 and 820 Squadrons from HMS *Courageous* and 801 and 822 Squadrons from HMS *Furious* being accommodated during the closing months of 1937.

The takeover was somewhat premature, as the new buildings required by the ATC were not ready until November 1937, the first course of flying instructors for air-firing commencing on November 29. At the same time, 7 and 99 Squadrons flew in from Finningley and Mildenhall respectively for a short stay.

Several more squadrons were attached in 1938 and such FAA units as 800, 820 and 821 came ashore. In February visiting squadrons and the TT Flight searched the north of Scotland for a missing Wellesley of the Long-Range Development Flight, but to no avail. As well as first-line units, training aircraft from 8 FTS Montrose and 6 FTS Little Rissington spent time here on courses.

The day before war was declared, 1 AOS was withdrawn from North Coates in Lincolnshire to Evanton. No 771 FRU Squadron had been here for a month, departing on August 20 and another naval squadron, 774, was to be here from July 3 to September 17 1940. Both flew Skuas, Swordfish and other types. The Advanced Training Squadrons of all the Scottish based SFTSs spent time at Evanton doing armament training. The fighter defence of the Fleet was the job of a detachment of 64 Squadron's Blenheims from Church Fenton between December 4 1939 and January 8 1940.

With the fall of Norway, Scotland found itself threatened with attack from

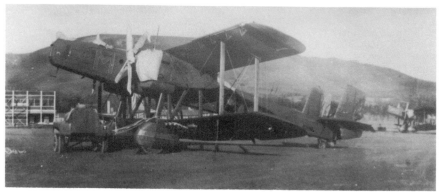

Top *Hampden* L4070 *of 83 Squadron parked at Evanton April 1939* (D. Garton, P.H.T. Green collection).

Above *Heyford* K5196 *of 99 Squadron with damaged rudders at Evanton circa 1938* (P.H.T. Green collection).

Below *Pre-war 'F' Type hangar at Evanton.*

this direction. One of the first effects was that cross-country flying, hitherto unrestricted, needed permission from the operations room at RAF Wick before a flight north of Helmsdale. The small stock of bombs at the airfield was now augmented by many more from Wick, which was considered too vulnerable to attack to carry a large supply. The Evanton dump allocated bombs to Wick, Lossiemouth and Kinloss when required.

To help train soldiers who were to be posted to the Middle East, the Lysanders of 'B' Flight 614 Squadron arrived on detachment on June 11 1940. The AOS aircraft dropped 1500 practice bombs on the Tain Ranges during July, one Harrow being fitted with five bomb sights which saved a lot of training time. Wallaces were phased out in July and in September four Henleys were exchanged with RAF Jurby for four Battle target tugs. The venerable Harrows were replaced by Bothas in April/May 1941 and a station pipe band was formed around the same time!

Wimpey & Co commenced the construction of two runways in March 1942, and completed them in the autumn. Both are in reasonable condition today, but very short, and since the landing ground was so narrow, it was impossible to make them intersect at right angles, so crosswinds were still a problem. This led to the loss of Botha L6242 on April 10 1943, when it got its port wing down in a crosswind, stalled and crashed on its back in the Cromarty Firth. The tide was out and the crew members were lucky to escape with minor injuries.

In April 1943, the Tain air-to-ground ranges ceased to function and a new site at Dornoch was opened. The unpopular Bothas were superseded in mid 1943 by Ansons fitted with a Bristol turret for gunnery training. The last Botha was flown to Abbotsinch for disposal on November 10 1943. A Manchester aircraft was flown in, its engines and mainplanes removed and the fuselage mounted on trestles for instructional purposes, including cockpit drill.

The last course of air gunners, No 138, comprised a polyglot collection of British, French, Norwegian, Czech, Polish and Belgian personnel. They were all awarded their brevets at a full station parade on August 18 1944.

From August 26, RAF Dalcross provided a Care and Maintenance party, the airfield being taken over by the RN on September 1 and commissioned as HMS

Fieldfare on October 9. No 4 OTU's TT Flight, which had lodged here for some time, departed from Tain on December 12 1944.

Many aircraft were stored at the RN Air Yard, on which £2 million was spent, particularly in the post-war period, the station being paid off in December 1947. Spasmodic use has been made of it since by civil aircraft. Loganair planned to operate services through here in 1966, but the idea was not developed.

Fearn, Highland

21/NH845760. 1 mile NW of Balintore on B9166

Fearn's mixed RAF/RN ancestry is betrayed by three runways, a three-storey tower and one surviving 'S' shed. (It once had some Bellmans too.) It was built as a satellite to Tain, opening late in 1941, but seems to have been used very little by the RAF. It was transferred to the Royal Navy and commissioned as HMS *Owl* on July 15 1942. Bomber Command wanted lodger facilities here for possible Norwegian operations and earmarked it for 83 Squadron, but the Navy refused permission.

It became a torpedo school with accommodation for two TBR squadrons and a number of units flew the Barracuda from here. The first, 747, formed on March 22 1943 but moved to Inskip in Lancashire the following June, only to return in January 1944 and stay until October.

No 717 Squadron formed in July 1944 and left for Rattray in November. No 714, which had re-formed at Fearn in August 1944, also went to Rattray in October.

Several first-line Barracuda squadrons

Beech Traveller at Fearn (Mrs E. Hall).

Standard naval tower at Fearn.

worked up at Fearn, including 816 from March to July 1945, 817 from April to August 1945, 841 between February 29 and June 28 1944, 837 from November 1944 to April 1945 and 860 from November 1945 to May 1946. The nearby Tain ranges were used for torpedo practice. Also after the war 719 Squadron re-formed for strike training in March 1946 but took its Barracudas and Fireflies to Eglinton in May. A fighter affiliation squadron, 736B, based its Seafires here for part of July and August 1945.

Very unusual was 708 Squadron, the Firebrand Tactical Trials Unit which arrived from Gosport in December 1945 and disbanded in March 1946 after evaluating this troublesome aircraft. HMS *Owl* was then paid off on July 2 1946 and reverted to Care and Maintenance.

After the war it is said to have been used as a satellite by the Oxfords of 8 AFTS at Dalcross. However, one ex-pilot

Expeditor HD763 *at Fearn 1946* (Mrs E. Hall).

told me that during his time at the school there were no RLGs available.

Loganair planned to link Fearn with several other Scottish airports, as it was the nearest aerodrome to the oil rig construction site at Nigg Bay. A long-term helicopter service direct to Nigg put paid to this idea.

Findo Gask, Tayside
58/NO010215. 2 miles N of Dalreoch Bridge off A9

I first visited Findo in 1974 and was pleased to find a large three-storey tower of the late war type that was built at Heathrow, Dumfries and Gaydon amongst others. A rusty 'T2' was the only hangar left, the seven Blisters having gone years before. The tower is only yards from the farm of Clathymore, which, surprisingly, was not demolished when the airfield was built. In 1981 things were much the same, except that the 'T2' had been reclad and renovated.

A grass satellite aerodrome, Findo had a lot of dispersed sites to the south-east and such ancillary structures as a Battle HQ and machine-gun range. SBA equip-

Findo Gask tower and adjoining farm.

ment was installed and there were a number of hardstandings displaced around the perimeter. Many of the buildings, including the Station HQ offices, were built of cellular concrete, a cheap and very nasty substitute for brick which has not stood the test of time!

The airfield was built originally as 25 SLG intended for 44 MU Edzell and opened on June 14 1941. It was, however, not used for storage purposes, but re-allocated to 309 Squadron, as it was near to the Polish Army camps for which the unit carried out co-operation. Pending Findo's completion as a full aerodrome, the Squadron was moved from Renfrew to Dunino, but Findo was only employed as a satellite until November 25 1942, when the squadron moved its HQ here. The aircraft were mostly Lysanders, 'B'

'T2' hangar with huts of cellular concrete construction at Findo Gask.

Flight's Mustangs being detached elsewhere for varying periods.

Surface deterioration caused a move to Kirknewton on March 6 1943, the HQ staff returning to Findo on June 21 after 309 Squadron was posted south to Snailwell at the beginning of that month. There were no aircraft until July, when a flight of 652 Squadron's Austers came over from Methven for a brief stay.

Flying Training Command took over on July 12 1943 and Findo became a satellite for 9 (P)AFU at Errol but it was not actually used as such until March 28 1944, when the Masters of 'C' and 'D' Flights were sent here. All the trainee pilots were naval at that time and destined for TBR Squadrons. The Admiralty had been interested in the station for development as the southern terminus of their Northern Air Transport Service up to Scapa Flow, but nothing came of it.

Findo still had Sommerfeld Track runways and suffered badly from poor drainage, so it was with some relief that it was given up in favour of Tealing with its hard runways on September 12 1944. The site then passed on loan to the War Department for the use of the Polish Army and finally to 260 MU for storage until 1948. Polish inscriptions were visible on the tower doors until well into the 60s. Aeroplanes returned years later when AST at Perth used the site for practice forced-landings.

Fordoun, Grampian

45/NO755775. 4 miles NE of Laurencekirk
B966 follows old runway

Fordoun was built as the two runway satellite of Peterhead, with six fighter dispersals, four Blister hangars and four dispersed living sites. No 2 FIS Montrose kept a detached flight here from

November 1942 until September 13 1944, flying mainly Oxfords.

In September 1943, two officers from 778 Service Trials Squadron at RNAS Crail inspected the station with a view to becoming a lodger unit. An ATC Gliding School was also mooted, but neither plan was proceeded with.

Fordoun was one of the aerodromes selected to take part in Operation *Tyndall* and duly received ten dummy Bostons. The ORB notes:- 'August 7 1943—A Czech pilot landed. His attention was drawn to the Bostons. He contended they were Marauders and left in the morning still unaware that they were dummies!'

Operation *Tyndall* was a cover plan mounted in the late summer of 1943, with the object of delivering a deceptive threat to pin down German forces in Norway during our invasion of Italy. The idea was to simulate invasion preparations in the east of Scotland by a considerable glider-borne force. Horsas and dummy Boston aircraft for 'tactical support' were displayed on a number of airfields on the East Coast. Despite all the effort involved, there is no evidence that German reconnaissance was deceived.

No 1632 Flight was at Fordoun in 1943 and became part of the newly formed 598 Squadron on December 1 1943. Four Lysanders and two Martinets were kept here. In March 1944, flying was stopped, as the concrete runways were cracking badly and temporary repairs had to be made. A third runway had been planned and, although it was never built, the perimeter track followed the expected contours. By December 1944 the aerodrome was on loan to the War Department.

Blister hangar at Fordoun.

Fordoun was reopened for private flying in May 1965 and became the base of the Fordoun Flying Club in 1967. A road now follows the line of one of the runways, but all four Blister hangars have survived, one roofless, and other buildings including the parachute store still stand.

Forres, Grampian

27/NH020580. One mile W of Forres, on A96

Like nearby Elgin, Forres was a grass-surfaced bomber OTU satellite. It was brought into operation on April 27 1940, when 'D' Flight of 19 OTU moved over from Kinloss. From then until October 22 1944, it was used almost constantly, day and night, by Whitleys, apart from short periods of unserviceability, such as in January 1942, when surface conditions closed it. No 19 (P)AFU Dalcross also used it as an RLG in 1943, until being allowed to use Brackla for the same purpose in November 1943.

The dilapidated state of many of 19 OTU's aircraft in the hands of inexperienced pilots resulted in a number of bad crashes on and around Forres. For example on November 11 1940, Whitley *N1440* dived into the ground in the circuit, and on September 3 1942 *Z6760* hit a bank on take-off. The obstacle was perhaps the slope leading up to the railway bridge on the north-east edge of the aerodrome, from which a good view of the site can be had.

After 19 OTU gave up the satellite, it was loaned to the War Department and there is no further record of military flying use. A short concrete strip was built in 1960. It was known as Mundole, after a house on the southern perimeter of the original airfield. This was to enable a director of United Biscuits Ltd to

Dummy camp at Forres with 'T2' hangar and Whitleys of 19 OTU (Public Record Office).

commute from and to the London area in company aircraft. It has also been used by Aztecs belonging to a distillery since about 1966.

A total of 16 hardstandings was built along the banks of the river Findhorn to the south of the wartime airfield and the modern strip is laid alongside them. The 'T2' hangar and almost all the original buildings have been demolished and modern houses have been built on other hardstandings to the north-east. All in all it is difficult to imagine that this was once such an important RAF station.

Fraserburgh, Grampian

30/NK040645. Adjacent to Inverallochy on B9107

The two runways of the old airfield are now blocked by poultry houses owned by a well-known frozen chicken firm. Almost all of its original buildings have been demolished, leaving only a few solitary huts and the parachute store. It was built as a satellite of Peterhead, opening on December 6 1941, and consisting of three

dispersed sleeping sites, a communal area and a technical site with one 'T2' hangar. The watch tower was a satellite type 17658/40.

Two days after the opening, Swordfish of 823 Squadron became the first lodgers, staying until the end of January 1942. No 883 with Sea Hurricanes then spent the first fortnight in February at Fraserburgh.

The station was transferred from Fighter to Coastal Command on May 18 1942, to accommodate 8 OTU which formed here on the same day. Policy was to remove the Photo Recce Conversion Flight of 3 School of General Reconnaissance from Squires Gate and 1 PRU/Advanced Training Flight from Detling. They were then to combine in one OTU the work of training Spitfire and Mosquito crews in the specialised task of PR. The first aircraft for the new OTU, 8 Spitfires and a Master, landed on May 24 and work was begun on erecting Blister hangars for maintenance and dispersal.

The Spitfires were sent out on long trips of up to six hours, a typical one taking in an entire circuit of Scotland, including the Western Isles and the English Border. As the training commitment built up, Fraserburgh was found to be too cramped to accommodate the OTU. The necessary programme of works services to improve the airfield would entail the evacuation of its staff so it was decided to move the OTU to Dyce. Ample accommodation existed here, and on completion of the transfer on March 9 1943, Fraserburgh was reduced to Care and Maintenance and a request to release it for use by the FAA was refused.

On April 6 1943, it was transferred to Flying Training Command, 21 Group, in preparation for a new job as satellite to 14 (P)AFU, expected to move into Banff in the near future from Ossington in Nottinghamshire. This was achieved by May 25 and Oxfords began to fly from Fraserburgh in large numbers.

An unusual visitor on July 24 was a battle-damaged B-17 from the 100th BG which made a crash-landing. The bomber had taken part in the 8th Air Force's first attack on targets in Norway.

Advanced pilot training went on without a break until September 1 1944, by which time a surplus of pilots was becoming apparent, so 14 (P)AFU and others were disbanded. A move would have been inevitable in any case, as Coastal Command needed Banff and its satellites for strike operations. The airfield had, incidentally, displayed ten dummy Bostons in July/August 1943 for Operation *Tyndall*.

RAF Fraserburgh was then returned to Coastal under 18 Group but does not appear to have been used much at first, except by 838 Squadron's Swordfish from October 23 to November 8 1944.

On Boxing Day 1944, a detachment of 279 Squadron arrived from Banff. It operated Warwicks carrying airborne lifeboats and acted as ASR cover for the Banff and Dallachy Strike Wings. On December 31, for example, a Warwick rendezvoused with four Mosquitoes, one of which was limping along on one engine. Losing height, it eventually had to ditch, and a lifeboat was dropped 200 yds from the crew's dinghy. The rockets which were supposed to shoot out lifelines from the boat failed to fire and a second boat was dropped by another Warwick from Wick.

The members of No 279 Squadron often acted as shepherds, for example, on the occasion when a Warwick escorted a Mustang with a rough-running engine into Sumburgh. It must have been a great morale-booster for the fighter pilots faced with hundreds of miles of icy sea on only one engine.

Apart from the ASR sorties, Fraserburgh was not very active and was thus able to find room for a maintenance team from Banff which did acceptance checks on new Mosquitoes for the strike units. The airfield finally closed at the end of June 1945, but was used by the Aberdeen Gliding Club in the 50s.

Gosforth (Newcastle), Tyne and Wear
See Newcastle

Parachute store at Fraserburgh.

Grangemouth, Central Region
65/NO940810. Just SE of town on A904

Now totally obliterated by the BP oil refinery and other industrial development, Grangemouth was opened on May 1 1939 as the Central Scotland Airport by Air Marshal Viscount Trenchard. Events passed it by, however, post-war use being restricted to a Gliding School up to 1946 and use by the Tiger Moths of 13 RFS between April 1 1948 and April 19 1949. It closed in June 1955.

The first quasi-military units at Grangemouth were 35 E&RFTS, which opened on May 1 1939 with Tiger Moths and Harts, and 10 Civilian Air Navigation School with Ansons, which also formed in 1939. Both schools were administered by Scottish Aviation, but the E&RFTS closed in September 1939 and the CANS was absorbed into 1 AONS at Prestwick in December.

Grangemouth is associated chiefly with fighter training, but in the early days of the war, operational squadrons used it for the air defence of the Clydeside area. Daily in September 1939, 602 Squadron dispersed one flight of Spitfires here from Abbotsinch and on October 19 1939, 141 Squadron moved over from Turnhouse with Blenheims and Gladiators. The squadron went back to Turnhouse on June 28 1940 and was relieved the same day by 263's Hurricanes from Drem. The expected heavy raids on the district had still not materialised, so 263 moved back to Drem on September 2 1940.

No 614 Squadron was also here from June 8 1940, operating Lysanders on coastal patrols and for training with the Navy. The unit moved to Macmerry on March 3 1941 as 58 OTU began to expand.

No 58 OTU formed here on December 2 1940 with Wing Commander J.R.

Hallings-Pott DSO, posted in from 7 OTU at Hawarden as CFI, bringing with him a wealth of experience in Spitfire training. The first four Spitfires were not delivered until December 31 and work on runway construction hindered flying. Two runways, a perimeter track and hardstandings were completed by mid-1941. The shorter runway is now Inchyra Road. Also that year, 4 Delivery Flight was based here for the ferrying of fighter aircraft, eventually moving to Turnhouse on January 8 1942.

The opening of the satellite at Balado Bridge on March 20 1942 took much of the load off the parent station, in that the latter could now concentrate on the ground training of pupils and initial conversion onto the Spitfire. Advanced instruction in operational flying was now concentrated at Balado. In addition, from September 1942, the large number of Polish trainees passing through necessitated the formation of a completely Polish section—'A' Squadron divided into 'A' and 'B' Flights. From October, *all* Polish fighter pilot pupils were sent to 58 OTU and it became the only OTU in 81 Group where British and Polish flying instructors worked alongside one another.

In an attempt to reduce the minor crashes caused by over-shooting, the east/west runway was extended by about 300 yds in the summer of 1942. Night flying was begun on Septmber 30 1942 and around the same time the OTU joined the *Saracen* Scheme, fielding 558 Squadron in the event of an invasion of this country.

At the end of 1942, the OTU was able to summarise in its ORB as follows: 'A year of achievement, a year of development and a year of change. In the course of the last 12 months, 400 fighter pilots have passed out from Grangemouth, men of many nations, men of varying skill and character, all imbued with a high fighting spirit, trained to the last degree, replacing the gaps in the old established squadrons, forming new squadrons, serving at home and overseas. Some have given their lives, some are prisoners of war, others have won renown with their skill and courage.'

By this time it was noted that Polish fighter pilots had now accounted for more than 500 enemy aircraft over Britain. Sergeant Turek, who was a graduate of 58 OTU, shot down three FW 190s, nos 497, 498 and 499. Three days later Flying Officer Langhamer, an ex-Grangemouth instructor, dispatched No 501, but sadly, on the same day, Pilot Officer Kosmoski,

another former 58 OTU instructor, was reported missing.

Several pilots failed to return from training flights in Scotland, claimed probably by the sea, but there is a remote possibility that one at least awaits discovery with his Spitfire in some untrodden corner of the Highlands. On November 11 1941, for example, Spitfire *L1083* from Grangemouth disappeared in cloud over the mountains and was never heard of again.

Flying into high ground was another ever-present danger, one of the worst incidents occurring on January 18 1943, when a formation of three Spitfires crashed in the Ochill Hills. Two of the pilots were killed instantly and the third lying injured in his cockpit was very fortunate to be found by a shepherd soon afterwards. Another pilot baled out safely over the hills on September 9 1943 but the wreckage of his Spitfire was never found.

Going back to the domestic details of running an OTU, we find a new system of flying beginning in January 1943. It took into consideration the number of pupils on a course, the number of aircraft available and the number of flying hours required per pupil. Maintenance was planned to meet these demands and permission was sought to carry out all-night inspections in the five Blister hangars under floodlights, despite the blackout. It was thus possible to increase the number of serviceable aircraft available for day flying. Brick ends were built on the Blisters, the open ends being screened by heavy curtains.

In May 1943 the station workshops in the pre-war civil hangars at Grangemouth were busy fitting Spitfires with light bomb carriers to take four 10 lb practice bombs under each wing. Another local modification was the clipping of the wings of bomb-carrying Spitfires, the first being taken up for a test flight on August 14 1943. The same day the unit's last Lysander was flown away, all target towing work now being done by Martinets. Spitfire Vs were being allotted to 58 OTU to replace the worn-out Is and IIs, some being veterans of the Battle of Britain.

The OTU was renamed 2 Tactical Exercise Unit on October 17 1943 under 2 Combat Training Wing. There was by now a temporary surplus of trained fighter pilots and the aim was to give as much experience of air warfare as possible whilst they were being held in reserve. No 2 TEU disbanded on June 25 1944 and the airfield was then used for storage by Maintenance Command.

Greencastle, Down

29/J285115. 2 miles S of Kilkeel on unclassified road

This station seems to have been planned to house a bomber OTU but in April 1942, just before it was opened, it was designated one of 12 aerodromes in Northern Ireland to be taken over by the USAAF. The original scheme envisaged that US fighters based at Ballyhalbert, Eglinton and Kirkistown would take over the entire air defence of Ulster, and that other operational units would use the remaining nine fields.

Greencastle opened on July 30 1942, but it was over a year before the Americans occupied it. In the meantime, it served as a useful bolt-hole for lost aircraft. On September 11, for example, Ventura *AE920* landed direct from Gander and on November 13 four P-38s arrived *en route* from Speke to Eglinton, having lost their way. Many other visiting aircraft on communications flights are mentioned in the Station ORB.

The FAA showed an interest in Greencastle for TBR training in January 1943. It observed that there were certain snags, including the proximity of the Mountains of Mourne and the fact that the airfield was close to the border, which might entail difficulties with sabotage and the salvage of force-landed aircraft. However, they were not offered the airfield and it was finally handed over to the USAAF as Station 237 on August 3 1943.

The 5th CCRC Group was to be activated at Greencastle and appears to have given ground training only for bomber crews. Air gunners were given practice in ground-to-air firing against drogues and after March 1944 all the gunners passing through the 2nd CCRC at Cluntoe were sent here for short courses.

Greencastle's main role was as satellite air depot to Langford Lodge and to this end multiple hardstandings were built on which up to 100 aircraft could be stored. Throughout 1944, B-17s, B-24s and other types were prepared as replacements for VIIIth Air Force losses. However, long-term storage was prevented by salt spray corrosion from the nearby seashore.

In February 1945, the 5th Airdrome Squadron assumed full control of all activities at Station 237. That month there were some 320 aircraft on the airfield and to keep track of the whereabouts of each one coloured pins were inserted in a plan of the field.

A lodger unit in 1944/45 was the VIIIth Air Force Anti-Aircraft Machine Gun School which trained ground AA gunners for airfield defence. The 4th Gunnery and Tow Target Squadron acted as the Luftwaffe, flying mainly A-20s and A-35s.

Greencastle was restored to the RAF on May 31 1945 and on that occasion the Ministry of Information allowed a little slightly inaccurate publicity: 'A chapter was ended in Ulster's wartime activities at Greencastle, County Down, when the last of the RAF aerodromes occupied by the USAAF was handed back. The 350-acre base, the runways of which have enough concrete in them to lay a 9 ft wide roadway from Belfast to Londonderry, was a vital link in the United States' constant flow of bomber crew replacements. To its broad acres overlooking the Irish Sea, trained aircrew came from the States. At Greencastle the bombers were crewed-up—skilled individualists becoming members of a team—and replacements for lost crews operating from British bases were flown over every day.'

The former airfield is now remarkable for the fact that almost all the buildings and works, including runways, have been removed. High land values and sand and gravel deposits are the reason for this. Only about a 300 yd length of one of the three runways is left intact and the broken concrete of others has been used to form new field divisions in place of the original Mourne granite dry-stone walls. Part of the only remaining group of dispersals is used as a base for holiday caravans. The tower, a 12779/41 type, still stands, the ground floor being occupied by a large and ill-tempered pig.

Greenock, Strathclyde

63/NS285765. Greenock Docks

As well as being a major wartime port, Greenock also had an RAF station which owed its beginnings to the pre-war licensed seaplane base. A flying boat maintenance base was established officially at Greenock on October 10 1940, the first aircraft received being Stranraer *K7295* which flew in for major inspection. Others of the same type were sent, some for the fitting of IFF and other equipment. Several Lerwicks were put into storage here in November 1940, pending a decision on the future of this disappointing machine.

A Singapore came in for hull repairs in December and on Christmas Eve the first Sunderland arrived, from 228 Squadron on Malta. Scottish Aviation had an outstation at Greenock and it was handed over to them for overhaul. The first of many Catalinas for Scottish Aviation docked on February 1 1941 and on February 12, *Golden Hind X8275* arrived for inspection and modification by Short Bros engineers.

The station suffered from lack of accommodation for personnel and there was considerable local opposition to the requisitioning of billets. An ex-servicemens' club and Greenock Social Club were taken over and it was not until September 1942 that a hutted camp was completed at Darroch Park.

RAF Greenock was responsible also for the storage of RAF marine craft until a shipyard at Dumbarton was requisitioned for the purpose. This became a separate unit—62 MU—on May 29 1941.

There was a heavy air raid on the port on the night of May 7 1941, a direct hit on a hangar and storage yard destroying a Swordfish, a Sunderland and two Catalinas. A new slipway had, meanwhile, been constructed at Gourock Bay and the undamaged aircraft were transferred there soon after.

By July 1941, many Catalinas were being fitted out for the RAF by SAL and others from Saunders-Roe at Beaumaris were awaiting delivery to squadrons. At the turn of the year, American MAD (Magnetic Anomaly Detection) equipment was installed in Catalina *FP191*. A Greenock test pilot and crew tried it out from Beaumaris with observers from RAE Farnborough and CCDU pronounced it highly successful.

Specialisation in Catalina preparation ended in April 1944 and Sunderlands were again handled. This was a result of a requirement by Coastal Command for Greenock to supply temporarily both 302 FTU and MAP with aircraft for dispatch overseas. A record number of Sunderlands and Catalinas passed through in June and Coronado *JX470* was also in for a mainplane repair.

Conversion of Sunderlands from Mk III to Mk V standard was begun in October 1944 and it was while at Greenock on December 3 that *DV978*

sank at her moorings in a gale. Sunderland work went on to the end of the war, a notable event being the station altitude record for this type. Whilst being airtested, *ML816* reached 19,200 ft and was still climbing at 200 ft per minute when further ascent was abandoned due to lack of oxygen.

On another lighter note, a Sunderland flew over to Woodhaven on June 29 1945 with the station football team, supporters and crew, a total of 25. They returned later with the 18 Group Victory Cup, having beaten RAF Milltown at Leuchars.

The last aircraft left Greenock on July 25 1945, Sunderland *ML819* to Calshot. A few weeks later the base reverted to Care and Maintenance under Maintenance Command. Civil flying boats, including Aquila Airways' Hythes, visited in the early '50s.

Hatston, Orkney

6/HY435125. 1 mile NW of Kirkwall on A965

Aircraft from Hatston destroyed one German cruiser, the *Konigsberg*, hastened the sinking of the battleship *Bismarck* and made an inconclusive attack on another cruiser, the *Scharnhorst*.

Long before dawn on April 10 1940, 16 Skuas from 800 and 803 Squadrons led by Captain R.T. Partridge barely got airborne from the small airfield, each armed with a single 500 lb semi-armour-piercing bomb, and set course for Bergen, 300 miles to the east. The Skuas had been disembarked to the shore station from *Ark Royal* and were flying to the very limit of their endurance.

Landfall was made exactly on track and within one minute of ETA, a commendable performance by the Observers. Three direct hits by the dive bombers and many near misses turned the *Konigsberg* into a blazing hulk. Four and a half hours after take-off the Skuas landed back at Hatston, three of them damaged but having lost only one of their number in the surprise attack. They thus earned the distinction of being the first aircraft to sink a major warship in battle.

On June 1 1940, six Swordfish from Hatston made the first torpedo strike against a capital ship at sea, again at maximum range. It was sadly unsuccessful as the crews had received insufficient training in this specialised form of attack. Two of them were shot down and the

Top *Swordfish taxiing out at Hatston. Kirkwall town behind. A photograph packed with atmosphere* (Imperial War Museum).

Above *US Navy Vindicator in pre-war markings. This type was a frequent visitor to Hatston in the spring of 1942.*

Below *Gladiator N2274 of 804 Squadron and Vega Gull* G-AETF *at Hatston March 1940* (Via R.C. Sturtivant).

Scharnhorst completed her trip from Trondheim to Kiel unscathed.

It was an aircraft from Hatston which discovered, on May 22 1941, that the Bismark had left her anchorage south of Bergen and thus started one of the greatest chases ever known on the high seas. A group of torpedo-armed Albacores was standing by at Hatston ready to intercept the Bismark the moment she left her fjord but the RAF reconnaissance aircraft were grounded by bad weather. Increasingly concerned at the lack of information, the CO of the Albacores arranged a search mission. Lieutenant N.E. Goddard, the CO of 771 Squadron, volunteered with his crew to fly an unarmed target tug, a Martin Maryland, over the anchorage 300 miles away.

Skimming the sea with hardly any forward visibility and the mountainous coast waiting somewhere ahead required tremendous faith in the navigator, Commander Rotherham, but the landfall over low ground was absolutely accurate. Bismark's anchorage was deserted and so were other nearby fjords. Bergen harbour too was circled and heavy flak peppered the Maryland without doing any vital damage. With no sign of the battleship, it pulled up into the clouds.

The news was too important to impose radio silence so the telegraphist tried to inform Coastal Command. There was no reply so he called blind on 771 Squadron frequency. A bored wireless operator towing targets around Scapa Flow picked up the faint morse and found himself copying one of the most important operational signals of the entire war. The message was passed to the Fleet which immediately put to sea and within a week the German ship was sunk.

Unlike other airfields in the North, Hatston had not been a civilian site before

Avengers of 846 Squadron on the same apron at Hatston shown on the previous page but several years later (Via R.C. Sturtivant).

the war. Highland had used Wideford and Kirkwall, although Captain Freeson had originally found what he considered to be a much more suitable spot at Hatston farm but the land owner would not agree.

Early in 1939 when an Admiralty representative asked Fresson for advice on the best site for an airfield in Orkney he immediately suggested Hatston. He went on to say that winter rain would make any grass airfield in the islands completely unusable for modern aircraft and that tarmac runways would be essential. This was revolutionary talk in those days and it is amazing that the advice was taken. Hatston, therefore, was almost certainly the first airfield built in the British Isles with hard runways.

Its only flaw was the steep slope on the east/west strip towards Kirkwall harbour, the trick being to fly just above the approach hill, whose slope corresponded to an average glide path angle. The runways at HMS Sparrowhawk, as it was known, were finished just in time for the war, the hangarage and accommodation taking somewhat longer. Scottish Airways was allowed to use the new airfield until nearby RAF Kirkwall was completed.

As over 200 naval squadrons spent time at Hatston during the war years and records are almost non-existent, it is only possible to give some examples. No 804 Squadron formed here on November 30 1939 with Gladiators and Martlets and remained until 1940. They are reputed to have evaluated the Brewster Buffalo fighter while at Hatston. It could only manage about 270 mph at 6,000 ft with armour and ammunition against the manufacturer's figures of 318 mph at 13,000 ft. Another aircraft tried out at Hatston and subsequently rejected was the Curtiss Helldiver. No 1820 Squadron brought some in from Burscough in November 1944.

No 771 FRU Squadron arrived from Donibristle at the end of September 1939 and flew various types until moving to Twatt on July 1 1942. A brief RAF detachment was made by 254 Squadron's Blenheims in April/May 1940 before they went on to Sumburgh. In April 1942, the USS *Wasp* was in Scapa Flow and her Vindicator aircraft, and probably other types, used Hatston as a shore base. The rest of the American Task Force there at that time comprised the battleship *Washington*, two heavy cruisers and six destroyers.

Amidst all the transit squadrons, another long-term resident was 712 Squadron which re-formed on August 2 1944, using Dominies and Expeditors for communications until disbanding in August 1945. The last based unit was 719 Helicopter Flight which was present with Hoverflies up to September 1945.

After the war, the station became Kirkwall's airport until 1948, when it proved too small for the safe operation of the Dakotas BEA was then introducing on the North Scottish routes. The former RAF Kirkwall was revived and Hatston, although used by the Orkney Flying Club from 1953 to 1957, was eventually closed. The hangars were put to industrial use and some of the huts turned into council housing. The control tower, an unusual wooden building, is now gone. In April 1981 it was announced that Air Orkney was assessing the possibility of reopening part of Hatston to avoid the increasing charges at their Kirkwall base but at the time of writing nothing has come of this.

Helensburgh, Strathclyde

63/NS272834. ½ mile S of Rhu on A814

The Marine Aircraft Experimental Establishment was evacuated from Felixstowe to Helensburgh in September 1939. Originally run by the Air Ministry, the base was transferred to the control of MAP in 1940 and often referred to as Rhu. Not far away at Dumbarton, Blackburn built Sunderlands and Bothas, the latter being test-flown from Abbotsinch.

Many flying boat types were to be seen here on trials. New types like the Lerwick were evaluated, in this case showing little promise. The first Mariner GR1 arrived in September 1943 via Saunders-Roe at Beaumaris and in 1943 a Coronado also flew in.

In 1940 a Bv 138 three-engined flying boat captured at Trondheim was flown to Helensburgh for evaluation. Around the same time, at least four Norwegian Navy He 115 seaplanes arrived after the fall of Norway.

Depth charge dropping tests were a common task and on one occasion a Sunderland was damaged when the weapon exploded on impact with the water. On November 28 1941, an MAEE Sunderland crashed in the sea off Rhu on flame damper trials and two members of the crew were killed.

A small land plane section of MAEE used Ayr and Prestwick in 1944/45 for affiliation trials, the types including Wellingtons. MAEE returned to Felixstowe in August 1945 and the station then closed.

Inchinnan, Strathclyde

64/NS475682. 1 mile NW of Renfrew on A8

A naval airship station was opened here for the construction of airships by Beardmore in 1916. An AAP was added in 1918 to receive Handley Page V/1500 aircraft built by Beardmore at Dalmuir. (A small airfield at the latter factory across the Clyde was used for testing smaller machines between 1916 and 1921.)

The Inchinnan site covered 360 acres and one of the airships built here was the R34. The 700 ft long × 100 ft high hangar was sold off for scrap early in 1923.

Invergordon (Alness), Highland

See Alness

Inverness (Longman), Highland

See Longman

Kidsdale (Burrow head) Dumfries and Galloway

83/NX445365. 2 miles NW of Isle of Whithorn on unclassified road off A747

One of the RAF's least-known stations in Scotland, Kidsdale, is closely linked with nearby Burrow Head, where there was an AA practice camp. There is much confusion between the two locations but it appears that Queen Bee target aircraft were catapulted from Burrow Head and target-towing aircraft used Kidsdale. The unit involved was 'W' Flight of 1 AACU with Henleys and Queen Bees. The HQ was Burrow Head from May 8 1937, moving to Kidsdale on December 1 1939.

Being one of the few aerodromes in this part of Scotland, it made a welcome diversion for weather-bound aircraft. On April 7 1942, an Oxford with an ATA pilot force-landed. Shortly afterwards, a Battle also put down because of bad weather but skidded into a derelict car on the edge of the runway. This was one of many around the perimeter intended for obstruction of the landing ground when necessary. A larger visitor on September 8 1942 was a Beaufighter on a delivery flight.

Pilotless Queen Bee 'shoots' were a regular occurrence, one on July 9 1941 being claimed as a record when it reached 14,000 ft in front of the guns without being hit. Another was trawled up by a fishing boat in Luce Bay and found to be one shot down nine days before.

The Taylorcraft of 651 Squadron were here from August 10 1942 until December 1942, flights being dispatched to take part in Army exercises at various temporary locations such as Redesdale in Northumberland.

In 1942 the site was offered to the Royal Navy, who were requesting new training stations. They considered it as a possible fighter or torpedo training base but it would have needed enlarging and furthermore was almost surrounded by existing firing ranges so the plan was soon dropped.

Kidsdale was handed over to the War Department, Scottish Command, on November 25 1943 and there is no record of further use for flying.

Killadeas, Fermanagh

17/H205525. 5 miles N of Enniskillen off B82

Beginning on January 29 1941 the Chiefs of Staff of Britain and the USA held secret talks in Washington to plan the co-ordination of strategy should America be drawn into the war, as seemed likely despite the strong lobby for non-involvement.

Much attention was paid to the problem of Atlantic security and agreement was reached about possible American naval bases in the UK. In May 1941 the basic details were circulated secretly to all those likely to be concerned. Two naval bases, Londonderry and Rosneath, were to be placed at the disposal of the USA, along with two flying boat bases at Lough Erne and Loch Ryan. These pairs of bases, in Northern Ireland and Scotland respectively, were selected in case the Germans bombed the US forces out of one of them.

The US Government was to be responsible for the construction of the necessary installations by US contractors under the supervision of American engineers. If and when the USA became involved in the war, these bases were to pass completely under their control. Lower Lough Erne, crescent-shaped and 16 miles long by 5 miles wide, was to accommodate four Catalina squadrons. Work did not begin until August 1941, but the whole programme, which included the main base at Ely Lodge, repair facilities at Killadeas, an ammunition depot and a hospital, was

Catalinas of 131 OTU, Killadeas, over Castle Archdale, June 1943 (M.E. Street, via Chaz Bowyer).

completed in five months. Much of the Nissen-hutted accommodation was sited on a wooded peninsula.

Commissioned by the US Navy early in 1942, it was, surprisingly, not used by them and in June the repair base at Killadeas was transferred to the RAF and the remaining sites to the US Army. The station was taken over by 17 Group Coastal Command and on July 20 1942, 131 OTU formed here and took over the Catalina training commitment of 4 OTU. It later added Sunderlands to its establishment and a target-towing detachment was based at St Angelo. For night flying the flarepath at neighbouring Castle Archdale was employed. A satellite at Boa Island/Rock Bay was used between May 1944 and April 1945 and was also located on Lough Erne.

In July 1944, it was decided that 12 (O)FIS at St Angelo should take on the extra duty of teaching flying boat instructors, its Sunderlands and Catalinas being based at Killadeas. Another lodger unit was 302 FTU which came here from Oban on April 15 1945 with Sunderlands. It left for Alness on July 1 1945 and 131 OTU disbanded at the same time.

The base was run down and closed by 272 MU which had formed here on August 1 1945 and also disposed of surplus aircraft before disbandment on February 28 1947. The CO of 4 OTU had flown in during June 1946 to see if Killadeas was suitable for the transfer of his unit but decided it wasn't.

Today most of the wartime buildings have been cleared and the large house which once housed Station HQ is now a hotel. The Lough Erne Yacht Club operates from the original slipway and aircraft hardstandings. The only real survivor from wartime days is an RAF pinnace in dilapidated condition but still on its original beaching trolley.

Kinloss, Grampian

27/NH070630. 3 miles NE of Forres on B9089

The B-17 Fortress was the backbone of the USAAF's strategic bomber force in Europe during the Second World War, despite the RAF's misfortunes with early operations on the type. The original model of the Fortress was flown by 90 Squadron in 1941, a detachment being sent to Kinloss in September. On September 5 four of them set off to bomb the *Admiral von Scheer* in Oslo Harbour. One came back early with supercharger trouble, the other, unable to spot the ship, bombed the docks from 30,000 ft.

Three days later, four Fortresses went back to Oslo, but this time were intercepted by fighters. One was shot down, another disappeared and the only one to reach the target found it obscured by cloud and thus brought its bombs back. The fourth aircraft suffered enormous punishment, one gunner being killed and another wounded. One engine was put out of action, the other three were all damaged and the aileron controls were shot away. Against all expectations, Sergeant Woods reached Kinloss, but the experience confirmed the RAF's worst fears about high altitude daylight bombing and it was left to the Americans to perfect the techniques.

Kinloss was a late Expansion Period airfield built in 1938/39 and showing a mixture of permanent buildings (three 'C' Type hangars for example) and the

Crew and Whitley of 19 OTU at Kinloss (RAF Museum).

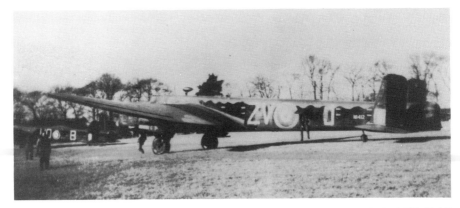

temporary structures of all subsequent aerodromes. It was planned to house an FTS far away from the likely operational area of East Anglia. At that stage, of course, a threat from the direction of Norway was not taken into account.

No 14 SFTS opened here in 1939, flying Oxfords and Harvards and a few biplanes for adanced training. In mid-April 1940, the school vacated the station for Cranfield and it was transferred to Bomber Command to accommodate Whitley Detachments of 77 and 102 Squadrons. It was not, however, the first time that bombers had flown from here as Nos 10, 49, 50, 51 and 102 Squadrons had already detached Whitleys and Hampdens to reinforce 18 Group Coastal Command attacks on Stavanger, Trondheim and other Scandinavian ports since the beginning of the war. No 609's Spitfires were also here in December 1939 and January 1940 but no combats materialised.

The Whitleys returned to Driffield on May 4 1940 but meanwhile 45 MU had formed as a lodger unit on April 15. The dispersed hangar sites were still under construction so the first aircraft, Harvard *N7013*, could not be delivered until May

Whitley N1412 ZV-Q *of 19 OTU* (RAF Museum).

31. During June, 26 aircraft were received, mainly Oxfords and Hawker biplanes but at the end of June the MU was told it was to specialise in the preparation of Halifaxes, Whitleys, Wellingtons and Spitfires for the squadrons, although other types such as the Tiger Moth would be held as required.

The other unit with which Kinloss was to be associated for the rest of the war, 19 OTU, formed on May 17 1940 for night bomber crew training. At the end of July, the OTU was informed that in the event of invasion in the north it was to attack troop-carrying surface craft. On receipt of the codeword 'Julius Caesar' all training was to cease and all available Whitley and Anson aircraft were to be prepared for operations.

A satellite at Forres came into use in April 1941, by which time the original allotment of Whitleys was in poor mechanical condition. All the early

Mosquitoes of 6 OTU at Kinloss (RAF Museum).

Beaufighter of 6 OTU at Kinloss (RAF Museum).

Whitley IIIs were therefore disposed of, leaving only Merlin Whitleys on strength.

In the spring of 1941, the MU was still struggling to maintain its output even though only eight out of 12 hangars were occupied and only four of these were completely finished. Many fields around the aerodrome were requisitioned for dispersals and the opening of SLGs eased the storage problems. In mid-1941, the Boston was added to the list of first-line aircraft handled by the MU.

The OTU took part in operations in May and June 1942. Twelve Whitleys used Abingdon in Oxfordshire as an advanced base for the Thousand Bomber Raid on Cologne, one aircraft being reported missing. Again flying from Abingdon, one Whitley failed to return from an attack on Bremen on June 25.

Owing to frequent bad weather, high ground and worn-out aircraft, 19 OTU had a higher than average accident rate, almost 200 aircrew being killed and 64 injured during its life. One drama had an amusing outcome, however, when a pilot reported an engine on fire and made a hurried landing. On investigation it was believed that the fire had been little more than red hot exhaust stacks, as the pilot had never flown a Whitley in the dark before!

Kinloss was chosen as an advanced base for Norwegian operations in 1942 and brought up to the standard needed for RAF and USAAF heavy bombers. Some American troops arrived in October 1942 for the purpose. Halifaxes had already employed the airfield for anti-*Tirpitz* raids and far ahead in November 1944

Lancasters of 9 Squadron flying from Kinloss would take part in the final destruction of the monster.

In 1943, 45 MU was responsible mainly for Halifaxes, Spitfires and Wellingtons, Warwicks joining this commitment the following year. All available manpower was diverted to Halifax production in March 1944 for 38 Group's Invasion effort. Also in March a Swedish Airlines DC-3, *SE-DAC*, did some familiarisation flying at Kinloss as it was to become the company's diversion field for Dyce. Another local event was the formation of a Mountain Rescue Unit in July 1944.

No 45 MU deleted the Spitfire from the types it prepared in February 1945, by which time it was heavily involved in breaking down large numbers of early mark Halifaxes. The end of the war brought flocks of surplus aircraft, chiefly Halifaxes, Ansons and Warwicks, the holding increasing by leaps and bounds to a peak of 1,059 aircraft in October 1946. After this, the numbers began to dwindle as the scrap dealers took them away piecemeal. As late as the '60s the corroded frames of a number of Ansons still languished in the sandhills bordering the aerodrome.

The last course, No 16, passed out of 19 OTU on May 25 1945, most of the crews going to 4 Group squadrons in Yorkshire. One of the OTU's pupils back in 1943 was Cyril Barton, who won a posthumous VC on the ill-fated Nuremburg raid of March 1944. The unit closed on June 26 and the station passed to Coastal Command for 6 OTU, equipped mainly with Beaufighters and Mosquitoes. Moving in on July 18, the OTU was redesignated 236 OCU on July 31. The OCU went on to train crews on Lancaster, Neptune and Shackleton aircraft.

No 120 Squadron flew Lancasters from Kinloss from December 1949, converted to Shackletons in April 1951 and moved to Aldergrove a year later. Still operating Shackletons, it returned on April 1 1959, converted to Nimrods in February 1971 and is still flying them from here at the time of writing.

At St Eval, 217 Squadron had received two Neptunes for conversion flying and in April 1952 moved to Kinloss where the squadron was equipped fully with the type. It was disbanded here on March 31 1957.

Other Shackleton units were 201 and 206, at Kinloss from March 14 1965 and July 7 1965, respectively. Both eventually received Nimrods. No 8 Squadron reformed here on January 8 1972 with Shackleton AEW 2s but moved to Lossiemouth on August 17 1973.

The airfield has been much extended since the war, one of the subsidiary runways being converted into a huge parking apron.

Kinnell, Tayside

54/NO610510. 1 mile N of Friochkeim off A933

Kinnell on a summer's day is a peaceful stretch of farmland divided by two crumbling concrete runways. The ruined tower stands in a rippling field of corn and cattle rest in the shade of some tumbledown huts. One tries with little success to imagine the ambulance and fire tenders racing out long ago in May 1943 to a Beaufighter damaged by Fw 190s off Norway. The navigator was grievously wounded and died later, despite his pilot's attempt to make a landfall as soon as possible. The aircraft was from 143 Squadron on attachment to Wick from its base at North Coates in Lincolnshire.

Kinnell's war was not usually so dramatic; it spent its brief life as a satellite

to Tealing, being first used on March 29 when 56 OTU sent four Lysanders over for target-towing. The course at this fighter OTU soon included a final three weeks at the satellite for such exercises as interception, dummy *Rhubarbs* and practice attacks on Hampdens from Leuchars. The aircraft used were Hurricanes.

As described in the section on Tealing, the latter airfield was too close to hills for safe night flying so on September 16 1942 night flying was started at Kinnell with circuits and bumps. The satellite's aircraft were also affiliated with the Peterhead Sector in emergency as 556 Squadron and were often to provide operational convoy escort. The first scramble took place on April 6 1943, two aircraft shadowing a convoy until relieved by aircraft from Peterhead. This became a regular occurrence and was a valuable taste of operational flying for the advanced pupils.

On October 5 1943, 56 OTU was reorganised into 1 Combat Training Wing, being later renamed 1 TEU. No 1 Squadron of the CTW was based at Kinnell, specialising in air-firing and evasive action, and each pilot was now required to complete five hours' night flying at the satellite. In 1944, the TEU received some Spitfires and these were often to be seen at Kinnell alongside the Hurricanes.

No 1 TEU closed on July 31 1944, Kinnell being taken over as a satellite by 2 FIS at Montrose and used by 'G' Flight's Oxfords. After the FIS disbanded in July 1945, the airfield became a site for 44 MU for a short time.

There is not much left today, apart from the tower, which is an unusual type.

Anson WD413 *parked on Kinnell runway June 1981.*

Hurricane after undercarriage collapse at Kinnell 1943 (P. Davies collection).

The four Blister hangars have all gone. A short stretch of runway is still used by aircraft for parachute dropping but the rest has been reduced to rubble.

Kirkistown, Down

21/J645595. At Kirkistown off B173

Opened in July 1941 as the somewhat rudimentary satellite to Ballyhalbert, Kirkistown possessed three runways and only four Blister hangars. Although an RAF field, its first user was the naval 888 Squadron which moved here from Ballyhalbert on November 4 1942, going to Lee-on-Solent in December. No 835 Squadron was here in January prior to a move to Macrihanish on January 29.

No 504 Squadron moved in from Ballyhalbert on January 22 1942, returning there on June 19, with Spitfires being used for air defence duties. Thereafter, Kirkistown was used solely as a satellite and RLG for Ballyhalbert-based units but could be very active, as on the occasion when a Spitfire's engine failed near the aerodrome. A practice scramble was in progress and red Verys were being fired so the pilot belly-landed with considerable skill on Kirkistown football ground.

On August 28 1943, the Northern Ireland Training School was set up here for the purpose of training RAF Regiment personnel in combat and defence duties. The airfield ceased to be Ballyhalbert's satellite on March 21 1944, being transferred to RAFNI for administration. However, this did not stop it from being employed for dummy deck landings by Seafires of 808 and 885 Squadrons in August 1944. A bombing target was constructed on the airfield, but after a

month's use the damage caused to the runways by stray practice bombs resulted in a ban on this activity. A range at nearby Gransha Point was allocated instead.

USAAF aircraft were frequent visitors, for example a C-47 on May 4 1944, which landed to check the weather forecast *en route* to Maghaberry. On July 30 1944, Liberator *42-50781* made an emergency landing and overran the runway into the fence, causing superficial damage. After repairs it was flown out to Langford Lodge.

Both Kirkistown and Ballyhalbert were transferred to the Royal Navy on loan on July 14 1945, the NI Training School having already left for Newtownards on May 11. Kirkistown was commissioned as HMS *Corncrake II* on July 17 and later returned to the RAF on January 15 1946.

About a quarter of the former airfield is now a motor racing circuit owned and operated by the '500' Motor Racing Club or Ireland. There has been partial removal or reclamation of the runways and taxiways on the remainder, the land being used for grazing. The reclamation takes the form of top soil spread over the concrete areas to a depth of a few inches and sown with grass. Free-fall parachuting also takes place at the time of writing.

Kirkistown has an unusual feature in the form of a hillock within 100 ft of one of the runway edges. As if this were not enough of an obstruction, some elaborate concrete defence positions have been built on top of it. One hates to think of the results if a Spitfire swung on take-off!

Kirknewton, Lothian

65/NT125655. 2 miles SW of Balerno between B7031 and A70

Kirknewton opened in November 1941, although it seems to have been used as a grass landing ground as early as October

1940. No 289 Squadron formed here on November 20 from 13 Group AAC Flight. This unit was responsible for army co-operation with AA batteries and stationed detachments at various airfields in Southern Scotland and Northern England. An assortment of Blenheims, Lysanders, Hudsons, Hurricanes and Oxfords was operated, the squadron moving to Turnhouse on May 20 1942.

The Refresher Flying Training School arrived from Moreton Valence in Gloucestershire late in May 1942, flying Master IIs, Oxfords and Tutors. This obscure and short-lived unit was established to provide a refresher course in elementary single- and twin-engined aircraft for pilots who had not been engaged in flying duties for a considerable time. It also gave conversion courses from single- to twin-engined aircraft. The standard required on completion of an RFTS course was that the pupil should be ready for further training at an OTU or FIS. Plans soon changed, however, and the RFTS disbanded at Kirknewton on October 31 1942.

After some time on Care and Maintenance the airfield became a satellite of Findo Gask and on March 8 1943, 309 Squadron moved in with Lysanders and Mustangs. Findo became unserviceable and the Station HQ was transferred to Kirknewton on May 1 1943. The squadron left for Snailwell early in June and on June 21 Kirknewton returned to Care and Maintenance under 21 Group Flying Training Command.

The Air Ministry Airfields Board visited in August 1943 to investigate the possibility of lengthening the runways but found it could not be done. On February 10 1944, the station was handed over to 44 Group Maintenance Command for use by 243 MU for bomb storage. This MU stayed on after the war, finally disbanding in January 1956.

On May 22 1944, RAF Turnhouse ORB recorded an amusing incident when a Ju 188 flew up the east coast. 'The Italian Co-operators at Kirknewton are reported to have dived under the bedclothes on hearing the sirens and registered even greater agitation on the sounding of the "all-clear". This report came from the AC2 who generally looks after them. He is Maltese and they call him Sir!'

In December 1944, the airfield is listed as having no hangarage but today one can see a Bellman and two Blisters. One of the original dispersed sites is now occupied by the First Battalion, Gordon Highlanders. It does not look a promising site for an airfield with its three short runways surrounded by rolling countryside and a large spoil heap just to the west.

In the 50s the USAF's 7535th Air Base Squadron used the airfield for storage but it reverted to British use during 1967. No 661 Gliding School commenced operations here on April 2 1967.

Kirkpatrick, Dumfries and Galloway

85/NY250700. 2 miles SW of Kirkpatrick-Fleming on unclassified road off B6357

When 15 EFTS was forced to move north to Carlisle because its former base at Redhill looked like coming into the front line, it soon needed RLGs because of the poor drainage at Carlisle. The first was found at Burnfoot in July and the second in September at Kirkpatrick just over the border. It was brought into use on November 25 1940, the aircraft being Magisters at first, later replaced by Tiger Moths. Night flying began here in July 1941.

The small airfield was closed in July 1945 when the EFTS operations were being reduced. Since the flight office was demolished there are now no buildings left, the five Blister hangars having been removed long ago.

Flight hut at Kirkpatrick 1976 (J. Huggon).

Watch office at Kirkton.

Kirkton, Highland

21/NH805985. 2 miles S of Golspie off A9

Now farmland beside the A9 trunk-road and the main line to Wick, this SLG gives away its position by conspicuous gaps in the hedges and walls where the runways once lay. The site, 41 SLG, is bisected by a track which leads past the old watch office bungalow to the plantation on the south perimeter where many of the aircraft were dispersed. Kirkton had an unusually large number of buildings for an SLG, over a dozen, although only a few survive, the rest being merely concrete bases.

It was opened by 45 MU Kinloss on August 24 1941 and used initially for the storage of Whitleys and Spitfires. An enforced visitor on September 16 1941 was a Battle target tug from Evanton which made an emergency landing resulting in the death of the drogue operator and injuries to the pilot.

Spitfires being precious to the RAF, it was agreed in May 1942 to concentrate on providing 100 per cent effective camouflage. In June 1942, Havocs began to join the fighters, along with the many Whitleys and Wellingtons which still needed dispersal from Kinloss. Another accident occurred on July 5 1942 when Anson *R3399* overshot on landing, fortunately without injuries.

The defence of the SLG was taken very seriously, an exercise in July 1942 involving an attack by 250 men of the Royal Norwegian Regiment. Detachments of the Cameron Highlanders, RAF Regiment and the Sutherland Home Guard defended it and although the Norwegians secured the neighbouring high ground, Kirkton was denied to them.

In March 1943, the total of aircraft stored here reached 70, some 20 more than the official capacity. It was still in use in October 1944 but the actual closure date is uncertain. It was, perhaps, in February 1945 when 45 MU took over Brackla for aircraft storage. Final de-requisitioning came on May 4 1945.

It is indeed an idyllic spot sheltered by the hills and woods and close to the sea, perhaps one of the most unlikely airfield sites in Scotland.

Kirkwall, Orkney

6/HY480085. 2½ miles SE of Kirkwall on A960

From October 17 1940, when the operations room staff moved here from Wick, Kirkwall, or Grimsetter as it was often known, was a Fighter Sector Station in 14 Group. The large ops room can still be seen on the airport road close to the town. The aerodrome was employed only as a satellite by Skeabrae at first, until 132 Squadron in its entirety arrived on June 11 1942. Its Spitfires left for Martlesham Heath towards the end of September. They were replaced by similar aircraft of 129 Squadron which stayed until January 19 1943 on local air defence.

No 234 Squadron was the last RAF fighter unit at Kirkwall, being present from January until April 24 1943, when it moved to Skeabrae. The airfield was then transferred on loan to the Royal Navy in July 1943 and commissioned as HMS *Robin* on August 15. No 846 Squadron with Avengers took up residence in September/October but it was not the first naval unit to be based there, as 800's Sea Hurricanes had already been there between January and March 1943.

Various squadrons spent time ashore at Kirkwall, including 848 with Avengers in November 1943, 1770 with Fireflies from December 1943 to mid-February 1944, and 842 whose Wildcats and Swordfish were there in June/July 1944.

The final naval units at Kirkwall were 881 Squadron with Wildcats early in 1945 and 801 with Seafires in February/March 1945. The airfield reverted to RAF control on July 31 1945 and later became Kirkwall Airport for services to the mainland. Faroe Airways operated a Copenhagen/Stavanger/Kirkwall service in 1966/67 with DC-3s and around the same time runway 10/28 was extended for Viscount aircraft. In the terminal is a memorial

Left *Modernised tower at Kirkwall* (J.C. Temple).

Below *Mainhill/'S' shed at Kirkwall* (J.C. Temple).

Right *Two examples of wall art at Langford, which survived until 1980* (E.A. Cromie).

unveiled in 1976 to Captain E.E. Fresson who pioneered scheduled air services to the Orkneys and Shetlands.

Two of the naval 'S' hangars remain and the control tower is the original building with a modern glasshouse on top. Not directly connected with the airfield but of local interest is the fact that the US Army Douglas DWC seaplanes on a round the world flight refuelled in Kirkwall harbour before setting off for Iceland on August 2 1924. Although one turned back because of fog, the others got there.

Langford Lodge, Antrim

14/J100760. 3 miles E of Crumlin on unclassified road

Langford Lodge was a large estate owned by the Packenham family, whose ancestor, General Sir Edward Packenham, had been defeated at the Battle of New Orleans by Andrew Jackson. It thus added insult to injury when the Americans

Langford's base hospital still close to the airfield (Via Harry Holmes).

came in the Second World War and virtually took over the land for a huge repair depot!

Its possibilities as an airfield had been recognised by MAP officials early in 1941, when it was selected as 20 SLG for 23 MU. Work was well advanced when a change of policy came in February 1942. The US Government had decided to set up a depot in Ulster for the repair and servicing of USAAF aircraft. Langford Lodge was allocated to them and plans were made under 'lend-lease' for the UK Government, through MAP, to bear the cost of constructing the base, estimated initially as £1¼ million, while the US Government would furnish the specialised equipment.

MAP prepared a scheme covering the erection of hangars, workshops, hutted camps on five sites and facilities for some 2,600 civilian employees of the Lockheed Overseas Corporation which was contracted to run the depot. Work was to begin on February 20 1942 and was to be completed within six months. Being highly secret, it was known as the 'Y Scheme' and such importance was attached to its completion on time that it was accorded absolute priority over all other construction in Northern Ireland.

The site was remote and not well-served by transport but to help bring in labour from the towns, the Great Northern Railway actually built a single-track line from Crumlin to the depot. The six months' target was not met and although HQ Langford Lodge opened on August 15 1942, it was some months before aircraft work could begin. 'Scheme Y' had by now been renamed HQ 1st Service Area and the airfield was numbered Station 597.

The first P-38 Lightning arrived at Sydenham on November 11 1942 and was promptly brought over to Langford for testing. The P-38s were usually towed on dollies or their own wheels, whilst P-47s were flown over. At the same time the depot was busy assembling Brewster Bermudas for the RAF. In July 1943, a glider, presumably a CG-4, was received and converted to carry a complete mobile repair unit to assist in retrieving force-landed aircraft. It is not known if it was used on a regular basis or merely for experiments.

The experimental engineering section turned out its first drawings, which consisted of a modified well gun, nose gun installation, scanning windows, armour plate and additional oxygen outlets for the B-24. Twenty B-24s were quickly modified at the same time as the first of many C-47s began to arrive.

Langford Lodge dispersal laden with war-weary A-20s and B-17s circa March 1945. Centre right is 379th BG Lead-ship (Via Harry Holmes).

Almost from the start, there was friction between Lockheed and the VIIIth AFSC regarding the running of the depot. The USAAF wanted to assume full control and operate the station with Air Depot Groups. With this in mind the 7th ADG arrived in September 1942 but contracts with Lockheed continued to be renewed at six-monthly intervals until 1944 and the 7th ADG was transferred to Warton in January 1943.

During 1943, the 3rd Base Air Depot, as Langford was now known, concentrated on P-38 conversion. Many 'E' models were re-worked and sent direct to the Mediterranean Theatre of Operations. Work was also started on B-17 nose gun modifications and on B-24 windshields as a result of recommendations arising from

Langford Lodge tower 1981. Note all *windows angled* (E.A. Cromie).

combat over Europe. The first P-39 Airacobras (about 20) to be handled at Langford were completed in March 1943. During this month, 125 aircraft were completed, including P-38s, P-39s, P-47s, B-17s and Bermudas.

To handle the deliveries, Detachment B of the 325th Ferrying Squadron was at Langford in 1943/44. The 325th moved to Heston in May 1944 at the same time as the 311th and 312th Ferrying Squadrons arrived from Maghaberry. They were anxious to sample the 'steam-heated and ice-cream-prevalent environs of Langford'.

Beginning in January 1944, the depot repaired electric propellors and manufactured kits for them and its engineering staff devoted much time to research and development. It was also possible to introduce assembly line methods which permitted maximum utilisation of the large number of unskilled soldiers who now helped man the BADs.

Langford was certainly one of the busiest stations in Northern Ireland and incredible numbers of aircraft were kept in open storage on the multiple hard-standings built out in the fields to the north. War-weary aircraft could be seen in all the markings of the combat units in East Anglia. For example, in September 1944, 322 surplus Liberators were parked on and around the airfield. In May 1945 the numbers of aircraft in store reached their highest—572, including 280 A-20 Havocs.

Although the BAD had closed officially on August 7 1944, Langford was retained as an experimental station and for storage. During its relatively short life the depot had re-assembled or modified 3,250 aircraft, serviced 11,000 more and overhauled 450,000 components, thus making a significant contribution to aerial supremacy over Europe.

The airfield was finally returned to the RAF in March 1946, later to be taken over by Martin-Baker for ejector seat production, the runways being used by company aircraft flying to and from Chalgrove in Oxfordshire.

At the height of its career, the base had nine 'T2' hangars, eight Robins, some 20 Butler buildings and a Lockheed-designed hangar which is still in use today. The control tower is particularly interesting because it shows almost certainly the first use in the UK of angled windows to cut down reflections, the curse of all vertically glazed visual control rooms, believe me! However, why *every* window in the building—including the lavatories—had to be angled is a mystery!

Largs, Strathclyde

63/NS200595. Just N of town centre off seafront

Largs was not an RAF station but merely a terminal administered by Scottish Aviation Limited for the reception of flying boats from across the Atlantic. The aircraft were moored in the lee of Great Cumbrae Island and the crews were ferried to and from Largs by launch. A small knot of spectators would usually gather on the seafront to watch the aircraft. On one occasion with a 70 mph gale blowing unusually from the east, a Catalina caused some consternation when it made a full stall landing pointing directly at them into wind.

Catalinas were the usual aircraft to be delivered here after the terminal opened around December 1942. Mariners were also to be seen on occasion, for example *JX110* which took off for Stranraer on February 2 1944.

In June 1944, a new service was inaugurated by 45 Group for the carriage of urgent freight to the UK and the return of ferry crews to Canada. It was operated by Coronados of 231 Squadron twice weekly, routing Boucherville–Gander–Largs eastbound and Largs–Reykjavik–Gander–Goose Bay westbound.

An Icelandic Airways Catalina *TF-ISD* made an exploratory trip in July 1945 from Reykjavik and back carrying passengers and mail. This was repeated in September, the return being made via Copenhagen. On September 25 1945, the Coronado service to Canada terminated with the departure of *JX498*.

Leanach, Highland

27/NH755455. 3 miles ENE of Inverness on B9006

Nearly 200 years after the Battle of Culloden, the site where once the rear-guard of the Royal Army took its position became an airfield. The battlefield is a melancholy spot, with mass graves commemorating an event which did little credit to either English or Scots, as a glance at the history books will show.

A pre-war ELG for Highland Airways when Longman was fog-bound, Leanach was selected as 43 SLG for 46 MU Lossiemouth, the first trial landing being made on May 10 1941. Hurricanes and Defiants were among the types dispersed here but the camouflage was severely compromised by other visiting aircraft, for example, Rapides diverting from Longman and trainers from the AGS at Dalcross. Action was taken to remind civil and military pilots that SLGs were prohibited for landing except in emergency.

On April 22 1942, the senior MU test pilot landed a Wellington at Leanach to see if it was suitable for aircraft of this size. He found it marginal and only selected pilots were to be allowed to ferry these aircraft here. Beaufighters also began to be stored here in the autumn of 1942.

No 19 (P)AFU at nearby Dalcross was without RLGs early in 1943 and representations were made to MAP for facilities to be provided at Leanach. After protracted negotiations, permission was finally given and the airfield was brought into use on June 6 1943.

Simulated night flying was done in Oxfords, sodium flares being lit on the

Flight hut at Leanach 1981.

ground and the pilot wearing blue goggles. This joint use was not very satisfactory and 41 Group decided to vacate Leanach (but keep it in reserve) and re-allocate the SLG at Dornoch to 46 MU instead. This was done on October 11 1943.

No 19 (P)AFU retained use of Leanach until the unit disbanded on February 25 1944 and the SLG does not appear to have been active after this, being de-requisitioned on March 30 1945. One small building by the roadside is all that is left now, the Robin hangars have been dismantled long ago.

Lennoxlove, Lothian

66/NT525715. 1 mile S of Haddington off A6137

In the 1930s the Marquis of Douglas and Clydesdale operated a private airfield from his estate at Haddington. This fact evidently did not escape the notice of officialdom as the site was chosen for 27 SLG, known usually as Lennoxlove but sometimes as Haddington.

The SLG was allocated to 18 MU at Dumfries and a Battle made the first trial landings on April 24 1941. The landing strip was declared serviceable and the following day the first aircraft to be stored, a Blenheim, was delivered. The runway was short, however, and it was decided that only small aircraft of around Hurricane size could be dispersed until the necessary permission to close the country road was obtained. Once this was done the strip was extended and more Blenheims were received.

In August 1941, 18 MU considered the possibility of flying Whirlwinds in. The chief test pilot commented that this type swung badly in crosswinds and therefore waited until the wind was in the right direction before making a successful test landing. Many Whirlwinds were then stored here and in the summer of 1945 the type's derivative, the Welkin, made an appearance. Only a limited number were built and most ended their days at Lennoxlove.

Flying Training Command was also interested in the SLG and Master *AZ538* from Drem visited on February 15 1942. Any further training use is uncertain, however, and perhaps doubtful as many Wellingtons and Blenheims were being flown in. When many of the SLGs were being inspected for the storage of four-engined aircraft in the summer of 1942, a

Halifax landed here, the strip and dispersal areas being pronounced ideal for this purpose.

With the enemy far away, camouflage was not so important and by November 1944 the SLG held 119 aircraft, most of them Wellingtons. A hazard virtually unique to SLGs was the damage caused by falling branches and even whole trees during gales. Several Wellingtons suffered in this way at Lennoxlove.

The process of closing down began in August 1945, the SLG finally ceasing operations the following month. Unconnected, but of local interest, was a landing ground for 77 (HD) squadron in 1918 at Gifford three miles SE of Haddington.

Leuchars, Fife

59/NO460205. 5 miles NW of St Andrews on A919

Scotland's answer to Duxford and Biggin Hill, so much has happened at Leuchars that it deserves a book to itself. The site dates back to 1911 when the Royal Engineers experimented with balloons, a proper airfield being established in 1918 by the RNAS.

Going back to 1914, some of the RFC's first aircraft landed at St Andrews on flights from Montrose. Duncan's Garage, owned by Mr Andrew Duncan, father of Dr Atholl Duncan who loaned many of the photographs for this book, supplied the necessary petrol and oil for the return trips. When it was decided to build an airfield at Reres Farm, Mr Duncan was contracted to level the ground.

No 203 Squadron re-formed at Leuchars on March 1 1920 with Nieuport Nighthawks, being redesignated 402 Flight on April 1 1923. No 205 Squadron also re-formed in April 1920, initially with Parnall Panthers, becoming 441 Flight three years later. In the meantime 'A' Flight became the nucleus of 3 Squadron in October 1921 and left for Gosport in October 1922. Nos 403 and 404 (Fleet Fighter) Flights were added to Leuchars' strength in mid-1923.

More flights were formed in 1924, some leaving for other bases, and by September 1926, 442 and 443 Flights were left, together with 'A' (Fighter), 'B' (Spotter), and 'C' (Recce) Training Flights. The fighter units operated Flycatchers and the recce flights Fairey IIIDs and Panthers. During 1927, 'A', 'B' and 'C' Flights were combined to form the Base Training

Top *Overstrand at Leuchars, Empire Air Day 1938* (Dr A.A. Duncan).

Above *Leuchars in 1928* (P. Geary/Roy Bonser collection).

Flight and 445 and 446 Flights arrived with Fairey IIIFs.

The aircraft were often away aboard carriers and the unit was re-formed into the Base Training Squadron in 1932. First-line squadrons, including 810, 811 and 822, were also housed for varying periods.

February 1935 saw a further name change to 1 FTS, the Army Training Camp at the nearby Tentsmuir Ranges coming under its jurisdiction. Aircraft in use now included Fairey IIIFs, Tutors, Harts, Nimrods, Ospreys and Seals, mainly providing instruction for Royal Navy officers.

No 1 FTS moved to Netheravon in August 1938 and Leuchars passed to Coastal Command control. With the arrival of 224 and 233 Squadrons at the end of that month the station became operational for the first time. Both units flew Ansons but re-equipped with Hudsons during 1939.

On the second day of the war, a Hudson of 224 Squadron became the first Coastal Command aircraft to attack an enemy machine, a Do 18 over the North Sea. On February 16 1940, a Hudson from the same unit intercepted the German prison ship *Altmark* from which 299 prisoners were rescued by HMS *Cossack*.

The only fighter squadrons to see service at Leuchars during the war were 605 with Hurricanes for a short spell in 1940 and 72 Squadron's Spitfires for the first three weeks of November 1940.

Left *Hawker Nimrod K3656 at Leuchars 1938* (Dr A.A. Duncan).

Below left *Swordfish K5940 at Leuchars 1938* (Dr A.A. Duncan).

After some time working up at several other airfields, the Dutch 320 Squadron assembled here at the end of March 1941. Their Hudsons replaced those of 233 Squadron which had gone to Aldergrove in December 1940 and 224 which left for Limavady in mid-April 1941.

The Dutch crews spent the next year on *Rover* patrols over the North Sea, reporting and harrying enemy shipping. The first such offensive sweep of the Norwegian coast on August 30 ended in disaster when only one out of four aircraft returned. Subsequent sorties were more successful until the squadron moved to Norfolk in April 1942.

A less warlike but nonetheless vital unit formed at Leuchars in January 1941—10 Blind Approach Training Flight with Ansons. It was renumbered 1510 Flight in November and often flew when weather grounded the operational aircraft. It finally left in August 1944.

The first Beauforts belonging to 42 Squadron flew in from Wick on March 1 1941 and two days later they were joined for a short period by the Blenheims of 107 Squadron for anti-shipping and mine-laying missions along the coast of Northern Europe. The Blenheims of 114 Squadron were here also between May and July 1941 on loan from Bomber Command.

It was a 42 Squadron crew who featured in the well-known saga of 'Winkie' the pigeon. Out on patrol on February 23 1942, their Beaufort suffered engine failure, and, unable to maintain height on one, was forced to ditch. A carrier pigeon was always taken along on these trips but on this occasion the bird struggled free without a message while the airmen were launching their dinghy. The bird duly arrived back with its civilian owner, exhausted, wet and oily. With some deduction the search was switched nearer

Above left *Oxford I L9655 at Leuchars 1939* (Dr A.A. Duncan).

Left *Gauntlet K7838 at Leuchars 1938* (Dr A.A. Duncan).

to the coast and the survivors were found almost immediately and picked up by HSL. 'Winkie' was awarded the Dickin Medal and royally entertained by the RAF. (This use of pigeons for operational purposes was finally discontinued in February 1944.)

On October 19 1942, 540 Squadron formed from 'H' and 'L' Flights of the Photographic Reconnaissance Unit which had been at Leuchars for some time. The squadron's chief task was to monitor the movements of the German Navy, with particular reference to those of the *Tirpitz*. Sorties were flown as far as Stettin and Berlin but the main area of operations was over the Norwegian coast. Detachments of 541 and 542 PR Squadrons were also at Leuchars at various times.

No 42 Squadron was posted overseas in June 1942 but 144 Squadron with Hampdens had arrived in April along with the Australian 455 Squadron. Most of the Hampdens were flown to Russia via Sumburgh in September 1942 and left there for Russian crews to use for Arctic convoy protection. In the meantime, more Hampdens, of 415 (Canadian) Squadron made a two-month visit. The Hampden however, lacking radar and adequate armament, could only be regarded as a stopgap. Beaufighters of 235 Squadron flew in from Chivenor in January 1943 staying up to August and during the following month 144 converted to the Beaufighter, leaving in May 1943.

The Norwegian 333 Squadron formed at Leuchars on May 10 1943 out of 1477 Flight, becoming a split unit flying Catalinas from Woodhaven (qv) on anti-

submarine patrols and Mosquitoes as 'B' Flight from Leuchars. Ostensibly for photo recce, the Mosquitoes were armed and had considerable success against enemy aircraft. During December 1943, for example, a Ju 88 and Fw 190 were shot down for the loss of one Mosquito. On February 13 1944, Second Lieutenant Jensen and his navigator, Flight Lieutenant Thorkildsen, destroyed a Bv 138 flying boat, the third enemy machine to fall to their guns.

Torbeaus of the New Zealand-manned 489 Squadron arrived from Wick in October 1943 and in December 455 Squadron stood down to convert to Beaufighters. Lodger units at this time included 18 Group Comm Flight and 3 Armament Practice Camp which had been here since December 1941 for weapons training with visiting units.

By March 1944, 455 Squadron was operational again with cannon-armed Beaufighters which flew as a Strike Wing with the Torbeaus of 489 Squadron. In April, the Air Torpedo Development Unit arrived from Gosport, displaced temporarily by operations in connection with the forthcoming invasion. Barracudas and Beaufighters were kept at Leuchars overnight but did most of their flying from Crail.

Amidst all the warplanes at Leuchars, BOAC had been running a service to Sweden, since 1941, first with Hudsons and then with Mosquitoes, the latter beginning on February 4 1943. Mail and one passenger were carried in the bomb bay of the Mossie along with limited cargoes of high quality engineering products brought back from Stockholm, particularly ball-bearings.

Despite flak from ships in the Skaggerak and attempted fighter interceptions, it was believed that no aircraft were lost to enemy action but several were destroyed

Lightnings of 23 and 74 Squadrons over the Tay Bridge (Via Dr A.A. Duncan).

in crashes. By the time the Mosquito service had moved to Croydon on May 17 1945, the aircraft had flown 520 round trips. A separate Norwegian unit with Lodestars had followed the same route, relying mainly on cloud cover to get through unscathed.

In March 1944, a detachment of the American 492nd Bomb Group, the 'Carpetbaggers', arrived at Leuchars for clandestine flights in support of the Norwegian Underground. The unit was commanded by Colonel Bernt Balchen, a famous Arctic flyer of pre-war days, and two projects were involved. *Ball* Project was the dropping of equipment and agents from black-painted Liberators whilst the *Sonnie* Project ferried ex-internees and escaped Norwegians of military age back from Sweden. The *Sonnie* aircraft were painted green and carried US civil registrations.

From April 1944 to June 25 1945, *Sonnie* Liberators and C-47s brought a total of 4,304 passengers from Stockholm to the UK, including Norwegians, American aircrew internees and the nationals of at least six other countries. The flights were almost the only dependable means of communication between the American Legation in Stockholm and the outside world. The Leuchars unit was eventually given the Meritorious Service Award in recognition of its achievements in all weathers. Seven aircraft of the *Ball* Project were shot down and one *Sonnie* Liberator lost in a collision with a Swedish mountain.

No 333 Squadron's Mosquitoes moved to Banff at the end of August 1944, the station's main operational commitment being taken over by 206 Squadron's Liberators. They saw a lot of action right up to the end of the war, most sorties after

Lightning XM989 *of 56 Squadron over the Fife coastline* (Via Dr A.A. Duncan).

November 1945 taking place at night with Leigh Light illumination. From September 1944, 547 Squadron operated alongside 206 with more Liberators on similar duties.

Leuchars' last operational flight of the war landed on June 3 and the operations room closed down the next morning. In July, 206 Squadron moved out to Oakington and its sister unit, 547, disbanded. Immediately prior to this, however, the Liberators of 120 and 203 Squadrons arrived. No 3 School of General Reconnaissance came in from Squires Gate with Ansons and soon resumed the training of observers and navigators. St Andrews UAS was set up in October with Tiger Moths to provide basic flying training for local undergraduates.

No 3 APC disbanded in September 1945 and on November 8, 519 Squadron's Halifaxes arrived from Tain, only to disband at the end of May 1946. No 203 Squadron departed in January 1947 and in June 237 (PR)OCU was established with a mixture of Spitfires, Mosquitoes and Oxfords. Another unit still sharing Leuchars at this time was 18 Group Comm Flight which had been formed in 1943.

In May 1950, Leuchars entered the jet age with its transfer from Coastal to Fighter Command and the arrival of 222 Squadron's Meteor 4s from Waterbeach. No 120 Squadron, which had long since re-equipped with Lancasters, left for Kinloss in December, whilst a second Meteor squadron, 43, arrived from Tangmere in November.

No 229 OCU was formed in 1951 with seven Meteor T 7s and 23 Vampires for the task of re-training Royal Australian Air Force pilots in the operation of Vampire aircraft with which they were being re-equipped in place of the Spitfire. By the end of the year, three jet fighter squadrons formed the Leuchars Wing—43 and 222 with Meteor F 8s and 151 (re-formed here on September 15) with Vampire NF 10s. In the spring of 1952, 264 Squadron arrived from Linton-on-Ouse with the all-weather version of the Meteor—the NF 11—but had departed again by the end of August.

Another important milestone was reached on July 29 1954, when the first of the second generation jet fighters arrived on the station. This was the Hunter F 1 to re-equip 43 Squadron. No 222 also began to receive Hunters and 151, by now flying Meteor NF 11s, converted to the Venom NF 3. July also saw the establishment of an SAR detachment of Sycamore helicopters of 'C' Flight, 275 Squadron.

The summer of 1956 was a quiet one for local residents, as the airfield was closed for runway extensions and essential maintenance. No 43 Squadron was detached to Turnhouse and 151 and 222 went to Acklington, all returning in August.

The Javelin arrived in 1957 for 151 Squadron but 222 disbanded on November 1. No 29 Squadron arrived from Acklington with more Javelins, joining 151 in the all-weather defence of Northern Britain. On September 1 1958, 275 Squadron, by now operating Whirlwinds, was renamed 228 Squadron.

In June 1961, 43 Squadron took its Hunters out to Cyprus and 151 was disbanded on September 19. Replacing 151 at Leuchars was another Javelin squadron, 25, which arrived in December but disbanded on November 30 1962. Its place was taken by Javelins of 23 Squadron in February 1963 and the next month 29 Squadron finally left for Cyprus.

A dramatic new shape came on the scene in 1964 when 74 Squadron's Lightnings moved in from Coltishall. In September, 23 Squadron gave up its Javelins in favour of Lightnings and on May 1 1965, 228 OCU was reopened, this time for the purpose of training crews for Javelin units in the Near and Far East theatres.

After 74 Squadron left for Singapore in February 1967, a new Lightning squadron, No 11, re-formed in April. The St Andrews UAS disbanded in April,

combining with the Edinburgh UAS at Turnhouse to form Lowlands UAS.

September 1969 saw the appearance of the Phantom when 43 Squadron re-formed with the type. No 11 Squadron went to Binbrook in March 1972 and 23 disbanded on October 31 1975. A second Phantom squadron, No 111, arrived from Coningsby in November 1975.

Today, Leuchars is Strike Command's premier air defence base in the UK and Phantoms are on permanent readiness to intercept Russian reconnaissance aircraft probing the UK Air Defence Region.

Limavady, Londonderry

4/C675255. 2 miles N of Limavady on A2

With a range of hills topped by Binevenagh at 1,260 ft rising in the circuit, Limavady was a strange choice for an airfield site. Perhaps when it was planned only daylight fair weather flying was envisaged. Coastal Command operations came later and no wonder the crews referred to the heights as 'Ben Twitch'!

Today, the old airfield reveals an interesting collection of buildings. The tower, once lived in, is a 518/40 type and a Dome Trainer is in a fair state of preservation. The operations block is kept locked by the owner with the result that it is unvandalised and even has an intact gas filtration plant. A tattered copy of Station Standing Orders still adheres to the wall but the most exciting survival is the original operations board for 224 and 502 Squadrons. It had headings for submarine movements, attacks made and all the details required for waging the air war over the Atlantic. Alas, it is painted directly on to the wall and incapable of removal for preservation.

The airfield site had been chosen in 1938 as an Armament Training Station to serve the bombing range in Lough Foyle. After Munich, construction was begun and it was envisaged that it would be part of a plan for the expansion of Coastal Command should this prove necessary.

The first recorded use was by the Whitleys of 'A' Flight 502 Squadron at Aldergrove from December 4 1940, equipped with the new and very secret long range ASV radar. The entire squadron moved in on January 27 1941. Other Aldergrove units kept detachments here around this time, including 272 Squadron with Blenheims and 224 with Hudsons.

Limavady 1945

Bellman hangar

T2 hangar

Bomb stores

←Cannon test butt

Control tower

Battle HQ

Station HQ

River Roe

Blister hangar

LIMAVADY

N

0   3000
                                    ft

Map based on information obtained from the RAF Museum — Crown Copyright reserved   .... Airfield boundary

Limavady 1982.

Hurricanes of 245 Squadron also used the airfield from time to time.

No 502 Squadron was soon in action from Limavady. On February 10 1941, Flying Officer J.A. Walker severely damaged a U-boat 300 miles west-north-west of Ireland and in June, Flying Officer Holdsworth made two attacks on submarines in four days. It was not all one-sided, however, as on July 17, one of the Whitleys had to ditch after combat with a Condor.

From December 1941, 502 based a detachment in the south-west for Biscay patrols, the whole squadron moving to St

Eval just after Christmas. Although it was destined to be February 1943 before an aircraft from Northern Ireland sank a U-boat, 502 Squadron served as a vital deterrent at a time when U-boats had almost free rein in the Atlantic.

From April 15 1941, 224 Squadron's Hudsons flew anti-submarine patrols to protect convoys moving into and out of the Clyde and Mersey, until the Hudsons left for St Eval in mid-December. No 53 Squadron filled the gap temporarily until 224 returned in February 1942 and went to Tiree on April 12. No 143 Squadron, whose Beaufighters were for the time being non-operational, arrived from Aldergrove on April 22 1942 and stayed until early June.

The Operations Board for 224 and 502 Squadrons which still exists in the old operations block at Limavady (E.A. Cromie).

SQUADRON STATES					
DATE	TIME				
B. SQUADRON					
T.YPE					
C. SERVICEABLE %					
D. RELEASED REF. REARM					
E. AT HOURS					
AT HOURS					
F. NO CREWS					
G. AVAILABLE STRIKE					
H. UNDER ORDER					
J. RECCE.					
K. AIR- STRIKING					
L. BORNE CONVOY					
M. A/s PATROL					
CREWS AVAILABLE					
STRIKE					

ENEMY FORCES					
FORCE	COMPOSITION	POSITION	TIME	CO SPEED	ORIGIN	REMARKS
DATE	FROM	TO	S.A.C.S.	SQDN C/S	O.C.S.
224					
502					
3					
FORCE OR CONVOY					
R/T CALLSIGN					
W/T CALLSIGN					
PENDANT					

The first Wellingtons on the station had belonged to 221 Squadron, here from May to the end of September 1941, flying Atlantic patrols. They returned briefly from Iceland in December to prepare for Middle East posting. During July 1941, the squadron flew 92 sorties, attacked four U-boats (two in one day) and had two air combats in which two Wellingtons were lost.

No 7 OTU, which was to carry out GR and ASV training, formed at Limavady on April 1 1942 to be equipped with Wellingtons and Ansons. The airfield now embarked upon almost two years of non-operational flying but there was no let-up in activity and first-line aircraft continued to use it as a diversion when other Ulster bases were weather-bound.

Aircraft were delivered to the OTU in a trickle and No 1 Course did not arrive until May 13. The torpedo training section of the curriculum was done at Abbotsinch but the rest of the navigation exercises and practice bombing was done from Limavady. On one occasion a rear gunner saw what he believed was a U-boat and the report was passed to Coastal Command.

The airfield attracted many Trans-Atlantic delivery flights, one of the first being a Hudson on May 20 1942. Two days later, Liberator *AM263* landed direct from Montreal and on June 17 Mitchell *FL178* and Hudson *EW916* arrived. There were numerous alerts for missing aircraft and an OTU machine was kept on stand-by for searches, although most of the strays eventually turned up safely.

With so many over-water flights in poor weather, the OTU's own accident rate was high. On one night, January 2/3 1943, three aircraft were lost. One crashed on Binevenagh, another near Ballykelly and a

third was found next morning just off-shore. Others simply disappeared and there were further hazards such as bird-strikes whilst low-flying and on one occasion an Anson from the unit was hit by a shell when it was unlucky enough to break cloud right over a convoy. Two of the crew were injured before its identity was established.

A change of policy resulted in 7 OTU being transferred to Haverfordwest in South Wales at the beginning of January 1944 and Limavady went back onto ops again. Towards the end of the month, 612 Squadron arrived from Chivenor with Wellington XIVs. Bad weather curtailed operations for much of February, the aircraft lacked de-icing equipment and there was no SBA or BABS system at Limavady to assist landing in poor conditions.

One aid which had been installed was a system of lead-in lights to assist aircraft in keeping clear of the nearby high ground. Projector lights were sited on the coast with a series of guide lights along a path to the aerodrome and obstruction lights on each of two hills to the east of this path.

One sortie on February 10 was highly successful. Pilot Officer Paynter and crew homed on to a radar contact which turned out to be a fully-surfaced U-boat. A perfect attack was made visually without need for the Leigh Light, the radar contact soon disappearing and débris and small orange lights were seen on the surface. Thus died the *U-545*, her crew being picked up by the *U-714*.

No 612 Squadron was not impressed with Limavady, its living sites were thought to be too far apart—'dispersal gone mad' was one way it was described. The food was poor too. From the flying point of view, it was recorded: 'The QGH procedure is complicated by the nearby

hills and will probably not be used except under the most favourable conditions. Few pilots would have confidence in it in really poor weather on the admission of most aircrew and ground staff. It looks as if Limavady QGH has been worked out by a wingless wonder or else the baker has not tested his own bread!'

Aircraft availability was low in February 1944, seven of the total establishment of 15 being detached, three at Chivenor where major inspections were still carried out, two at CCDU for rocket projectile experience and two at Defford for radar fitment. The last straw came on February 20, when all the Wellingtons of both 612 and 407 Squadron, which was also based here, were grounded because of spar defects. Three days later the ban was lifted after a local modification was approved.

On March 1 1944, 612 Squadron was informed that it would move to Chivenor owing to enemy submarines having changed their area of operations. The air party left on March 6.

No 407 Squadron had been at Limavady since the end of January 1944, flying Leigh Light Wellingtons. They were engaged in concentrated training prior to D-Day, coupled with operational sorties. An almost certain U-boat kill was made on February 18 and the aircraft were loaned occasionally to 612 Squadron to make up the latter's aircraft depletion.

No 407 Squadron left on April 28 1944 for pre-Invasion patrols and Limavady was bereft of Coastal Command whilst the centre of activity swung to the southwest. The Royal Navy seized the opportunity to base several squadrons here temporarily during the summer of 1944. The first were 846 with Wildcats and 811 with Swordfish which came from

HMS *Biter* in June. No 850's Avengers arrived from Perranporth on August 1 and moved on to Maydown on August 13. No 811 Squadron came back on August 25 and embarked on HMS *Vindex* on September 29 and 850 was here again from August 26 to November 5 when it moved to Mullaghmore. Also to Mullaghmore on the same day went 825 Squadron, which had been here since September 29 with Swordfish and Sea Hurricanes.

As the Brittany ports were denied to the German Navy their submarines withdrew to the north-west and Limavady was host once more to Leigh Light units. Nos 172 and 612 Squadrons arrived early in September 1944, the operational situation being summarised as follows: 'A number of U-boats have been attacking and sinking our shipping in the Western Approaches and the Navy, although it has large escort groups in the area, has not yet had any concrete success against them. Consequently a number of anti-submarine squadrons of Coastal Command have been moved to 15 Group area. It appears that the squadrons will once more revert to their original role of flying only by night.'

In an attempt to combat the new *Schnorkel* breathing pipe, by means of which U-boats could remain submerged and undetected for several days at a time, a comprehensive anti-*Schnorkel* training programme was begun in November. Few crews had any confidence in the ability of their existing radar to detect the tiny objects and there were no successes.

No 612 Squadron went to Langham in Norfolk on December 17 1944 but 172 Squadron stayed for Atlantic patrols until disbanding on June 4 1945. No 281 Squadron arrived from Mullaghmore on

Left Looking through the watch tower window towards Binevenagh, on which several aircraft came to grief during Limavady's operational life (E.A. Cromie).

Right *AA Dome Trainer at Limavady* (E.A. Cromie).

March 31 1945, with Warwicks and Sea Otters for ASR duties, leaving for Bally-kelly on August 13 1945.

The final RAF presence here was 22 Aircrew Holding Unit which transferred to Aldergrove on August 18 1945 and the Coastal Command Anti-U-boat Devices School. After four months of existence, VJ-Day spelled the end of the School and Limavady then closed.

Loch Doon, Strathclyde

77/NX483948. On the shore of Loch Doon

With the mountains of the Rhinns of Kells so alarmingly close, this beautiful scenic area seems an unlikely place to site an aerodrome. Nonetheless, a School of Aerial Gunnery formed here in January 1917 with such types as the BE 2c. A School of Aerial Fighting was also set up in 1917 and disbanded the following year.

There is a very unusual concrete structure on the eastern shore of the Loch at Portmark with a slipway leading to it. This was possibly a winch shed for the seaplanes which are reputed to have flown from here with an RNAS training unit.

Long Kesh, Down

20/J230615. 3 miles SW of Lisburn off A3

Better known as the site of the notorious Maze Prison, Long Kesh's origins as a busy wartime RAF station have tended to be obscured by this unfortunate fact.

It opened in November 1941, taking over Maghaberry on November 15 as satellite on Care and Maintenance. No 231 Army Co-operation Squadron moved in from Newtownards on December 11 with 12 Lysanders and six Tomahawks. On January 15 1942, 88 Squadron's Bostons arrived from Attlebridge, Norfolk for three weeks' intensive training which included low-level close support during Army exercises.

To help with the continuation training of the operational crews of 88 Squadron and also that of ground defence personnel in Ulster, 1494 TT Flight was formed with Lysanders at Long Kesh in February. It moved to Sydenham on April 14 1942. The Spitfires of 74 Squadron carried out defensive patrols for two months before going to Atcham on March 24. Another temporary attachment was 'A' Flight of 651 Squadron with three Taylorcraft from May 6, which returned to Old Sarum in mid June.

Two scheduled services were started in 1942, the first on April 1 by the US Navy. A Lockheed Electra would operate a thrice weekly run between Hendon and Eglinton calling at Long Kesh to drop and collect passengers, light freight and mail. The second was more ambitious, so much so that weather conditions resulted in many cancellations. It was a towed glider service from Netheravon in Wiltshire to Long Kesh via the shortest sea crossing from Stranraer. The aim was to provide a useful ferry route, give crews experience in long distance glider towing and navigation, study the effects of fatigue on tug and glider pilots and to develop and test airborne equipment. The aircraft generally employed were Whitleys, Hotspurs and Horsas.

Like most other airfields in Northern Ireland, Long Kesh attracted its quota of strays after the Atlantic crossing. In April 1942, for example, Venturas *FH308* and *FH381* landed from Newfoundland and on November 16 1943 landed a USAAF B-17 originating from the same place. Another B-17 had been forced to land at Shannon in Eire owing to petrol shortage. After re-fuelling and a meal for the crew it was allowed to leave for Nutt's Corner but the radio failed and the aircraft landed at the first airfield it came across, which happened to be Long Kesh.

The site was inspected by a USAAF major in August 1942 with a view to American occupation. This did not materialise, nor did the proposed formation of an AFU. What did happen was the transfer of the station to Coastal Command on December 29 1942 for 5 OTU.

No 231 Squadron was dislodged to Nutt's Corner to make room for 33 Beauforts. The OTU also had 11 Hampdens and a couple of Martlets which were to be operated from the satellite at Maghaberry. Its job was to convert pilots to Beauforts and Hampdens after which they were crewed-up and given training in navigation, bombing and gunnery.

The Beaufort was a real handful to an inexperienced pilot and accidents were frequent at 5 OTU. Many resulted from uncontrollable swings on take-off or landing which ended up with the undercarriage collapsing. The Irish hills claimed others and several just disappeared over the sea on navigation exercises. Engine failure caused many fatalities and as a result of an accident in April 1943, due to engine seizure, all the Beauforts were

Long Kesh on March 26 1944; 807 Squadron dispersal upper left, 809 and 879 Squadron dispersal in centre (P.H.T. Green collection via Major R.C.L. Fitzwilliams).

grounded until a modified oil pipe joint was fitted. In all there were 56 serious accidents to the type whilst operating from here.

In October 1943, the OTU received 12 Hudsons and five Oxfords from Thornaby for a new Hudson training commitment. Limited Ventura training was also begun, the five crews from the first course being posted to 519 Squadron. By the time the OTU moved to Turnberry in February 1944, the unpopular Beauforts were no longer in use, having been entirely replaced by Hudsons and a few Venturas and Oxfords.

Things were quiet until March 20 1944, when 20 Seafires of 809 Squadron landed. They were joined a few days later by 807 and 879 Squadrons with 36 more aeroplanes, mostly Sea Hurricanes. These fighters were intended for use in battle exercises around Lough Beg and some took part in training with American aircraft over Lough Neagh.

On March 25, 190 Squadron moved in from Newtownards with Oxfords and Martinets. The squadron was transferred to Turnhouse on August 28, leaving only a detachment at Long Kesh. This stayed until December 1 1945 when it, too, rejoined the main party in Scotland.

The King and Queen and Princess Elizabeth made their first visit to Northern Ireland by air, landing at Long Kesh in a Dakota, on July 17 1945. Another VIP—General Eisenhower—passed through on August 24. The airfield closed in 1946.

It should not be forgotten that Short Bros assembled and flight-tested Stirlings here as an out-station of Sydenham. The first one flew on August 26 1942, followed by a second on October 10 and others at regular intervals thereafter. The Ulster and Short Gliding Club was here until at least 1968 when the building of the prison drove it elsewhere.

Close inspection of the former airfield today is impossible for obvious reasons but published photographs show at least one 'T2' hangar (there were two during the war, plus two Bellmans and five Blisters) and in addition, the fact that the H-blocks are built amongst the old frying pan hardstandings. Military units, including a helicopter flight, occupy most of the wartime accommodation.

Longman (Inverness), Highland

26/NH670465. 1 mile N of Inverness city centre

In 1932, Highland Airways Ltd proposed an airmail and newspaper service between Inverness, Wick and Kirkwall. Captain E.E. Fresson asked Inverness Council if they would consider making Longman Fields (once used for public executions!) into a municipal airport. Carried on the wave of fervour which attended civil aviation in those days, they agreed and it was opened officially by the Duke and Duchess of Sutherland on June 17 1933.

Bellman hangar at Longman.

As the site was close to the water's edge, flying-boat operations were also envisaged but were never destined to be of any significance. For example, a Saro Cloud visited in August 1933 with spectators from the Isle of Man to see the Highland Gathering.

Flying had actually started in April 1933 with some joy-riding and on May 8 an Orkney service had begun with a Monospar ST 4 and, later, Dragons. It stopped at Wick and provided one return trip each weekday timed to connect at Inverness with trains to and from the south. On May 29 1934, there was a small ceremony to inaugurate the first regular British internal airmail.

The scheduled services expanded to embrace Renfrew, Perth and Sumburgh, Highland Airways having in the meantime merged with Northern and Scottish Airways to form Scottish Airways. The war, however, resulted in the temporary suspension of all operations by the company.

During the summer of 1940, 'A' Flight of 614 Squadron was detached here, being re-designated 241 Squadron on September 22 1940. Operating Lysanders and a few Blackburn Rocs—the latter for dive-bombing demonstrations—the squadron took part in exercises and flew coastal patrols.

Longman was taken over officially as an RAF station on April 1 1941 but when 241 Squadron left for Bury St Edmunds on April 15 it found itself almost devoid of aircraft. The opening up of RAF Dalcross at the end of June occupied some of the airmen and a visit by HM The King was a highlight in August. The same month Lysanders of 309 Squadron were detached for an exercise, an event which was to be repeated on several occasions for Army co-operation work with the 51st Highland Division on manoeuvres.

The airfield and its facilities were still somewhat under-employed, so in February 1942, the Ferry Pool at Prestwick requested accommodation for one Oxford, one Manchester, two Hurricanes and eight Masters. These aircraft were destined for delivery to Lossiemouth and Kinloss but both aerodromes were temporarily unserviceable. One of the Hurricanes featured in an unusual incident when the guns were accidentally fired by an armourer working on the aircraft. Fortunately nothing was in the way and the bullets whizzed harmlessly over the aerodrome. The following day a visiting Blenheim lost an engine on take-off and ditched in the Moray Firth. Three of the crew were rescued but one was reported missing.

Another unexpected event happened on March 1 1942, when a cargo ship tied up at a quay about 400 yds from the aerodrome and proceeded to fly a barrage balloon. The local pilots were not pleased and the naval authorities promised there would be no repetition!

In April 1942, Dalcross, although having tarmac runways, was unusable due to heavy rain and permission was given for the AGS to operate six aircraft from Longman's well-drained grass until things improved. The small airfield suddenly assumed potential importance when it was realised that, should an enemy invasion of north east Scotland ever materialise, operational squadrons would have to be based here if Dalcross were flooded. Still in April several Vindicator dive-bombers of the US Navy, temporarily based at Hatston, visited Longman. Another unusual movement on May 18 was a Lockheed Electra conveying the then Vice Admiral Louis Mountbatten, Chief of Combined Operations, to Hendon.

In the spring of 1942, Longman housed a detached flight of 289 Squadron with Oxfords and Hurricanes, 70 Wing Calibration Flight with Blenheims and 56 MU, an aircraft salvage unit. The HQ staff considered the airfield of great strategic importance, Inverness being at the entrance to the Caledonian Canal and controlling the petrol supply for the north of Scotland, as well as being at the hub of the only railway running north, east and south. Its loss would mean the gradual strangulation of the north of Scotland. Scottish Command of the Army was difficult to convince, however, so priorities for defence personnel were given to the RAF stations at Wick and Peterhead, more vulnerable but of less strategic importance.

Elaborate defence exercises were arranged, such as the one at dawn on September 27 1942, when three flying boats alighted in the Firth just off the aerodrome. The 'umpire' stated that 50 Germans had landed from these boats, the RAF countered with the retort that the defences were ample to cope with the situation!

Moving on to July 1943, a twice-weekly RAF ferry service was begun between Longman and the Orkneys, calling at RAF Castletown when necessary. On June 15, 526 Squadron had formed from 70 Wing Calibration Flight. The duty was still radar calibration for local ground and naval units with Blenheims as the main equipment. Some Hornet Moths and Oxfords were used also and the squadron provided communications flights with Dominies for units in northern Scotland.

Just how a Liberator managed to get into the small field, and better still, how it flew out again, defies the imagination but a USAAF aircraft did it on January 19 1944. On a direct flight from Newfoundland it probably got lost on the way to Prestwick. On January 23 Anson *LV127* from Dalcross was not so lucky. Trying to land in heavy rain and bad visibility it overshot into a Blister hangar at the south end of the airfield. The aircraft was wrecked along with an Oxford of 598 Squadron standing in the hangar. All the crew were injured, the gunnery instructor dying later. Only five minutes before another Anson had overshot and hit an earth bank but the crew had escaped unhurt.

Visitors in March 1944 ranged from two Luftwaffe airmen under escort who had been shot down over the Orkneys to C-47s of the USAAF from Bottesford in Leicestershire. The Luftwaffe returned on May 21 when a Ju 88 flew over Inverness very low without attacking. The next day Spitfires from HQ 13 Group Comm Flight patrolled the area until midnight in the vain hope that the raider might return.

Longman was proud of its record of uninterrupted operation but on January 19 1945 it became unserviceable for the first time in its history because of snow. This was not to be for long, however, for rollers and vehicles cleared an 800 yd strip along the east to west run and it became the only usable aerodrome in the north apart from Hatston.

April 19 1945 saw a visit by B-17 *43-38130* from Polebrook, a veteran of 78 bombing missions. On May 1 1945, 526 Squadron was disbanded and absorbed by 527, whose HQ was at Digby in Lincolnshire. A flight of three Dominies of 527 Squadron was left at Longman for communications by 70 Signals Wing and remained here until the squadron disbanded on April 15 1946. A naval communications squadron, 782, which had been a lodger for some time, left for Donibristle on July 27 1945.

Wartime restrictions on civil flying were revoked on January 1 1946 and the British European Division of BOAC was set up the same day. The BEA internal services were carried on by private operators under charter until February 1947 when BEA took over complete responsibility for them. Most of the Inverness routes were now flown by Jupiter class aircraft which were ex-German Ju 52/3ms. These aircraft were plagued by technical problems and were soon replaced by Dakotas. Longman was now considered too small for the safe operation of these larger aircraft, so all flying was moved to Dalcross which became Inverness Airport in 1947.

Today, Longman has been almost obliterated by a by-pass road and an industrial estate. During the war it had two Bessonneaux, one Bellman, one Blister, one 'T1' and one Super-Robin hangar. Of these only the Bellman survives in the middle of the industrial estate and there appear to be no other original buildings left.

Longside, Grampian

30/NK030425. 2 miles S of Longside on unclassified road

Although there is no trace of it today, there was an airship patrol station here from 1916 to 1918. In 1917 a sub-station was established at Auldbar, four miles north-west of Montrose.

Airship C10A *emerges from the hangar at* Longside (Via Chaz Bowyer).

Lossiemouth, Grampian

28/NJ210695. 5 miles N of Elgin south of B9040

Built as a permanent station at the same time as its neighbour at Kinloss, Lossie opened in 1939 for 15 SFTS. An accident on September 28 1939 was one of several which caused Flying Training Command to change its markings, the trainer yellow undersurfaces being extended halfway up the fuselage sides. A Harvard pilot taking off failed to see a camouflaged Oxford in his path against a background of fir trees and gorse in bright sunlight and there were two fatalities in the resulting collision.

Throughout the war, Lossiemouth had a dual role as a bomber training and maintenance base. Starting off as a grass field, it acquired runways in 1942 and the MU dispersals and hangarage gradually encroached on the surrounding countryside. Three 'C' Type hangars had been built but when the war began, the rest of the accommodation had to be put up in a hurry and was therefore of the austerity type.

No 46 MU opened officially on April 1 1940, receiving two Hurricanes on April 9 and then many Hinds, Harts, Tiger Moths and Audax. The first of five 'J' Type hangars was not ready for use until June and seven more 'L' Types were being constructed on dispersed sites. At the end of September, the MU held 243 aircraft, 32 of them Wellingtons and since space was at a premium some were picketed out on the playing field at the rear of the main site.

In August 1940, machine-gun posts were placed on the roofs of the 'L' hangars, a wise precaution because on October 26 three He 111s made a low-level attack. Three men were killed on the ground, a Blenheim destroyed and several others damaged but one Heinkel was shot down right in the middle of the airfield.

The Blenheims belonged to 21 Squadron, which had moved in from Watton on June 24 1940 for anti-shipping patrols off the Norwegian and Danish coasts. They returned to Watton in October but came back for a few weeks in May/June 1941. A detachment of 110 Squadron, also equipped with Blenheims, spent the last two weeks of April 1940 attacking aerodromes during the German invasion of Norway. Yet another Blenheim squadron, No 57, was here between June 24 and August 13 1940 on anti-shipping operations.

On April 20 1940, 15 SFTS went to Middle Wallop leaving Lossie free for an intended establishment of two operational bomber squadrons. This policy was changed, however, and 20 OTU activated instead on May 27 1940 for night bomber training with Wellingtons and Ansons. Under Plan *Banquet* the unit would have had a defensive role in the event of an invasion of Scotland.

The airfield must have been becoming very crowded as the MU was dealing with more and more aircraft, mainly Hurricanes, Wellingtons and Defiants. In May 1941, three Irish Air Corps officers visited to inspect three Hectors with a view to purchase, going on later to Kinloss to look at some more. (The Irish later took delivery of 13 Hectors.)

The Air Ministry's short-sightedness in not laying runways from the start, severely affected the OTU's training programme in the autumn of 1941. Things were so bad that aircraft had to be detached to Lakenheath about 400 miles away so as to keep up with the flying! The following year, in September 1942, 11 Wellingtons from 20 OTU took part in a raid on Dusseldorf, taking off from a forward base at Elsham Wolds in Lincolnshire.

No 46 MU, meanwhile, was getting even more busy dealing with a variety of types, principally Wellingtons, Hurricanes, Masters and Tiger Moths. Beau-

Top *Oxford* N6323 *of 15 FTS at Lossiemouth* circa *March 1940* (R.D. Cooling).

Above *Harvard* P5849 S *of 15 FTS at Lossiemouth February 1940* (R.D. Cooling).

Below *Bent Blenheim IV* L8784 *of 254 Squadron at Lossiemouth March 1940* (R.D. Cooling).

Bottom *Refuelling a Master I at Lossiemouth March 1940* (R.D. Cooling).

fighters began to arrive in 1942 and the first Lancasters on the unit in December 1942. The nearest Ferry Pilots Pool (No 4) was at far off Prestwick, so, to improve the situation, a sub-pool of 4 FPP was opened at Lossiemouth on February 11 1942, being expanded later into 10 FPP. SLGs were now available and there was much ferrying of aircraft between them and the parent station and also on behalf of 45 MU at Kinloss.

The runways were finally built in 1942 and Lossie was then designated as an advanced base for two 5 Group squadrons if anti-*Tirpitz* operations became necessary. Sorties by the 8th USAAF were also envisaged and it was decided that the runways would be extended and more hardstandings laid. All raids from northeast Scotland were to be controlled by the existing operations block at Lossiemouth.

A USAAF engineer battalion arrived in November 1942 and within three weeks extended the north/south runway. This was useful experience for the airfield construction soon to be undertaken by the Americans in East Anglia. At the same time the AMWD built a new watch office.

At the end of May 1943 the MU's aircraft holding was reduced with a view to specialisation in types. Primary production now consisted of the Beaufighter and Lancaster with a lesser commitment for Defiants, Ansons and Oxfords.

No 20 OTU, meanwhile, was soldiering on with the job of supplying crews to Bomber Command. The accident rate on the often elderly Wellingtons was high, being aggravated by bad weather, high ground and long over-water navigational exercises. Six Wellingtons simply disappeared in 1943 taking with them 32 men. Sometimes there was a faint *Darkie* call, but more often than not silence, and then an empty dinghy might be picked up far out to sea. No 46 MU, too, had its accidents. During what should have been a ten minute test flight in a Beaufighter in July 1944 the aircraft just vanished after take off in good weather and the pilot was never heard of again.

Lossiemouth and Milltown played an important part in the raids on the *Tirpitz* late in 1944. On September 11, Lancasters of 9 and 617 Squadrons made a refuelling stop on the way to an advanced base in Russia. Badly damaged, *Tirpitz* was attacked again on October 29 from Lossiemouth and its satellite but cloud cover prevented any hits.

The *coup-de-grace* came on November 12 when 32 grossly over-loaded Lancasters set course for Tromso Fjord. This time the ship was capsized by the impact of the massive *Tallboy* bombs. Now this threat was removed, British heavy ships were free to move to the Far East.

Three additional types came on the MU's books in April 1945 for preparation and storage—the York, Lincoln and Warwick—and with the running down of the OTU more hardstandings became available for them. No 10 FPP disbanded on July 10 1945 and 20 OTU went the same way a week later. The station was transferred to Coastal Command 17 Group on July 28 and received 41 Liberators and crews of 111 OTU from the Bahamas in August. The number of Liberators had been reduced to 17 by February 1946 but ten Halifaxes had been taken on as well.

A detachment of Warwicks from 280 Squadron was here for ASR duties up to June 1946 and 111 OTU disbanded in August 1946. Lossiemouth had been taken over by the Royal Navy on July 12 1946 and commissioned as HMS *Fulmar* but the MU was still busy flying aircraft out and breaking down the surplus ones. The task was completed in January 1947 and 46 MU closed the following month.

Lossiemouth thus began the second stage of its career, this time as the Navy's largest air station in Scotland. Training and maintenance were still the routine. No 766 Squadron, an Operational Flying

DH Dragon G-ACCZ at Lossiemouth February 1940 (R.D. Cooling).

School, with Fireflies and Seafires, arrived in August 1946 and stayed until October 1953, when a move was made to Culdrose. Other squadrons in the immediate post-war era included 741 with Fireflies and Seafires and 767 with Seafires.

An Aircraft Holding Unit was set up and large numbers of surplus Ansons and Oxfords were flown in for open storage. The unit grew in size and at one time 362 aircraft were held. Oddities were eight Mosquitoes reconditioned for the Israelis. The AHU was renamed Naval Air Support Unit in 1966 and by then occupied three hangars in the south-east corner of the airfield.

Every type in the naval inventory was to be seen at Lossiemouth at some time, 736 (Attackers), 738 (Sea Fury/Sea Hawk) and 759 (Sea Vampire) being among the squadrons based here in the 50s. Hellcat *KE209* was still flying from Lossiemouth as a 'station hack' as late as August 26 1954, when it visited Turnhouse, but it was grounded for good a week later. Miraculously, it avoided being scrapped and ended up in the Museum at Yeovilton.

The airfield had undergone a large expansion programme in 1953 which included the lengthening of two of the runways and improvements in radio aids, lighting and parking facilities. While this was going on, Milltown was employed for all flying until May 1953, when the parent reopened.

The Naval Air Fighter and Strike School now moved here from Culdrose to take advantage of what is said to be the best weather factor of any airfield in Britain. In addition, new naval types such as the Buccaneer (700Z Flight) and Scimitar were proved at Lossiemouth before entering service.

On September 29 1972, Lossiemouth

Oxford N6279 of 15 FTS after overshoot at Lossiemouth (Via S.G. Jones).

was transferred from Royal Navy to RAF control. The naval squadrons based there at that time were 809 (Buccaneers) and 750 (Sea Princes) and both moved elsewhere. The station closed in 1972/73 for more major alterations.

When it reopened, the HQ and 'B' Flight of 849 Squadron with Gannets returned as lodgers, until February 1979, when the Navy gave up its fixed-wing aircraft. The first RAF squadron was No 8 with Shackletons from August 17 1973, followed by No 54 with Jaguars from March to August 1974 and 6 Squadron, also with Jaguars in October/November 1974.

No 226 OCU re-formed at Lossie on October 1 1974 with the renaming of the Jaguar Conversion Unit which had been providing operational conversion for all Jaguar aircrew since January 1974. No 2 Tactical Weapons Unit formed in June 1978 from the parent TWU at Brawdy to solve the problem of overcrowding at Brawdy and its ranges until new facilities became available at Chivenor.

Lough Erne (Castle Archdale), Fermanagh
See Castle Archdale

Lough Neagh (Sandy Bay), Down
See Sandy Bay

Low Eldrig, Dumfries and Galloway
82/NX11-42. 6 miles N of Drummore off A716

No 11 SLG, as it was designated, was an unfortunate choice of site but this only became apparent when preparation was well advanced. Its first mention in the records of 18 MU, Dumfries, is on December 7 1940 when the unit's CO inspected it and decided where the equipment and guard huts would be placed. A further visit was made at the

beginning of May 1941 and even though there had been no recent rain the southern third of the landing strip was very soft. Some exploratory digging revealed one foot of peat and, worse still, another soft patch in the centre of the SLG was found to be formed of peat 4 ft deep.

After rolling to compact the surface it was decided that the site would not be abandoned but restricted to aircraft of Blenheim size. A Dominie made a trial landing on June 3 1941 and the SLG was then brought into use as a summer dispersal area only. However, the bogging problems continued and although the peat was excavated and replaced by earth and stones the site was considered unsafe for further landings. At the end of October, 18 MU test pilots collected the aircraft stored here, including Battles, and it was closed for the winter.

It reopened in May 1942, 19 aircraft being present in July, but it was still unsuitable and was closed permanently on September 30 1942 although not finally derequisitioned until November 13 1944. A recent visit revealed that one hut and the tractor shed still stand.

Macmerry, Lothian

66/NT445735. 2 miles E of Tranent on A1

From 1929, the airfield, which is sometimes referred to as Tranent or Penston, was operated by the Edinburgh Flying Club. North Eastern Airways also flew some scheduled services between 1936 and 1939 with Airspeed Envoys and Couriers.

The RAF took it over in 1941 and eventually added a 'T2' and eight Blisters to the original civil hangarage and built six dispersal pens. A detachment of 607 Squadron's Hurricanes was based from January 16 1941, rejoining the rest of the Squadron at nearby Drem on March 2. It was replaced three days later by 614 Squadron equipped with Blenheims and Lysanders.

Late in May 1942, Blenheims of 614 flew to West Raynham to take part in intruder attacks on night-fighter airfields in support of the 1,000-bomber raid on Cologne. In August, part of the squadron was detached to Thruxton for the Dieppe Raid. Prior to April 1942, half of 58 OTU's air firing squadron was stationed at Macmerry pending the opening of Grangemouth's satellite at Balado.

The airfield was greatly enlarged in 1942, absorbing the site of the First World War flight station at Penston. This had

been used by 77 (HD) Squadron between 1916 and 1918. The Blenheims of 13 Squadron were here from August 1942 until the personnel embarked for North Africa in November. Other army co-operation squadrons based were 63 with Mustangs from November 1942 until July 1943 and 225 with Hurricanes and Mustangs in September/October 1942. Many sorties were flown in support of local army exercises with the British 5th Corps assigned to Operation *Torch*. One 225 pilot observed that Macmerry looked like a postage stamp compared with their previous airfield at Thruxton.

The OTUs at East Fortune used Macmerry as a satellite from an undetermined date. The first was 60 OTU for night-fighter training with a mixture of Defiants, Blenheims and Oxfords. It was just beginning to re-equip with Beaufighters when it was transferred to Coastal Command on November 24 1942. Redesignated 132 OTU with a new role of long-range fighter and strike training, it continued to use Macmerry.

Cunliffe-Owen had a works on the eastern fringe of the airfield for the overhaul of Hudson aircraft and another ancillary use was the occupation of about 200 USAAF ground personnel from October 15 1943 until early the following year. The RAF Regiment also had a training school here from the beginning of 1943. An Elementary Gliding School was inaugurated on April 1 1944 and remained until 1946.

The Royal Navy, too, had a presence in the shape of 740 Communications Squadron which re-formed on December 30 1943. It operated a variety of aircraft including Dominies, Ansons, Swordfish and Reliants, until it disbanded at Macmerry in September 1945. The airfield was commissioned as HMS *Nighthawk II* on June 6 1945 as a satellite to Drem but was returned to the RAF on December 1 1945.

Macmerry was reopened with a formal ceremony by the Edinburgh Flying Club on August 31 1946. It was in a poor state, having been partly ploughed up for crops the previous spring, which severely restricted the landing area. Closed in 1953, it reverted to agriculture and an industrial estate was built on part of it.

Machrihanish, Strathclyde

68/NR665225. 3 miles W of Campbeltown

Unusual in that it had three separate periods of existence, Machrihanish began life in August 1918 as a sub-station of the airship base at Luce Bay. It also housed 272 Squadron, whose DH 6s flew coastal patrols over the Clyde and in the Hebrides until the Armistice, disbanding in December 1918 when the station closed.

It was rebuilt at the beginning of the Second World War, becoming HMS *Landrail* on June 15 1941. Like other Scottish naval aerodromes, it housed over 200 squadrons at various times, but incomplete records and space limitations allow only a handful to be mentioned.

In support of disembarked units, 772 FRU Squadron came here in July 1941 from adjacent Campbeltown and absorbed 790 Squadron, which was already at Machrihanish, having formed in October 1940. An assortment of aircraft was operated, including Swordfish, Chesapeakes, Blenheims, Masters and Fulmars, the whole fleet moving to Ayr in July 1944.

For night torpedo attack training, 766 Squadron formed at Machrihanish on April 15 1942 with Swordfish, moving to Campbeltown in February the following year. First-line squadrons like 800 and 804 with Sea Hurricanes and 818 with Swordfish were seen in 1943. Spitfires of 65 Squadron spent a week here in January practising deck landings on *Argus*, in the Clyde, with Seafires. This was in preparation for future amphibious landings.

A detachment of the Carrier Trials Unit, 778 Squadron arrived in August 1945 and stayed until January 1946. No 787Y Flight for fighter affiliation was here early in 1945, disbanding on March 1 1945.

The station was then disused but maintained until December 1 1951, when it recommissioned for Firefly training. No 799 Squadron was also based between December 1951 and August 1952 for refresher flying on a variety of types.

Flying ceased again in 1953, but the airfield underwent major reconstruction for NATO in 1960/62, also becoming a US Navy weapons facility and Master Diversion Airfield. The four runways were superseded by a new 10,000 ft strip. BEA/BA services were flown to Islay and Glasgow until taken over by Loganair in April 1977.

Maghaberry, Antrim

20/J180645. 3 miles NE of Moira off A26

Maghaberry was built as a satellite to Long Kesh and taken over on November 15 1941. It was used occasionally by Tomahawks and Lysanders of 231 Squadron based at the parent station, until the whole squadron moved its HQ to Maghaberry on January 15 1942. Its duties were mainly exercises with the Army and it stayed until November 20 1942, when it was displaced by the pending arrival of 5 OTU.

The first ten days of the New Year were taken up by the OTU's move, bad weather delaying the delivery of aircraft. The main type on charge was the Beaufort but a Hampden Flight and two Martlets were stationed at Maghaberry. No 306 FTU moved in from Templeton in South Wales on June 15 1943, mainly responsible for Wellington training but left for Long Kesh on August 15. 'A' Flight of 104 OTU (Wellingtons) also used the airfield as a lodger from September 7 to October 4 1943.

On October 15, about 200 USAAF personnel arrived in advance of the planned transfer of the station to that service. The forward party of the 311th Ferrying Squadron was posted in from Watton on November 7, the squadron having been activated, on paper at least, on November 1. Maghaberry was officially handed over as Station 239 on November 15 with the customary colour-changing ceremony and marchpast.

It had been intended to become a fighter CCRC but instead was developed as a base for the delivery of aircraft to mainland Britain. The 312th Ferrying Squadron and 321st Air Transport Squadron formed here at the same time as the 311th in 8th Air Force Service Command and on December 9 1943, the 325th FS was also initiated. All four units came under the control of the 27th Air Transport Group at Grove in Berkshire.

The field was employed also by casualty evacuation transports as the US 79th Station Hospital was nearby at Moira. On December 20, two aircraft of the 9th Troop Carrier Command evacuated American military patients from Maghaberry to Pershore in Worcestershire, marking the Command's first genuine operational mission.

The pilots for the new units were almost all experienced in ferrying duties and wise to the ways of the British weather and terrain. The CO of the 311th FS was 1st Lieutenant Gregory P. Thomas, who had already spent three years with the British ATA.

'T2's used for Stirling assembly at Maghaberry (E.A. Cromie).

Despite its title, the 312th FS did not actually ferry aircraft at first but acted as a training squadron for the 27th ATG to convert pilots on to all types of tactical aircraft, particularly Mustangs and Thunderbolts, and later heavy bombers and transports. After checkout and until such time as they were transferred, the pilots delivered aircraft on behalf of the 311th.

Mechanics were trained also, aircraft ranging from P-38 to B-17, and C-47 to B-24 being borrowed from the 311th. Early in May 1944, the 312th participated as an attacking force in a practice beach-landing in Northern Ireland by British troops. The 311th moved to Langford Lodge on May 8 1944, the other squadrons at Maghaberry following later that month.

During the American occupancy, Private John A. McAlpine and Private B.C. Owings Jr were awarded the Soldiers Medal for an act of bravery on March 4 1944. A Marauder crashed on take-off from Maghaberry and they managed to rescue one of the crew alive from the burning wreckage at great personal risk. They also pulled out three others in the vain hope that they might still be alive.

No 5 OTU continued to operate from here, now mainly with Venturas and Hudsons, until the unit returned to its original base at Turnberry on February 15 1944. The USAAF handed the station back to RAFNI on June 6 1944, but as it was not required immediately it was put on Care and Maintenance and made available for emergency landings only. There was one exception, however, Shorts, who had been assembling Stirlings here for some time, were allowed to make test-flights several times weekly as before.

On January 1 1945, the airfield was transferred to Maintenance Command as an Aircraft Storage Unit under the administration of 23 MU at Aldergrove. Several hundred Stirlings were stored here and eventually scrapped.

A maximum security prison has been built on the site to replace The Maze and most of the airfield buildings, including the early tower and its replacement, have been cleared for security reasons. However, in September 1982 the Bombing Teacher building still stood, along with several other structures on the Instructional Site.

Maydown, Londonderry

7/C485210. 4 miles NE of Londonderry off A2

Conditions were primitive, a collection of Nissen huts often in a sea of mud and a toy-like control tower. This unlikely setting was the HQ of the squadron which would grow to be by far the largest in the Navy. No 836 Squadron was to provide personnel and aircraft for the MAC-ships or merchant aircraft carriers which would become operational during 1943. As each ship neared completion a new flight of Swordfish would be formed for her at Maydown. The pool of aircraft eventually reached over 90, the flights joining a ship when required and disembarking at Maydown on the return voyage. Somewhat late in the war, this ensured that no North Atlantic convoy would lack air cover at any stage.

The airfield, however, had opened as a satellite to RAF Eglinton in the summer of 1942. On August 7 1942, the 2nd FS of the 52nd Fighter Group was detached to Maydown from the parent station. The Spitfires flew some convoy escorts before moving to Goxhill in Lincolnshire on August 24, to be joined later by the rest of the group. When the 82nd FG arrived at Eglinton its 97th FS occupied Maydown on October 6 1942. The unit's P-38s made some long training flights in company with USAAF Fortresses, eventually being posted to North Africa via St Eval late in December 1942.

On January 3 1943, the ground staff of the USAAF units and RAF HQ personnel were withdrawn from Maydown and the six airmen running the Q-site were stood down. On the following day the station was closed for building and expansion. Whilst this was in progress, a Fortress from Marrakesh, low on fuel, put down on March 20.

With effect from May 1 1943, Eglinton and its satellite were loaned to the Royal Navy, the RAF establishment being reduced to a minimum compatible with requirements to maintain RAF fighter units on a lodger basis. Both airfields were to be returned by October 1944 for planned used by the Americans but this never happened and Maydown remained HMS *Shrike*. Having only two runways with no room for a third to be laid it was also considered unsuitable for night-flying and too close to Eglinton for both to operate large numbers of aircraft simultaneously.

No 836 Squadron, the operational pool mentioned above, was active from June 1943 until disbandment on May 21 1945 and was supported by 744 which re-formed here on March 6 1944 for MAC training. This squadron later reverted to anti-submarine training with Barracudas and moved to Eglinton on November 29 1945.

A second pool squadron, 860, arrived on December 6 1943 and was crewed mainly by Dutchmen until it disbanded on August 1 1945. Avengers of 856 Squadron were here for the first two weeks of August 1944 and more Avengers of 846 and 850 Squadrons were attached in November 1943 and part of August 1944 respectively. The other based units included 822 with Barracudas in June and July 1945 and a detachment of 794 for ADDLS circa November 1945.

Maydown closed at the end of September 1945 but was re-activated briefly as HMS *Gannet II* until closed to flying in January 1949. It is now an industrial estate, but, from the air, stretches of runway and most of the perimeter track can be discerned.

Maydown (FAA Museum).

Methven, Tayside

58/NO055255. 4 miles W of Perth on A85

Now totally farmland, with only the standard tractor shed and a few pieces of SMT to reveal that it was an SLG, Methven was brought into use by 44 MU in April 1941 as 24 SLG. Ansons and Wellingtons were among the types stored here during its first year of operation.

In May 1942, a naval officer from RNAS Donibristle visited to explore the possibility of using the SLG for the transportation of naval stores to and from the nearby depot at Almondbank. This was approved but the flights were confined to small communications types like the Proctor and Dominie. (Almondbank, by the way, is still used by the Royal Navy and a Whirlwind helicopter was displayed on the gate in July 1981).

A Stirling was landed and taken off from Methven on July 30 1942 and it was then pronounced serviceable for four-engined aircraft, although it was the end of the year before Stirlings were flown in on a regular basis. Otherwise, the aircraft here were such types as the Beaufort, Defiant and Hurricane.

Auster squadrons were based at intervals; for example, 652 from March 26 until July 2 1943. Flights were detached to places as far apart as Dumfries, Morpeth and Findo Gask for training with the Army.

Methven's closure date is uncertain but it was still active in April 1944.

Milfield, Northumberland

75/NT945330. 5 miles NW of Wooler on A697

Much of the success of the RAF and USAAF ground attack units on the

Continent after D-Day stemmed from the training given at a little-known airfield in Northumberland. When Milfield opened as the Fighter Leader School on January 26 1944, the original intention was to give experience in strafing, dive-bombing and rocket firing with live ammunition to pilots of 2nd TAF but American units were soon invited to attend the courses as well.

The FLS was divided into five squadrons, 1, 2 and 3 with Spitfires forming a Tactics Wing and 4 and 5 with Typhoons and Hurricanes as an Armament Wing. Any attached USAAF aircraft would temporarily form 6 Squadron.

The exercises were extremely elaborate and each course lasted three weeks. The first week was devoted to fighter bomber attacks and fighter cover, the second to strafing on typical targets and the third to further development of the previous training. During this period, a typical battle situation of establishing a bridge-head was developed. The Goswick Ranges had six old Churchill tanks for rocket practice, a 10 ft square moving target and 50 vehicles forming a dummy convoy. Real 500-pounders were dropped and a section of railway line was laid at Goswick for practice train-busting, while real trains were often the subject of vigorous dummy attacks.

Milfield 1981 (F. Neal).

On February 20 1944, the first American pupils arrived in 16 P-47s from various groups in the 9th Air Force then being established in Southern England. Many Mustangs and Lightnings were also seen at Milfield in the following months and their pilots were allowed to fly Spitfires and Typhoons for comparison. A few Royal Navy pilots brought their Seafires here too.

The FLS forged a close link with the USAAF's School of Air Tactics at Orlando in Florida for the interchange of information and personnel where possible. Intensive training went on until December and the graduates used their experience to further the Allied advance in Europe. On December 27 1944, the FLS moved south to Wittering, ending its separate existence when it merged with the Central Fighter Establishment.

Milfield's career went back further than 1944, however, as it was first occupied on August 6 1942 when 59 OTU moved in with Hurricanes and a few Masters. The same site, then known as Woodbridge, had been used as a landing ground by 77 Squadron in 1917.

Ex-56 Squadron Typhoon at Milfield (Via J. Huggon).

The exotically titled No 1 Specialised Low Attack Instructors School was part of 59 OTU in 1943, flying Hurricane IVs for RP and 40 mm cannon firing. No 184 Squadron brought its Hurricanes here on February 3 1943 for a short course before returning to Colerne on February 22. Fighter Command considered setting up an Armament Practice Camp here in March 1943 but chose Acklington instead.

Its first Typhoon was delivered to 59 OTU in May 1943 and it soon became a specialised OTU on this type, although supply difficulties meant that many Hurricanes remained on strength. Under the *Saracen* Scheme, advanced pupils and their instructors would form 559 Squadron in an emergency. This nominal unit was at the Brunton satellite initially but moved to Milfield in May 1943, where it occupied a dispersal hut next to the watch office.

The OTU closed down on January 26 1944, No 1 SLAIS being absorbed by the newly formed FLS. No 59 OTU had a very fine record, having in its 34 months of life completed 101,355 flying hours and trained 1,485 pupils. It was noted that life had never been easy as the training commitment was always a little greater than the resources of the OTU.

Before the FLS left, 56 OTU re-formed here on December 14 1944, equipped with Typhoons and Tempests and a few Hurricanes and Masters. Frantic efforts were made to get the OTU into shape so that training could begin on January 2. Almost without exception, the incoming instructors were new to OTU work and had to be briefed and trained themselves, as most had not flown a Tempest before.

The Spitfire OTU syllabus was modified to accommodate the capabilities of the Typhoon and Tempest and the first course of pilots arrived on schedule. Brunton was employed for the final phase of training. After Germany surrendered, the intensive courses became more leisurely. Three, of nine weeks each, were to run concurrently, with output each three weeks of ten Tempest and ten Typhoon pilots.

For Battle of Britain Day 1945, 53 Typhoons and Tempests flown by instructors and pupils were despatched to 51 RAF stations. The OTU closed on February 14 1946, the pilots still under training at that time going to 61 OTU at Keevil.

Much of the technical site is still intact, with two 'T2' hangars in good condition,

although the 518/40 tower has gone. The NE perimeter track is incorporated into a minor road.

Millisle, Down

15/J560755. 2 miles W of Millisle on B172

Crossing a country road on the Ards Peninsula is a long ribbon of concrete, part of an action station that never was. Intended for a USAAF CCRC, it was abandoned when construction was quite well advanced. The usual three runways in a triangle were planned and two thirds of one and about one third of another were completed. A section of perimeter track leads off to nowhere and the technical site has now been taken over by light industry.

The whole concept is astonishing and one is tempted to say that it could only happen in Ireland! Fortunately the local farms and cottages were not demolished and still sit beside the abandoned strip. Army Air Corps Beavers have landed here occasionally, the concrete being in excellent condition. Kells Point to the south of Cluntoe and Ballymoney in Antrim were other projected airfields but neither was ever started.

Milltown, Grampian

28/NJ265655. 3 miles SE of Lossiemouth on B9103

Starting life as a Q-site for nearby Lossiemouth, it was soon suggested as suitable for development into a real airfield. The decoy was thus abandoned on October 27 1941 and construction of three runways was undertaken at a leisurely pace. It was expected that it would be completed by the end of April 1943 and was intended to house a Coastal Command OTU. A secondary function as an advanced base for Bomber Command was also established to replace the temporary facilities at RAF Peterhead.

The new airfield was brought into use on June 14 1943 as a satellite for 20 OTU's Wellingtons, the Coastal OTU plan having been shelved. It was also employed briefly in December 1943 for the display of gliders under Operation *Tyndall*. No 20 OTU used Milltown until September 1 1944, when it was needed by Coastal Command to accommodate one of the squadrons redeployed from south-west England to combat the U-boats now operating from Scandinavia.

Liberators of 224 Squadron arrived from St Eval early in September 1944 and began to fly patrols against U-boats and shipping off the Norwegian and Danish coasts. On September 19, in a typical action, depth charges were dropped on a submarine, which submerged, leaving a 50 yds wide oil patch. No 224 returned to St Eval in July 1945, having flown its last operational sortie from Milltown on June 2.

The airfield played its part in the sinking of the *Tirpitz* on November 12 1944, when 32 Lancasters of 9 and 617 Squadrons took off from Lossiemouth, Kinloss and Milltown. (The squadron ORBs do not record the particular aircraft which left each base.)

No 20 OTU was allowed to use Milltown for circuits and bumps in February 1945, whilst runway repair work was going on at Lossiemouth. When Lossiemouth was transferred to 17 Group Coastal Command on July 28 1945, Milltown became its satellite once more.

Early in August 1945, the Liberators of 111 OTU from the Bahamas began to arrive, soon joined by 1674 HCU from Aldergrove. The HCU disbanded, however, the following month, but 111 OTU soldiered on until August 1946, when it, too, disbanded.

Lossiemouth and its satellite were taken over by the Royal Navy on July 2 1946, Milltown becoming HMS *Fulmar II*. It was later equipped with a complete mirror landing installation so that student pilots from Lossiemouth could carry out MADDLS (Mirror Aerodrome Dummy Deck Landings).

The airfield was returned to the RAF in September 1972 and was then used several times for exercises by Harriers with Hercules in support. No 663 Gliding School operated from here until it was closed for flying in March 1977, to become a radio transmitter site used by 81 Signals Unit. The single 'T2' hangar was used by the DOE for storage. (There used to be a 'B1' hangar as well.)

Montrose, Tayside

54/NO725600. 1 mile N of Montrose beside A92

Montrose is the oldest military airfield in Scotland, dating back to 1912 and displaying the hangar architecture of several different periods. The site is steeped in aeronautical history and one hopes that it will be preserved for posterity before it is too late. The First World War hangars resemble the Belfast type but are

built entirely of timber with none of the usual brickwork. An air raid destroyed two of them and the Bellman replacements still stand today, their stark austerity contrasting with the intricate wooden buildings alongside.

A crescent-shaped block of hangars dates from this period and a ruined control tower and machine-gun butts date from the Second World War. The top storey of the tower has been crudely demolished, probably to remove an obstruction to night helicopter training a few years ago. A disused railway runs past the airfield and a bridge over it has been fortified with an elaborate pillbox with an AA gun mount on its roof. This was the original Battle HQ, replaced later by a standard building on the eastern perimeter. Wartime runways were of army track and sections of this are now peeping through the grass.

One of the original squadrons of the REC, No 2, came north from Farnborough in January 1913 and flew various types of reconnaissance aircraft from here until June 1914, when it returned to Farnborough. During its occupation of Montrose, 2 Squadron made some very long flights indeed, considering the aircraft of this period. For example, six aircraft flew to Limerick, in Ireland, and back and in November 1913 Captain C.A.H. Longcroft flew from Montrose over Portsmouth and back to Farnborough in a BE 2, covering the distance of 650 miles without landing. These and other long distance flights were remarkable for their lack of incident and showed that aeroplanes were becoming far more reliable than before. Experiments were also carried out in fitting machine guns and the lighter Lewis gun was selected as the most suitable weapon.

When the war started, the aerodrome was developed into a training station, the first unit being 6 Reserve Squadron which formed on July 17 1915 with many different types, including the Maurice Farman Shorthorn and Longhorn. Various training units used the field until 32 TDS formed out of Nos 6, 11 and 18 Reserve Squadrons in July 1918 for single-seat fighter training. The aircraft used included SE 5As, Camels and Avro 504Ks.

Three squadrons formed here during the First World War. These were No 25, which flew several types including Maurice Farmans, Caudrons and Avro 504s and came into being on September 9 1915, going to Thetford in December of

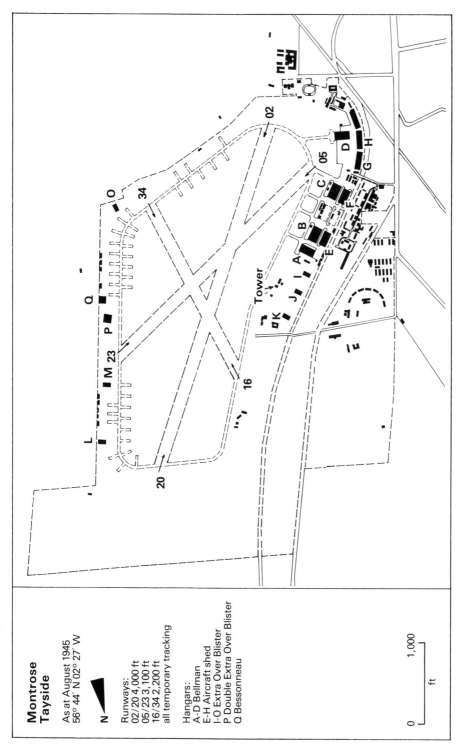

Montrose
Tayside

As at August 1945
56° 44' N 02° 27' W

N

Runways:
02/20 4,000 ft
05/23 3,100 ft
16/34 2,200 ft
all temporary tracking

Hangars:
A-D Bellman
E-H Aircraft shed
I-O Extra Over Blister
P Double Extra Over Blister
Q Bessonneau

0   1,000
                ft

Tower

02
05
34
20
23
16

O
Q
M
P
L
D
H
G
C
F
B
E
A
J
I
K

Top *Sopwith Camel C6753 serving as a trainer at Montrose early in 1919. It had previously been with 151 Squadron (L.V. West).*

Above *Pre-First World War hangars at Montrose.*

Below *First World War hangar and Bellman at Montrose.*

Bottom *Original Battle HQ at Montrose with AA gun position on roof.*

that year; No 80, formed as a Fighter Squadron on August 1 1917 with Camels, moving to Beverley in Yorkshire in November 1917 and No 83 Squadron, formed in January 1917 but moved almost immediately to Spitalgate for training. The American 41st Aero Squadron was here from March 1918 with Spads and Camels, moving to Gullane the following month.

The airfield was abandoned after the war ended but the RAF's 1935 Expansion Scheme resulted in its re-activation, the land being bought back for £18,600. Six new FTSs were being formed to train officers and airmen pupils and on January 1 1936, 8 FTS opened at Montrose. The aim was to give three months *ab initio* flying to each course of 48 trainees, followed by three months of advanced instruction, by which time they would be able to join RAF squadrons as qualified service pilots.

The landing ground had obviously suffered from neglect and it was still being levelled and returfed. Meanwhile, the first Hart and Audax aircraft had been delivered for the school but aircraft movement had to be limited until ground conditions improved. The biplanes were still being operated when the war started but began to be replaced by Masters in May 1940.

The Ansons of 269 Squadron were based between August 25 and October 10 1939 as part of a plan by the Admiralty to concentrate available aircraft on the east coast and prevent an enemy surface raider breaking out into the Atlantic undetected. The main Coastal Command effort was thus put into forming a barrier to ships getting out round the north of Scotland from the north German ports. The aircraft patrolled from Montrose out to the Anson's operational limit which was 50 miles south-west of the Norwegian coast. The gap up to the coast was to be covered by British submarines until sufficient Hudsons were available to bridge it.

On November 1 1939, the personnel and aircraft of 13 FTS, comprising ten Ansons and four Harts, arrived at Montrose. The unit had recently disbanded at Drem and was now amalgamated with 8 FTS. Perth aerodrome became unserviceable for heavy aircraft in the winter of 1939/40, so customs and handling arrangements were made at Montrose for BOAC's Lockheed 14 service from Perth to Stavanger to operate through here until conditions improved.

Being right on the coast, the airfield's vulnerability was obvious and in June 1940 hasty attempts were made to improve the defences. Nine pillboxes were erected at strategic points on the boundary, each accommodating ten riflemen and one Lewis gunner. Fifty airmen of above average marksmanship were selected as 'parashots' in case of an airborne landing attempt. The expected strike from the air came on July 18 1940 but it was not paratroops but bombs which landed on the aerodrome. A lone raider dropped its load, causing 11 casualties, two of them fatal, and damaging 13 aircraft, two of them later being declared write-offs. Five days later, another bomb was dropped close to the tarmac but no damage was caused.

Fighter protection was now given by a detachment of 603 Squadron's Spitfires from January 17 to April 14 1940. If an approaching raider was reported, a red Verylight was fired to clear the circuit of training aircraft and three Spitfires would leap into the air. Often, low-flying raiders would make their attacks unmolested owing to the element of surprise. On October 25 1940, three Ju 88s bored in from the south at 50 ft and dropped 24 bombs, strafing as they came. Five men were killed, 18 wounded, two hangars were destroyed and the officers' mess was completely gutted. A detachment of Hurricanes of 111 Squadron had been here since October 12 resting after the Battle of Britain but they had no time to get airborne. The difficulty was that Montrose and other airfields with detached flights were not linked to the

Maurice Farman Longhorn at Montrose circa *1914* (RAF Museum).

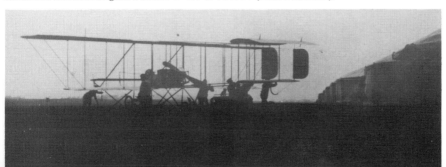

main Fighter Command operations system.

One of the last recorded visits by an enemy aircraft occurred on February 19 1941, when an He 111 made two runs across the aerodrome in snow and low cloud but did not open fire although the defences shot at it. No 111 Squadron left for North Weald in April 1941 and on April 29, 232 Squadron flew its Hurricanes into Montrose prior to embarkation at Gourock on May 10 for overseas service.

No 8 SFTS had continued instruction throughout this hazardous period. Night-flying training in aircraft with no radio was particularly dangerous in the blackout with the tiny goose-neck flares on the airfield easily lost to view and the Grampians lying not far to the west. No wonder one pilot on night-flying detail has since confessed that discretion was the better part of valour and he would sometimes taxi to a far corner of the aerodrome and return to the hangars after a decent interval, unnoticed in the general melée. He was not the only one either! The remains of a number of Montrose Masters still lie on the hills where they crashed, including one which was missing for six months.

An RLG at Stracathro was opened in July 1941 for both day and night flying, being occupied by 'A' Squadron of the FTS. No 8 FTS disbanded on March 25

Receipt for oil and petrol to the sum of 17s-6d (87½p) supplied by Duncan's Garage, St Andrews on April 4 1912. Signed by the CO of 2 Squadron (Dr A.A. Duncan).

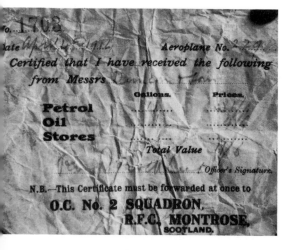

1942, its place being taken by No 2 Flying Instructors School which had already formed here on January 3 1942 with Masters and Oxfords. The FIS trained instructors for both single- and twin-engined FTSs and the new (P)AFUs and also operated special courses for OTU instructors.

A detached flight of 2 FIS flew from Dalcross until October 10 1942 and other RLGs used in 1942 included Tealing, Edzell, Stracathro and Fordoun. The training routine was occasionally enlivened by such exercises as dive-bombing and low-level dummy attacks on troops in the Forfar district.

A long dry spell in the early summer of 1942 resulted in much sand being blown about the airfield, bottles of eye lotion being issued to each flight. If the sand got into eyes, it also got into engines, causing excessive wear and a request for desert-type filters.

Montrose displayed a couple of dummy Bostons in connection with Operation *Tyndall* in the late summer of 1943, but attempts at simulating an army camp were very half-hearted. An officer, inspecting the 'camp', found it very unconvincing, with no paths worn in the grass between tents and dummy soldiers sprawled over tables in the open like the aftermath of some booze-up!

In February 1944, Flying Officer S. Thompson was awarded the AFC after one engine of the Oxford he was flying caught fire at 3,000 ft. He ordered his three crew to bale out but by the time they had done so the fire had spread to the wing centre-section. The aircraft was now too low for Thompson to bale out so he crash-landed at Montrose, sustaining only minor injuries.

The FIS received two Hudsons in July 1944, joining a Beaufort 1 for heavy twin experience. On June 20 1945, instructional flying ceased and the unit disbanded on July 11. During its life, the FIS used three separate locations for practice forced-landings. They were Cairnbeg *(NO697758)*, Wakefield *(NO682697)* and Balhall. The latter is said also to have been an ELG for Montrose in the First World War. They were never more than large fields and all have returned to cultivation.

Since the RAF vacated the airfield soon after the war, it has been used occasionally by light aircraft, by British Airways heli-copters for night training in 1977/78 and by RAF Hercules on tactical exercises in October 1978. The story of the Montrose ghost has been told so many times that I shall not repeat it here. Suffice it to say that a Second World War instructor told me that although he had never heard of a 'sighting', the airfield had a strange atmosphere which he could not quite define and there were a couple of inexplicable accidents while he was there.

Morpeth, Northumberland

NZ/170820. 3 miles SW of Morpeth off A6087

The first aircraft, a couple of Lysanders, were delivered on April 12 1942. Bothas, however, were to be the main equipment and some arrived in time for the opening of 4 Air Gunner School on April 17. The new station needed some organisation, so it was nearly five weeks before the first course of pupils was posted in, the flying training programme not getting started until May 31.

A skeleton staff had occupied the airfield since January 1942, finding it extremely primitive, with lighting by paraffin lamp only and problems with the contaminated water supply. These teething troubles were gradually overcome and the school began to function with great efficiency. Spitfires appeared briefly in August 1942 when 72 Squadron was stationed here before moving to Ayr.

Most of the Botha pilots were Poles who found their second-line duty tedious and often livened it up with low flying and beat-ups. A basic mistake and non-existent flying control, however, was the cause of an accident at a runway intersection on November 16 1942. A Botha took off on the wrong runway and collided with a similar aircraft. It was a miracle that there was only one death and one injury as a result. A few months later, on March 29 1943, two Bothas collided in mid-air and this time there were no survivors.

Martinets had mostly replaced the Lysanders by the spring of 1943 and the school looked forward to the unpopular Botha being phased out in favour of the Anson in the near future. During July 1943, the total number of air gunners trained here reached 2,000 and the Botha was used for the last time on air-to-air firing. The Anson proved to be much more suitable for the task, the instructor in particular having a good view of his pupil in action.

A total of 240 airmen were under instruction during August 1943, the standard course lasting for six weeks.

Various nationalities were requisitioned, including Dutch, Free French and Norwegian. The amount of live ammunition expended in training was staggering, some 325,400 rounds being fired during August.

The Austers of 'A' Flight 652 Squadron were detached to Morpeth during June 1943 directing the practice artillery shoots at Otterburn. Employees from several local firms making parts for Barracuda and Swordfish aircraft were invited to visit Morpeth on September 25 1943 to watch flying demonstrations by both of these types. This sort of thing was quite common during the war and was a shrewd means of keeping up the workers' morale.

In November 1943, the last surplus Botha was ferried to Abbotsinch for breaking up and the next event of note took place in February of the following year when a Flying Control Officer was at last posted to Morpeth. It seems incredible now that flying had gone on daily for nearly two years without any proper control. Early in 1944, an unusual experiment was tried; the airfield possessed a number of Blister hangars as well as three of the more substantial 'T1's and some of the former were in inconvenient positions. Without being dismantled, one was moved successfully about half a mile to a better site. Eight more were moved, a cine film record being made of the job. One wonders if a print still exists in the Crown Film Unit archives. It is hardly a box office smash like *Star Wars* or perhaps more appropriately *Gone With the Wind*, as this is exactly what did happen in November 1944. An 80 mph gale lifted two of the hangars bodily and dropped them upside down, both being totally wrecked.

While all this removal work was going on, Morpeth became parent station for RAF Usworth on April 21, when the latter was reduced to Care and Maintenance. Morpeth in turn passed to Care and Maintenance under Woolsington when 4 AGS closed on December 9 1944. The last of 69 complete courses was passed out and the 70th, consisting of 73 cadets, was transferred to 3 AGS at Castle Kennedy to complete its training.

Gunnery training was this small airfield's main contribution to the war effort but its active days were not over yet by any means. After a brief lull in training a new unit, 80 OTU, was formed here on April 23 1945, specialising in training Frenchmen to fly single-seat fighters. Spitfires,

Masters and Martinets were used. When the OTU moved to Ouston in July 1945, Morpeth closed to flying and was then used for storage by 261 MU from September 1945 until July 1948.

Many of the airfield's buildings were demolished by 1950. One of the 'T1's still exists in somewhat rusty condition, as does one of the Blisters. The watch office was a bungalow type with bay windows but there is no trace of it now. Much of the area is now wooded, engulfing the old technical site, although a few buildings have survived, but most are just heaps of rubble. The old flying field with its curious dip in the middle has been given over to heavy goods vehicle training, and, in the south-west corner, steeple chase jumps for the Morpeth point-to-point. Open-cast mining has eroded the southern perimeter.

Morpeth, like so many other disused airfields all over Britain, still serves one humble aeronautical function, that of being a visual reporting point, in this case for the northern extremity of Newcastle Airport's Special Rules Zone.

Mullaghmore, Londonderry

8/C900210. 7 miles S of Coleraine on A54

This airfield's part in the war effort was a humble one but nonetheless a positive contribution to victory. Early in December 1943, Brigadier General James Gavin of the US 82nd Airborne Division was touring Northern Ireland looking for a suitable building in which to dry 30,000 parachutes. They had been used in Italy, were water-soaked and it had not been possible to unpack and dry them up to that time. An unused 'T2' hangar at Mullaghmore proved to be ideal and seven officers and 105 enlisted men of the 505th Parachute Maintenance Company were brought in for the job. It was completed early in February and the parachutes would later be used in training drops and the Normandy Invasion.

Otherwise, Mullaghmore's history was one of constant changes of plan. It seems to have been planned originally for a bomber OTU when construction began on November 20 1941 and was then variously considered as a gunnery school, forward fighter airfield and satellite to the Coastal Command base at Limavady. Only two runways were considered necessary because of local topography, the north-south strip being practically parallel to the

River Bann valley, through which blow the prevailing winds.

A firm decision on its future had still not been reached when a Care and Maintenance party opened it on August 17 1942, the runways being obstructed to prevent possible enemy landings. A Major from the USAAF made a tour of inspection on August 24, indicating possible American interest in the airfield as the 8th Air Force began to consolidate its support organisation in the UK.

The obstructions were removed in October 1942, so that the runways would be usable in emergency. Other local flying obstructions, including a mill chimney and Droghed School, were demolished by the Royal Engineers, so that the airfield could be used as a satellite by 7 OTU Limavady from December 29 1942. Wellingtons were the aircraft in use and on February 28 1943, a maintenance party from the OTU was detached here for servicing them in one of the four 'T2' hangars.

A foretaste of USAAF occupation came on September 13 1943, when a B-17 landed *en route* to Prestwick, having failed to make radio contact with its destination. On September 21, a B-24 with two dead engines spotted the field from the coast and made an emergency landing.

Part of 104 OTU moved in from Maghaberry on October 3 1943 with more Wellingtons on a lodger basis and was joined by the advance party of Americans on November 21. Mullaghmore was handed over officially to the USAAF as Station 240 on December 20 1943. The 7 OTU detachment, meanwhile, continued to operate, finally leaving on January 4 1944. No 104 OTU disbanded on January 18 1944 and its Wellingtons also left.

The 6th Replacement and Training Squadron (Bombardment) and HQ and HQ Squadron of the 6th CCRC were activated here on December 16 1943. The initial task of these units was to hold the station for any purpose the exigencies of war might bring. It was thus kept open for flying 24 hours a day, but for the moment was used only by administration aircraft and any strays in the area.

Personnel of the 320th Glider Infantry Regiment were present in February 1944 and on February 20 Major General Matthew B. Ridgway of the 82nd Airborne presented a Silver Star to one of its Staff Sergeants for his conduct at Salerno. Later in the month, the 6th CCRC was sent to Cheddington in Buckinghamshire and Station 240 was warned to expect up to 80 aircraft for short-term storage.

The first arrived on February 28 in the form of three Marauders. On the same day, 25 C-47s and C-53s brought in freight and passengers from Stansted. March 11 saw the arrival of 25 more Marauders from Gosfield and Earls Colne in Essex, some refuelling at Andreas in the Isle of Man on the way.

Mullaghmore was returned to the RAF on May 1 1944 and preparation was made to receive Coastal Command squadrons. Plans changed yet again, however, and the first operational aircraft which arrived on November 1 1944 were six Avengers detached from 824 Squadron at Benbecula. After only three anti-submarine patrols, they returned to base the following day to be replaced on November 3 by the Swordfish of 825 Squadron and the Avengers of 850.

The Loran Training Unit with Wellingtons was a lodger at this time and apart from long navigational flights it often flew ASR sorties for missing aircraft. One of its own aircraft disappeared at night on November 10 and several fruitless days were spent searching for it. This gap in specialised ASR coverage was filled when a detachment of 281 Squadron's Warwicks were based from January 2 1945, the ground crews being flown in by USAAF C-47s.

The Loran Training Unit was a purely temporary expedient stemming from the introduction of American Loran navigation equipment to long-range Coastal Squadrons in August 1944. As a critical stage in the anti-U-boat war had been reached, the operational squadrons could not undertake the training of their own navigators without seriously curtailing their activities.

It was decided that 4 Refresher Flying Unit, now redundant at Haverfordwest in Wales, would be re-equipped for Loran training and moved to a more northerly station within the Loran Chain of master and slave radio transmitters. Limavady was the airfield chosen at first but this was changed to Mullaghmore and the RFU moved here in October becoming the LTU on October 5. Each course consisted of 24 navigators and lasted for about five days.

By March 1945, so many squadron navigators had been trained in the use of Loran that it was proposed shortly to discontinue training and transfer responsibility for it entirely to the squadrons. Loran became the major aid to oceanic

flying for the airlines after the war and has only been superseded quite recently. The LTU moved to Limavady on March 3.

Nos 825 and 850 Squadrons had left in the meantime and another FAA Squadron, 1771, flew its Fireflies in on January 7. On February 7, it was moved to Ayr, being now replaced by the Barracudas of 815 Squadron. A Barracuda attacked a smoking wake with depth charges on March 5 but no results were observed. Two days later *G* of 815 Squadron made another inconclusive attack on an oil streak with bubbles.

On March 31, 281 Squadron moved to Limavady and the station went to Care and Maintenance in May 1945. So passed into history an airfield which one airman described as 'Like being on a bog and sometimes in it!'

Like most other disused airfields in the Province, Mullaghmore now has a variety of uses, including open storage of wood products on the main runway, a stock car racing track, and repair of agricultural machinery. Several locally-owned aircraft are kept here in a modern hangar erected on the site of one of the wartime 'T2's. Some of the old airfield buildings are used to house farm livestock and the control tower has been converted into an attractive dwelling.

Murlough, Down

15/J405350. 1 mile S of Dundrum off A2

Sometimes referred to as Dundrum, this was 19 SLG under 23 MU Aldergrove for the whole of its lifespan. The first test landing was made on March 11 1941 by a Blenheim, the site opened four days later and two more Blenheims, the first for storage, flew in on March 21.

There was a serious shortage of airfields in Northern Ireland at this time pending completion of a number of new ones, so 'A' Flight of 88 Squadron with Battles used Murlough between May 26 and June 23 1941 for special training. The SLG closed for the winter and was reopened in May 1942 when the ground had dried out, guard duty being provided by a detachment of the Royal Irish Fusiliers. During the summer of 1942, 'A' Flight of 651 Squadron detached from Long Kesh was allowed to use the airfield for practice.

The aircraft stored here included many Wellingtons and when 23 MU vacated the site on February 14 1945, there were still four ancient Wellington 1cs waiting to be broken up by 226 MU. The latter was

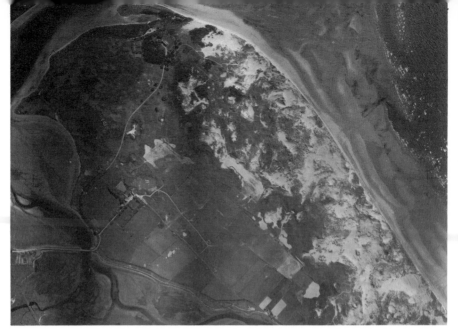

Above *Vertical of Murlough taken by 231 Squadron on June 3 1942. At least 15 aircraft are discernible on the original print.*

Below *Murlough landing strip in middle distance. Slieve Donard in the Mountains of Mourne rises in the background.*

based on a ground station at Mullusk and was responsible for salvaging crashed and surplus aircraft in Northern Ireland.

The former SLG site is now part of a conservation area and only the tractor shed and another small building remain to show where it was.

Newcastle (Gosforth), Tyne and Wear

88/NZ243668. 2 miles NE of Newcastle beside A1

A naval aerodrome was opened on the racecourse here in 1915 and was developed later into an Aircraft Acceptance Park (9AAP) to receive such types

as the Blackburn Cuckoo and Bristol F2b built by local sub-contractors.

Armstrong-Whitworth built BE 2s at Gosforth and flew them from a 150 × 600 yds area of Newcastle's Town Moor, moving in mid-1916 to a slightly larger part of the Moor and in 1918 to Cramlington.

A small RNAS unit was at Gosforth in 1915 and Major C. Draper, then a Lieutenant, was in command. One day they had a report that a Zeppelin was crossing the North Sea and the Admiralty ordered an aeroplane to go up and destroy it. It was dark but off Draper went on what was his first night flight. They had no W/T or guns but the passenger was a private in the Royal Marines armed with a service rifle and four single rounds of incendiary ammunition. The airship came over at 13,000 ft—it took them an hour to reach 3,000 ft!

'Immediately after this', Draper recalls, 'the Mayor of Newcastle asked me to make a night flight and let him know if he had 'blacked out' properly, but as he had only darkened the top half of the street lamps, the whole place looked like fairyland!'

Newtownards, Down

15/J495725. 1 mile SE of Newtownards on A20

Newtownards grew out of Northern Ireland's lack of a proper airport during the 1920s and early '30s. Regular air services connected the province with Britain but its terminal at RAF Aldergrove was ill-equipped to handle passengers. Potential private flying was also being handicapped by the lack of a suitable aerodrome.

A solution was provided by the Marquis of Londonderry, who was himself an enthusiastic aviator and Secretary of State for Air from 1931 to 1935. A 50-acre portion of his estate was turned into an airfield and opened as Ards Airport on August 31 1934. Its facilities included a hangar and clubhouse and Airwork Limited of Heston was contracted to run the airport.

Newtownards rapidly eclipsed Aldergrove and became part of an airline network extending to Glasgow, the Isle of Man, Blackpool, Liverpool and London. The airlines involved included Blackpool and West Coast, Olley Air Services, Northern and Scottish and Railway Air Services and the aircraft were Spartan Cruisers, Dragons and DH 86s.

It was a sad day for Newtownards when the new airport at Sydenham opened on March 10 1938 and airline operations were transferred there. The Northern Ireland Flying Club went on operating from Newtownards but with the war everything came to an abrupt halt.

The airfield was requisitioned and judged to be a suitable place for training and army co-operation. Its area was increased to 234 acres and the original buildings supplemented by many new ones including four Blisters around the perimeter. Seven dispersed living and communal sites were added, construction work being carried out by the Royal Engineers under the direction of AMWD. Two tarmac runways were laid, along with

Pillbox at Newtownards decorated like a New York subway train! The pole for the wind-sock is a tail-boom from a Miles Aerovan.

an unconventional third one which was half tarmac and continued as a grass strip.

Flying meanwhile went on with little interruption, the airfield serving as RLG for the Tiger Moths and Battles of 24 EFTS Sydenham. The first army co-op flying began in June 1940 with Lysanders of 416 Flight Aldergrove. The flight was developed into 231 Squadron and made Newtownards its HQ on July 15 1940.

The airfield suffered 13 fatal casualties from among its army defence personnel when a stick of bombs intended for Belfast fell on it during the night of April 14/15 1941.

No 231 Squadron moved to the new airfield at Long Kesh on December 11 1941, leaving Newtownards to bear the brunt of a new requirement. This was to provide target-towing facilities for AA and air-to-air firing practice in connection with the build-up of ground and air forces in the Province. By April 1942, there were four flying units on the station; 1480 Flight with Defiants and Lysanders, 1493 TT Flight with Lysanders and one Master III, 'S' Flight of 1 AACU with four Henleys and 82 Group Comm Flight with an assortment of small aircraft.

Although there were only 21 aircraft based at Newtownards in April 1942, they represented six different types with eight different varieties of engine and the

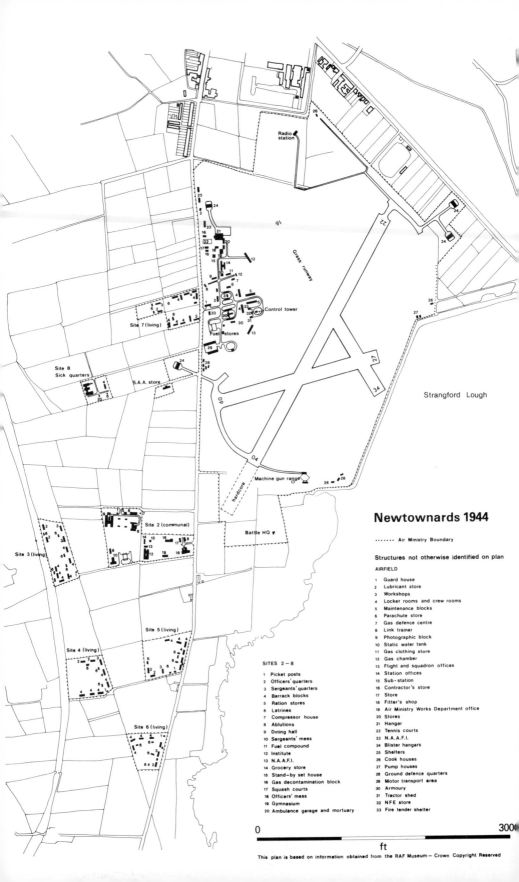

Newtownards 1944

.... Air Ministry Boundary

Strangford Lough

Structures not otherwise identified on plan

AIRFIELD

1 Guard house
2 Lubricant store
3 Workshops
4 Locker rooms and crew rooms
5 Maintenance blocks
6 Parachute store
7 Gas defence centre
8 Link trainer
9 Photographic block
10 Static water tank
11 Gas clothing store
12 Gas chamber
13 Flight and squadron offices
14 Station offices
15 Sub-station
16 Contractor's store
17 Store
18 Fitter's shop
19 Air Ministry Works Department office
20 Stores
21 Hangar
22 Tennis courts
23 N.A.A.F.I.
24 Blister hangars
25 Shelters
26 Cook houses
27 Pump houses
28 Ground defence quarters
29 Motor transport area
30 Armoury
31 Tractor shed
32 N F E store
33 Fire tender shelter

SITES 2 – 8

1 Picket posts
2 Officers' quarters
3 Sergeants' quarters
4 Barrack blocks
5 Ration stores
6 Latrines
7 Compressor house
8 Ablutions
9 Dining hall
10 Sergeants' mess
11 Fuel compound
12 Institute
13 N.A.A.F.I.
14 Grocery store
15 Stand-by set house
16 Gas decontamination block
17 Squash courts
18 Officers' mess
19 Gymnasium
20 Ambulance garage and mortuary

Radio station

Grass runway

Control tower

Fuel stores

Site 7 (living)

Site 8 Sick quarters

S.A.A. store

Site 2 (communal)

Battle HQ

Site 3 (living)

hardcore

Machine gun range

Site 5 (living)

Site 4 (living)

Site 6 (living)

0   3000

ft

This plan is based on information obtained from the RAF Museum – Crown Copyright Reserved number of maintenance personnel was insufficient to ensure a reasonable level of serviceability. In August, the CO of 1480 Flight was driven to report on its Defiants: 'The whole problem of this aircraft is one of serviceability. There is probably no single-engined aircraft which is less suitable for AA co-operation duties. It is under-powered, which leads to constant engine troubles, it is too complicated, too inaccessible and finally the spares situation is not good.'

In contrast, the eminently suitable Lysanders were kept extremely busy, often operating temporarily from other aerodromes. During November and December 1942, for instance, 1493 Flight was almost continually engaged with 501 Squadron at Ballykelly. This Flight was transferred in its entirety to Ballykelly on January 26 1943 and on December 1 of the same year, 1480 and 1617 Flight merged to form 290 Squadron. (No 1617 Flight had, itself, been formed out of 'S' Flight of 1 AACU late in 1942.) An Oxford detachment of 6 AACU also spent time here in 1943 between May 30 and August 21.

On December 24 1943, B-17G *42-31599* made a precautionary landing after a direct flight from Gander and was sent on to its proper destination at Nutt's Corner. Another transatlantic Fortress diverted in on February 7 1945 and on June 9 1944 a Halifax from Linton-on-Ouse landed after operations over France.

Apart from these highlights, the aerodrome was little used after March 21 1944, when 290 Squadron moved to Long Kesh. This transfer was forced by insufficient hangarage and the poor state of the

airfield's surface. Newtownards was then kept on a Care and Maintenance basis administered by RAF Long Kesh. With the establishment of 203 EGS early in 1945, gliding was the only use made of the airfield, apart from an RAF training school, until the time of its reversion to the Londonderry Estate shortly after the end of the war.

The next 15 years were marked by the establishment on the airfield of a number of enterprising but short-lived ventures. These included the manufacture of Messenger aircraft and car ferry services to and from Stranraer (West Freugh) by Silver City Airways. However, it has been private and club flying which has kept Newtownards alive and it is now Ulster's chief centre for these activities.

The dispersed living sites were cleared to make way for a housing estate, but some wartime defence positions remain on the fringes of the aerodrome, including a half-demolished Seagull Trench near the shore.

Nutt's Corner, Antrim

14/J190775. 2 miles E of Crumlin on A52

Nutt's Corner was built in record time under the direction of AMWD No 16 Works Area. The Airfield Board had selected the site in the summer of 1940 and within months the War Cabinet had accorded the very highest priority to aerodrome construction in Northern Ireland. This would enable Coastal Command to have more bases from which to mount its anti-U-boat operations at a time when shipping losses were rising to unprecedented levels.

No 120 Squadron re-formed at Nutt's Corner on June 2 1941, at the same time that the station opened. The first three Liberators arrived on June 8 and others were delivered during the following weeks. After two months working up on the new type, the first operational sweep

ATC cadet discovers the workings of a machine-gun in a Lysander of 231 Squadron. Newtownards May 11 1941 (Via E.A. Cromie).

was made by *AM924* on September 20 and convoy escort sorties were begun five days later.

The first action did not come until October 4, however, when an Fw Condor was encountered near a convoy. A lumbering combat ensued and the Condor made off when the Liberator had to abandon the chase with a damaged engine. On October 22, Liberator *AM926*, piloted by Flight Lieutenant T.M. Bulloch, made a head-on attack against another Condor scoring hits with its front guns. The Liberator took a hit in a propellor which was not noticed until after it had got back to base. The Focke Wulf escaped into cloud but an hour later a U-boat was seen with conning tower awash. The Liberator dived steeply and straddled the disappearing track with three depth charges, one possibly being on target.

An officer on attachment to 120 Squadron noted that the 1,600 yd runways available were marginal with a fully-loaded Liberator and the aircraft were often pulled off the ground at 125 mph with 50 yds to spare! To service a 110 ft wingspan aircraft in a 90 ft hangar meant that it had to be lifted on trolleys and dragged in sideways.

He also commented: 'The aerodrome at Nutt's Corner is built on what is partially a bog, and as the runways are of tarmac they give trouble. If an aircraft leaves the runway it gets bogged at once. The dispersal parks have concrete taxi tracks and these have been covered with tar and stone chippings for camouflage. The stones come loose and damage to propellors results. It is a pity they did not use wood chippings instead of stones. The hardstandings are excellently arranged, being a series of circles round which an aircraft can easily be taxied, and are far superior to a narrow track terminating in a concrete square on which it is impossible to turn a big aircraft.'

No 220 Squadron moved in from Wick on January 9 1942 with Hudsons but soon began to convert onto Fortresses, flying the initial operational sortie on April 29 1942. The unit transferred to Ballykelly on June 20. No 160 Squadron's Liberators spent May 1942 at Nutt's Corner flying AS patrols over the Atlantic to gain experience before leaving for the Middle East in June.

Some 31 sorties were flown by 120 Squadron in April 1942, ranging from Iceland to the coasts of Spain and Portugal. St Eval was employed as an advanced base for some of these. On April 25 *P* of 120 Squadron dropped depth charges on a U-boat, but, as usual, the results were unknown.

In June 1942, seven Lancasters of 44 Squadron from Waddington arrived for training in anti-submarine tactics and convoy escort. On June 14, a Lancaster on escort duties was forced to ditch, the crew being picked up by a destroyer and taken to Freetown in West Africa. The detachment returned to Lincolnshire on July 19 1942.

As Nutt's Corner had been selected as a transatlantic reception centre, 120 Squadron was moved to Ballykelly on July 21 1942. The station, however, was not transferred to 44 Group Ferry Command until January 19 1943 and there was little activity apart from the regular glider ferry service to the mainland. In the meantime the runways were lengthened and spectacle hardstandings were built out into the surrounding fields.

No 231 Squadron was a lodger between January 2 and March 21 1943, with Tomahawks, Mustangs and Lysanders and detachments returned in July. No 104 OTU formed here for transport crew training on March 12, flying Wellingtons. Some of the crews were posted to BOAC on completion of their courses and the OTU disbanded on January 18 1944.

The first USAAF B-17s began to arrive from Gander in July 1943, B-24s and C-47s following in August until a steady stream built up. There were occasional dramas such as the day when a B-17 crashed on landing in bad weather and the crew of a sister aircraft baled out successfully with an engine fire and little chance of getting down safely at Nutt's Corner.

No 1674 HCU used the airfield as a satellite between February 20 and March 18 1944, while the runways at Aldergrove were being repaired. USAAF C-54s became quite regular visitors on diversion, particularly if headwinds forced a fuelling stop on the way to Prestwick. Operational diversions involved 18 Lancasters and seven Halifaxes on June 9, when weather closed their bases on return from Northern France. Twelve more Lancasters diverted the next morning.

Less warlike was a daily training shuttle service from Bramcote or Nuneaton to Nutt's Corner, flown by 105 OTU crews for experience. Another HCU, No 1332, arrived from Longtown on October 6 1944 bringing initially one C-87 Liberator

Nutt's Corner 1945 (Via M.J. Burrow).

transport, two Stirlings and a York. Transatlantic deliveries were few now, most going direct to Prestwick.

Early in 1945, Nutt's Corner became the nerve centre of Training Area Flying Control (TAFC), covering aircraft flying in the north of Scotland and north-west Atlantic. HF/DF fixer stations were available at Nutt's Corner, Stornoway, Prestwick, and Doncaster and a lost aircraft could rapidly be given a position. One wonders how many lives could have been saved had this system been devised earlier in the war. In March 1945 new standardised training routes were introduced for the whole of the British Isles with a series of set turning points, particularly for aircraft on cross-country flights under the control of TAFC.

Another contribution to flight safety was rather more mundane, consisting of about 1,000 4-gallon kerosene tins painted white and placed at intervals along the perimeter tracks to assist taxying at night.

Towards the end of May 1945, 1332 HCU left for Riccall in Yorkshire. An advanced party of Royal Navy personnel arrived in June, preparatory to the station being taken over by that service on July 9 1945. Two days later it was commissioned as HMS *Pintail* but did not see much use before being given back to the RAF on April 1 1946.

After BEA threatened to withdraw services to Northern Ireland unless a better site than obstructed Sydenham was made available, Nutt's Corner became the new Belfast Airport on December 1 1946. Ex-RAF buildings were cleverly converted into a terminal and with some improvements the airport gave good service until replaced by Aldergrove on September 26 1963.

The McCandless Autogyro *G-ATXW* flew from here in 1968 but since then the former airport has been taken over for various purposes, including broiler houses, go-cart racing and a road transport training centre. One of the runways has been used as the base of a new road across the site. The two 'T1's and two 'T2' hangars of the war period are long gone. From an aircraft climbing out of Aldergrove Airport, Nutt's Corner's runways look operational and all the diamond hardstandings are intact. It is only when one gets closer that the numerous obstructions can be discerned.

Oban, Strathclyde
49/NM855300. Oban Bay

The first recorded use of Oban Bay by a flying boat took place in 1933 when a Saro Cloud of British Flying Boats Ltd brought passengers from the Isle of Man to see the Lochaber Games. The RAF too recognised Oban's potential as a base and began to use it in December 1937, although at first only as a convenient refuelling point on round-Britain cruises.

It was elevated to full station status when the war started. On October 7 1939, 209 Squadron's Stranraers were sent here from Invergordon for Atlantic patrols and in December the unit began to re-equip with Lerwicks. This twin-engined design was not a success, amongst its short-comings being an inability to maintain height on one engine. Two were lost in accidents before 209 moved to Pembroke Dock on July 16 1940. No 10 Squadron Royal Australian Air Force was also at Oban in 1941, flying Sunderlands and using Lochboisdale on South Uist as an emergency diversion.

No 210 Squadron moved in on July 13 1940 to operate Sunderlands, converting to Catalinas in April 1941 and transferring to Sullom Voe on February 28 1942. Whilst at Oban, one of its flights became the basis of 95 Squadron on January 15 1941 and moved to Pembroke Dock the next day.

On July 28 1941, Catalina *W8416* of 210 Squadron left Oban via Invergordon for Archangel on a mission of vital impor-tance. The squadron ORB does not identify the 'special passengers' but they were Harry Hopkins, President Roose-velt's personal representative to Europe and two USAAC officers. The trip's objective was to obtain for the President first hand information, till then not forth-coming from the Russians, from Stalin himself of the Russian war situation and the country's armament requirements.

In direct contrast, and perhaps epitomising Britain's role as the sole bastion of civilisation at that time, it is reassuring to note that a Catalina was allotted to Professor Julian Huxley on August 31 for a trip to St Kilda and round the Western Isles to make observations of bird life.

More Sunderlands, this time from 228 Squadron, arrived in March 1942 for patrols, leaving for Pembroke Dock in December. The Norwegian 330 Squadron brought its Catalina IIIs in towards the end of January 1943 but soon gave them up in favour of Sunderlands. The initial operational sortie on the new type was flown on April 20 and on June 7 Crown Prince Olav of Norway inspected a parade of squadron personnel. A few days later two of the unit's obsolete Northrop N-3PBs were flown over from Reykjavik for dismantling at Oban and storage until the end of hostilities. No 330 Squadron left for Sullom Voe on July 12 1943.

No 422 Squadron's Sunderlands were also based from November 1942 to May 1943 working up for operations. They had been preceeded by 423 Squadron, which had formed at Oban on May 18 1942 to fly

Sunderlands. It became operational in August and moved to Castle Archdale in November 1942.

An advance party of 302 FTU arrived from Stranraer on July 9 1943, followed by four Catalinas on July 21. The FTU eventually specialised in Sunderland training and absorbed 308 FTU on January 14 1944. The unit flew many thousands of hours from here until it moved to Killadeas on April 16 1945.

Going back to October 20 1943, 524 Squadron formed on this date at Oban for the purpose of gaining experience with the Martin Mariner. Although the type was to be used with some success by the US Navy after the war, it was found unsuitable for RAF service, partly because of its poor single-engine performance, and the squadron disbanded on December 7 1943.

Oban was reduced to Care and Maintenance on April 28 1945 and little remains to remind one of the flying boats once moored off Kerrera Island where the bomb dumps can still be seen. The crews used to be billeted in hostels in the town and maintenance was done at Ganavan Sands *(NM862328)* at which the old slip-way and steel door runners of the hangar betray the site.

Ouston, Northumberland

88/NZ080700. Just N of B6318 at Harrow Hill

In late 1938, a small group of civilian officials gathered on a Northumbrian hill as a result of receiving a secret signal sent by the Air Ministry in distant London stating that an airfield site was projected at Ouston. An earlier glance at the map had shown two Oustons—one a few miles south-west of Hexham and the other, a hamlet set in a wild moorland area 12 miles west of Newcastle and north of the Roman Road to Carlisle. Only two farm houses braved the blast of the elements there to form a pocket-sized parish. The south-westerly Ouston seemed clearly indicated but the chagrin of the officials was tempered with incredulity when it was realised that it was, indeed, the wild improbable site that was intended. Never-theless, some of the officials went to the other Ouston first.

Construction work proceeded slowly because of the inaccessibility of the area and some opposition from agricultural interests, although the land at Ouston was hardly of the first quality. The station was built to a fairly regular pattern, having a

A Spitfire (P9448 FD-P *of 81 Squadron) in dire trouble at Ouston on February 7 1942* (Via J. Huggon).

mixture of pre-war-style buildings and the utility types which came later. A 'J' Type hangar dominated the airfield, the control tower being located in front of it.

Ouston opened on March 10 1941 as a Fighter Sector HQ under 13 Group to replace Usworth, its staff being drawn mainly from that station. Its first squadron was 317, which moved over from Acklington at the end of April. Equipped with Hurricanes, this recently-formed Polish unit claimed its first kill on June 2 when a Ju 88 was sent into the North Sea. Relieved by 122 Squadron from Turnhouse on June 26 1941, 317 went to Colerne.

No 122 Squadron's Spitfires transferred to Catterick in August 1941, leaving 232, which had been here since the previous month, and which eventually left for the Middle East in November. Another squadron, 131, re-formed at Ouston on June 30 1941 with a large proportion of Belgian pilots but soon moved to Catterick.

Another squadron which did not fire its guns in anger whilst at Ouston was No 81 which moved in from Turnhouse early in 1942. Its Spitfires returned to Edinburgh five weeks later and a further month was

Another pranged Spitfire at Ouston, this time around 1947 (J. Harris).

spent at Ouston during the early summer.

Throughout its first year of existence, the station had also served as a satellite for 55 OTU's Hurricanes from Usworth but was given up when the OTU moved to Annan at the end of April 1942.

No 242 Squadron was here for two weeks in May 1942 with Spitfires, being replaced by the re-formed 243 Squadron on June 1. No 243 became operational within a fortnight and flew coastal patrols and scrambles in defence of the north-east until moving to Turnhouse at the beginning of September. No 72 Squadron appeared briefly in the autumn of 1942 to re-equip before overseas posting.

To cover the need for ASR off the east coast, 281 Squadron had been formed at Ouston on March 29 1942, equipped initially with Defiants. In February 1943, Walrus amphibians were added and by June, when the squadron moved to Woolsington, the Defiants had been replaced by Ansons.

Also in 1942, a flight of 410 Squadron was detached here for night-fighter patrol. Defiants were used first, but, despite some reluctance on the part of the crews, a change was made to Beaufighters.

An Army co-operation squadron, No 613, arrived in August 1942 flying Mustang Is and took part in many local exercises before going south again at the beginning of March 1943. It was joined for a short period in August by 226 Squadron's Bostons, which had the misfortune to lose three aircraft in crashes on their first day at Ouston. Other

Chipmunk WG470 at Ouston in March 1962 with 'J' Type hangar beyond (J. Harris).

unusual lodgers were the Hurricanes of 804 Squadron which flew in from Macrihanish on June 3 1943 and left for Twatt on February 4.

Austers appeared on January 31 1943, when 657 Squadron formed at Ouston, flying many Army exercises until leaving for North Africa in August. No 198 Squadron flew its Typhoons in from Digby late in January 1943 but soon transferred to Acklington to complete its working-up period on the new type.

Ouston's last operational squadron was No 350, which spent most of June and July 1943 flying monotonous convoy patrols before returning to Acklington. On June 21 1943, 62 OTU began to move in from Usworth, which had been found increasingly unsuitable for its work. The unit continued to train radar operators for the night-fighter force until disbanding on June 6 1945. Ansons were used at first but in the final months Wellingtons began to replace them.

No 80 OTU which specialised in training French pilots on Spitfires came over from Morpeth in July 1945 and flew from here prior to disbandment on March 8 1946. The Harvards of 22 SFTS were displaced from Calveley in Cheshire to Ouston in May 1946 but the school soon disbanded.

Under the Royal Auxiliary Air Force, 607 Squadron re-formed with Spitfires on May 10 1946, converted to Vampires in 1951 and operated them up to March 1957 when it disbanded. No 1965 Flight of 664 Squadron was also based in 1953 with Austers.

Continuing in a reserve role, the station housed Durham UAS, 11 AEF, 641 Gliding School and was employed as an RLG by the Jet Provosts of 6 FTS Acklington. In 1967 it became the North East Regional Airport for five months while Newcastle's runway was being lengthened and renovated. Today Ouston is occupied by the Army and known as Albemarle Barracks.

Perth, Tayside

58/NO155285. 4 miles NE of Perth on A94

The aerodrome known locally as Scone has been associated with pilot training for almost 50 years. The first school established here was 11 E & RFS operated by Airwork Limited from January 27 1936. Tutors, Harts and Battles were flown at first but after the unit was re-designated 11 EFTS on September 3 1939 it standardised on Tiger Moths.

The airfield was opened officially on June 5 1936 by Lord Swinton, the Secretary of State for Air, and was managed by Airwork on behalf of Perth Corporation. The company also ran 7 CANS which opened on January 9 1939 at Perth with Ansons, being renamed 7 AONS on November 1 of that year. Both schools were run by civilians, but on January 1 1940 all the flying instructors were mobilised.

To allow for further expansion of the training programme, an ELG was opened at Scone Park and an RLG at Whitefield. The establishment of Tiger Moths was also increased from 72 to 90 at the end of December 1940.

A detachment of 6 AACU had been operating from Perth since May 2 1940 and in November and December other lodgers were a small detachment of 44 MU Edzell ferrying in non-operational wooden types of aircraft for temporary storage. This was a stop-gap until SLGs became available, the aircraft involved being mainly Proctors. A further short-term use was made early in 1941, by one flight at a time of 309 Squadron from Renfrew, for essential training, including night-flying, pending completion of their new base at Findo Gask. No 5 FIS was also at Perth in 1942/43 flying Tiger Moths and a few Masters.

Joint user of the aerodrome in the early war days was British Airways, which began a Perth-Stavanger service on September 4 1939. Dyce was sometimes used as the Scottish terminus for the Lockheed 14s. From Stavanger in November 1939 there started a joint Norwegian-Swedish service using Swedish-registered

Ju 52s. The routes were suspended in April 1940 when the Germans invaded Norway and Denmark.

No 11 EFTS was so busy turning out scores of pilots for onward postings to AFUs that its records make dull reading. The system was literally a conveyor belt with targets of trained pilots fluctuating mainly according to the demands of the bomber offensive. The fickle Scottish weather often delayed the output and there were the inevitable accidents.

On August 14 1942, for example, a Tiger got into a flat spin and both occupants baled out after futile attempts to recover. Again on October 6 1942, the pilot and instructor abandoned a Tiger over Methven when the port wing failed during aerobatics, a rare occurrence on this type.

Pre-AFU courses were begun in March 1945 to acclimatise Dominion-trained aircrew to the vagaries of British weather and geography. As the war drew to a close UAS courses were restarted and in October 1945 seven officers of the rejuvenated Danish Air Force arrived for 20 hours elementary flying training. Pupil strength in December 1945 was 135 but the hectic activity of previous years, with flying went on 24 hours a day, except Thursday and Saturday nights, was no longer apparent or needed.

The school became 11 RFS on March 11 1947, still operating the faithful Tiger Moth. No 666 Squadron formed here on May 1 1949 with Austers and by 1953, No 1966 AOP Flight and the Squadron HQ were in Perth. No 11 RFS was one of the longest surviving of these units, finally disbanding on June 20 1954, by which time it had re-equipped with Chipmunks.

Airwork Services eventually bought the airfield outright from the local council and carried on the tradition of pilot training. As well as providing comprehensive courses for professional and private pilots, Air Service Training Perth, as the School is now known, also trains ground engineers. So good is ASTs reputation that over 40 overseas airlines have sent students here. To cope with the large number of aircraft movements two asphalt runways were laid in 1969.

Peterhead, Grampian

30/NK080470. 4 miles W of Peterhead on A950

On the morning of November 30 1941, a single Ju 88 made a surprise low attack, dropping two bombs and machine-gunning the aerodrome. A Spitfire was damaged, a Flight Lieutenant was killed and three airmen slightly injured. Both the officer and aircraft belonged to 416 Squadron, which had formed here on November 18.

Thus was the war brought home to the newly completed airfield known locally as Longside. It had been occupied somewhat prematurely since July 1941, at which time it was reported that work was proceeding very slowly and that during wet weather the workmen could not be induced to carry on. The living sites were unfinished and all personnel had to be billeted in Peterhead.

No 143 Squadron had re-formed here on July 7 1941 with Spitfires, becoming operational on July 19 for air defence patrols despite the fact that one of the three runways was not yet available and only two thirds of the perimeter track was built. This squadron left for Skeabrae on February 15 1942, having shared the station with the Hurricanes of 883 Squadron since January 31. The latter flew to Macrihanish on May 11 preparatory to embarkation on a carrier. No 416 Squadron, the other occupant, left for the

RAF Peterhead in April 1943 with dispersal pens showing prominently (RAF Museum).

south of England in June 1942, having encountered only one enemy aircraft but being unable to claim it.

Another FAA squadron in the shape of 802 from St Merryn was attached from May 1942, its place being taken by seven Fulmars of 884 Squadron from Turnhouse on July 6. It was hoped to celebrate Peterhead's first anniversary by 'shooting up a Hun' but, alas, every contact turned out to be friendly. The next day Fulmars of 884 on convoy protection chased a Ju 88 but it showed them a clean pair of heels.

Six more Fulmars, this time from 886 Squadron, arrived on August 13 1942 but this obsolete type was of little use against fast aircraft like the Ju 88. A regular reconnaissance flight, known to the RAF as 'Weather Willie', was stalked on several occasions but it was many weeks before one of these aircraft fell to the guns of two Beaufighters of 125 Squadron 130 miles east of Stonehaven. Later in the war, when the codes had been cracked, the RAF made good use of the weather information so gained and fighter pilots were forbidden to fire on the met aircraft. Mock interceptions were made from time to time, however, so as not to invite suspicion.

Another new fighter squadron formed at Peterhead on April 6 1942, No 164 with Spitfires. They worked-up for a few weeks and went to Skeabrae on May 4. The unit returned for two further short periods in 1942 before it went to Fairwood Common to convert to Hurricane IVs at the end of January 1943. No 602 Squadron was also detached here twice in 1942 with Spitfires.

Typhoons appeared on January 29

Demolished remains of Peterhead's watch office, a 518/40 type.

1943, flown by 245 Squadron, who were converting from Hurricanes at this time. They left for Gravesend on March 31 and were replaced by the Spitfires of 165 Squadron, which flew routine convoy protection until a move to Ibsley in July 1943. The next squadron for a rest period was No 313 and its Spitfires duly flew up from Devon at the end of June, leaving for Hawkinge towards the end of August.

Apart from fighter squadrons, the airfield hosted several other units on a lodger basis. In February 1942, for example, Masters and Hurricanes from 8 SFTS at Montrose practised circuits and bumps and an Autogyro did some flying for an unspecified purpose. No 1479 AAC Flight was available for target towing work with Defiants and Oxfords, using Fraserburgh as well. This flight, by now operating Martinets instead of Defiants, disbanded on December 1 1943 to form part of 598 Squadron under a reorganisation of the AA co-operation resources of 70 Group. The new squadron was tasked with providing co-operation for certain defended areas in the north of Scotland and the Islands. There was also an Anson and Walrus detachment from 282 Squadron.

From about September 1942, the aerodrome was used by 2 FIS because that unit's satellite at Stracathro was unserviceable. The detachment returned there on May 25 1943, when the field dried out. In July 1943, Spitfires of 556 OTU Squadron from Kinnell made the first of many visits

Spitfire of 164 Squadron rests in the snow at Peterhead 1942 (R.E.G. Sheward, via C.H. Thomas).

under Peterhead Sector Control for convoy escort.

In mid-1942 Bomber Command was looking for advanced bases from which to attack German capital ships in Norwegian waters. Peterhead was one of the airfields it had in mind and was earmarked for 50 Squadron's Lancasters. The USAAF too was offered facilities here when the airfield was brought up to the standard required. It was anticipated that up to 12 heavy bombers from either force would be accommodated, all controlled from the operations block at Lossiemouth. However there was a snag; extending the runways would be impracticable except over a long period, so Peterhead was only to be used by bombers if absolutely necessary. Its temporary commitment was taken over by Milltown when the latter was completed in mid-1943.

Peterhead played its part in Operation *Tyndall* in the summer and autumn of 1943 when 100 tents were erected to simulate an army camp. Twenty dummy Boston aircraft were displayed, being dismantled at night and covered with nets to give an illusion next morning to enemy reconnaissance aircraft that they were being flown in and out. Two real Bostons were also kept here to 'show life'.

Returning to its original fighter role, the station was occupied by 118 Squadron's Spitfires from September 20 to October 19 and this unit was to be back in August 1944 for a second short stay. No 504

Squadron spent a longer time here than was customary (October 1943 to January 1944) but saw no action before joining the Hornchurch Wing.

No 129 Squadron in turn left Hornchurch for Peterhead and stayed until March 16, its place being taken by 350 Squadron's Spitfires, which moved to Friston towards the end of April 1944. A detachment of 278 ASR Squadron was based in the early spring of 1944 but soon moved back to covering the East Anglian coast. There was also a short stay by 899 Squadron Seafires in June/July 1944.

One of 350 Squadron's pilots, Sergeant M.J. Morel, was involved in an unpleasant ordeal on March 21 1944. Just off the Aberdeen coast, the engine of his Spitfire failed, and, unable to reach land, he decided to bale out rather than ditch. Unfortunately the cockpit hood jammed so he had to ditch anyway. Sinking with the aircraft, he managed to break out despite the drag of his parachute, which his struggles had accidentally released. This incredible balance of luck and misfortune continued when he was immediately picked up by a fishing boat!

No 309 Squadron's Mustangs flew from Peterhead in November/December 1944, not for the first time, as the unit had occasionally detached sections of aircraft here since January 1943. Other Mustangs at Peterhead marked a new role in its short history, that of long range escort to the Coastal Strike Wings at Banff and Dallachy. No 315 was the first on November 1 1944, moving to Andrews Field in mid-January 1945. It was replaced by 65 Squadron which was to fly many sorties from here until May 6 1945.

Another Mustang squadron, No 19, was also present from February 13 until it moved to Acklington on May 23.

Peterhead's last operational units carried on the duty of escort out to the Norway coast with Mustangs until the war ended. They were 122 and 234 Squadrons which both moved to Dyce on July 3 and 611 Squadron which disbanded here on August 15 1945.

No 598 Squadron had already departed to East Anglia on March 12 1945, a farewell party being held at the Royal Hotel in Peterhead. It had taken some days to assemble all the aircraft from the far-flung detachments at Sumburgh and Skeabrae. The airfield was soon closed and was eventually auctioned in September 1959. It was reopened in 1975 for helicopter operations and improved so that fixed-wing flying could begin in 1977.

North Scottish Helicopters has built a hangar on the northern side of the airfield. The wartime main site is fenced off from the active part but easily accessible and used for pipeline storage. The control tower, a 518/40 type, has been demolished, but since the rubble still lies there it must have been for practical rather than aesthetic reasons, ie, an obstruction to helicopter flying. Of the 12 dispersal pens and eight Blister hangars around the perimeter there is no trace. The old Battle HQ is in a field across the road south of the airfield and the operations block can be found about two miles down the road towards the town.

Port Ellen, Strathclyde

60/NR325515. 4 miles NNW of Port Ellen on A846

This airfield, also known less frequently as Glenegedale or Islay, was opened as early as August 1940, but throughout its wartime career never had a definite role. It was, however, strategically placed to accept lost aircraft and those in emergency in a district singularly lacking in landing facilities. One of the first strays was probably an Anson of 48 Squadron from Aldergrove, which put down with engine trouble on September 19 1940. A detachment of the same squadron was based here in later months.

In 1941, it was decided to construct three runways in the special sand mix and bitumen reserved for boggy and ill-drained land when better ground was unavailable. Hangars were built at the same time and the first runway was completed by July

1942. Dispersals were located along a road to the east of the airfield and in an old quarry.

The landing ground was used spasmodically whilst work was going on, but, on December 17 1941, a Hudson of 59 Squadron taxied into an unmarked peat bog and sank 6 ft. These areas had deliberately not been marked as this would tend to give away the aerodrome to aerial reconnaissance, so local flying orders were hastily amended to ensure that aircraft would not taxi off the runways or perimeter track without instructions from the duty pilot.

Many naval aircraft from Macrihanish, mainly Swordfish but sometimes Blackburn Rocs, began to visit Port Ellen in July 1942 but a bigger arrival on September 9 1942 was Liberator *41-11874* with an oil leak. It was escorted by six Lightnings, all of which had taken off from Stornoway.

One of Port Ellen's few based units was 304 FTU which formed here on February 5 1943. Seven Beaufighter crews flew their aircraft in from the OAPU at Filton. The function of the FTU was to prepare Beaufighter (and a few Beaufort) crews from OTUs to navigate and fly their aircraft on long ferry trips overseas. The course was only two weeks but they made extended training flights out over the Atlantic and in the process discovered the exact fuel consumption of the new aircraft. This could vary markedly between identical types. The crews also flew searches for missing aircraft, both from their own unit and others.

No 304 FTU suffered a fairly high accident rate, surrounding hills, bad weather, inexperience and the Beaufighter's tricky handling characteristics all contributing. September 9 1943 was the worst night when three Beaufighters were written off. One crashed on rising ground just after take-off, a second also flew into the hills, perhaps because he was watching the first burning on the ground, and a third made a very heavy landing and burst into flames. Prompt action by the station fire party saved the crew.

No 304 FTU was to absorb 306 and 307 FTUs on January 15 1944 but a week before this actually happened it was transferred to Melton Mowbray. The airfield, which by then had acquired a control tower and bomb dumps, was now put on Care and Maintenance. It still performed its duties as ELG and many aircraft continued to make routine visits as well. One diversion ended in disaster for Stirling *LJ529*. The captain requested homing on *Darkie* with one engine out of action but crashed on the south-east corner of the aerodrome.

A happier fate befell a USAAF Liberator which had missed Valley in Wales after the long flight from Marrakesh on April 10 1944. He landed safely and, ten days later, an Anson just got in with only 5 gallons of petrol left in the tanks!

FAA aircraft from Macrihanish often found Port Ellen a useful diversion field, but distinctly unusual was a rare JT-serialled Dauntless forced down by bad weather whilst in transit from Wick to Prestwick on June 1 1944. On May 13 1945, Corsair *JS714* got lost on a local trip out of Eglinton and was looking for somewhere to land when he spotted Port Ellen. This was rather ironical as the latter was once nominated as a Fighter Command forward airfield for Eglinton but seems never to have been used for this purpose.

In 1945, a detachment of Mosquitoes from the MAEE used the airfield as a base for weapon dropping trials until June 21. They returned on September 21, one Mosquito, a *Highball* conversion, being lost in an accident on October 25. The last Mosquito left for Wisley on November 13 1945.

The airfield passed to the MoA in 1947, scheduled services being operated to Campbeltown and Glasgow by BEA, later BA, and then transferred to Loganair in 1977. A few years ago, some fragments from a Beaufighter crash and cannon shells were found on the airport. The original tower is still in use and the operations block has been turned into offices.

Bristol 'Britain First' prototype with Anson and Tiger Moths at Prestwick circa 1938.

Prestwick, Strathclyde

70/NS365270. 1 mile N of Prestwick town on A 79

'Captain E.P.M. Eves walked across to the duty pilot's office to report. Answering routine questions, he said that he had come from Gander after a flight of 10 hours 45 minutes. "That seems a long way off," remarked the duty pilot. "Where is it that you've come from?" Then it dawned upon him that the captain had flown the Atlantic. Other captains later noticed the good weather for landing at Prestwick and for this and other reasons the Atlantic Ferry's eastern terminal was officially transferred to that airfield.'

This extract from *Merchant Airmen*, the official Air Ministry account of civil aviation during the Second World War, relates how Prestwick Airport (opened as a grass field on February 17 1936 by the Marquis of Clydesdale and the late Group Captain D.F. McIntyre) became a trans-atlantic terminal in 1941. A 6,600 ft runway was built in that year and a second 4,500 ft strip was added in 1942, along with extensive new apron areas. The circuits of Prestwick and RAF Ayr over-lapped, which required some care, and the outer circles of the Drem lighting systems were joined.

Going back to the early days, 12 E & RFTS formed here on the official opening date. It was operated by Scottish Aviation Ltd and flew Tiger Moths and Harts. It became 12 EFTS on September 3 1939, by which time Ansons and Battles were also in service. SAL formed 1 CANS on August 15 1938 with Ansons, a unit which was re-designated 1 AONS on November 1 1939. Three ex-KLM Fokker airliners (F.22s and an F.36) were also used as flying class-rooms until the school closed down on July 19 1941. (No 12 EFTS had already disbanded on March 22 1941.)

Pending the construction of RAF Ayr, fighter squadrons were based at Prestwick, beginning with 603 Squadron from Turn-

Above *SC-54D Searchmaster O-72624 of 67th Air Rescue Squadron just airborne from Prestwick, Easter 1964.*

Below *C-118 Liftmaster 53-3261 about to unstick from Runway 13 at Prestwick, Easter 1964.*

Above *Anson N9739 at Prestwick 1941* (R.D. Cooling).

Below *Shell of Prestwick's pre-war HQ and clubhouse after it caught fire one afternoon in 1941* (R.D. Cooling).

house on December 16 1939, some of whose Spitfires were also detached to Dyce and Montrose. They moved to Drem on April 14 1940. More Spitfires, this time from 610 Squadron spent a month here before going south to Biggin Hill on May 10 1940.

An intimation of what the air was like in the South reached Prestwick when the remnants of the mauled 141 Squadron were withdrawn here on July 21 1940. The Squadron had just lost six out of nine Defiants in a battle with Bf 109s over the Channel and the defencelessness of the type against single-seat fighters had now become evident. The unit left for Turnhouse on August 30 1940. Other refugees included airliners from Croydon and 253 Squadron's Hurricanes stayed for five days before flying to Kenley on August 29 to relieve 615 Squadron, which then withdrew to Prestwick for a rest.

The Whitleys of 102 Squadron flew in from Leeming on September 1 1940 on loan to Coastal Command for convoy escort duties until October, before resuming bombing operations from Yorkshire. Another Coastal unit, 1 OTU at Silloth based a Blenheim detachment here from August 9 to November 1 1940.

No 615 Squadron left for Northolt in October 1940, the next fighter squadron posted in being 602, from Westhampnett, in December. No 1 (Canadian) Squadron flew Hurricanes from Prestwick late in 1940 before transferring to Castletown on December 8. On April 15 1941, soon after Ayr opened, 602 Squadron went there. No 3 Radio School was a lodger with Bothas and part of its role was to teach AI interception. The school moved to Hooton Park, Cheshire at the end of 1942.

Despite all this varied activity, Prestwick will be remembered chiefly as a transatlantic ferry base through which were delivered many thousands of American- and Canadian-built aircraft. ATFERO (the Atlantic Ferry Organisation) was set up by MAP and administered by BOAC. The first steps towards its creation were taken by the Canadian Pacific Railway and Canadian Pacific Air Service. To inaugurate the ferry a number of British airline pilots went to Canada and many Canadian radio operators volunteered their services. The first aircraft to be flown across the Atlantic—Hudsons—left Gander in Newfoundland on November 10 1940 and arrived in Northern Ireland on Armistice Day. Thereafter most flights made Prestwick their terminus.

A Return Ferry Service was organised with Liberators to fly the crews back for more aircraft. These operated mainly from nearby Ayr. As the volume of traffic grew ATFERO was transferred to the control of RAF Ferry Command in July 1941. A mixture of civilian and service personnel continued to work together both in the air and on the ground and in March 1943 the newly-established RAF Transport Command absorbed Ferry Command.

Atlantic Ferry reduced the time taken for delivery of aircraft from the Canadian and American factories from at least three months to just a few days and saved a lot of shipping space. Up to the end of the war, some 37,000 aircraft would be delivered via Prestwick and the experience built up was invaluable when airline services began in the immediate post-war period. Trans-Canada Airlines' service, for example, stemmed directly from its Lancaster run which started on July 22 1943 from Dorval via Montreal to Prestwick with mail for Canadian servicemen and other freight.

Hudsons, Liberators, Fortresses, Dakotas, Mitchells and Canadian-built Mosquitoes and Lancasters formed the majority of the movements. The first Mosquito was delivered on August 8 1943 and made the Gander/Prestwick trip in 5 hours 37 minutes, then a record. On July 1 1942 the first B-17 (assigned to the 97th BG) landed in Scotland. This was the first of 12,357 aircraft for the US 8th Air Force (mostly flown by their own combat crews) which passed through. In 1944 a detachment of the 311th Ferrying Squadron was on hand to assist with onward delivery to the depots.

The peak month for aircraft movements was August 1944, when 7,847 were logged. The USAAF's Air Transport Command operated its own scheduled services using the new C-54 Skymasters. A detachment of the RCAF's 168 Heavy Transport Squadron began to operate Fortresses early in 1944 on mail runs. The USAAF, too, ran a schedule for the US Postal Service for a few months in 1944 flying transit mail in C-47s to Lichfield.

A major innovation after D-day was the rapid evacuation of casualties from the Continent straight back to the USA via C-47s from forward airstrips and onward from Prestwick in C-54s.

Prestwick was one of the few UK airfields with a radio range facility for letting down through cloud, the descent leg being to the south-west over the sea, clear of the mountainous Isle of Arran. One approach, however, ended in tragedy on August 28 1944, when a C-54 trying to do a low visual circuit at night missed the control tower by 30 ft. It then struck a wireless mast and crashed into Hillside Avenue. Five civilians were killed along with the 20 occupants of the aircraft.

As late as July 1945, aircraft were still being delivered in quantity, some 55 Dakotas passing through in that month. In August, ten Soviet naval Cansos made a refuelling stop en route from Elizabeth City, New Jersey to Kolberg. They were not, however, Prestwick's first Russian visitors—a number of TB-7s had landed during the war. During the same period, 41 Liberators landed from Nassau on the move of 111 OTU to its new base at Milltown.

On September 17 1945, 24 Squadron, which had run a shuttle service to Hendon for some years, began an all-weather run to Blackbushe with Dakotas, once daily in each direction.

Somewhat overshadowed by the glamour of transatlantic flying, 4 FPP of ATA had been based here since September 1940 and slipped into oblivion on October 31 1945. Its early days had been marked by the bizarre HQ which consisted of a derelict motor coach weather-proofed and divided into tiny offices. (Prestwick was not unaccustomed to improvisation—a temporary fighter operations room under the Turnhouse Sector was set up in the attic of a water mill on the fringe of the aerodrome in January 1941!) The Ferry Pool later added a Grumman Martlet packing case with door and windows cut out. Expansion had begun! It was years before a proper brick building was built for them but the lack of facilities made no difference to the vital work carried out.

September 1945 saw the departure of the USAAF support units and a significant reduction in aircraft movements. On October 22, the first post-war flight by a commercial aircraft was made by a Skymaster of American Export Airlines from New York to Prestwick via Labrador and Iceland. Stop-gap Liberators and Lancasters were soon replaced by DC-4s and Constellations, as BOAC, KLM, TCA, SAS and other airlines began regular transatlantic services through the airport which had been transferred to State ownership on April 1 1946.

SAL had prospered during the war years, many of the aircraft passing through

being modified or given pre-acceptance checks on behalf of the RAF. Components were manufactured and a batch of 50 Queen Bee target aircraft was assembled in 1943/44. The 'Palace of Engineering' was moved from its original site at Bellahouston, Glasgow in 1941 and re-erected at Prestwick, where it still stands today. More hangarage was built alongside, including 'A1's and 'R'-Types and after the war ended SAL was well placed to convert and overhaul ex-military C-47s and C-54s for the civil market, soon becoming the official Douglas overhaul centre for Great Britain. Over 300 transports were civilianised by SAL and many refurbished for the re-emerging European air forces.

SAL went on to design and build the Pioneer and Twin-Pioneer utility transports. A total of 59 Pioneers and 87 Twin-Pioneers had been completed when production ceased in 1962. The Company's ability to use its capacity to the best advantage in lean times brought contracts ranging from the overhaul of RCAF T-33s, CF100s and CF104s to the conversion of Convair 240s to turbo-prop propulsion. In the early '70s Bulldog and Jetstream production was taken over when the respective parent companies failed.

Although Scottish Airways fell beside the wayside after starting services to Belfast, Denmark and Iceland with Liberators and Dakotas, most of the other operators through Prestwick progressed through Stratocruisers, DC-7s, Super Constellations and Britannias to jets. The North Atlantic ferry route continued to be used by military aircraft en route to the USAF's European bases. The reverse direction saw the delivery of Doves, Herons, Viscounts and other British types to North America.

The USAF base was reactivated in 1951 to provide support for MATS and other military aircraft flying between the USA and Europe and to provide rescue coverage over the Atlantic. The subsidiary runway was closed to enable a huge parking apron to be constructed. The main 13/31 runway was lengthened by stages to 2,987 metres and an entirely new cross runway added which encroached upon the former RAF Ayr.

In the mid-'60s a modern terminal and tower were built and the old hotel with the tower on its roof and surrounding hut complex were pulled down. The 67th ARS left for Spain in 1966 and the former American site became HMS *Gannet* on

November 23 1971 for 819 Squadron's Sea Kings.

Amongst its many claims to fame, Prestwick saw the only glider crossing of the Atlantic made by an RAF Hadrian towed by a Dakota. It took place in July 1943 but was deemed to be too chancy an operation to become routine. On October 3 1949, two Thunderjets completed the USAF's first transatlantic jet ferry flight and on July 31 1951, two Sikorsky H-19s landed after the first helicopter crossing, having been escorted by a C-47 and an Albatross amphibian.

Raploch (Stirling), Central Region

See Stirling

Rattray (Crimond), Grampian

30/NK070580. Just N of A952 at Crimond

This airfield was almost unique in that the site was discovered by the Admiralty independently of the Air Ministry Aerodromes Board which was responsible for choosing sites for both services. It stemmed directly from the wrangle over Dallachy (qv), a station which was totally unsuitable for naval requirements. However, the RAF still tried to foist it upon them. The new airfield was known initially as Crimond after the neighbouring village but was later renamed Rattray, after a local headland.

In September 1942, an Admiralty Planning Officer was moved to write: 'It is imperative to the national interests that naval requirements for air stations and facilities should be treated on their merits and given equal consideration with RAF requirements, irrespective of the fact that the RAF, being first in the field, have earmarked all suitable facilities. The present system, whereby the Royal Navy has to

Barracuda ME248 flying from Rattray in 1945 (Via R.C. Sturtivant).

adapt itself to sites which the RAF with its wider scope of interests has found of no value can but lead to naval and national disaster.'

After Dallachy was turned down in September 1942, the Navy decided to build its own Observer School to be ready, hopefully, by September 1943 with Arbroath being used in the interim. A promising site was found at Crimond but letting the contract took time and work was not begun until March 1943. It was built in the standard Navy style with four runways but took so long to complete that it was not commissioned until October 3 1944 as HMS *Merganser*. No 774 Squadron however had already been here since the previous July for TAG training.

Events had overtaken the need for a new Observer School so the airfield became host to several Barracuda training units. No 774 was the first, disbanding in August 1945. No 714 Squadron moved in from Fearn in May 1944 for TBR training, followed by 717 in November in a similar role.

Their task was to take batches of young pilots who had just gained their wings after little more than a 100 hours in the air, and teach them to fly operational aircraft. The course included formation flying, dive-bombing, low-level bombing, navigation exercises and night landings. Torpedo and deck landing training would follow at other units and most of the graduates were destined for the Pacific if the war lasted long enough.

The Barracuda was an unpopular aircraft with characteristics which did not allow for any mishandling. Fatal accidents were frequent, four Barracudas being wrecked on one occasion when another trying to land in mist hit the tower aerials and ploughed into the aircraft park.

Two first-line Barracuda squadrons reformed at Rattray in 1945, 817 on April 1 and 818 on May 1, moving away on April 27 and June 26 respectively. There was also 753 Squadron from Arbroath on October 15 1945, operating a variety of

Pentad Hangar at Rattray.

types for observer training until it disbanded the following August, and 766 Squadron with Fireflies and Seafires from January 20 to August 13 1946, when it left for Lossiemouth. The RNAS then closed on September 1 1946 and went to Care and Maintenance.

Today Rattray is covered with 900 ft radio masts but vestiges of the old airfield are still discernible. The guardroom is derelict, one 'S' shed survives but the tower has now gone. Much of the hangarage was in dispersals to the north of the field towards Loch of Strathbeg but it all seems to have gone now.

Renfrew, Strathclyde

64/NS505665. M8 motorway follows line of runway

From 1915, Renfrew was used for testing W. & J. Weir-built aircraft, including the FE 2b and DH 9. It also housed the Beardmore Flying School from 1915 to 1918 and 6 Aircraft Acceptance Park from 1918. The latter took delivery of aircraft built in the Clyde Valley by various contractors and shared accommodation in the Belfast hangars with 6 (Scottish) Aircraft Repair Depot.

The aerodrome lay dormant from 1919, but the following year it began to be used for private flying. On September 22 1920, the first King's Cup Air Race included a stop at Renfrew and in 1926 the Scottish Flying Club was formed. No 602, the first Scottish Auxiliary Air Force squadron,

The one and only Blackburn CA.15C, K4241, at Renfrew in the mid-1930s (Via S.G. Jones).

was formed here on September 15 1925, the first DH 9 being delivered from Henlow on October 7. Fairey Fawns joined the unit in October 1927, a type ideal for the awkward steep approaches into Renfrew necessitated by the surrounding houses. The Wapiti replaced the previous types in 1929 and in January 1933 the squadron moved to nearby Abbotsinch.

Thereafter, Renfrew was operated by the Scottish Flying Club on behalf of the local council and an excellent clubhouse was built with a control tower on top. A network of scheduled services linking Glasgow to England, the Western Isles and the North was soon built up. The operating companies included Northern and Scottish Airways, Railway Air Services and Midland and Scottish Air Ferries. The services were suspended when the war started but soon restarted on a reduced scale which was maintained until the end of hostilities.

No 309 Squadron began to fly Lysanders from Renfrew on November 6 1940 on army co-operation duties. The Polish pilots found the Scottish countryside very confusing because it was too full of woods, roads and railways. Another cause of alarming experiences was the fact that the throttle control worked in the opposite sense to that on Polish aircraft!

The airfield was found to be generally unsatisfactory, being too small, too near the Glasgow balloon barrage and often enveloped in industrial smoke. It was shared with Scottish Airways and Airwork which overtaxed the already boggy surface and allowed civilians to wander about at will. The landing ground was so undulating that bombs constantly dropped off the racks whilst the Lysanders were taxying. Detachments to Perth enabled essential training to be performed and on May 8 1941 the whole unit moved to Dunino so as to be nearer to the Polish Army camps.

In April 1942, 54 Spitfires were flown into Renfrew for loading on to the carrier USS *Wasp* in the adjacent docks. They were needed urgently for service on Malta but Abbotsinch was a morass and unlikely to dry out for days. Renfrew was considered too small for the operation of Spitfires but the ATA decided to try, as otherwise the ship would not be able to sail on schedule. All landed safely and went on to make a vital contribution to Malta's survival.

A few months later, another Spitfire came to grief at Renfrew when the pilot's trouser leg caught in a cockpit lever and he was unable to correct a swing on take off with rudder. The fighter struck the roof of a house and dropped into the street on the other side, the pilot being almost unharmed.

During 1942/43, the MAP built runways at Renfrew, Abbotsinch being used in the interim by Scottish Airways' services. Lockheed Overseas Corporation established a facility at Renfrew to assemble fighters shipped over from the USA and landed at King George V Dock, Shieldhall. The aircraft were mainly Lightnings and Mustangs. From December 1943, only partially dismantled machines brought over as deck cargo were handled, boxed aircraft being sent direct to the Base Air Depots for assembly.

After the war, BEA took over all the Renfrew services and the former Lockheed hangars became the maintenance base for their Scottish Division. Piecemeal expansion had left the airport in a state of chaos. SAL also had a base here for RCAF CF100 and F-86 overhauls between 1954 and 1960.

A new terminal building and control tower were opened on November 26 1954, the first State-built one since the end of the war. The airport was the base of the Scottish Air Ambulance Service operated by BEA with Rapides and later Herons and covering airports and airstrips

Wildcat at Renfrew, believed to be in 1944 (Via R.C. Sturtivant).

throughout the Highlands and Islands.

Only one mile separated the eastern boundary of Abbotsinch from the western edge of Renfrew and it was easy to mistake runway 08 at the latter with 06 at Abbotsinch. The problem was solved when Renfrew closed on May 2 1966, Abbotsinch opening the same day as the new Glasgow Airport. The main runway was incorporated into the M8 motorway and a large housing estate has now been built on the site.

St Angelo, Fermanagh

17/H230500. 3 miles N of Enniskillen on B82

One of the four sites intended for use by 23 MU Aldergrove, St Angelo opened in April 1941 as 18 SLG, runways being provided, it is said, because of the poor drainage. This did not escape the notice of the RAF, which was still short of airfields in Northern Ireland, and it was taken over in August 1941. It opened as a fighter sector station on September 15, remaining as such until October 1942. It was, however, only occupied by small sections of various squadrons such as 133 and 134 in an endeavour to intercept enemy reconnaissance aircraft off the west coast of Ireland.

On March 28 1942, two Defiants of 153 Squadron arrived for a short detachment from Ballykelly and it was then used as a Station HQ for 131 OTU at nearby Killadeas until accommodation was built at the latter. A satellite station at Lisnaskea was planned but never built, perhaps because the site was too close to the border.

In the meantime, various aircraft passed through, including a captured Bf 108 used by the RAF for liaison duties. The airfield was used regularly as a diversion on the transatlantic ferry route to Prestwick, the first visitor being a Hudson from Canada on May 4 1942. On June 17 Liberator *FK228* landed from Gander flown by Clyde E. Pangborne, a well-known American barnstorming pilot of the '30s. The occasional Mitchell arrived

from June onwards and many Venturas found a haven here.

American troops having arrived in the Province by this time, the station defence came under their jurisdiction in May 1942. The airfield was expected to become a CCRC for USAAF fighter pilots in 1942 but was never used for this purpose. It continued to serve no definite role in 1943, a rare highlight being glider dropping exercises in May with Whitleys, Albemarles and Horsas.

The transatlantic diversions went on as before, USAAF B-17s now appearing regularly and joined by one of the new C-54s on May 22. A 24 hour *Darkie* watch was maintained for lost aircraft and on May 28 five aircraft were homed into St Angelo, four of them short of fuel and one with engine trouble. Signal mortars were often employed to illuminate the airfield in bad weather.

St Angelo was transferred from the control of RAFNI to Coastal Command 17 Group as a satellite to Killadeas on August 4 1943. Lodgers between October 9 and 27 were the Swordfish of 824 Squadron. The airfield was now used by the TT and Comm Flight of 131 OTU whose flying boats operated from Killadeas. Fighter aircraft, including Spitfires, also spent time here for affiliation duties with the Sunderlands and Catalinas. A Beaufighter Squadron, 235, was here from February 21 until March 27 1944, when it returned to Portreath in Cornwall.

St Angelo finally found its own little niche in RAF history when 12 (Operational) Flying Instructors School formed on May 1 1944. It was designed to train ex-operational pilots for instructional duties at OTUs in Coastal Command and to familiarise them with the types of aircraft they would be required to fly as instructors. The syllabus was designed to ensure that the students could fly their aircraft with precision and confidence and thus their future pupils would learn by good example. It would also weed out pilots who were temperamentally unsuitable as instructors and teach those who were the art of imparting their knowledge to others.

The first month was spent in preparation, the aircraft being collected from various sources and consisting of four Wellingtons, eight Beaufort IIs and two Mosquito IIIs. The first course of 17 pilots was posted in during the middle of June for a stay of 24 days. In July it was decided that the FIS should take on the extra job of teaching flying boat instruc-

tors, the flying taking place from Killadeas in Sunderlands and Catalinas.

The school, redesignated Coastal Command Flying Instructors School on February 23 1945, maintained its valuable contribution to the training programme with little drama, apart from an accident on July 27 1944 when Mosquito *HJ887* suffered engine failure on take-off and overshot into the river at the end of the runway. The crew was unhurt but the wrecked aircraft had to be dragged out with a crane.

Just before the unit moved to Turnberry on June 8 1945, it received its first Bristol Buckmaster, a long-awaited type to replace the ancient Beauforts. On the last day, one of the latter beat up the mess at Killadeas as a farewell gesture. The airfield was then transferred to Maintenance Command on August 1 1945 to become a satellite of 272 MU at Killadeas. Before the MU disbanded on February 28 1947, 24 Ansons were stored and eventually broken up at St Angelo.

In the '60s the airfield was reopened by Fermanagh District Council and renamed Enniskillen. Only the 15/33 runway is kept in use, the other being bisected by a public road. The result is an extremely attractive little airfield and one can see why the two runways had to be built in an 'L' shape in plan view—this was the only layout the terrain would allow. Small hills rise on all sides and some interesting defence positions are built on them, consisting of pillboxes connected by a concrete zig-zag trench some 6 ft deep. The Battle HQ to 11008/41 design is on a hilltop and fighter pens in various states of disrepair are dotted around the perimeter track. The second runway is disused and occupied by a sawmill and military helicopter base.

Sandy Bay (Lough Neagh), Antrim

14/J115715. 2½ miles SW of Glenavy off B12

The largest lake in the United Kingdom was once the British terminal for a little-known regular service operated by Coronados of the US Naval Transport Service. It linked New York with Northern Ireland via Botwood in Newfoundland or Port Lyautey in North Africa, coming under the operational control of the US Navy Commodore at Londonderry. RAF Station Nutt's Corner supplied briefing and control facilities and looked after messing and accommodation for transit crews and permanent staff. Coastal Command provided buoys, moorings and local marine craft. The service began in May 1944, two aircraft arriving and departing each day from Sandy Bay. No less than ten Coronados arrived on May 23 but the schedule proved short-lived and ceased on October 15 1944.

Going back to the First World War, Lough Neagh was suggested by the Admiralty in May 1916 as a suitable site for an airship construction works as it was thought to be immune from enemy action. The plan was not proceded with, however, nor was a second proposal in 1917 for the building of a shed for non-rigid airships.

Like many similar stretches of sheltered water, the Lough had been used spasmodically by marine aircraft since well before the war but was never a proper flying-boat base. It had, for example, no night lighting and the proximity of Langford Lodge's circuit and the air firing and bombing ranges out in the Lough caused problems.

Coastal Command Squadrons frequently detached individual aircraft to Lough Neagh for APC under the control of Aldergrove. One such was Sunderland *DD858* of 423 Squadron, which landed heavily on October 23 1943 and overturned, injuring all seven of the crew.

As a footnote, it is of interest to record that Lough Neagh was the first bombing range where crews, usually from 1674 HCU at Aldergrove, could carry out low-level bombing at night, using radar homing and Leigh Light techniques and receive an accurate assessment of their errors.

Scatsta, Shetland

2/HU385725. Near Sullom Voe oil terminal beside B9076

The most northerly airfield in the British Isles was born out of the lack of a fighter station in the Shetlands, Sumburgh then being too small and even with extension thought unsuitable for Spitfires. It was expected that sites could be found in the islands

for 'strip aerodromes', ie, a site where two or three concrete runways could be laid irrespective of the ground between them and joined by taxiways. Scatsta was planned originally to have three runways but the third was abandoned because of labour shortage. A plan to cut dispersal pens into the peat was also dropped. It eventually served the dual purpose of Sumburgh satellite and landplane support base for the flying boat station at Sullom Voe. It was literally carved out of the Shetland coastline, the shorter of the two runways started at the base of an 800 ft hill, climbed a hill itself and then descended to the sea. Some 13 ft of peat had to be taken out during its construction.

The first aircraft to land was a Hornet Moth with a visiting Air Vice-Marshal on April 25 1940. Numerous communications flights and diversions followed, examples being a Blenheim of 59 Squadron on April 28 1941, a Hampden of 172 Squadron and a Whitley of 612 Squadron on November 6 1941. There was only one runway during this period, the second being built later.

In an effort to combat enemy reconnaissance aircraft, two Spitfires were detached to Scatsta at the end of January 1943, but appear to have been unsuccessful, as most of the uninvited guests came in at low level and gave the radar stations little or no warning.

Apart from a detachment of 282 Squadron with an Anson and Walrus on ASR stand-by, few aircraft movements are on record for 1943, but they include a Grumman Goose amphibian on August 9 and Harrow *A* of 271 Squadron from Hatston on August 21. October 1944, however, saw two Lancasters of 617 Squadron land on October 29 for fuel, having taken part in a raid on the *Tirpitz* at Tromso. Cloud had begun to cover the target just as the force arrived. Some

View from HS 748 on short final to Runway 24 at Scatsta. Terminal on disused runway to right (J.G. Smith).

Lancasters bombed blind, others brought back their 12,000 lb *Tallboy*, including one of those which arrived at Scatsta. Surprisingly, the pilot had no difficulty in landing and taking off again from the short runway with this heavy load.

The airfield was used also as a refuelling stop by Mosquitoes acting as photo reconnaissance support for the *Tirpitz* raids and by more Lancasters in November. From about September 1944, a Martinet target tug was detached from 3 APC at Leuchars until mid-1945 to give practice to Shetland units.

At the end of 1944, the station records list visits during the year by a wide variety of aircraft types, including the Barracuda, Mohawk, Corsair, Liberator, Ventura, Fulmar and Wellington. The only accident was a Dakota which made a heavy landing.

Examples of visitors in 1945 were a Barracuda of 703 Squadron in June which remained for a few days on radar exercises and Anson *NK730* from Lossiemouth on December 14.

Scatsta reverted to Care and Maintenance in 1946 but was re-activated in 1952 for Exercise *Mainbrace*. It was used mainly by Dakotas of 18 Group Comm Flight on a mail run linking Kinloss with Sullom Voe and Norway. At least one Anson, an Oxford ambulance and a Devon also called in.

The airfield was left to nature for many years, but in 1978 the operators of the Sullom Voe oil terminal obtained planning permission to restore it. One runway was resurfaced and a control tower built on the old north-south strip. It has since been used mainly by Dan-Air HS 748s and Loganair aircraft to take some of the load off Sumburgh. A C-130 Hercules landed on May 24 1969 in connection with the Loran monitor station which the US Coast Guard service had opened the previous year to serve its international chain of stations in northern Europe.

Skeabrae, Orkney

6/HY275205. On A967 7 miles N of Stromness

No 804 Squadron received an excellent Christmas present in 1940 when a Martlet patrol just airborne from Skeabrae after lunch sighted a Ju 88 over Scapa Flow. Lieutenant Carver and Sub-Lieutenant Parke chased it for some distance and managed to put an engine out of action. The German crew crash-landed in a field and were taken to Kirkwall for interro-

gation. The Martlet thus gained the distinction of being the first American fighter to destroy an enemy aircraft during the Second World War.

An advanced party of airmen first occupied the station on August 15 1940 and although the Battle of Britain skies over Southern England were blue, the far-off Orkneys were suffering almost incessant rainfall which the locals claimed was most unusual for the time of year. The RAF was sceptical, however, and those buildings which were completed lay in a sea of mud. The severely delayed construction work meant that there was no water, sanitation or electricity laid on.

As there were no local workmen available, the labour force was apathetic because there was no competition for jobs and therefore no incentive to work. There was also criticism that the HQ and Technical buildings had apparently been sited with little or no tactical consideration, as they were crammed together and made an ideal target for a few incendiary bombs. The hangars, in contrast, were well dispersed.

The airfield's earlier history was unusual in that it was already under construction by the Admiralty for its own use and was handed over to the Air Ministry on May 2 1940 in order to meet urgent Orkney fighter defence requirements. As part of this arrangement, the Naval and Air Staffs agreed that all aerodrome construction on the Orkneys was to be carried out by the Admiralty and that in the Shetlands by the Air Ministry.

The first recorded landing here was by a Miles Whitney Straight, of the Station Comm Flight on September 15. The anticipated two RAF fighter squadrons turned

518/40 type tower at Skeabrae (J.C. Temple).

Spitfires of 164 Squadron on dispersal at Skeabrae 1942 (R.E.G. Sheward, via C.H. Thomas).

out to be 804 Squadron, FAA, equipped with Gladiators and a solitary Martlet. The RAF was hard-pressed to defend the south, let alone this far-flung outpost.

No 804 arrived on October 25 1940 and, apart from the victory described above, had an uneventful stay, leaving for Skitten early in the New Year. It was replaced on January 7 by 3 Squadron's

Seafires of 801 Squadron ashore at Skea-brae from HMS Implacable *in December 1944* (FAA Museum)

Hurricanes from Castletown, 'A' Flight of this unit being detached to Sumburgh. No 3 Squadron transferred its HQ to Castletown on February 10 and 253 Squadron flew up from Leconfield to fill the gap.

The squadron's Hurricanes had several engagements with the enemy, the first being on May 11 1941 when a Ju 88 was fired on without effect at 20,000 ft over Scapa. Another patrol left a Ju 88 with an engine smoking but were themselves damaged by return fire. On May 5 1941, Flying Officer Eckford, DFC, with call-sign 'Hopeful 2' stalked a Condor about 50 miles NW of base. Although it was in the early hours of the morning, the bomber presented a clear silhouette against the north eastern twilight. It was raked

Massive generator building, now lived in, which served both Skeabrae and RNAS Twatt (J.C. Temple).

with gunfire but escaped into thick cloud and no claim was made.

At the end of May 1941, civil aircraft of Scottish Airways used Skeabrae for the first time, because of adverse weather at Kirkwall. The airfield was also one of the keystones of an ambitious exercise in August to test the island's defensive capacity. A force of 18,000 men, supported by tanks and artillery, was landed on the south-east coast, with the airfields at Skeabrae and Twatt as the objectives via Kirkwall and Stromness. The Hurricanes of 253 Squadron supported the attackers and escorted Blenheims against their home airfield. Both dromes were eventually overrun but valuable lessons were learned all round.

No 253 Squadron left for Hibaldstow in September 1941, being replaced by 331 from Castletown with Hurricanes, although they converted to Spitfires in November. More Hurricanes joined them in December, this time from 801 Squadron. No 331 flew uneventful patrols until the beginning of May 1942, when they flew south to North Weald.

Another Spitfire Squadron, 132, spent a little time at Skeabrae between February 15 and June 11 1942 when it repositioned to Grimsetter. Air defence patrols were shared with 164 Squadron, which had formed recently at Peterhead and was based in Orkney from May 4 until September 10 1942. On the day the squadron arrived, they lost one Spitfire when its tail was chopped off by another aircraft landing too close behind on a downhill runway.

The next resident was 602 Squadron from Peterhead which arrived in September, staying until January 1943 when it moved to Perranporth in Cornwall. It was relieved by 129 Squadron already operating Spitfires in the islands from Grimsetter. This squadron, too, went south to Ibsley in February, its place being taken by 66 Squadron, supported by 234 Squadron from April 24. Both squadrons left for Churchstanton in Devon towards the end of June. A longer term resident was 1476 Advanced Ship Recognition Flight equipped with Ansons. It arrived in December 1942 and stayed until January 1944.

As there was little to shoot at nowadays, the squadrons were kept in practice by Master and Lysander target tugs of 1494 Fighter Gunnery Flight. One of the Lysanders was involved in a regrettable incident on March 30 1943, when it took off with a member of the ground crew on the tail. It climbed to 200 ft, stalled and crashed, the unfortunate passenger being killed and the crew receiving superficial injuries. Later in the war, 289 and then 598 Squadrons kept detachments here for target towing.

No 312 Squadron was next in line for duty at Skeabrae, staying from June to September 1943 with Spitfire Vs. After this date, there were temporary attachments by the naval 801 Squadron operating as a lodger alongside 453 Squadron which was here until January 1944. No 801 Squadron embarked on HMS *Furious* on February 8 1944 and meanwhile another RAF unit, 602 Squadron, had arrived in mid-January from Detling.

On February 20, two of its Spitfires were patrolling 50 miles east of the Orkneys at 32,000 ft when they saw a vapour trail. The aircraft, a long-range Bf 109, was chased in a dive, the ASI of one of the Spitfires registering 400 mph. The enemy fighter was hit in the wing and spun into the sea leaving only wreckage on the surface.

No 602 Squadron returned to Detling in March, 118 Squadron having already flown up from there to Skeabrae two days before. The Seafires of 801 and 880 Squadrons also spent a lot of time here in the spring of 1944 when not flying from *Furious*. No 118 Squadron left for Detling in July, its replacement being 313 Squadron from Lympne. This squadron in turn was ousted by 611 Squadron early in October. The latter shot down a Ju 188 attempting to photograph the Fleet at

Scapa and a few days later, during escort to Coastal strike aircraft, they shot down a Ju 88 off the coast of Norway. The squadron left for Hawkinge on New Year's Eve.

Domestic affairs on the station featured the erection of a new Callender-Hamilton hangar in November 1944 and the inauguration on November 11 of a twice-weekly RAF air service to Inverness. More warlike was the diversion on January 29 1945 of nine Mustangs of 65 Squadron after an escort operation to Beaufighters off the Norwegian coast. They had taken off from Banff and run into heavy snow on the outward trip, their CO subsequently being reported missing.

A Canadian Squadron, 441, had taken over Scapa defence from January 1, being replaced by 329 on April 3. The final squadrons posted here for this routine but nevertheless vital duty were 451 from May to September 1945 and 603 in June and July 1945.

With the end of the war in Europe, there was no further threat to the Fleet Anchorage and Skeabrae's task over, it was soon reduced to Care and Maintenance, being by now nominally a satellite to Grimsetter. The RN finally disposed of it in 1957.

In 1973, an American oil company applied for planning permission to develop the old airfield for use by aircraft up to Boeing 747 size, linking the Orkneys direct to Texas and other oil centres! This grandiose scheme, needless to say, came to nothing. Slightly more feasible were NATO studies on using the site as the basis for a military airfield in the event of US forces being asked to leave Iceland.

By 1981, there were about 25 buildings still intact, including the 518/40 watch office, gymnasium, cinema and decontamination centre.

Skitten, Caithness

12/ND325570. 3 miles NW of Wick on B876

Skitten is mentioned in the Norse *Orkneyinga Saga* as the site of a battle in the ninth century, but curiously the name does not appear on modern maps. The airfield is associated with a gallant failure, Operation *Freshman*, the attack on the heavy water plant at Vermork in Norway. Bombing had been tried, to deprive the Germans of the means to manufacture an atomic bomb, but the plant was well

The RAF is long gone but the 'bull' remains! Station HQ at Skitten.

protected by the terrain. The answer seemed to be a glider assault force.

A total of 32 volunteer airborne troops made up the attackers and two Whitley crews from 38 Wing were rapidly converted on to Halifaxes, the aircraft being delivered direct from MAP. With the codename *Washington Party*, the detachment arrived at Skitten on November 17 1942, the starting point chosen because of its long runway. Two days later the aircraft left separately but the *Rebecca* navigation equipment malfunctioned and it was impossible to locate the *Eureka* beacon placed on the ground by Norwegian agents.

The Halifaxes and gliders flew around in some confusion for a while until just north of Stavanger a tow rope broke because of icing and the Horsa crash-landed in the mountains. The tow-plane just managed to reach Skitten on its last drops of fuel. The other combination flew into a mountain, all on board being killed including the Skitten Medical Officer who had volunteered at the last moment to fill a vacant crew position. The survivors from the force were later executed by the Gestapo but the plant was eventually destroyed by SOE agents and the Norwegian Resistance.

One of the least known of the Scottish wartime airfields, Skitten was begun early in 1940 on a plateau in the rolling treeless country near the road to John O'Groats. It was used first by 232 Squadron's Hurricanes which moved in from Castletown, then the parent aerodrome, on December 5 1940. The aircraft were then detached to Drem for a few weeks, returning on

November 11 and finally leaving for Elgin on December 4 1940. No 260 Squadron, also with Hurricanes, replaced them until transferring back to Castletown on January 7 1941. They came back to Skitten on February 10 1941, departing for Drem on April 16.

To cover the gap between January 7 and February 10, 804 Squadron of the FAA was based with Martlets and a pair of Gladiators. Blizzards in January 1941 blocked all the roads in Caithness for days and an airlift of rations had to be made by Harrows from Castletown to Skitten.

No 607 relieved 260 Squadron in April 1941, but by this time Wick was interested in Skitten as a satellite for Coastal Command operations and a preliminary survey of the available accommodation was made in May. On July 27 1941, 607's Hurricanes went to Castletown and 404 Squadron's Blenheims moved to Skitten from there. The latter flew patrols until October 1941.

No 48 Squadron's Hudsons were posted in from Stornoway on October 20 1941, moving to Wick on January 6 1942. Beauforts arrived in February in the shape of 217 Squadron from Thorney Island but they were transferred to Leuchars at the beginning of March.

For a station designed to accommodate a single fighter squadron, Skitten was becoming seriously overcrowded. At one time in February 1942, the Sergeants' Mess was catering for almost 200 men with staff to serve only 38! The runways, too, were marginal for the safe operation of medium-sized aircraft and all three were extended early in 1942.

The increases in length met the secondary purpose of allowing emergency use by Bomber Command aircraft if operations against naval anchorages in Norway demanded it. On June 30 1942, three Lancasters of 44 Squadron were here on a short detachment. No 86 Squadron's Beauforts were also on the station from March to July, and on April 22 had carried out an exercise with US Navy aircraft. These are recorded as six Devastators which landed at Skitten but

they were more than likely Vindicators from the USS *Wasp*. If they were Devastators it must have been the type's only visit to the UK.

A Halifax force-landed on March 28 1943 with compass trouble after a raid on Berlin. As its base was in faraway Yorkshire, the crew was very much off course and lucky to make a landfall.

A detachment of Leigh Light Wellingtons from 172 Squadron was based from August 17 to September 14 1943 and during this period one flight became the nucleus of 179 Squadron which formed here on September 1. Many ships were torpedoed by Hampdens of 489 Squadron flying *Rovers* from Skitten between August 1942 and October 1943, when they moved to Leuchars.

Early in 1943, the airfield was officially designated as a reserve base for Bomber Command to accommodate 24 heavy bombers, meaning that the Coastal Command units would have to move elsewhere at short notice. Although it had good approaches, it was noted that, as at so many of these hastily-built airfields, the prevailing wind favoured the shortest runway. The latter was thus to be further extended to 1400 yds.

Skitten's most intriguing unit formed on April 1 1943 for 'anti-submarine duties' under 18 Group. Numbered 618 Squadron, it was in fact intended primarily for dropping modified bouncing bombs on the *Tirpitz* timed for the day before its sister unit, 617 Squadron, was to attack the Ruhr Dams. Problems with the weapon and subsequent delays in training crews resulted in the shelving of the project, the Mosquitoes being transferred to Wick on December 11 1943 and never used in anger.

One of the final units to be based was 519 Squadron with Hampdens, Spitfires, Hudsons, and Venturas. Arriving from Wick in December 1943, the sphere of operations was the North Atlantic, North Sea and out towards the Arctic. The twins

Gas decontamination centre at Skitten.

were used for long and medium range met flights and the Spitfires for high altitude ascents. The motto on the squadron badge was 'Undaunted by Weather'. The squadron returned to Wick on November 29 1944. It was not much used after this date and closed soon after the end of the war.

Skitten is a pleasant enough spot in summer but one needs little imagination to see how bleak it would be in winter. The runways are badly deteriorated, but, nevertheless, *The UK Air Pilot*, the official procedures and navigation manual, warns: 'There is a disused wartime airfield (Skitten) three nautical miles NW of Wick aerodrome. The approach path to runway 14 at Wick passes directly over this airfield and aircraft have touched down there in error on occasions in conditions of poor visibility.'

There were once eight Blisters and a single Bellman hangar but all have gone now, along with seven dispersal pens and the watch tower. Prominent among the surviving buildings is a decontamination centre.

One feels that there should be some memorial to that gallant glider operation so long ago when the aircraft and their troops set off in cold and drizzling darkness, most of them to a tragic end.

Smoogro, Orkney

6/HY36-06-*. 7 miles SW of Kirkwall south of A964

When HMS *Furious* was in harbour at Scapa Flow, her pilots used to practice flying from the small naval airfield at Smoogro. It occurred to them that it might be possible to land back on the flying-off deck instead of ditching or landing ashore. After some experimental rolling of the wheels along the deck it was considered possible to land provided the ship was sailing into wind at 25 knots or so.

The first trial was made on August 2 1917. That day there was a steady wind of 21 knots into which *Furious* steamed at about 26 knots, there being insufficient space in the Scapa anchorage to work up to her maximum of 31 knots. Commander Dunning piloted a Sopwith Pup and landed on successfully, a ground handling party grabbing rope toggles hanging from the aircraft. Tragically Dunning was to

*At the time of writing the complete map reference is not available.

drown five days later when his engine choked on an overshoot and the aircraft went into the sea. The experiments, however, led to the development of the aircraft carrier and the conversion of *Furious* for a landing-on deck.

Smoogro continued to be used as a shore station by naval aeroplanes until the end of the war. There was also a seaplane base in Scapa three miles south of Kirkwall. It opened in August 1914 and was a Fleet Aircraft Repair Base and Stores Depot in 1918. After the Navy left, it was for many years the county TB hospital.

Stannergate (Dundee), Tayside
See Dundee

Stirling (Raploch), Central Region
57/NS785945

This aerodrome was used as a training station from 1916 until 1917, when it ceased to be used for flying. In 1917 it was used also as a landing ground for 77 (HD) Squadron, mainly with BE 2s. At Kincairn near Stirling there was another landing ground for 77 Squadron in 1916/17.

One training squadron based here, was 43 which formed here on April 15 1916 with various types such as the BE 2 and 504 K and moved to Netheravon in August/September 1916. The other was 63 Squadron,, forming on August 31 1916 and originally intended to train as a light bomber unit for the Western Front. The types used were BE 2s and Martinsydes and the squadron moved to Cramlington on October 31 1916.

The aerodrome was an open space just under the Castle hill which has now been developed into a housing estate. It was said to be an ancient tilting ground and there were no proper buildings except for a commandeered farmhouse in which the senior officers lived. Everyone else lived in tents and the aircraft were housed in some temporary wooden hangars. In the 30s Northern and Scottish Airways also used a field near here.

Stornoway, Western Isles
8/NB455335. 1½ miles E of Stornoway on A866

Yet another Scottish wartime airfield which owed its position to pre-war civil flying, Stornoway absorbed the Melbost

Golf Links on which Dragon *G-ACIT* had landed in 1934. Captain Fresson demonstrated that four 600 yd strips could be levelled if some bunkers were filled in and it would still be possible to retain 18 holes. The Golf Club, however, did not want the ground altered and negotiations dragged on for four years until the site was finally approved. Unfortunately, completion coincided with the outbreak of war and it was never used. The Air Ministry then tore it up and built a large runway airfield for Coastal Command instead. It was to be May 1944 before the planned Inverness–Stornoway service begun.

The RAF Station HQ was established at Stornoway in April 1941 but it was the end of July before an operational squadron was based, 48 Squadron from Hooton Park. Even then many of its Ansons were detached to other places such as Aldergrove and Islay. Hudsons had almost entirely replaced the Anson by the time the unit moved to Skitten on October 20 1941.

Mention should also be made of HMS *Mentor* at Stornoway Harbour from which Walruses of 701 Squadron flew between November 1940 and June 1941. Other naval activity at Stornoway included 827 Squadron's Albacores, here from March to May 1941 and 842, a Wildcat Squadron, here in August/September 1944.

At the beginning of April 1942, 500 Squadron came from Norfolk with more Hudsons, detaching some of them to Limavady to increase the radius of action for U-boat patrols. Two submarines were attacked in April 1942 but in neither case was there a definite sinking. Success came to Flying Officer M.A. Ensor on August 24 when he dropped four depth charges on a surfaced U-boat, blowing off the bows. He was awarded the DFC for this exploit but on a later patrol he dropped

USAF Sabre at Stornoway in the '50s (Via J. Bricknell).

his depth charges, only to see a very dead whale rise to the surface, an all too common happening in this type of warfare.

Stornoway was not a popular posting because of local restrictions on drinking hours and the playing of football on Sundays. One crew rebelled, it is said, and beat up the town in a Hudson at 3 am on a Sunday morning. Unfortunately an Admiral was on board a battleship moored in the bay which probably contributed to their swift transfer to a mainland squadron.

No 500 Squadron left for St Eval on August 31 1942, its patrols being taken over by 58 Squadron with Whitleys, until this Squadron moved to Hampshire in December. The station was then occupied by 303 FTU which formed here on December 15 1942. This unit was tasked with holding up to 20 Wellingtons and their crews at any one time and dispatching them to overseas squadrons.

During June 1943, about 100 officers and men from the USAAF were brought in to handle the ever increasing numbers of American aircraft using the airfield as a transatlantic staging post. There had been spasmodic visits since July 1942 when some of the first P-38s to reach Europe had flown in via Iceland with a B-17 to navigate for them. In June 1943 alone, 68 aircraft passed through on delivery.

On July 9 1943, around the same time as the USAAF began a shuttle met service between Iceland, Stornoway and Prestwick, 518 Squadron formed at Stornoway for met reconnaissance with Halifaxes. Perhaps because of the congestion caused by the FTU and aircraft on ferry flights, 518 moved to Tiree on September 25 1943.

A total of 108 US aircraft of various types passed through in September 1943 and on November 1 the station was transferred temporarily to the control of Transport Command. No 303 FTU continued to operate but moved to Talbenny in South Wales in March 1944. On June 24, Marauder *43-34120* on a ferry trip overshot on landing, killing the two pilots.

Stornoway's most active contribution to the war, however, was as the base of a pair of Halifax squadrons which wreaked havoc on German shipping in Scandinavian waters during the closing months of the war. By August 1944, targets off the French coast were non-existent, so both 58 and 502 Squadrons moved to the Outer Hebrides and commenced anti-submarine patrols. Again, there were no results so at the beginning of October they were ordered to switch their efforts to night anti-shipping patrols. Their general area of operation would be the Skaggerak and Kattegat but they were to concentrate on the shipping lanes between Oslo, Kristiansund and the Danish ports.

In October, the two squadrons operating in conjunction made 27 attacks but as usual with night engagements, results were difficult to assess despite the use of slow-dropping flares. One exception occurred on October 25, when a 58 Squadron Halifax set a motor vessel on fire with a stick of bombs. Neither did they neglect the occasional U-boat found lurking off the Norwegian coast. On October 27, two 502 aircraft shared in the destruction of the last of many enemy submarines credited to the squadron.

At the end of April 1945, the Stornoway squadrons received a letter from the Air Officer Commanding, Coastal Command, saying in part 'Hearty congratulations on the fine operational achievement of both

Warrant Officer Jones holding up Wellington GR XIV NB773 of 36 Squadron at Stornoway in May 1945 (G. Jones).

squadrons, particularly during the last two months. You have sunk more than 25,000 tons of shipping and damaged 50,000 tons since the beginning of the year . . .'

In April 1945, the Halifaxes reached a new peak of success. Shipping movements between Norway and Denmark almost came to a standstill. On a tons sunk or damaged per sortie basis for the three months ending April 10 1945 the Halifax's effectiveness was claimed to be three or four times that of the average for all other types of Coastal Command aircraft, including the Beaufighters and Mosquitoes.

On May 10 1945, the Squadrons' work was rewarded when four aircraft flew out over the western Baltic. Their crews estimated that they sighted over 100 enemy craft from U-boats to houseboats, all heavily laden with German troops heading towards the Kiel area and all flying flags of surrender. Their job finished, the two squadrons disbanded at Stornoway on May 25 1945.

The airfield passed to the Ministry of Aviation in 1946 and in 1948 it saw the start and finish of the first double crossing of the Atlantic by jet aircraft—Vampires of Fighter Command. In 1973 it was designated a Strike Command forward base, the main runway being lengthened and other improvements carried out. At the time of writing it is being developed further for NATO maritime patrol aircraft, interceptor aircraft and tanker aircraft which would use it in wartime to strengthen the defences on Britain's western flank.

Stracathro, Tayside

45/NO645635. 4 miles NE of Brechin off A94

The old airfield is just another expanse of green in a fertile valley with the Grampian Mountains rising to the west. There is little left apart from a few buildings which include a long barrack hut recently employed for calf rearing. Eight Blisters were erected during the war and a concrete

track was built around three sides of the almost square landing ground. Up the road to the south-east, the one-time communal site can still be seen.

Stracathro came under the control of Montrose for almost its entire life, the first recorded use being on July 16 1941 when 'A' Squadron of 8 FTS was detached here for both day and night flying on Masters. Within a fortnight the new RLG suffered its first fatal accident when Master *T8407* crashed.

When 2 FIS took over at Montrose in January 1942, the RLG remained in operation. In July, the FIS' Master Flights were detached here, leaving the parent station free for twin-engined training. The personnel, normally some 200, were not billeted at the airfield but taken there each day by bus and lorry.

No 1541 BAT Flight formed here on April 15 1943, affiliated to 2 FIS and flying Oxfords. Masters still used the RLG but it was a passing Hurricane which collided with an Oxford over the field on December 23 1943, killing two in the trainer. Details are sparse, but it would appear that the BAT Flight had the airfield to itself some of the time. For example, 'B' Flight of 2 FIS began flying from Stracathro on April 26 1944 but moved to Edzell on June 30.

When 2 FIS disbanded on July 11 1945, 1541 Bat Flight went with it. The field was then taken over by Edzell who passed it to 260 MU, Errol. The latter used it as a Sub-Storage Site until July 1948 when the MU, too, closed down.

Stranraer (Wig Bay), Dumfries and Galloway

See Wig Bay

Stravithie, Fife

59/NO540125. 3 miles SE of St Andrews on A959

The former watch office, converted into a dwelling, and an adjacent tractor shed betray the position of what was once 26

SLG. It came into use on May 9 1941 as a dispersal field for 44 MU Edzell, which at this time was mainly concerned with Hurricanes and Wellingtons. During this first month, 44 aircraft were flown in and under a grazing agreement, livestock were allowed on the field when it was not in use.

Not unusually, because of surface conditions, the SLG was closed down for the winter, reopening on May 25 1942, when 50 men of the 30th Battalion Highland Regiment were posted here for anti-sabotage patrols. Four days later a Defiant crashed on landing but fortunately the pilot was unhurt. The small field was found suitable for four-engined bombers when a Halifax made a test landing in July 1942. It is possible that a Stirling was also landed here around the same time.

The SLG was used by Lysanders, probably from 309 Squadron, and it is known that a field close to the site was used before the war by Leuchars as an RLG. The exact date of the SLG's closure is uncertain but it was derequisitioned on May 4 1945.

Sullom Voe, Shetland

2/HU390740. 25 miles N of Lerwick on B9076

To Derek Gilpin Barnes, author of the memorable but alas long out of print book *Cloud Cover*, Sullom Voe was a place haunted by 'the clash of remote Scandinavian swords and the grinding of Norse keels upon forgotten sands'. His striking pen picture captures the atmosphere perfectly:

'The station lay like a sullen explorer's encampment by the deserted shores of a black and evil loch. Yet in this austere landscape there was the utmost beauty as well as forbidding gloom. One sensed that

Catalina over Shetland desolation in March 1944. JX574 of 210 Squadron (M.E. Street via Chaz Bowyer).

the noise of aircraft and the prolonged shouting of a thousand men were but a momentary echo in the long Northern silence that would again irrevocably descend (on) . . . the sullen waters of the Voe, ablink with the riding lights of aircraft at their moorings. In the camouflaged huts, huddled on that desolate shore, were many young men all dreaming of trams and girls, fish bars, pictures, "the dogs" and home, and all shouting or singing or turning on radios—to drown the thin, insistent voices of an earlier age.'

Now engulfed by the oil terminal, there is little trace of the RAF's most northerly wartime station in the British Isles, apart from some Nissen huts. It was set up in 1939 to cover the gap between Norway and Iceland, the first aircraft here being the Sunderlands of 201 Squadron which flew up from Calshot on August 9 1939 and patrolled until November 6. They were then replaced by the Londons of 240 Squadron from Invergordon which stayed until April 1 1940. The ageing flying boats were reinforced at Sullom by a detachment of 210 Squadron Sunderlands which went back to their base at Oban on May 21.

Satellite moorings at Lerwick were used early in the war and other aircraft were dispersed around Garth's Voe and Voxter Voe. This was partly for shelter as during the hunt for the *Scharnhorst* and *Gneisenau* in October 1939, a Sunderland put down safely in the Voe in a 60 knot gale and tossed helplessly at her moorings for over ten hours before the crew could be taken off. Until shore accommodation was built, the station was controlled by 100 Wing aboard the depot ship *Manela*.

No 201 Squadron returned to the Shetlands on May 26 to join 204 Squadron, which had already been here for seven weeks on Norway patrols. On April 3, Sunderland *F* of 204, captained by Flight Lieutenant Phillips on his first operational flight, had shot down the first enemy aircraft credited to RAF Shetlands. The flying boat was circling a convoy when Ju 88s appeared. Waiting until the range closed to 200 yds, the gunners fired on the leader, which crashed into the sea almost immediately.

In January, Sullom itself had seen some action, starting off with several false reports of enemy aircraft which turned out to be Gladiators from Sumburgh or stray Sunderlands, but culminating in an actual attack on January 29. Two raiders flew over the Voe in daylight, dropping bombs without hitting anything and were

driven off by gunfire and two Sumburgh Gladiators. On November 13 1939, the neighbouring village had the distinction of suffering the first bomb on British soil of the Second World War.

A Norwegian Northrop floatplane arrived on April 13, having flown with three crew via Lerwick. Bombs and ammunition were no longer available in Norway so they decided to go to Britain and offer their services to the RAF. Another escapee four days later was an Arado 196 seaplane captured at Christiansand and flown back by two more Norwegian airmen.

When hostilities ceased in Norway during June 1940, four He 115As set out for the UK. Three were Norwegian aircraft, the other a captured Luftwaffe example. Three reached Sullom, including the former German aircraft, but one ran out of fuel and had to be sunk after ditching.

Several other notable events took place in June, beginning on June 4 when a Swordfish landed on the beach adjacent to the RAF camp, having been unable to get down at Hatston because of weather conditions there. Later it took off from the football pitch and returned to base. The following day a Do 17 appeared over the Voe and was chased by Gladiators but lost in bad visibility.

Sunderland *A* of 204 Squadron failed to return from a reconnaissance of Trondheim on July 21, but on August 26 an aircraft of the same unit destroyed four He 115s at their moorings at Tromso and damaged four others. Short-range patrols to the west of the Shetlands were made by Walrus aircraft of 700 Squadron from December 1940. On Christmas Eve one dropped two 100 lb depth charges on a submerged U-boat. Bubbles were seen but there was no other evidence to confirm a kill.

On the morning of March 23 1941, two Me 110s made a low level attack on the camp but it was Sullom church and village and a naval supply ship which took most of the fire. One aircraft was shot down by a Bofors gun and crashed in flames into the water. The pilot's body was washed up later, along with the auxiliary fuel tanks which had made the long flight from Norway possible. An unexploded 250 kg bomb was made safe and mounted with an inscription and small fence round it! A month later, on April 28, a Sunderland of 201 Squadron engaged a Condor and compelled it to jettison the bomb load but unfortunately could not catch it.

No 204 Squadron was posted to Reykjavik on April 5, leaving 201 at Sullom to help with the search for the *Bismarck* in May 1941. No 201 left for Castle Archdale on October 9 1941. The Canadian 413 Squadron then flew Catalina patrols until March 1942 when 210 Squadron returned, by now having re-equipped with Catalinas. They went to Pembroke Dock on October 4 1942. A new Catalina squadron, No 190, formed at Sullom Voe on March 1 1943 for Atlantic patrols, being disbanded on paper and renumbered 210 Squadron on January 1 1944.

In the meantime, the Norwegian 330 Squadron had moved its Sunderlands here from Oban on July 12 1943, again for Atlantic patrols. During the first half of 1944 many of these were uneventful but an exception occurred on February 25 when Squadron Leader French in *M* of 210 Squadron out on convoy escort homed on to a radar contact and sighted a U-boat with decks awash. Two depth charges, all that could be carried on an extreme range patrol, were released to good effect; the submarine sank stern first 30 seconds later. This was claimed to be the first U-boat kill north of the Arctic Circle and French was awarded the DFC for his exploit.

On May 16 *V* of 330 Squadron attacked another submarine with uncertain results. Return fire damaged the aircraft so badly that it had to run up on the beach at Sullom before it sank. The front gunner was killed and two other crew members injured. Two days later, *S* of 210 Squadron sank a U-boat but not before its tail was holed by flak. The last fortnight in May saw a total of three subs sunk and three more probably destroyed, it being considered that a massed sortie destined for the convoy lanes had been broken up.

Enemy aerial opposition was almost nonexistent but *T* of 330 Squadron was unlucky enough to be intercepted by two Me 110s on June 8. The fight went on for 35 minutes, during which the starboard inner engine was hit and put out of action. This deprived the front and tail turrets of their power. Fortunately only the tail gunner was wounded but the depth charges had to be jettisoned in order for the Sunderland to reach base.

An action on July 17 1944 led to the award of the Victoria Cross to Flight Lieutenant J.H. Cruikshank of 210 Squadron. In the middle of a routine 14-hour patrol from the Voe in Catalina

JV928 a radar contact was picked up at a range of 15 miles. Believing it to be a friendly destroyer, the crew fired a recognition cartridge. Their answer was a heavy box barrage—it was a U-boat. On the first run-in the depth charges failed to release so Cruikshank circled for a second attack. This time they straddled the sub but just before the point of release the flying boat was badly hit by flak. The navigator was killed and the flight engineer and second pilot injured. Cruikshank was also wounded but the actual extent was not apparent until much later; some 72 separate injuries being recorded when he eventually reached a hospital.

He refused a morphia injection as this would numb his mental capacity and there was still a five hour flight back to base. When they made the Shetlands he insisted that they remain airborne for another hour until there was sufficient daylight to ensure a safe landing. This they accomplished successfully but had to beach the Catalina when water began to pour through all the holes in the hull. Both Cruikshank and Flight Sergeant John Garrett, the second pilot, recovered from their injuries and two months later received medals, a VC for the captain and a DFM for Garrett. The U-boat was subsequently confirmed as sunk.

Despite intensive efforts during August 1944 by aircraft based here, only four submarines were sighted and none was claimed as sunk. No 210 Squadron commenced a concentrated Leigh Light and radar training programme in preparation for the long winter nights to come and a detachment of Catalinas of 202 Squadron was sent to help with the operational commitments.

A summing up of the station's achievements in 1944 showed 14,080 operational flying hours and a total of 1,064 sorties. Apart from the VC award and the numerous sub sinkings, another notable event was the rescue of six survivors of a downed Liberator from the Arctic Circle on July 21. Catalina *X* of 210 Squadron, captained by Squadron Leader French and a volunteer skeleton crew, landed in a heavy swell and took them off successfully.

The Voe's operational area covered the vast distance from the Norwegian coast to the Lofoten Islands, 68° north to The Naze and patrols north-east, north and north-west of the Shetlands. Some 41 Russian convoy sorties had been carried out plus three flights by 210 Squadron to and from Grasnaya in North Russia. There had been problems with weather diversions

as the nearest east coast base was Alness, 200 miles away and that on the west coast was Oban, over 300 miles distant.

The closing months of the war saw little action for the Shetlands aircraft, only two inconclusive attacks being made in March 1945, one on a probable *Schnorckel*, the other on a firm radar contact. A historic flight was made by Sunderland *G* of 330 Squadron on May 7 via Woodhaven, where it picked up VIPs, to Oslo, the first Norwegian aircraft to return there. The rest of 330 Squadron moved to Stavanger on May 30 and 210 Squadron's Catalinas also vacated the Voe. One of their last sorties from here took place on June 10 when two members of the RAF Film Unit were flown along the Norwegian coast photographing wrecked ships, the victims of the Coastal Strike Wings. From then on there was very little flying, only an occasional visit by a Sunderland from 4 OTU at Alness.

The station and its supporting landplane base at nearby Scatsta reverted to Care and Maintenance in 1946. Natural deterioration and storm damage made conditions very primitive when both locations were used during Exercise *Mainbrace* in the summer of 1952. No 201 Squadron's white-painted Sunderlands shared the Voe with dark blue PBM Mariners of the US Navy, together with the seaplane tender USS *Timbalier*. When the flying boats left, the American ones took with them at least three Shetland ponies!

Sumburgh, Shetland

4/HU395105. 25 miles S of Lerwick on A970

'Sea circled loneliness with the great lion of Sumburgh Head snoozing in the circuit' was how one wartime pilot described this criss-cross of runways on one of the few flat strips of land in the Shetlands.

Like so many Scottish airfields, it owed its origins to Captain E.E. Fresson of Highland Airways, having been established in 1933, with scheduled services starting in 1936. The RAF required it in

Rapide G-ADAJ *of Highland Airways at Sumburgh* circa *1936* (Via J. Huggon).

1939 for a fighter flight of three Gladiators and in November an Air Ministry report declared that it would not be suitable for the operation of modern aircraft without considerable improvement. Sand dunes were levelled to remove obstructions and allow for additional hangarage but it was 1941 before three runways were actually built. One required a cutting 200 ft wide and some 40 ft deep at one end through the sloping ground to the seashore.

When finished, it was a fine airfield for post-war Shetland, an airfield which could never have come into existence had it not been for the war, as the cost of construction with imported Irish labour was enormous.

A Station HQ formed on May 13 1940 to administer one squadron of Blenheims, No 254, which arrived from Hatston three days later and the 'Sumburgh Fighter Flight' equipped with Gladiators. The latter constituted the sole air defence of the Shetlands and probably destroyed two enemy aircraft during its brief attachment to the Wick Sector. In July, the biplanes were sent to Roborough, a grass airfield too small to accommodate Spitfires or Hurricanes. Their new role was the defence of Plymouth and the Flight became 247 Squadron on August 1.

'B' Flight of 3 Squadron was detached to Sumburgh from Wick on July 17 to maintain the fighter presence and simultaneously was formed into 232 Squadron under the Wick Sector. Flying convoy patrols for the most part, it was scrambled occasionally and on August 23 Blue Section managed to destroy an He 111 off Fair Isle.

No 232 Squadron left for Castletown on September 18, 254 Squadron having already gone to Dyce in July. No 248's Blenheim IVs took its place and flew shipping patrols off Norway until early in January 1941, when 254 returned and stayed until the end of May.

There was rarely a whole fighter

squadron available for service in Shetland, so detached flights of Hurricanes from the mainland filled this gap in the northern defences. They included parts of 3 Squadron from January 2 to March 29 1941 and 17 Squadron from April to June 1941, and again in August. Two Naval squadrons, 821 with Swordfish and 880 with Sea Hurricanes were here on short detachment in the autumn.

If the fighters saw little action over the islands, the Coastal Command aircraft based here did. One of the Beaufort's biggest operations in its early days came on June 21 1940. The battle cruiser *Scharnhorst* was known to be off Norway and it was decided to launch an attack on her from Sumburgh with a detachment of 42 Squadron. Nine aircraft took off carrying bombs as the crews were not yet trained in torpedo dropping. North of Bergen, Bf 109s fell upon them, shooting down three, although two of the fighters were claimed as destroyed.

Moving on to February 1 1942, a Ju 88 strafed the airfield and damaged some Blenheims of 404 Squadron which were detached at that time and riddled a hangar with cannon fire. A Magister was also hit and two airmen were killed and six injured. Flights of Spitfires from 132 and 331 were based but were unable to engage.

A bomb was dropped close to the airfield on March 10 1942, but ten days later one of our own aircraft almost caused a disaster. A Beaufort with engine trouble swung on landing and ran into the squadron offices, setting fire to both huts and aircraft. The crew got clear and the torpedo on board exploded soon afterwards, completely wrecking the offices and crew rooms. Fortunately a warning had been broadcast on the tannoy system so everyone was well away.

Flying from Sumburgh was a hazardous undertaking. The airfield was sited on a spit of land with the sea on two sides and a 1200 ft hill less than three miles from one end of the runway, with a smaller hill in line with the other end and close to the edge of the airfield. The trick on black nights was to come in high and make a steep descent but it needed good judgment and accidents were frequent. One Beaufort pilot lost control trying to avoid the hill and spun in. A Mosquito of 143 Squadron was forced by the hill to make a right hand circuit with, rather than against a dead engine, landed much too fast and ran into a brick wall with one fatality.

It was not only flying which could be

unpleasant. The Station Medical Officer recorded in 1942 that he had treated an unusual number of airmen for neurosis, some of whom had been on the island longer than the recognised 12 months and he recommended that they be posted. He also suggested, somewhat ambiguously, that the presence of WAAFs on the camp would do much to improve the general happiness of the men! Another domestic problem was the shortage of green vegetables and it was arranged that Harrows would fly them up regularly from the Mainland, RAF Sullom Voe also making use of this service.

Beaufighters had appeared for the first time on September 29 1941, when 143 Squadron had brought theirs in from Dyce. East Coast convoy patrols were flown until they moved to Aldergrove in the middle of December 1941. In October 1941 the squadron flew 156 sorties from Sumburgh on shipping escort, fighter patrol and Faeroes patrol. On October 19, two Beaufighters probably destroyed a Ju 88, the unit's first success.

By August 1942, the station had been increased in size until it was capable of accommodating three Coastal squadrons. These were 248 with Beaufighters (here since May 30 1942), 404 with Blenheims and a detachment of 608 with Hudsons. Targets off the Norwegian coast were attacked and convoys on their way to North Russia were protected. Notable visitors on September 25 1942 were three Mosquitoes of 105 Squadron refuelling on the way back from the celebrated bombing of the Gestapo HQ in Oslo.

For anti-submarine patrols, Hudsons of 48 Squadron were here between September 23 and November 19 1942. A detachment of four Beaufighter VIs of 125 Squadron was sent to the Shetlands in October to try to intercept enemy reconnaissance aircraft over the North Sea. Although they damaged three, they did not succeed in shooting any down and returned to Fairwood Common in December 1942.

During August 1942, Sumburgh was employed as the jumping-off point for Hampdens of 144 and 455 Squadrons. Fuelled to the limit, they set off for North Russia, several crashing or disappearing *en route*. Well over 30 years later one of them was found on Tsatsa Mountain in Lapland. Two of the crew had survived but the remains of the others were still in the wreck.

The fighter detachments continued in 1942 with Spitfires of 602 Squadron, being taken over by 234 in January 1943. On March 24 1943, one of the latter's pilots shot down an Me 210 off Fitful Head. This detachment left in April, being relieved successively by flights of 313, 310 and 453 Squadrons.

Equipped with Mosquitoes, 307 Squadron was having a quiet life at Drem, so a detachment was sent to Sumburgh in November 1943 to fly *Rhubarbs* over Norway. Two He 177s and a Ju 88 fell to their guns and several aircraft were destroyed on the ground before the whole squadron was withdrawn to Lincolnshire in March 1944. A typical sweep on January 19 1944 took in the seaplane station at Stavanger. Several moored Bv 138s were set on fire and the Mosquitoes made off when Fw 190s were seen scrambling from the nearby airfield.

Other Mosquitoes, including those from 333 Squadron, used Sumburgh as an advanced base for recces of the Norwegian coast. It was also a convenient staging post for PR aircraft based at Wick and Leuchars. No 540's first operational sortie was launched from the Shetlands during which the *Tirpitz* and *Admiral von Scheer* were photographed in Ofot Fjord.

In 1944, Cansos of the Canadian 162 Squadron based at Reykjavik were flying armed transits between Sumburgh and Iceland on the lookout for submarines and the station continued to be used by a variety of operational aircraft for refuelling stops. On one occasion (November 7) a Swedish Airlines Fortress made a night landing with engine trouble, and, eight days later, a badly shot-up Liberator crash-landed returning from ops with a dead gunner and several wounded.

From June 14 1944, the Ansons of 1693 (GR) Flight began close-in anti-submarine patrols to the west of the Orkneys. This was perhaps the last operational use of the type and the Ansons remained at Sumburgh until transferring to Bircham Newton at the end of May 1945. The only other operational aircraft now at Sumburgh were the fighter detachments, including 118 Squadron from March to July and 611 from October to December 1944. No 598 Squadron had a detachment here in 1945—and probably earlier—for target towing.

Cripples continued to find the airfield a haven. On January 12 1945, for example, a Lancaster with battle damage put down, three of its crew having baled out over enemy territory. Beaufighters from the

Dallachy Wing were frequent visitors, mauled by the enemy and escorted in by ASR Warwicks. Escort Mustangs with rough engines were also grateful to be shepherded in on occasion.

The end of the war in Europe cut off Sumburgh's importance at a stroke. The Coastal Command operations room closed on June 4 1945, and, apart from communications flights, the only visitors in that month were Spitfires of 129 and 165 Squadrons in transit to Norway. The station went to Care and Maintenance under Sullom Voe on August 29 1945.

BEA began scheduled services in 1947, first with Dakotas, until the main runway was extended in 1966 to take Viscounts. Unfortunately, persistent bad weather and cross-winds often disrupted the services. In the summer of 1973, for example, one in six Viscount flights had to be cancelled and the construction of an entirely new airport was considered. It was decided instead that the east-west runway be extended and the ground levelled to a distance of 350 ft on either side.

The oil boom turned Sumburgh into a very busy airport almost overnight and a large capital expenditure programme resulted. The wartime control tower on its hill is still in use, albeit modernised. In 1975, nearly 200,000 passengers and 1,000 tonnes of freight were flown to and from the oil rigs, but, at the time of writing, long-range helicopters are coming into service, thus bypassing Sumburgh and causing a considerable decline in its traffic.

Sumburgh was the scene of an accident to a Dan-Air HS 748 in 1979 when it failed to get airborne and crashed in the sea. The death roll would have been much higher had it not been for the courage of the stewardess. In similar crashes during the war, a 307 Squadron Mosquito was lost with both crew and a Warwick of 281 Squadron ditched near Sumburgh Head. Four of the crew managed to reach the shore but the other was drowned.

Sydenham, Down

15/J375765. 2 miles NE of Belfast city centre on A2

In the 1830s and 1840s the Belfast Harbour Commission had begun extensive widening and deepening of the harbour. In the process, the artificial land formed was named Queen's Island, sites on it being offered to shipbuilders. One small firm which set up business here was Harland &

Wolff who later moved into aircraft construction with Short Bros.

Land alongside the shipyard was converted into an aerodrome in 1933, but the surface was at first inclined to be soft and was not considered suitable for use by passenger aircraft on regular services. After Harland & Wolff built a large factory on the site and improved the landing ground as part of the country's rearmament programme, it was ópened officially as an airport on March 16 1938 by the wife of the then Prime Minister, Neville Chamberlain.

The airlines, recognising the value of an airport within five minutes' drive of the city centre, moved their operations from Newtownards. On January 1 1939, Short Bros set up 24 E & RFTS, pupils doing their basic training on Tiger Moths and Magisters and going on to the more advanced Harts and Demons.

In 1940, the airport was taken over by the RAF, the first units to be based being 88 and 226 Squadrons with Battles from June 23. This was a token measure to strengthen Ulster's defences. 'Fighter protection' for the airfield itself that summer was a flight of four elderly Hawker Demons flown by Battle pilots.

On September 29, a Dishforth-based Whitley just managed to glide into Sydenham with all its fuel exhausted after a raid on Berlin. Other visitors included nine Ansons of 48 Squadron detached from November 18 to December 2, when they moved to Stornoway.

Stirling production was by now well under way at the Short Bros and Harland factory, despite delays caused by the air raid on August 14 1940. The attack was made by 15 He 111s of KG100, five Stirlings on the production line being destroyed, but the factory went on to produce a total of 603 aircraft of this type.

Both 226 and 88 Squadrons now had a Blenheim and two Bostons for pilot conversion pending re-equipment with the American type. They left for East Anglia in May and July 1941 respectively, where they received their full complement of Bostons.

Sydenham in July 1941 was used by several units, ranging from 804 Squadron with Sea Hurricanes to 8 Ferry Pilots Pool which had formed here in August 1941 to deliver Stirlings to the mainland and also Wellingtons and other aircraft to and from 23 MU at Aldergrove. Throughout the war, DH 86s and Dragon Rapides continued to run services out of Belfast. No 24 Squadron also operated a Hendon service for military personnel for much of the war.

The station was renamed RAF Belfast on November 27 1941 and a foretaste of its future role as an RNAS came with the increased presence of Naval squadrons during 1942. Those attached included 808, 881, 886, 887 and 891. There was, too, a detachment of 6 AACU which had been flying from here since approximately January 1942 and from August, Queen's UAS kept a Tiger Moth here. There was also the RAFNI Comm Flight which had formed out of the Station Flight on November 19 1942 and was to remain here until April 30 1945.

Unusual visitors on May 5 1943 were two USAAF transport aircraft bringing cargoes of depth charges from Honington for the escort carrier USS *Bogue*. Using some of these weapons her Avengers sank a U-boat the following month. The 6 AACU detachment went to Newtownards at the end of May, and on June 21 1943, the station was handed over to the Royal Navy and commissioned as HMS *Gadwall*.

Between July 1943 and April 1944 some 950 USAAF fighters, mainly Lightnings and Thunderbolts, were landed at Belfast either cocooned as deck cargo or dismantled in boxes. At Sydenham, within 500 yds of the unloading point, they were rapidly assembled and flight-tested by employees of the Lockheed Overseas Corporation and then flown to Langford Lodge for thorough inspection before delivery to England.

Stirling III prototype R9309 at Sydenham (RAF Museum).

The Admiralty placed one of its hangars at Sydenham at the disposal of Lockheed and four canvas Bessonneaux were erected adjacent to the wharf. It was then possible to assemble six aircraft a day and if necessary, by increasing the ground staff, up to 24 a day.

The Swordfish aircraft of 818 Squadron disembarked from HMS *Unicorn* on October 13 1943, being absorbed by 838 Squadron on November 1 when the aircrew left for Ceylon. A Corsair Squadron, 1831, was here for six weeks in November/December 1943 before disbandment. No 819 with Swordfish and Martlets came over from Inskip on November 14 prior to embarking on HMS *Activity* on January 12 1944. No 899 Squadron with Seafires followed on January 17, leaving on April 1 1944. No 857, an Avenger squadron, was here between July 15 and September 9 1944 and two more Corsair squadrons, 1850 and 1851, disembarked from December 6 to February 12 1945 and from January 14 to March 6 1945, respectively. The station was renamed HMS *Gannet III* on April 30 1945.

Belfast was unique in the UK in having fuelling facilities, an aerodrome and a wharf adjacent to deep water, all of which made not only the servicing of aircraft carriers relatively easy, but also allowed aircraft to be hoisted directly on to escort carriers. When the Royal Navy took over Sydenham, plans were prepared for the building of a second airport wharf, so as to enable the increased number of aircraft carriers coming into service to be berthed without delay. Construction was delayed, however, as the only possible site fouled the approach path to one of the runways. Only when a new runway had been built was construction approved but it was not completed until the end of the war.

Shorts found some work in the late '40s civilianising the Seaford flying boat as the Solent. The main runway at Sydenham

Hudson N7263 of 24 Squadron at Sydenham on October 21 1940 (Via E.A. Cromie).

was extended to 2,000 yds in the mid-'50s for the test-flying of Short-built Britannias and the firm was also building Canberras under sub-contract. The adjacent wharf came into its own again in 1954/55 when the company gained a contract to handle cocooned aircraft brought over from the USA as deck cargo. The types handled were Harvards and Sabres at first and then F-84s and T-33 trainers.

The Royal Navy ran an Aircraft Maintenance Yard on the other side of the airfield employing much local civilian labour in the repair of such aircraft as the Barracuda and Sea Otter. It went on to overhaul Sea Hawks, Sea Vixens and then Buccaneers. The facility was transferred to the RAF in July 1973 and closed in April 1978.

Shorts built and flew the SC 1 VTO research aircraft which contributed directly to the later success of the Harrier. At the opposite end of the scale, the firm designed the giant Belfast freighter, but, after the ten ordered by the RAF, it failed to attract any more orders. It was the Skyvan which made its first flight from Sydenham on January 17 1963 which has provided Shorts with a steady income up to the present. The SD3-30 airliner, built on the same 'box with wings' principle, but with a much longer fuselage, more powerful engines and retractable undercarriage, is a worthy successor and looks fit to keep the work-force busy for a long time to come.

The airfield was renamed Belfast Harbour in the '70s to give a better indication of its convenient position and it serves as a useful diversion for Aldergrove on occasion. The control tower is a three-storey naval type and many distinctive naval hangars can be seen along with RAF varieties like the Bellman and 'T2'.

Tain, Highland
21/NH830820. 2½ miles E of Tain

Developed from a pre-war landing ground serving the Tain Ranges, Tain opened on September 16 1941 as a Fighter Sector Station to bridge the gap between Scapa

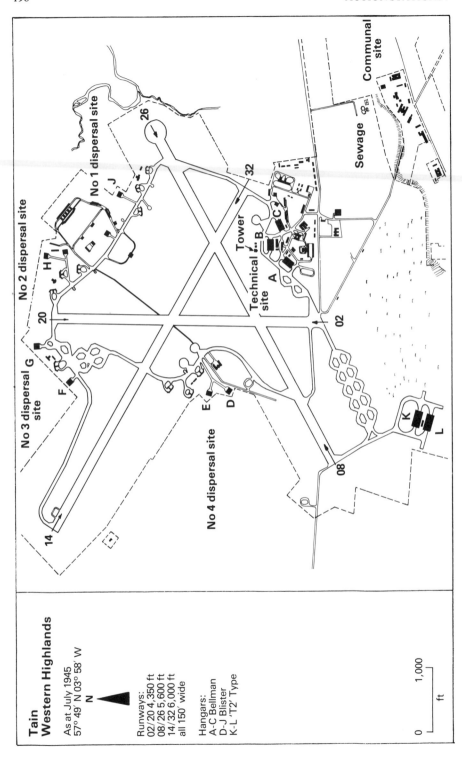

Tain
Western Highlands

As at July 1945
57° 49' N 03° 58' W

N

Runways:
02/20 4,350 ft
08/26 5,600 ft
14/32 6,000 ft
all 150' wide

Hangars:
A-C Bellman
D-J Blister
K-L 'T2' Type

0   1,000

ft

No 1 dispersal site
No 2 dispersal site
No 3 dispersal site
No 4 dispersal site

Communal site
Sewage
Technical site
Tower

26
32
02
08
14
20

A
B
C
D
E
F
G
H
J
K
L

and the northern flank of the Turnhouse Sector. The satellites were Fearn and Elgin and Hurricanes of 17 Squadron began to operate immediately. They moved to Catterick on October 31 and were replaced the following day by 'B' Flight of 123 Squadron detached from Castletown for sector reconnaissance and convoy patrols. The expected action in this part of the world was not forthcoming, all the *X-Raids* intercepted turning out to be friendly aircraft.

In March 1942, 801 Squadron of the FAA took over the patrols with sea Hurricanes in expectation of enemy resistance to a number of Bomber Command raids being carried out from Tain against the *Tirpitz* and other warships at Trondheim.

The Halifaxes of 76 Squadron had landed at Tain on March 27 1942 and after some preparation at the advanced base, they took off for Norway on the evening of March 30. The results were inconclusive and one aircraft failed to return. After five days on standby for further sorties, the squadron left for base at Middleton St George.

The Halifaxes returned late in April and made further attacks on the *Tirpitz* on April 27 and 28. Bombs of 4,000 lb were dropped but no hits could be seen through the smoke-screen. On April 29, 801 Squadron went to Turnhouse and the next day 76 Squadron left also, leaving the station bereft of operational aircraft.

The first American aircraft to land here was a Vindicator on April 23 1942. Although quite a familiar sight in Royal Navy marks, to whom it was known as the Chesapeake, this was a US Navy aircraft operating from the USS *Wasp* then in Scapa Flow. The pilot had lost his way flying from Hatston to Longman. In May

Albemarle P1431 of Coastal Command Development Unit at Tain on October 21 1942 after crash-landing with a runaway propellor. The picture was taken before the fire tender arrived! (P.J. Blandford).

a Liberator landed at Tain, a foretaste of the aircraft to be stationed here later in the war.

In June 1942, the station ORB commented: 'A strong west-wind made the aerodrome rather like the Libyan Desert with flying sand. There is no doubt the completion of the station and its efficient appearance has reacted favourably on general morale and discipline. A few months ago it was nothing more than a contractor's dump; there was no incentive for smartness.'

Flaming June was something of a joke in the North, despite rumours of heatwaves in Southern England, there was snow on the hills north of Dornoch and the airmen had to look at their diaries to reassure themselves that it really was summer. The airfield was still without aircraft and the staff began to wonder if Tain was marked on the maps at Whitehall and Kingsway!

A further indignity occurred when the satellite at Fearn was reallocated to the Admiralty. However, matters did improve slightly on June 15, when CCDU moved in from Ballykelly with a small collection of Beauforts and Hudsons, an Oxford and a Wellington.

Tain was already a designated advanced base for Bomber Command and the USAAF was now also to be allowed to use it if necessary. At the end of October 1942, a party of American engineers arrived to lay down extensions to the north-east/south-west runway and in the process to gain valuable experience in airfield construction. During the same month, arrangements were made with Fearn for FAA aircraft to carry out night-flying from Tain twice a week. As there were better facilities here, maintenance of FAA aircraft was also carried out until Fearn was developed.

The New Year saw some activity when aircraft from three squadrons—Beaufighters of 254 and Wellingtons of 311 and 547—arrived in January. The station was transferred to the control of Coastal Command on February 22 1943 and there now followed a rapid turnover of strike

Tain's operations block.

and shipping recce squadrons for varying periods. On March 11, for example, the Hampdens of 415 Squadron carried out an armed recce off Norway with torpedoes. Although no enemy ships were sighted, one aircraft failed to return and five diverted to Dyce on the way back.

In April, 404 Squadron's Beaufighters made their first sorties from Tain, attacking shipping off the Norwegian coast with cannon fire. On April 8, the Beaufighters of 144 Squadron arrived from Leuchars and were to make many operational flights from Tain before going north to Wick on October 20 1943. April 21 serves as a typical example of the Squadron's operations. Four Beaufighters took off on a patrol and sighted a motor vessel of 4,000 tons with two escorts. The ship was left listing heavily and covered in smoke and steam. The escorts, too, were strafed and severely damaged. Two more Beaufighters went out again in the afternoon but were intercepted by Bf 109s. One of the Beaufighters, too late to make cloud cover, was hit badly, the radio being wrecked and the navigator wounded. The fighters finally broke off, probably out of

Watch tower at Tain.

ammunition, leaving the Beaufighter to limp back to Tain. The undercarriage collapsed on landing and the crew just managed to escape before the aircraft caught fire.

Non-operational movements at the station were generated by No 1 Torpedo Refresher School, which, as its name implies, kept Coastal Command crews up to date in the skills of weapon delivery. A Rocket Projectile Flight was also part of the school, using a ship-towed target. Royal Navy crews also attended the courses in association with nearby Fearn, 815 and 817 Squadrons with Barracudas being attached for the first two months of 1944. No 1 TRS had, incidentally, formed in January 1943 as an offshoot of CCDU, which left Tain for Dale in April 1943.

No 186 Squadron was here from January to March 1944, during which time it converted from Typhoons to Spitfire VBs before moving south to Lympne. In mid-March the North Coates Wing was posted to train for a special operation (presumably against the *Tirpitz*) which in the event did not materialise. A total of 40 Beaufighters landed, supported by eight Dakotas of 271 Squadron with spares and ground crews. Further back-up was provided by four Warwicks of 280 Squadron on detachment from Thornaby and three Wellingtons from Bircham Newton. All this preparation came to nought however, and the aircraft left a few days later.

In the meantime, the north-east/south-west runway had been further extended with PSP by a Works Flight from RAF Oban. Diamond-shaped hardstandings had also been built and the station was now ready to accept Coastal Command Liberator Squadrons. No 86 Squadron had already been operating a Liberator detachment from here for a week in July 1944 to meet a concentration of U-boats off the Norwegian coast and even before that, an 86 Squadron aircraft flying from Tain on June 26 had sunk a U-boat.

No 311 Czech Squadron arrived on

August 7 for patrols off the Norwegian coast, also with Liberators. Other lodgers were a detachment of 547 Squadron with Wellingtons and the TT Flight of 4 OTU with two Oxfords and five Martinets. The latter moved here from Evanton on December 10 1944.

In March 1945, 86 Squadron began to use Mk VIII Liberators with an endurance of 10½ hours. Patrols were uneventful until May 5 when G of 86 Squadron spotted three fully surfaced U-boats off Denmark, one of which was being attacked by a Wellington of 547 Squadron. The Wellington was hit by flak and dived into the sea leaving one airman clinging to a dinghy. Two of the submarines had by now submerged but the third was bombed by the Liberator. Straddled by depth charges it sank stern first leaving 40 survivors in the water. A light ship about a mile away lowered a boat to pick them up and the circling Liberator was able to direct attention to the Wellington crewman, who was also rescued.

The last days of the war were spent in shadowing surrendering German U-boats and in June, 311 Squadron was transferred to Transport Command and left for Oakington. No 86 Squadron went to the same base on August 14 and left the station to 519, the Met Squadron, which arrived from Wick on August 17 with Halifaxes, Spitfires and a few Fortresses. The stay was short and they moved to Leuchars on November 8 1945. No 1 TRS, by now renamed 1 TTU, occupied the airfield for its final year and when the Beaufighter Xs left for Thorney Island on November 13 1946 it reverted to Care and Maintenance.

Back in January 1945, the Navy had requested an airfield near the Moray Firth for torpedo training, Tain or Leuchars being suggested, but events overtook the requirement.

There is still an RAF Tain, but the name applies to the permanently staffed air-to-ground weapons range on the coast adjacent to the old airfield. It is heavily used by the RAF, USAF and other NATO air arms and there are two helipads near to range control. These are available as a forward refuelling base for Lossiemouth helicopters on search missions when necessary.

There was a range here before the war and in 1940 it was obstructed with coils of barbed wire and old cars to prevent German troop carrier landings. The airfield was built on part of the original ranges.

In a small copse about a mile from the airfield is an impressive and atmospheric survival—the operations block. It was originally intended to control the Tain Sector and the usual miniature theatre with raised balcony was provided. Surprisingly, it is unvandalised. One enters through a door marked 'All Aircrew' and an arrow points down the steps. Other readable inscriptions include 'Tactical Library'. A good torch is essential to penetrate the gloom as no windows were provided of course. The trunking for the gas filtration and air supply is all still in place.

One feels an intruder in this building, it seems like a piece of history suspended in time. It needs to be preserved as a memorial to all the Beaufighter and Liberator crews who jostled through its doors with their charts and wind forecasts and flying gear to the waiting truck for the dispersal point. So many never saw Scotland—or anywhere—again.

Tealing, Tayside
54/NO405370. 3 miles N of Dundee off A929

Just after dawn on April 29 1942 a strange four-engined aircraft appeared in the circuit at Tealing; it was one of the first Russian TB7s to visit Britain and brought Molotov and a Military Mission. This airfield was probably chosen in order to attract as little attention as possible to the visit. Another arrived on May 20, leaving for the USA via Prestwick on the 24th.

No 56 OTU opened up Tealing when it moved from Sutton Bridge at the end of March 1942 equipped with Hurricanes, Masters and some Lysanders for target-towing. The new airfield had apparently been located without regard for local weather and topography, for it lay in a hollow plagued by fog and bad visibility and was overlooked by a range of hills to the west which made night-flying impossible. The OTU was anxious to resume its training programme delayed by the move from Lincolnshire but poor weather in April hindered it even more.

Most of the Hurricanes were well worn, some being veterans of the Battle of Britain and accidents due to technical failures were frequent. Others were typical of fighter OTU casualties—collisions and hitting trees whilst low-flying. One unfortunate accident was caused by a pupil pilot pressing the wrong button and firing at another Hurricane on which he was making practice attacks. The other pilot thought his aircraft was on fire and baled out to safety.

The courses during this period comprised about 40 pilots, many of whom were posted to the Middle East on completion. Three weeks of the course were spent at the satellite at Kinnell and all night flying was done from here.

In November 1942, some realistic training exercises were devised and soon became a regular part of 56 OTU's curriculum. For operational tactics training and formation practice, groups of up to 30 Hurricanes escorted Masters acting as bombers on simulated attacks against tagets as varied as Kinnell airfield, naval craft off Dundee and the Tay Bridge.

These exercises became highly elaborate and went under the codename *Swankpot*. *Swankpot* 15 on June 12 1943, for example, was a practice *Roadstead* with the object of locating an 'enemy' convoy with fighter-bomber and anti-flak sections, plus two support squadrons. Top cover was provided by Spitfires from 2 TEU who also gained valuable experience from these operations. The whole thing was supervised by the dummy ops room at Tealing.

The Bell Rock Lighthouse, Balado Bridge airfield and various factories along the east coast were among the recipients of these spectacular and realistic attacks which often included dive-bombing. The local population took it all without complaint!

On March 22 1943, 56 OTU was affiliated to the Peterhead Sector under a scheme first started in 1942 under the codename *Saracen*, whereby each fighter OTU would be turned into an operational squadron in the event of invasion. 'E' and 'F' Flights at Kinnell formed 556 Squadron and a section was at readiness during certain periods for convoy patrols under Peterhead. In August the airfield took part in Operation *Tyndall* with the arrival

of two gliders and the creation of a dummy Army camp.

Moving on to October 1943, 56 OTU was reorganised into 1 Combat Training Wing and subsequently retitled 1 Tactical Exercise Unit. The three courses currently passing through were redirected to 55 and 59 OTUs and replaced by a new intake of 150 pilots who had already completed their OTU training. No 1 Squadron was based at the satellite to specialise in air firing and evasive action and 2 and 3 Squadrons at the parent station. The former taught low-flying navigation and did dummy *Rhubarbs*, the latter undertook *Circus* and *Roadstead* operational exercises in conjunction with 2 TEU at Grangemouth.

Experimental landings were made by a Typhoon on November 7 and on January 4 1944 a flight of three Austers from 658 Squadron arrived with a Rota Autogiro for an exercise with the 52nd Lowland Division. At this time the TEU operated up to 110 aircraft, mostly Hurricanes with a few Masters and Lysanders. There were also two Typhoons for type conversion. RAF Tealing exchanged 40 Hurricanes for 38 Spitfires from Grangemouth on February 21 1944.

Nine Mustangs of 63 Squadron appeared on March 23 on a three-day detachment from Turnhouse to take part in training with the TEU and ground forces. The April weather in 1944 was such that nearby Craigowl Hill was cloud covered most of the time and there were 17 days of rain. Just prior to D-Day, 1 TEU was put on operational readiness to reinforce the regular squadrons as a contingency in the unlikely event of a counterattack from Norway. The unit was stood down on June 15.

The TEU disbanded on July 31 1944 but during this final month the airfield was host to a large number of Dakotas. On July 27, 30 of them landed to enable locally based troops to practice embarkation. The men were later flown to Broad-

Left *The Monolith of the Glen. Tealing tower in retirement.*

Right *Russian TB-7 at Tealing in May 1942 after bringing Molotov to Britain. Hurricanes of 56 OTU can be seen in the background* (Via Dr A.A. Duncan).

well. More troops were flown out on July 29 and 30 but the big day was July 31 when no less than 90 Dakotas ·arrived from airfields in the Cotswolds.

In August, Tealing was taken over by Flying Training Command, officers from 9 (P)AFU Errol having already visited with a view to taking it over as a satellite in place of Findo Gask. The changeover was made on September 12, the AFU hoping that the hard runways would enable them to maintain the flying task during the winter months. The observation was made that the district was known to suffer from very high winds and the airfield was unsuitable for night-flying. The latter was nevertheless attempted, although only one runway could be used because of the proximity of the hills.

The unit was gradually replacing its Masters with Harvards and by the end of October was entirely re-equipped. No 9 (P)AFU disbanded on June 21 1945 and Tealing was placed on Care and Maintenance under the wing of RAF Montrose.

The old aerodrome has not stood the test of time very well. One of its runways is covered with poultry sheds and the other is badly broken up. The tower, a large 518/40 type, remains but the hangars have long gone. It is just possible to trace where the TB7 was once parked in the well-known photograph but it is now all weed-grown concrete. The original entrance to the station is difficult to find, being near the church on the northern perimeter.

Tiree, Strathclyde

46/NM000445. 3 miles W of Scarinish on B8065

This was a particularly unpopular posting owing to its remoteness. It was close to the sea and on one occasion the officers' mess windows were broken by a mine exploding on the beach and on another the RAF helped rescue the crew of a trawler. It was driven ashore about midnight and the master later presented his fish catch to the station in gratitude.

The airfield's origins went back to 1934 when Midland and Scottish Airways selected a landing strip on The Reef, Tiree. A new service between Glasgow and Skye was meant to call at Reef but a dispute about rental delayed the start of a daily summer service until 1937. This continued with some breaks during the Second World War, when a civil grass strip remained open alongside the sprawling RAF station.

In 1940, when Atlantic convoys were forced to reroute round the north of Ireland, new airfields in the Hebrides became an urgent requirement. The civil airfield was requisitioned and contractors imported hordes of unruly labourers.

The airfield was first occupied in November 1941 but no electricity or water supply was available. The first Christmas was a miserable affair and the only highlight if it can be called that, was a pilot officer playing in the New Year on his saxophone! Things improved when RAF Tiree became operational and a roster was kept by the station adjutant of all personnel who wished to travel on leave to the mainland. When possible they were given seats on the Station Comm Flight aircraft or any other available service machine.

Before its own aircraft arrived, the airfield was used by several others in emergency. On February 20 1942, a Liberator of 120 Squadron diverted from Nutt's Corner was filled with 1,250 gallons of petrol from tins and sent off on an operational patrol. A Harrow from Limavady brought stores and equipment on April 8 1942, heralding the arrival of 224 Squadron four days later. Its Hudsons were dispersed on the adjacent Scottish Airways' landing ground.

More operational aircraft arrived on May 13 in the shape of the Wellingtons of 304 Squadron which had just been transferred from Bomber to Coastal Command.

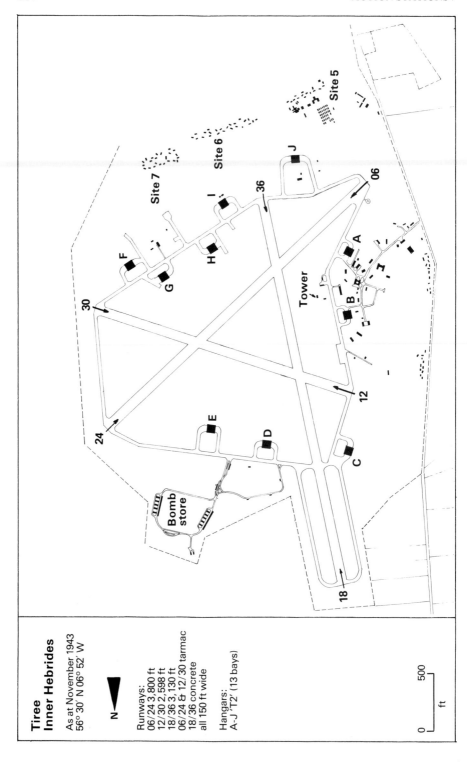

Tiree
Inner Hebrides

As at November 1943
56° 30' N 06° 52' W

N

Runways:
06/24 3,800 ft
12/30 2,598 ft
18/36 3,130 ft
06/24 & 12/30 tarmac
18/36 concrete
all 150 ft wide

Hangars:
A-J 'T2' (13 bays)

0   500
ft

Halifax V LK966 of 518 Squadron off the coast of Tiree (J.O. Friend, via Chaz Bowyer).

Anti-submarine patrols were begun on May 18 and on May 31, one of the Wellingtons sighted a U-boat wake and dropped depth charges on it. An elongated oil patch was seen and the wake stopped completely but no confirmation could be made.

Wellingtons and Hudsons lacked the range to venture very far out into the Atlantic, where they were desperately needed for convoy protection, so 304 Squadron was withdrawn to Dale in Wales and 224 Squadron converted to Liberators at Tiree in July 1942. The enormous range of this aircraft compared to its contemporaries successfully plugged the gap in air cover over the middle of the Atlantic. No 224 Squadron was sent to Hampshire on September 9 1942, its duties being taken over by aircraft based in Northern Ireland.

Tiree reverted to Care and Maintenance in October 1942, only coming to life again on September 25 1943, when 518 Squadron's Halifaxes were repositioned from Stornoway. This was a meteorological reconnaissance unit, with the motto (in Gaelic) 'We hold the key', which stayed until September 18 1945. From October 28 1943 until disbandment on February 14 1944 the associated Met' Conversion Unit trained Halifax crews at Tiree.

The met' flights penetrated 700 miles out into the Atlantic and from January 1945 the aircraft carried depth charges in case an enemy submarine should be sighted.

Another specialist unit arrived on February 27 1944. This was 281 Squadron from Thornaby, equipped with Warwicks carrying airborne lifeboats. The squadron, which also had some Ansons, was active until September 1945, although the HQ had moved to Mullaghmore on

February 7 1945, leaving only a detachment at Tiree. Hurricanes from 516 Squadron were detached for short periods in March 1944 on local exercises.

Tiree's war was low-key but the met squadron did an invaluable job, along with 517 Squadron in Wales, in providing the raw information on which the weather experts based their meteorological forecasts for the bomber offensive against Germany and other operations. Several aircraft were lost without trace over the ocean but the worst incident was a head-on collision right over the airfield between two Halifaxes, with the loss of 16 lives.

Early in 1944, the AMWD finally responded to endless requests to provide thicker gauge steel sheeting to re-cover the station's Nissen huts, which were not standing up to the island's climatic conditions. Another building peculiar to the airfields on the Western Isles was the '½ T2' which, as the name implies, was a standard 'T2' but half the usual length, presumably because there was less side area offered to the gales. Tiree had ten of these structures and since there were very few hardstandings the aircraft were probably hangared when on the ground. Because Tiree had been planned also as a Fighter Sector Station an operations room was sited just to the east.

On July 1 1946, Tiree was transferred to the Ministry of Civil Aviation, the island being left littered with derelict buildings. On the credit side, however, the RAF had brought a taste of the outside world to the island. The NAAFI canteen had constituted Tiree's first licensed premises and many islanders saw their first live concert at the camp theatre. The RAF water supply was adapted after the war to serve much of the island and the airfield diesel power station had its capacity doubled for civilian electricity needs.

To date, services to Barra and Glasgow have been operated first by BEA and then by Loganair. There are also occasional visits by light aircraft.

Toome, Londonderry

14/H970905. 1 mile W of Toome on A31

Toome was yet another of the Northern Ireland stations which had a prolonged opening-up period and whose birth was attended by visits, conferences and discussions. The first RAF airmen were posted in on January 2 1943 but the USAAF was interested in acquiring the airfield and a number of officers inspected it in March.

It had been planned originally in 1941, possibly as a bomber OTU satellite to Cluntoe but the requisitioning of the land proved to be a lengthy process, since about 50 landowners were involved. As a result, work did not begin until January 1942, when the firm of Farran's Ltd, an offshoot of Sunley who had built Birmingham Airport and Hawarden amongst others, established a site office in a cottage. Progress was delayed by the water-logged ground, most of which was only a few feet above the level of Lough Neagh and the nearby Rivers Bann and Moyola.

Such was the dearth of suitable airfield sites in Ulster that these factors were accepted at the planning stage. Even more unusual was the fact that the Station HQ and domestic sites were separated from the airfield by the River Moyola, the only connection being by a narrow bridge. Given the concern about sabotage, it is remarkable that the Air Ministry planners decided to risk the disruption which would have been caused by the loss of the bridge.

During its first months, Toome attracted the normal quota of aircraft lost or forced down by bad weather. On July 5 1943, for example, two Ansons landed, one from Cark and the other from Wigtown. Five days later a B-17 diverted in on its way to Prestwick from the USA. The same day a detachment of eight Wellingtons of 104 OTU Nutt's Corner arrived to make up Toome's first active flying unit, although it was only destined to be here until September 7 1943.

The station was formally handed over to the USAAF as Station 236 on July 26 1943 and from then until October 1944 was its busiest period. At least 600 and possibly as many as 800 combat crews were given training and sent to Marauder and Havoc groups, almost all of them going to the 9th Air Force following its absorption of 8th Air Force medium bombardment groups in October 1943.

On August 23 1943, the Combat Crew Replacement Centre units were activated with the provisional designations of 2902nd HQ & HQ Squadron and 2905th Replacement and Training Squadron, each of which was redesignated '3rd' on November 21 under 3rd CCRC Group. The first contingent of 22 crews arrived at Toome on September 21 1943 for a three-week course, being sent to units in England.

Despite training crews exclusively for 9th Bombardment Command, the 3rd CCRC Group remained assigned to 8th Air Force Composite Command. As the newly reconstituted 9th Air Force grew in strength, so did Toome. By November, there was a standardised 15-day course designed to familiarise airmen straight from the States with the special peculiarities of combat flying in Northern Europe.

During the first four months of 1944, a total of four new Marauder and three new Havoc groups was added to the 9th BomCom and there was a corresponding upsurge in activity at Toome. The first A-20 crews arrived at the end of February but did not depart for combat units until April, possibly because of problems which had been experienced in getting the 416th BG's Havocs operational.

In March and April the school was functioning close to its normal maximum capacity of 100 crews and in August a new

AM Bombing Teacher with gunnery and crew procedure training building in left background, Toome (E.A. Cromie).

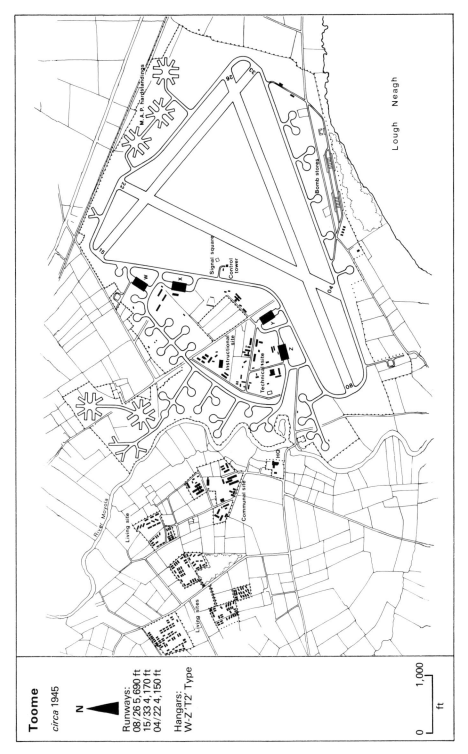

Toome

circa 1945

N

Runways:
08/26 5,690 ft
15/33 4,170 ft
04/22 4,150 ft

Hangars:
W-Z 'T2' Type

Lough Neagh

M.A.P. hardstandings

Bomb stores

Signal square

Control tower

Instructional site

Technical site

HQ

Communal site

Living site

Living sites

River Moyola

0 1,000 ft

record was set when 112 B-26 and 42 A-20 crews passed through. Every effort was made to provide the highest standards of instruction and to keep up to date with the latest experience and techniques.

Close links were maintained with actual front-line units, to which instructors were detached for short periods of operational duty. In the second half of June 1944, Lieutenant McKee, an A-20 flight commander from the 3rd R & T Squadron took part in five missions, one of which was the final attack on Cherbourg prior to the assault by the ground forces. In July, Lieutenant Galkins, another A-20 flight commander, completed three missions.

Toome's subsidiary function during the American occupation was the temporary storage of up to 50 aircraft on behalf of the Air Depot at Langford Lodge. For this purpose, five MAP multiple standings, which resembled snowflakes in shape, were constructed early in 1944 around the perimeter. It is doubtful, however, if they were ever used to the extent envisaged.

Some time after the 3rd CCRCs HQ was moved to Cheddington, Toome was transferred back to the RAF on November 7 1944, but it was not used again by flying units before the war ended. The staff were ordered to display a 'Landing Prohibited' sign in the signals square with effect from November 24. Prior to its display, three aircraft, an Avenger, Wildcat and C-47, landed because their respective destinations in Northern Ireland were weather-bound.

The station was inspected by a party from Bomber Command on February 1 1945, to assess the possibilities of it being used as a training school for up to 340 aircrew. The domestic site was found inadequate and the proposal was subsequently abandoned. So also was the suggested use of the airfield for Dakota training by 109 OTU. What was allowed was the grazing of sheep!

No 257 MU arrived at the beginning of June 1945, using the buildings for equipment storage until March 1947. Prospects looked good for a return to flying in February 1953 when 2 FTS reformed at Cluntoe and Toome became a satellite. Extensive runway resurfacing had been carried out but all in vain, as the school was withdrawn to the mainland in the spring of 1954. Interestingly Toome is recorded in April 1954 as being a 'station in reserve' under RNAS Eglinton.

The airfield was then handed over to the Admiralty as a repair facility for naval

gun turrets until the work ceased around the beginning of 1959. From 1961 onwards the site was gradually returned to its former owners. Most of the hardstandings were broken up, along with almost all of the living accommodation. The two most easterly hangars have gone but the other two are used for brick manufacture. In contrast, the control tower, a 12779/41 type, has been renovated as a smart dwelling. The bomb storage area is in good condition and the Bombing Teacher building still stands.

Turnberry, Strathclyde

70/NS205070. 6 miles N of Girvan on A77

Usually assumed to be a Second World War airfield, Turnberry actually came into existence in 1917 when 2 (Auxiliary) School of Aerial Gunnery was formed. This unit became 1 School of Aerial Fighting and Gunnery in May 1918 and then 1 Fighting School later the same month. Lionel W.B. Rees VC assumed command in 1917 and stayed until the end of the war. The casualty rate was high and an impressive memorial lists all the names. The airfield then closed but was revived as an AA Landing Ground in the '30s.

The Turnberry memorial (J. Huggon).

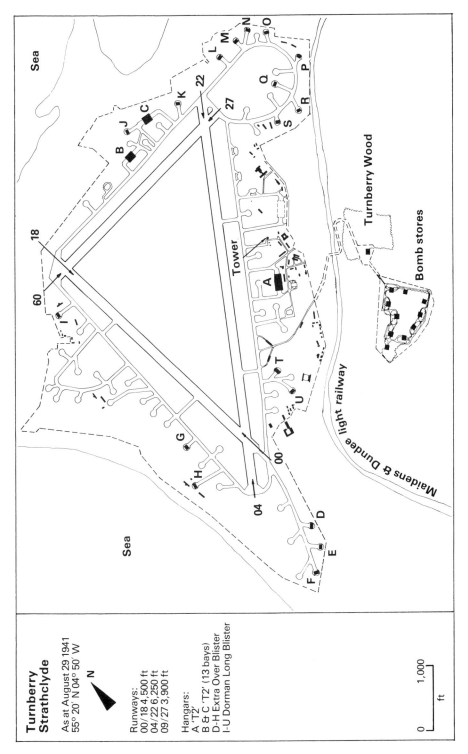

Turnberry
Strathclyde

As at August 29 1941
55° 20' N 04° 50' W

N

Runways:
00/18 4,500 ft
04/22 6,250 ft
09/27 3,900 ft

Hangars:
A 'T2'
B & C 'T2' (13 bays)
D-H Extra Over Blister
I-U Dorman Long Blister

0   1,000

ft

Sea

Sea

Tower

Turnberry Wood

Bomb stores

Maidens & Dundee light railway

After an opening-up process dating back to February 9 1942, Turnberry's second phase of active existence began in May 1942 with the move of 5 (Coastal) OTU from Chivenor. This unit's primary task was to train Beaufort crews but it only stayed until December 29, being then transferred to Long Kesh. No 1 Torpedo Training Unit formed at Turnberry in its place on January 1 1943, using Beauforts and Hampdens, the airfield still providing lodger facilities for one fighter squadron if necessary. 'B' Flight of 652 Squadron was detached here in January 1943 for Army exercises.

Because of overcrowding, part of the TTU was kept at Abbotsinch. The local topography so cramped the aerodrome that the construction of further hardstandings was impossible. However, in May 1943, this did not prevent Mosquitoes of 618 Squadron being detached from Skitten for *Highball* trials.

On September 29 1943, 2 TTU moved from Castle Kennedy to Turnberry, its Hampdens and Beaufighters being absorbed by 1 TTU. The latter in turn was taken over on April 25, soon after 5 OTU had arrived back at Turnberry on February 15 1944. The intention was to concentrate several different types of Coastal training within one unit. Specialised courses were run, for example, with Ventura aircraft to provide crews for 519 Met Squadron which still operated the type. Hudsons were used for refresher flying and Beaufighters for strike training. A further diversification came with the absorption of the Air Sea Rescue Training Unit on May 15 1944, Warwicks then joining the establishment.

In common with most airfields on the west coast, Turnberry collected its fair share of strays. Two of the most significant were a Liberator from Montreal bound for Prestwick on March 27 1944 and a USAAF C-47 two days later. The C-47 landed downwind but pulled up safely after a 16½ hour flight from North Africa. An operational diversion came on June 9 1944 when 22 Lancasters arrived because of bad weather over their Lincolnshire bases.

The Coastal Command Flying Instructors School was repositioned from St Angelo on June 8 1945 with Wellingtons and Beauforts on strength. No 5 OTU disbanded on August 1 1945 but 1 TTU seems to have re-emerged at this point under the wing of the CCFIS. Both units moved to Tain on November 12 1945 and

Turnberry then closed. In the '60s it was reopened for light aircraft use, especially during tournaments at the adjacent golf course.

Most of the wartime buildings have been demolished, including the 12779/41 watch office and the five 'T2' hangars.

Turnhouse, Lothian

65/NT60735. 5 miles W of Edinburgh on B9080

The first enemy aircraft brought down over Britain during the Second World War was credited partly to 602 and partly to 603 Squadrons.

The latter had formed at Turnhouse as long ago as October 14 1925, first with DH 9As, then Wapitis in 1930 and Harts in 1934. Redesignated as a fighter unit on October 24 1938, it re-equipped with Hinds, and flew them until Gladiators arrived the following March. Spitfires in turn soon replaced them and were operational just in time to meet the raids on eastern Scotland.

Turnhouse's history went back further than this, however, as it opened in 1916 with 26 Reserve Squadron forming here in May. Late in 1916 it also became a Flight Station for 'A' Flight of 77 (HD) Squadron but was reduced to landing ground status only for home defence purposes in July 1917. No 26 Training Squadron, as it was now called, left at the same time. No 73 Training Squadron moved in from Thetford on September 17 with Sopwith Camels, leaving for Beaulieu the following February. The airfield then became a Fleet Practice Station and Fleet Aircraft Repair Depot.

Moving forward to the '30s again we find 83 Squadron, a day bomber unit with Hinds, re-forming here on August 4 1936 and going to Scampton in March 1938. In February 1938 one of 111 Squadron's new Hurricanes flown by Squadron Leader J.W. Gillan set a record for the Turnhouse/Northolt trip of 327 miles in 48 minutes at an average speed of 408.75 mph. The attempt deliberately coincided with a strong tailwind but his navigation must have been incredibly accurate. Many years later, in August 1954, Squadron Leader R.L. Topp in a Hunter of 43 Squadron flew the same route in 27 minutes 46 seconds, an average of 717 mph.

Turnhouse became a Sector Station in September 1939 under 13 Group and was to see many fighter squadrons come and go. No 141 Squadron re-formed here on October 4 1939, transferring to Grangemouth two weeks later but returning at the end of June 1940, operational with Defiants. They went south in July but the Defiant soon proved easy meat as a day fighter and was withdrawn for other duties. Throughout September and most of October 1940, 141 was based at Turnhouse to train for night fighting.

No 603 Squadron had left in mid-December 1939 and concrete runways were then hastily laid to replace the worn out and ill-drained turf. The next fighter unit based was 245 with Hurricanes from Drem on June 5 1940 until allocated to Aldergrove for the defence of Belfast on July 20. They were replaced by 253 Squadron from Lincolnshire with more Hurricanes but a month later they moved to Prestwick.

No 65 Squadron, withdrawn from the Battle of Britain for a rest, filled the gap and flew the usual routine sector patrols and convoy escorts. Some fighter affiliation with 263 Squadron's Whirlwinds was also done before 65 went to Tangmere at the end of November. Concurrently, 3 Squadron's Hurricanes had also been at Turnhouse for most of September and October 1940, followed by 607 Squadron's aircraft into November.

Two squadrons re-formed here in May 1941, both with Spitfires. The first was 122 on May 1, moving to Ouston on June 26, the other was 123 on May 10. No 123 went to Drem in August to continue training Spitfire pilots fresh from OTU prior to postings to operational squadrons in the south.

The first Free French fighter squadron, 340, formed at Turnhouse on November 7 1941, becoming operational on Spitfires for defensive patrols on November 29. It

Above *Dutch Navy Neptune at Turnhouse in 1968.*

Below *Varsity taken from the control tower at Turnhouse in 1968.*

moved to Drem on December 20 but returned for brief periods in March/April 1943 and February 1945.

After leaving its Hurricanes with the Russians, following service near Murmansk, 81 Squadron's personnel reassembled at Turnhouse in December 1941 to work up on Spitfires. A detachment was kept at Ouston and eventually the whole unit moved there in April 1942. No 4 Delivery Flight was based from January 8 1942 to ferry fighter aircraft within 11 Group.

No 242 Squadron re-formed on April 10 1942, but its Spitfires were still not operational by the time it moved to Ouston in May. No 801 Squadron with Sea Hurricanes was also here around this time and the second line 289 Squadron moved its HQ over from Kirknewton on May 20, being destined to stay until May 7 1945. It was equipped with Hurricanes, Oxfords, Defiants and other types for a variety of co-operation duties.

FAA units were often attached for short periods, particularly when they disembarked from carriers in the Forth. Examples include 882 with Martlets in February/March 1942, 884 with Fulmars from March to July 1942 and 808 with Seafires in June/July 1943.

After serving in support of the Dieppe Raid, 232 Squadron came north to prepare for a move to North Africa in November 1942. No 234 was also here at the same time pending a similar move overseas. A second French squadron, 341, formed on January 15 1943 and after working up, moved to Biggin Hill in March, although it did return briefly in February 1945.

A tactical reconnaissance squadron, 63, with Mustangs, arrived in July 1943 to participate in intensive training exercises before going to Thruxton in November. Returning in January 1944, it re-equipped with Hurricanes and trained for bombardment spotting with the Navy

Canberra used by Ferranti for radar development over Turnhouse (Via R. Bonser).

pending attachment to the Invasion forces in May. Another Mustang squadron, 268, was also here from November 1943 to January 1944.

Turnhouse had many visiting aircraft, a large proportion being American towards the end of the war. The RAF staff did not appreciate the numbers of USAAF heavy bombers squeezing into the airfield on 'rest and recreation' flights to the capital. One genuine visitor, however, was a Fortress bound for Prestwick from Iceland which had flown round Scotland for three hours on March 18 1944 before being led in by a Mosquito from Drem.

A second target-towing squadron, 290, joined the station in August 1944 from Long Kesh, staying until the following January when it moved to Belgium to help with the training of AA gunners defending the Allied bases.

Spitfires returned in March 1945 when 329 Squadron was withdrawn from the Continent, but within a month they had gone to Skeabrae. Another squadron posted back to Britain, 164, appeared in June to re-equip with Spitfires, leaving for Fairwood Common in November and coming back for a couple of months in January 1946. No 303 Squadron's Mustangs spent December 1945 at Turnhouse then went on to Wick on January 5.

No 603 Squadron came home from the war in April 1945 only to disband on August 15. It was re-formed in 1946 with Spitfires, re-equipped with Vampires in July 1951 and went the way of all Auxiliary squadrons in March 1957. No 1968 AOP Flight of 666 Squadron was here from 1949 until about 1953 and Edinburgh UAS was another long serving resident with Tiger Moths and Chipmunks.

The US base at nearby Kirknewton attracted numerous USAF transports to Turnhouse and one American military aircraft was chief suspect in an unusual incident. On April 2 1954 a US Army Cessna Bird-Dog appeared in the circuit low level from the direction of the Forth Bridge, landed and spent the night in the RAF hangar. The next day the newspapers published a report of a high-wing light aircraft having flown under the Forth Bridge the previous evening. By this time the Bird-Dog was well on its way back to Germany!

The airport closed in 1961 to allow the main runway to be strengthened for Vanguard operations, East Fortune being used in the interim. At the same time, the Visual Control Room from the recently closed Blackbushe Airport was re-erected at Turnhouse on top of the original wartime tower.

The British Airports Authority assumed control in April 1971 and rectified Turnhouse's major shortcoming; the main runway, which had been laid during the war with more regard for fitting it in to the existing perimeter than the direction of the prevailing wind. Severe cross-winds were common, the subsidiary runway was too short, with a hill at one end, and diversions to Glasgow were embarrassingly frequent. An entirely new runway was built just to the north-west of the airport and a new terminal was constructed at the same time, giving Edinburgh an airport of equal standing to that of Glasgow.

Twatt, Orkney

6/HY265230. 9 miles N of Stromness on A967

Just before the new airfield opened, the captain-designate sent a memo to the Admiralty suggesting that RNAS Twatt might give rise to unseemly mirth. He was ignored, the name stuck and laugh they did!

This 'clearing in the primeval heather', as it has been described, was commissioned as HMS *Tern* on April 1 1941. (Even the date was unfortunate.) It had been built partly by the Auxiliary Battalion Royal Marines, later renamed the 19th Royal Marine Battalion, who also guarded the site during construction and for some time after it opened. (Royal Marines engineers did much of the heavy construction on airfield projects in the Orkneys.)

One of the first squadrons to spend time here was 818 with Swordfish in July/August 1941. No 809's Fulmars disembarked from *Victorious* to Twatt on a number of occasions, as did many other units during the station's operational life. No 700 moved in from Hatston in June 1942 with Walrus amphibians, which it detached to several locations around the islands until disbanding on March 24 1944.

No 771, a fleet requirement squadron, came from Hatston in July 1942 and flew a variety of types, including Blenheims, Martinets, Rocs and Beauforts. There is insufficient space here to list all the units disembarked briefly, but they included 822 Squadron with Albacores in October 1942, 819 with Swordfish in January/February 1942 and 804 with Sea Hurricanes in February 1943.

One of the last squadrons was 802 with Seafires from June 21 until July 20 1945. Five days later, 771 moved to Zeals in Wiltshire. Twatt remained a reserve station under Lossiemouth's control until January 1949 and was then retained by the Navy until sold off in 1957.

Swordfish target tug of 771 Squadron on the perimeter track at Twatt 1944. Note TT stripes (FAA Museum).

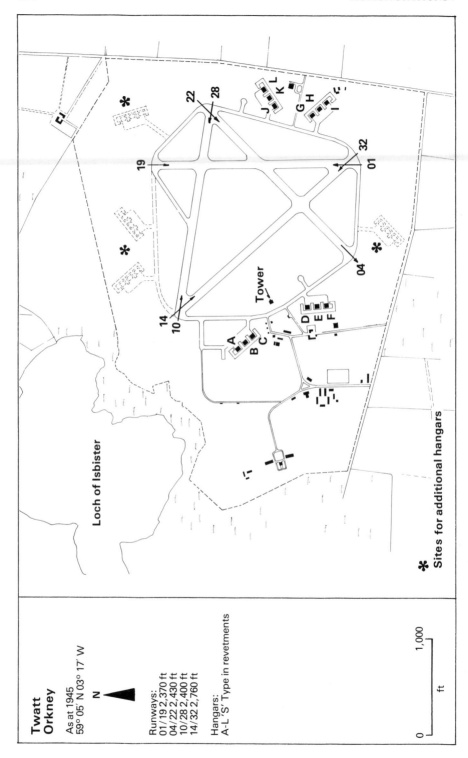

Twatt
Orkney

As at 1945
59° 05′ N 03° 17′ W

N

Runways:
01/19 2,370 ft
04/22 2,430 ft
10/28 2,400 ft
14/32 2,760 ft

Hangars:
A-L 'S' Type in revetments

Loch of Isbister

Tower

* Sites for additional hangars

0   1,000
            ft

Two views of Twatt: **Top** *the tower perched on top of the operations block and* **above** *the remains of the cinema* (J.C. Temple).

It had the usual four 90 ft wide runways and four dispersals off the perimeter track, each with three earth-traversed 'S' sheds. Twelve more hangars were planned in 1945 but never erected. A number of buildings are left today, the most interesting being the control tower perched on top of the operations block. The entrance and projection room of the station cinema are still standing and the former squash court can also be seen.

Usworth, Tyne and Wear

88/NZ340585. 2 miles SW of Boldon on A1290

Despite being a training station for most of its wartime career, Usworth had the distinction of being singled out for a major Luftwaffe attack during the Battle of Britain. On August 15 1940, a large force of He 111s of KG26 inadequately escorted by Bf 110s of ZG76 were detected approaching the east coast. Spitfires from 72 Squadron Acklington met them off the

Farne Islands and although heavily out-numbered claimed several destroyed.

The German formation then split in two, one portion making for Tyneside, while the other turned south. The second Acklington squadron, No 79, encountered the northern group just off the coast and a wild dog-fight with the escort ensued. Re-forming, the Hurricanes caught up with the bombers approaching Newcastle, where their primary objective would seem to have been Usworth. Harried by the Tyne guns and by more Hurricanes from Drem, the Heinkels made off, scattering their bombs to little effect, and leaving Usworth untouched. The southerly force, fired on by 14 and 607 Squadrons from Catterick and Usworth, jettisoned their bombs in the area of Seaham Harbour. The enemy lost eight bombers and seven fighters and since no military target was hit it was certainly a highly successful action on the part of 13 Group and the AA guns.

Their intended target started life in October 1916 as a Flight Station for 'B' Flight of 36 Squadron known as Hylton. In August 1917 it was in use by 'A' Flight and continued as such until the Armistice when it was just beginning to be called Usworth. (Early in 1916 when being laid out it had been named West Town Moor.)

On March 17 1930, 607 Squadron was formed as a day bomber unit in the Auxiliary Air Force and the former airfield was reactivated as its base. However, it was not until September 1932 that personnel were able to move to the site. Next month, the first aircraft, a Gypsy Moth, arrived for flying training, and in December, the first Wapitis were received. These were operated until September 1936, when Demons replaced them, the squadron's role being changed to fighter. These in turn were replaced by Gladiators soon after the Munich crisis.

A regular squadron, 103, flew Hinds and Battles alongside 607 at Usworth from February 26 1937, until moving to Abingdon at the beginning of September 1939. The first Battle had been delivered on July 18 1938 and the unit was completely re-equipped by the time it left. 'G' Flight of 1 AACU was also here from February 1 until May 19 1939.

No 607 Squadron moved to the new satellite at Acklington on September 10 1939, subsequently serving in the Battle of France and returning to Usworth in June 1940 to re-equip with Hurricanes. The squadron, now in fine fettle, went south to Tangmere in September in time for the height of the Battle of Britain. Apart from a brief stay in December 1940 and January 1941, 607 did not return to the north-east until it re-formed after the war. No 43 Squadron, also flying Hurricanes, was sent up from Tangmere in September for a well-earned rest, seeing no more action until it left for Drem on December 12 1940.

After a short period of inactivity, Usworth received fighter aircraft again, this time Hurricanes of 55 OTU which began to arrive from Aston Down on March 14 1941. They were mainly the Canadian-built Mk X variety which the OTU used for fighter and later fighter bomber training. Ouston was employed as a satellite until the OTU moved to Annan

on April 28 1942. Shortly before they left, the large Beehive hangar which still stands today was hit by an overshooting Hurricane, injuring the pilot.

The station was left in the charge of a Care and Maintenance party but not for long. The formation here of 62 OTU on June 23 1942 was intended to improve the quality of training given to radar operators for the night-fighter squadrons. No 3 Radio School at Prestwick had previously been responsible for this task, despite a dearth of facilities and efficient ground trainers.

No 62 OTU took over the AI Training Flight from 3 RS, which consisted of ten Ansons and 24 pupils for the initial course. The unit's establishment was to be three squadrons, each with 14 pilots, 14 observer-instructors and 14 Ansons. AI was to be fitted in each aircraft with two cathode ray tubes so that the instructor could monitor the pupil's interpretation of what was being seen on the screen while a second pupil watched the target's behaviour visually from the front seat as he listened to the commentary over the intercom.

After six weeks of carefully graduated exercises, the majority of trainees had gained such a sound grasp of the principles involved that they were soon able to adapt themselves to the higher speeds of operational aircraft. From Usworth they then went to one of the night-fighter OTUs to be crewed-up with their future pilots.

The OTU also trained a number of American airmen as AI operators for USAAF Beaufighter squadrons early in 1943. Indeed there was a detachment of the 416th Night Fighter Squadron at Usworth between May 14 and June 10 1943. For some time bad weather hindered the output of the night-fighter OTUs and some 49 pupils having passed their courses were held at 62 OTU until vacancies

Usworth 1978 (F. Neal).

enabled them to graduate on to the final stage of training.

Usworth proved to be inadequate for the rapid growth of 62 OTU and accommodation was stretched to the limit. The last straw was the advent of a balloon barrage at Sunderland whose proximity to the aerodrome made it a serious hazard, especially in a locality where industrial haze often obliterated all landmarks in a very short space of time. The unit accordingly moved to Ouston at the end of June 1943. In April 1944, Usworth was administered by RAF Morpeth for Care and Maintenance until an Aircrew Disposal Unit arrived in June, remaining until January 1945.

The airfield then seems to have been used very little for flying until after the war, when 23 RFS formed here on February 1 1949 with Tiger Moths, Ansons and eventually Chipmunks, disbanding at the end of July 1953. Other post-war units were 1965 Flight of 644 Squadron with Austers and 2 Basic Air Navigation School with Ansons. The latter was formed at Usworth by Airwork Ltd in March 1951 and closed in April 1953.

In July 1963, the site became Sunderland Airport and is now a thriving light aviation centre. The North East Aircraft Museum is also on the airport, its aircraft parked on the concrete floor which is all that is left of the former Callender hangar. The collection includes an F-100, T-33, Vampire, Meteor and Valetta. Another 'resident' of local folklore is George the Ghost, a Canadian pilot killed in a Hurricane crash it is said. He haunts the Beehive hangar and has even been seen in the Flying Club bar!

The Beehive is actually an original pre-war Lamella design. There was also a Callender hangar and one Blister during the war, with eight dispersal pens around the perimeter track which joined the two runways. Airfield defence was taken care of by a number of pillboxes, including at least one with a gun-post on its roof, a Battle HQ and reputedly three Pickett-Hamilton retractable forts.

West Freugh, Dumfries and Galloway

82/NX110545. 5 miles SE of Stranraer on A757

The only airfield in this part of Scotland to survive into the 80s, West Freugh dates back continuously to August 1936 when the building of a camp and associated ranges was begun, the land costing £19,400 for some 2,700 acres. It took its name from a farm engulfed by the aerodrome.

Difficulties were encountered at first with the bombing targets in Luce Bay—even piles driven 6 ft into the sand failed to withstand wind and tide. Although 4 Armament Training Camp opened on January 1 1937, it was the end of April before new targets had been completed. These were made of steel plates and girders bolted together to form three towers on wooden piles driven 18 ft into the sand.

A succession of squadrons was attached for training, 63 Squadron with Battles, which was here from August 29 to September 26 1938, being a typical example. No 4 ATC became 4 Armament Training Station on April 1 1938, receiving some Heyfords for training air observers in bombing and firing. A year later came a further redesignation to 4 Air Observer School, Battles being added to the establishment. As a more accurate description of its role, 4 AOS became 4 Bombing and Gunnery School on November 1 1939.

The same day, the Air Ministry issued instructions for action to be taken against enemy submarines if they were seen during range practice. 'E' Flight of 1

Lincoln SX930 of Bombing Trials Unit at West Freugh in September 1951 (H. Quinton).

AACU with Henleys towed targets from May 1939, Defiants being added in October 1942 preparatory to the flight becoming part of 298 Squadron on November 16.

A Heyford caught fire over the Luce Bay Ranges on March 3 1940, when a faulty gun mounting caused a bullet to pierce a fuel tank. The pilot brought the aircraft back over the airfield, baled out his crew and then jumped to safety himself.

A new training scheme was introduced in April 1940 when the Armament Training Squadron and ground instructors amalgamated into the Armament Training Wing. Three squadrons formed within this wing—Bombing Squadron with Battles (formerly 'C' Flight), Gunnery Squadron with Heyfords and Battles (formerly 'B' Flight) and the Towing Squadron with Henleys and Wallaces (formerly 'A' and 'D' Flight). In addition, the station was now a recognised alternative aerodrome for fighter squadrons in an emergency but it was destined never to be used for this purpose.

Re-equipment with Bothas began in April 1941, to an eventual total of 66, plus 27 Battles for target-towing. These unpopular aircraft were replaced by Ansons later that year and in yet another reshuffle on June 14 1941, 4 B & GS became 4 AOS once more. Its final renaming took place on June 11 1943 to 4 (Observer) Advanced Flying Unit.

Early in 1942, the Bomber Command Experimental Unit was based at West Freugh for weapons trials on the ranges, leading to the formation of the Bombing Trials Unit on August 1 1942. The BTU was to operate a variety of aircraft types, including Hampdens, Mitchells, Lancasters and Lincolns. A dummy factory target was built from concrete on the moors above Stranraer and is still to be seen today, the whole area being pitted with bomb craters.

The station served also in an *ad hoc* ASR role for aircraft missing in the northern Irish Sea. A particularly black day was February 9 1942 when two Spitfires from Kirkistown and two Hurricanes from Crosby-on-Eden were lost. Despite an extensive search with two Ansons no trace was found. The airfield's relatively good weather resulted in many diversions, notably several Hudsons from Newfoundland on delivery in June and August 1941 and a USAAF B-17 on July 14 1943. A Spitfire squadron, No 130, stayed for a

week in August 1942 although this had no connection with West Freugh's secondary duty as an emergency satellite for Ayr.

In April 1945, the pressures of training observers eased sufficiently to allow metal tracking to be laid on aircraft parking areas. There had never been any hardstandings, which made things very awkward in wet weather. There were, however, seven Bellman hangars to protect most of the aircraft from the weather.

The station was transferred to 41 Group Maintenance Command on July 31 1945, 4 OAFU having disbanded on June 21. It now became 103 Sub-Storage Site for 57 MU Wig Bay. The BTU and 1353 AAC Flight with Spitfires and Vengeances remained as lodgers but most of the hangarage was taken up by stored Mosquitoes, reaching a peak of 75 in November 1945.

The BTU moved to Wigtown in June 1947 but returned in May 1948 at the same time as 275 MU, which had been here since the previous November, disbanded. There was also a Mountain Rescue Team in residence.

The BTU was subsequently absorbed into the Royal Aircraft Establishment at West Freugh and many new types passed through on weapon development trials. In recent years there has been a concentration on missile tests for such aircraft as the Buccaneer. Air and ground crews are provided on contract by Marshalls of Cambridge. The airfield is obviously 'hush hush' and it is therefore impossible to get very near.

As a footnote, I should mention that part of the site, then known as Luce Bay, was an airship patrol station from July 15 1915 to 1918 and also an aerodrome for 523, 524 and 529 Flights of 258 Squadron engaged in Coastal Patrol. DH 6s flew anti-submarine searches over the Irish Sea and the Firth of Clyde, the Squadron disbanding on March 15 1919. The station was relinquished by the RAF in May 1920, its buildings being close to East Freugh which is still shown on some maps. There is also a record of its use as a non-rigid airship patrol station in 1918, being a parent to Ramsey, Macrihanish, Larne and Ballyliffin.

Whitefield, Tayside

53/NO170345. 5 miles SW of Coupar Angus off A94

This small airfield, whose longest grass runway was only 1050 yds, opened late in 1939 as a satellite to Perth. No 11 EFTS

flew from the latter and needed an RLG to spread the load.

Available records have neglected Whitefield but it must have been a busy little place as the EFTS had over 100 Tiger Moths on strength during the mid-war period. A few accidents happened at the RLG, mostly bad landings and none causing injury. During July 1943 there were three separate mishaps, one of them during night-flying, which was carried out from here with a gooseneck flarepath. On one occasion Mosquito *HP856* of 8 OTU force-landed with smoke in the cockpit from faulty radio equipment.

The RLG closed on July 9 1945, the demand for pilots obviously having decreased, and soon reverted to farmland. The eight Blister hangars were removed and only a flight office remains today to show where the airfield once was.

Wick, Highland

12/ND360525. 1 mile NW of Wick

RAF Wick was built on land adjoining the pre-war civil aerodrome at Hillhead Farm used by Highland Airways. The traditional grass surface of the time rapidly became a quagmire and there was a rush to lay down tarmac runways. Flying continued from the sea of mud alongside the construction works.

Four massive 'C1' hangars were built, in retrospect a mistake, as the two surviving ones are visible for miles across the bleak and treeless landscape. No wonder Wick was attacked so often, you just couldn't miss it. A decoy with dummy Blenheims

'C2' hangar at Wick.

was set up on a peat bog at Sarclet to the south and attracted many bombs at night.

Station HQ had been formed hastily at Wick on September 15 1939 and enough equipment and stores had been delivered by the end of the month for 803 Squadron's Skuas to disembark here for fighter patrols. No 269 Squadron arrived on October 10, bringing Ansons from Montrose to patrol the northern coastline round to Cape Wrath and as far north as the Faroes. They were reinforced by a Battle Flight of three Hudsons from 224 Squadron at Leuchars, but these returned to base on December 2, as there seemed to be little enemy activity in these waters.

On November 24 1939, 24 Hampdens of 50 and 61 Squadrons were attached to Wick under 18 Group Coastal Command but these, too, saw no action and soon went south again. No 803 Squadron moved to Hatston on February 10 1940, by which time Wick sported three canvas Bessonneaux hangars, hardly suitable to face the rigours of the Caithness winter. Indeed, one of them collapsed one night.

The Spitfires of 41 Squadron made a brief appearance in October 1939 but after Wick became a Sector Station in December 1939 (with its operations room in an elementary school) many fighter units were based for the protection of Scapa Flow.

The 518/40 type tower still unmodified at Wick.

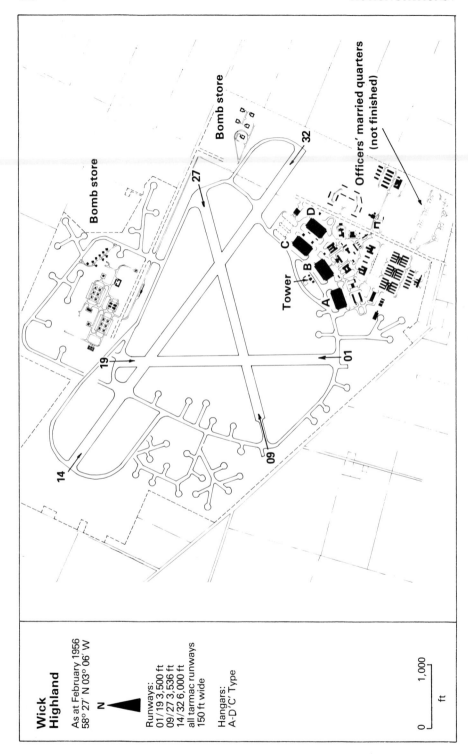

Wick Highland

As at February 1956
58° 27' N 03° 06' W

N

Runways:
01/19 3,500 ft
09/27 3,536 ft
14/32 6,000 ft
all tarmac runways
150 ft wide

Hangars:
A-D 'C' Type

Bomb store

Bomb store

Officers' married quarters (not finished)

Tower

A   B   C   D

19   14   27   32   01   09

0   1,000

ft

No 43 Squadron brought its Hurricanes from Acklington in February 1940 and was soon in action. On April 8, two attacks were met in which three He 111s were shot down and two damaged. One of the latter force-landed on Wick aerodrome with two of the crew dead. No 605 Squadron was here also with Hurricanes from February to May 1940, when it left for Hawkinge. The squadron's first victory was scored during a great air battle over Orkney on April 10, when seven enemy bombers were destroyed. As FAA Skuas and AA defence were involved too, it proved impossible to apportion credit but it was certainly a 'good show' all round.

No 504 Squadron took over Scapa defence towards the end of May 1940 and moved to Wick's new satellite at Castletown on June 21. No 43 Squadron left for Tangmere at the end of May 1940 but not before it was relieved by 3 Squadron which was to re-equip and train new pilots after heavy losses in France. Its Hurricanes moved to Castletown on September 2 and on October 17 the Fighter Sector HQ moved to Kirkwall, leaving Wick solely to Coastal Command.

No 269 Squadron was still here and converted to Hudsons in April 1940 for shipping attacks off Norway, often using Sumburgh as an advanced base. On June 11 1940, for example, Trondheim harbour was attacked and two Hudsons failed to return. The squadron also performed a special duty on June 22 when six Finns piloting Hurricanes were escorted to Stavanger *en route* to the Finnish Air Force.

With the German occupation of Norway, Wick found itself in the front line. The town was bombed on July 1, killing 11 civilians and a soldier, and the airfield's turn came on October 26 1940, when three He 111s first raided the Q-site at Sarclet, then found the real airfield and dropped a stick of bombs across the southern boundary. One Hudson was destroyed, a hangar received superficial damage and three civilians were killed.

No 42 Squadron had Beauforts at Wick from June 1940 but engine unreliability caused the type to be grounded. The Beaufort crews at Wick were incensed that a chance was being missed after the *Scharnhorst* was reported off Norway at reduced speed after a torpedo hit on June 21. Coastal Command was pressed to lift the ban and permission was given to mount an attack. The dive-bombing,

however, was inconclusive and Bf 109s swarmed after them. Three Beauforts did not return to Wick.

More air raids took place in 1941, the torpedo store being narrowly missed on March 17 but a sergeant was killed. On April 26, an enemy raider followed a Hudson in to land and dropped four bombs on the flarepath, killing an airman on duty.

The last attack, however, was the worst in terms of material damage. On June 4 1941 a Ju 88 dropped three bombs on No 3 hangar. One Whitley was burned out and another badly damaged. Three more were pushed clear of the flames at considerable risk, as an unexploded bomb was found under the debris the next morning. Most of the hangar roof was burned away and it was not repaired until long after the war.

In 1940, the Photographic Reconnaissance Unit at Heston maintained flights of Spitfires at St Eval and Wick to cover the Biscay ports and the Norwegian coast, respectively. It was from Wick on May 21 1941, using Sumburgh as a refuelling stop, that one of the most famous of all the early photographic sorties took place; the flight from which Pilot Officer Michael Suckling returned with the electrifying news that the *Bismarck* was on her way out to the Atlantic for the first time. Six days later she was sent to the bottom but tragically Suckling too was lost, flying from St Eval exactly two months after his epic trip.

The first of the new Mosquitoes was allocated to PRU in 1941 and it was decided that they should operate from Wick. They arrived here in October and each aircraft was named after a type of alcoholic drink including *Whisky, Benedictine* and *Vodka*. Before long it was found that Wick's isolation often meant that spare parts could take days to get there from the South and it was difficult to get photos to PR HQ in Buckinghamshire. The Mosquito's greater range made it less necessary to operate from the extreme north of Scotland so by December 1941 the detachment had moved to Leuchars.

No 269 Squadron, which went to Iceland at the end of May 1941, had shared the station with 42 Squadron since the latter arrived in June 1940. No 42's Beauforts were employed on anti-shipping and mine-laying sorties until it moved to Leuchars on March 1 1941. After one action in February a Beaufort landed back at Wick with extensive damage and a dead crew member.

The Whitleys and Ansons of 612 Squadron at Dyce moved in on April 1 1941, staying until December 15 when they left for Reykjavik. In December 1941, 404 Squadron's Blenheims were detached to support the Vaagso Commando raid, claiming one Bf 109 destroyed.

A detachment of 220 Squadron's Hudsons was based here in March/April 1941, followed by the whole squadron until January 9 1942 when it left for Northern Ireland to convert to Fortresses. On October 29 1941, nine aircraft of the squadron made a shipping strike against Alesund, sinking or damaging seven ships and setting fire to harbour installations, a feat which was considered to be the most successful shipping attack by a single squadron up to that time.

More Hudsons, this time from 608 Squadron, flew in from Thornaby in January 1942 and immediately began harrying ships off the Norwegian coast. Again, Sumburgh was used as a refuelling base and the squadron eventually moved there on August 5 1942 to increase its radius of action. No 86 Squadron, equipped with Beauforts, was also here between March and July 1942 for strikes off Norway and anti-submarine patrols were in the hands of 48 Squadron whose Hudsons were here from January to September 1942.

No 489 Squadron's Hampdens moved in from Skitten on September 24 1942 but left for Leuchars the following month. Another short-lived resident was 179 Squadron, which formed on September 1 1942 from a detached flight of 172 Squadron with Wellingtons. Anti-sub sorties were flown until the unit moved to Gibraltar in November.

A detachment of Hampdens from 144 Squadron was based in July 1942, and, moving on to the following year, the whole unit returned to Wick with Beaufighters on October 20. Many *Rover* patrols were flown with a steady drain on aircraft and crews. On January 14 1944, 25 Beaufighters, ten from 404 (which had been at Wick since April 1943) and 15 from 144, attacked shipping in Norwegian waters, three aircraft being lost. In May 1944 both squadrons left for Davidstow Moor in Cornwall to cover the west flank of the Normandy Invasion.

No 1406 Met Flight had been flying Hampdens and Spitfires from Wick since early in 1942 and on August 15 1943 it became the nucleus of 519 Squadron. The unit moved to the satellite at Skitten on December 11 1943 to help relieve the congestion at the parent station. By the time the squadron returned to Wick on November 29 1944, the Hampdens had long been replaced by Hudsons and Venturas. In November 1944, Fortresses were received for longer range flights and after the end of the war the squadron standardised on Halifaxes.

A posthumous Victoria Cross was won by a Wick-based pilot, Flight Lieutenant David E. Hornell, on June 24 1944. His Canso amphibian was one of a detachment of the RCAF's 162 Squadron. Out on a patrol in northern waters they found and depth-charged a U-boat. The submarine was destroyed but not before return fire had set the Canso on fire. The aircraft was ditched but soon sank. After 24 hours either in a dinghy or clinging to it—there was not enough room in the only dinghy left for all the crew—they were rescued, but Hornell and two members of his crew died from the effects of exposure.

No 618 Squadron reached Wick in June 1944, still working-up on Mosquitoes (see Skitten) but now destined for mine-laying in the Pacific. The aircraft were embarked on a carrier for Australia in October but never saw any action.

Wellingtons were at Wick again in August 1944, flown by 407 Squadron on AS patrols. Apart from three U-boats depth-charged in October, there was little excitement and the aircraft moved to Chivenor in November.

A Mountain Rescue Unit was formed in October 25 1944 to provide cover for the far North. November was spent in training and the first call-out came on December 16 to a crashed Barracuda near Berriedale. Three injured survivors were carried down from a 519 Squadron Fortress on the moors near Loch Rangag in February 1945.

Moving on to the end of November 1945, the Mustangs of 316 Squadron arrived from Andrews Field and commenced intensive training known as *Dodgem* Exercises. Simulated raids were made on such targets as Montrose aerodrome, Scapa Flow and Dalcross. Defending forces were made up of other Scottish-based squadrons, including No 91, No 164 and No 303. (The latter was at Wick from January 1946).

By February 1946, the local council was complaining of low and noisy flying over the town but it was not to last much longer as 303 left for Charterhall on March 3, while 316 went to Hethel on March 15.

Thereafter, the airfield reverted to a civil use with regular BEA services to Inverness, Glasgow, Edinburgh, Orkney and Shetland. The routes were never profitable, particularly when Viscounts were introduced and part of the Wick network was taken over by Loganair in 1976 with more suitable aircraft.

Once an action station, now in honourable retirement, Wick was totally devoid of aircraft when we visited it in June 1981. A horse grazed incongruously near the tower and the dilapidated 'C1' hangars, only two remaining of the original four, were full of steel pipes. The one behind the tower was one of those damaged in the air raid. Most of the station offices and technical buildings are still standing neglected but not yet derelict.

Wig Bay (Stranraer), Dumfries and Galloway

82/NX035680. 5 miles N of Stranraer on A718

In the autumn of 1945, the western shores of Loch Ryan resembled the fabled elephants' graveyard. No less than 177 big flying boats were in open storage, most waiting to be cut up for scrap at one of the biggest marine aircraft maintenance bases in Britain.

Before being relegated to an MU, Loch Ryan had seen operational squadrons of Coastal Command, the first, No 240, arriving from Pembroke Dock on July 30 with Stranraers. It moved to Northern Ireland on March 28 1941, following 209 Squadron, which had left two days previously. No 209 had been here since December 9 1940 operating the unsuccessful Lerwick on patrols.

Another squadron, 228, was transferred here from Pembroke Dock on October 9 1941 but moved to Oban on March 10 1942 to extend its radius of action out into the North Atlantic.

The station had a training role beginning in mid-1940 when the Flying Boat Training Squadron moved north from vulnerable Calshot. The unit flew a mixture of Singapores, Londons, Stranraers and Lerwicks. When Catalinas began to be delivered to the RAF, the FBTS was allotted one of the first, *W8406*, and in June 1941, three US Navy Catalina instructors were attached to the unit.

The FBTS was redesignated 4 (C) OTU

Over 150 flying boats, mostly Catalinas, can be discerned in this aerial view of the 57 MU dispersals at Wig Bay in October 1947 (Via J. Huggon).

on March 16 1941 and moved to Invergordon in June of that year. When the OTU was reorganised a detachment returned to Wig Bay on March 11 1942 to concentrate on the initial training of pilots in marine aircraft flying. The operational training of crews was to remain at Invergordon. This plan was subsequently altered and the detachment returned to Wig Bay on November 10 1942.

No 302 FTU now took up residence with effect from December 1 1942 but left for Oban on July 21 1943. No 1 FBSU had been here since March 12 1942 and it is probable that its gradual expansion had forced the other units to leave. The FBSU continued to function under 15 Group Coastal Command side by side with 57 MU which formed here in October 1943, absorbing 11 FBFU which had itself formed on July 15 1943.

The MU's task was the preparation, modification, repair and storage of Sunderlands, Catalinas and the new Martin Mariner which was just entering service. On February 1 1944, 57 MU and 1 FBSU were amalgamated and taken over by 41 Group Maintenance Command.

Loch Ryan was now dotted with moored flying boats, some 50 successfully riding out an overnight gale in April 1944. Two Shetland hangars were built, along with 26 hardstandings at Scar Point to accommodate the ever increasing numbers of aircraft. The Walrus and the Sea Otter had joined the variety of types being handled. Just to the North the Marine Craft Training Unit at RAF Carsewall used time-expired flying boats to practice mooring.

Typical of the work being done was the conversion of Catalina IVs to British standards. All possible aircraft were being beached on the Scar Point dispersals but there was still an average of 30 aircraft moored on the loch.

The Mariner having proved disappointing in RAF service, there were large numbers at Wig Bay awaiting disposal. On November 3 1944 *JX117* was being taxied to a slipway when it burst into flames after an explosion in the auxiliary power unit. The crew jumped into the water and were soon rescued but the Mariner was burned out and sank in 12 ft of water. Today one of its fuel tanks with the Martin Company insignia can still be seen near the shore.

During November 1944, heavy gales hit the Stranraer area, damaging a number of flying boats on their hardstandings. On November 17, a Sunderland was sunk at its moorings and a Catalina was driven ashore.

Poor but rare photo of a captured He 115 in RAF markings at Stranraer (Wig Bay) in July 1942 (Via J. Huggon).

The first direct transatlantic delivery into Wig Bay was made by Catalina *JX603* on December 14 1944. Unfortunately, the sea was very rough and after a safe landing the aircraft was blown ashore and damaged beyond repair. An accompanying Catalina, *JX590*, was slightly damaged and the third was forced down in the sea off Girvan and was later flown on to Loch Ryan.

The unit's holding and output commitment had almost doubled by the end of 1944 with considerable strain on the staff but they managed to keep up with the requirements. The conversion of Sunderland IIIs to V standard almost broke the camel's back but this was achieved as well, the first being test flown on May 18 1945. Around this time, Icelandic Airways Catalinas made a few familiarisation flights into Wig Bay as a possible diversion if the normal terminal at Largs was weather-bound.

West Freugh and Castle Kennedy were taken over in June 1945 as sub storage sites, Mosquitoes being kept here by 57

Sunderland ML817 *tied down on a hardstanding at Wig Bay in September 1951* (H. Quinton).

MU. The MU was also given storage facilities at Killadeas in Northern Ireland on the understanding that this station would close down in the near future.

After the war ended, the unit's work was almost wholly storage on a long-term basis, but a few unusual jobs included the overhaul of Catalinas for the Royal Norwegian Air Force. At the end of June 1945, 157 aircraft of various types were held, comprising the Walrus, Sunderland, Mariner, Coronado and Catalina. No 57 MU finally disbanded in October 1951, maintenance being taken over by Short Brothers under contract. Other work such as the reconditioning of 16 Sunderlands for the Royal New Zealand Air Force was also undertaken. The small RAF element was finally withdrawn on September 11 1957.

To set the record straight on the relationship between RAF Stranraer and RAF Wig Bay, some of the pre-war RAF moorings were just to the north-east of the boat pier, five were laid off to the east and five more in Wig Bay. In north-west gales, flying boats were advised to moor in Wig Bay and subsequently the adjacent shoreline was utilised for the wartime RAF station. RAF Stranraer remained a separate entity until disbanding on February 2 1944, but the two stations were inevitably interlinked.

There is very little to show where the base once stood. The bases of the hangars, two Shetlands and a 'J' Type, remain, with the steel door channels still in place. On the beach I picked up a corroded piece of aircraft alloy, perhaps a fragment of one of the flying boats which sank in a gale.

RAF Wigtown in October 1942 with Bothas and Ansons in large numbers (RAF Museum).

Wigtown, Dumfries and Galloway

83/NX435535. 1 mile off Bladnoch on A714

The airfield site had been chosen in 1938 and was intended provisionally for use by an AACU for target-towing on the Burrow Head ranges and as an Aircraft Storage Unit but this dual role was changed to that of a Bombing and Gunnery School.

When the war began, the landing ground was obstructed to prevent enemy aircraft landing and does not seem to have been used until 1 Air Observer School formed here on August 19 1941 with Bothas. The first aircraft were not ferried in until September 13 and the initial course of 40 British pupils arrived three days later.

There were no runways and the airfield became unusable in October/November 1941 because of flooding. It is believed that two runways were built in 1942, there being insufficient space for the more usual three. No 1 AOS became 1 (Observer) Advanced Flying Unit on February 1 1942, Bothas mainly replacing Ansons in July. It was almost a year later, however, that the Ansons completely ousted the unpopular Blackburn type. On May 28 1942, the maintenance and administration formerly done by Airwork Ltd was handed over to the RAF.

One of the Ansons featured in a drama on the night of November 4/5 1942 when *R9576* on a navigation flight over Northern Ireland ran into thick fog on the return leg. As if this were not enough, there was then a complete electrical failure and the crew was unable to find its base. They decided to return to Northern Ireland and pick up a landmark there but the fog had closed in behind them. Setting course once again for base their dilemma was solved when the lights of a ship were seen. The pilot, Sergeant MacKenzie, circled it

while the wireless operator signalled with a torch. The aircraft was then ditched near the ship, which turned out to be a trawler, and the crew was picked up unharmed and taken to Fleetwood.

The mountains to the north were a constant hazard to the station's aircraft and others from the training fields around the Irish Sea. Wigtown soon found itself with the added responsibility of organising search and rescue parties. This stemmed from the old pre-war responsibility of any flying station for dealing with crashes in its vicinity.

In the words of Air Vice Marshal (Rtd) D.M.T. MacDonald, the former CO of 1 (O)AFU: 'Unfortunately, being a training unit, Wigtown had many men with limited medical categories, which meant that the servicing personnel, all fit men, had to provide the rescue parties. This hindered routine maintenance and since there was no specialised equipment such as jeeps available to carry the injured, the party size was based on 16 men per casualty to allow for reliefs. In addition, some rough feeding facilities had to be provided, with a cook or two, for the men might be out for some time. Medical personnel and a signaller to keep in contact with base were also provided. If the crashed aircraft had a large crew, a lot of work stopped on the station because no manning or establishment allowance was made for rescue purposes.

'At the end of 1943 or the beginning of 1944 we were given a Jeep and a four-wheel-drive ambulance but in practice they were only of limited use because they could only get a shortish distance off the roads. To illustrate the kind of difficulties we were up against, I recall an Anson which flew straight into the side of Cairnsmore of Fleet. The scene of the crash was about four miles from any road and the bodies had to be carried up to the top of Cairnsmore before starting the journey back. Before they got to the road the men were so exhausted—it was by this time almost two in the morning—that I had to give orders to leave the dead under the lee of a wall and send out a fresh party to collect them the following morning.'

These untrained mountaineers performed well and the CO was justly proud of their efforts but a specialised Mountain Rescue Unit, less wasteful of manpower, was obviously necessary. The Medical Officer visited Llandwrog in North Wales in November 1943 to gain an insight into that station's pioneer Mountain Rescue Service (see *Action Stations 3*) and this resulted eventually in a proper organisation being set up at Wigtown.

Twenty-four Typhoons of 174, 175 and 182 Squadrons were attached to the station between September 18 and 22, to take part in a combined exercise involving the landing of seaborne troops in daylight under smoke cover on the west coast of Scotland. Ten Lancasters of 463 Squadron landed at Wigtown on August 27 1944 after operations over Konigsberg. They had only 45 minutes' fuel left and were unable to land elsewhere because of bad weather.

A Battle of Britain display was held in September 1945 but on October 15 all flying training ceased and 1 (O)AFU disbanded on November 12. The airfield was transferred to Maintenance Command as a sub-site of 220 MU Dumfries. The Bombing Trials Unit was also based at Wigtown from June 1947 but moved to West Freugh in May 1948 leaving the station to close on July 15 1948.

The runways gradually decayed, but not so badly that they could not be used, as several light aircraft still fly from here and are kept in lock-up hangars on the south side of the field. The ten Blister hangars around the perimeter were removed long ago and only the concrete floors of the seven Bellmans remain on the main site. Light industry has preserved some of the technical buildings but the majority are roofless.

The watch office still stands and the concrete letters 'JO' are overgrown in front of it. This is curious because the letters were allocated by the Royal Navy as an aircraft fin code when that service was considering taking over Wigtown in 1945/46. The wartime code letters for the station had been GO.

Sadly, by the times these words are read, all Wigtown's buildings may have been bulldozed to provide hardcore for a new harbour project in the nearby town.

Winfield, Borders

74/NT895505. 6 miles W of Berwick upon Tweed on B6461. Unclassified Road follows NW/SE runway

Built on the site of a First World War landing ground known as Horndean, which had been used by 77 Squadron, Winfield remained a satellite to Charterhall for 54 OTU throughout its brief life. It was in fact completed before its parent,

Winfield in 1981 (F. Neal).

but lacked certain important facilities at first, like a fuel installation and a watch office. A small opening-up party was sent over from Charterhull on April 30 1942 and flying began early in May with Blenheims.

From July 1 1942, when the OTU was reorganised, the Advanced Squadron (later known as 'C' Flight) was based at Winfield for AI training. On August 2 1942, 88 and 222 Squadrons with Bostons and Spitfires respectively arrived to take part in an exercise, staying until August 10.

'C' Flight received the first of six Mosquitoes on May 28 1944 for conversion of crews to the type on completion of their course at Winfield. On June 19, two Beaufighters with pupil crews on a training flight from here were diverted to intercept hostile aircraft in the vicinity but failed to make contact

The airfield shared many bomber diversions with its parent station in 1944/45. For example, on June 8, seven Lancasters of 50 Squadron landed here from operations over France when weather closed in at their base.

Winfield closed on May 31 1945 and all personnel moved back to Charterhall. The Royal Navy considered a take-over but it remained unused until re-opened in 1963 by the Border Reivers Flying Club, which has since operated a number of light aircraft from here. Some privately owned aircraft have also been based over the years and free-fall parachuting is currently done.

Winterseugh, Dumfries and Galloway

85/NY165705. 3 miles NW of Annan off B7020

Winterseugh opened as 37 SLG On May 1 1941, although in April a representative from the AMWD had visited regarding its suitability as a single squadron station, unwaware that the land was already earmarked for an SLG. A test landing was made by 18 MU on April 30 and an agreement was reached with the owner for the use of parts of a wood near the landing strip for hiding dispersed aircraft.

By the end of its first month an average of ten aircraft was stored here, a maintenance party being supplied and transported

Watch office at Winterseugh (J. Huggon).

by the parent MU when required. Two Super Robin hangars were being erected and workmen were still busy rolling, levelling and draining the very soft ground. Heavy aircraft could not be flown in yet until the grass runway had been extended.

In November 1941, Winterseugh was deemed unsuitable for Blenheims, Beauforts and Wellingtons after a Wellington sank in to a depth of over 2 ft after landing. Storage was to be restricted to Fairey Battles but in December Winterseugh was closed for the rest of the winter until the surface dried out and improvements could be made. Even so, it was never very successful and was de-requisitioned on April 20 1944, since it was too small for the types of aircraft then in service. It was considered also that retaining it for summer use only for small aircraft was unjustified.

As a footnote, the site was used originally by 10 B&GS as an RLG shortly after the School's move to Dumfries in July 1940. There is a wartime building well away from the MAP type buildings which could once have been a flight office.

Woodhaven, Fife

59/NO408271. 1 mile SW of Newport on Tay, on coast

The movements of German warships in Norwegian coastal waters were a constant anxiety to the British Admiralty. They also wanted information on the merchant shipping which supplied the German garrisons and returned with iron ore. It was imperative, therefore, that we should have some means other than air reconnaissance of watching their activities. The answer was to post observers equipped with radio transmitters on lonely headlands or deep in the fjords. The Norwegians who had this dangerous and difficult task were landed in smooth water close to the shore in Catalinas flown by their countrymen and there was a steady traffic from Scotland bringing agents in and flying them out.

The clandestine flights to Norway were operated in the early years by a captured He 115 seaplane flown from Woodhaven by Lieutenant K. Skavhaugen. The risks proved too great, however, and the operations were abandoned temporarily, the Heinkel later being broken up for scrap on the Tay.

No 1477 Flight, a Norwegian-manned unit, formed on February 17 1943 out of the previous Norwegian Detachment here since February 8 1942. Many long-range patrols were made from the Tay to the North Cape and the ice edge in the Jan Mayen Sea. They were uneventful until April 13 1943, when a U-boat was sighted off Dunnet Head. Three depth charges were dropped as it disappeared and many large bubbles were seen but a sinking was impossible to confirm.

The flight was absorbed into 333 Squadron which formed on May 10 1943 with Mosquitoes at Leuchars and Catalinas at Woodhaven. The main duty was anti-submarine patrol but the special duty operations continued to be flown and it is a pity that for contemporary security reasons the squadron records give few details.

On May 17 1944, Catalina *D* of 333 Squadron attacked a U-boat but was hit by return fire and came back with a dead crew member. Exactly a month later, on June 17, a 333 Squadron Catalina evened the score by sinking a submarine, 40 survivors being seen in the water as the vessel disappeared stern first.

No 333 Squadron went home to Norway in June 1945 and the wide river just upstream of the Tay Bridge is now just an empty expanse where it was once dotted with moored Catalinas.

There was also a Coastal Command squadron, 210, based at Tayport with Singapores and Sunderlands between September 29 1938 and October 8 1939, when it returned to Pembroke Dock. It is also of interest to recall that the Tay was used by the Short Maia/Mercury composite aircraft on October 6 1936 as the starting point for an attempt on the world's absolute distance record. Capetown was the destination but fuel transfer problems forced the Mercury to alight on a river about 500 miles short of her goal. It was, nevertheless, recognised as an international seaplane record for distance. Captain D.C.T. Bennett of later Pathfinder fame and I. Harvey comprised the crew.

Woolsington, Northumberland

88/NZ195715. 6 miles NE of Newcastle upon Tyne on A696

Unlike many other airports in Britain, Newcastle does not owe its present expansion to wartime improvements and runways. It was requisitioned but remained a grass field and was not used very much, although nominally a satellite first to Acklington then to Ouston from April 1 1941. Around this time it acquired three Pickett-Hamilton retractable pillboxes.

Back in 1933, Newcastle Corporation had been looking for a site for an airport but the area was honeycombed with old mine workings and resultant subsidence. The operators of Cramlington, by now well-established, smugly suggested that the city confine its attention to seaplanes! However, a site at Woolsington was found and opened on July 26 1935.

During 1940, 72 Squadron kept detachments at Woolsington for night patrols and on one of these Flying Officer Thompson found a Ju 88 illuminated by searchlights and shot it down, one of the few night victories in a Spitfire.

Later in the year, the aerodrome was strewn with anti-invasion obstacles which caused a Spitfire to overturn on December 3 when the pilot failed to notice them and swerved violently.

On July 26 1940, 83 MU was set up and Woolsington found itself acting as a scrap dump. The unit was tasked with the salvage of crashed aircraft in the counties of Northumberland, Durham, Cumberland and Westmorland and had parties of men under an NCO operating throughout the area.

Much of the Lake District came under their jurisdiction and many an aircraft was removed from the crags and ridges by sheer hard work. As well as being strenuous, salvage work could sometimes be dangerous as one group from 83 MU dis-

covered when they tried to rescue a force-landed Tiger Moth from a sandbank in the Solway Firth. A sudden freak tide almost engulfed their small boat and they were lucky to struggle ashore.

No 281 Squadron moved here from Ouston on June 14 1943 for ASR duties with Ansons and Walruses, leaving for Drem on October 6 1943.

The only other unit to use Woolsington was 62 OTU which employed it as a satellite for their Ansons from Ouston. The dates were from November 22 1943 until August 8 1944.

After the war, when commercial flying restarted, the airport expanded slowly, helped by the establishment of a subsidiary base of Lancashire Aircraft Corporation. Hunting Clan began operations in 1953 with Dakotas and routes included several international ones. Soon after a hard runway was laid in 1954, Viscounts were brought into use on some of the routes. The passenger figures were insufficient, however, and Hunting withdrew from the north-east in 1956.

BKS Air Transport restarted the London route in 1959, eventually becoming North East Airlines until absorbed by British Airways in 1976. A new terminal complex had been built in 1966/67 and today Newcastle boasts one of Britain's most modern provincial airports.

Walrus at Woolsington 1943 with, left to right, Phil Birkett, Ken Dale, Jack Hoult and George Durose (Via F. Neal).

Supplement

Additions, alterations and updates since the first edition

Abbotsinch, Strathclyde

Glasgow Airport is spending some £47 million on increasing the size of its terminal building by 70 per cent. It is hoped to encourage more transatlantic services but inevitably this will be at the expense of Prestwick.

Below Abbotsinch in 1934 (RAF Museum). **Bottom** *Derelict Avengers XB375 and XB378 at Abbotsinch during April 1963 (S.G. Jones).* **Above right** *Sea Venoms, including WW276 and XG700, await the scrapman at Abbotsinch in April 1963 (S.G. Jones).*

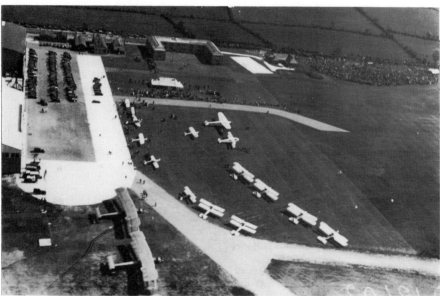

Above Aldergrove *on July 1 1933, the day of the first public air display held at the station. Two of 502 Squadron's Vickers Virginias can be seen, as well as a variety of civil and military types* (Via E.A. Cromie).

Ayr, Strathclyde

Adjacent to the graves of the crew and passengers of Liberator *AM260* in Ayr Cemetery is a small memorial stone inscribed: 'A token of respect to 22 victims of air crash at Whitletts 14th August 1941. Subscribed for by inhabitants of Whitletts. FOR FREEDOM.'

The aircraft crashed attempting to take off in the dark part of the way along the short runway. The tragic error was exacerbated by the customary radio silence imposed on these transatlantic trips. Together with the loss of two more ATFERO Liberators the same month, including 22 deaths on the Isle of Arran, this incident almost put paid to the Atlantic Ferry, such was the blow to the morale of American and Canadian civilian volunteers.

One of the passengers killed in the crash was Arthur B. Purvis, Chairman of the British Purchasing Commission. A British-born industrialist, Purvis had settled in Canada in 1924 and had many allies in the US government. Virtually single-handed, he had persuaded the US administration both to sell to Britain essential munitions of war and raw materials and to deny those raw materials to Germany. His death was a grievous blow, a fact which Churchill emphasises in his memoirs, but by that time he had laid the foundation for future co-operation with America and eventual victory. An unsung hero indeed, and richly deserving of a posthumous knighthood had he retained British citizenship.

Banff, Grampian

Efforts by north-east Scottish aviation enthusiasts to provide a memorial to aircrew of the Banff Strike Wing who lost their lives are approaching fruition. A recent £2,000 donation from the MacRobert Trust has increased the sum so far raised to over £6,000 and it is hoped to have construction work completed in time for an official unveiling during the summer of 1989. It is intended that the memorial will be sited on the A98 Elgin to Banff road and close to the Wing's one-time base.

Brackla, Highland

The function of the Aircrew Allocation Centre was explained in the October 1944 issue of *Tee Em*, the RAF Training Memorandum. 'It had for some while been realised that the system of posting in the RAF was vaguely unsatisfactory. Sergeant Winde, for instance, finishes his tour of aircrew duties and gets shot off somewhere as an instructor, merely because gunnery instructors are urgently needed at that time, and regardless of the fact that few people could make worse instructors than Winde. Flying Officer Fixe, on the other hand, who is of the born instructor type, finishes his tour a month later and gets posted to the Air Ministry, when they happen urgently to

A red-spinnered Mosquito of the Banff Strike Wing (Charles E. Brown, via RAF Museum).

want a navigational type in an office. And so on. Many a round peg thus gets shoved into a square hole.

'In order to obviate this sort of thing, the Aircrew Allocation Centre at Brackla has been brought into being. It is nothing more nor less than the practical realisation of A Good Idea. This Good Idea is that, instead of distributing people into jobs willy-nilly, helter-skelter, and at random, there shall be a central pool where the personal abilities of officers and NCOs of post-operational aircrew (except pilots) can be discovered and recorded with a view to avoiding unsuitable postings. In other words, at Brackla the bundles of round and square pegs are sorted out so that they can be fitted into the appropriate holes without the aid of a sledge-hammer.

'There are sports of every kind from football to fishing, and from clay-pigeon shooting to darts; the food is good and so is the local beer; there are discussion groups, lectures on all sorts of subjects by all sorts of experts; and *above all* NO BULL... No one stays at Brackla longer than about a month.'

Castle Archdale (Lough Erne), Co Fermanagh

The former flying boat base is now a thriving holiday centre with a combined caravan and country park and a purpose-built marina. In one of the restored outbuildings of the original country house, demolished soon after the war, a permanent exhibition was opened in June 1985. Called 'An Extra 100 Miles — Castle Archdale at War', it details the wartime history and is open from spring to autumn.

Iain Henderson has made a special study of Lough Erne's flying boat operations (see *After the Battle* magazine No 53) and one of

his discoveries was that a control tower on stilts was erected on Gay Island in the middle of the lough. The original Flying Control position was on the roof of Archdale House but too far away from the flarepaths to be effective.

Charterhall, Borders

Having read my account of author Richard Hillary's death whilst flying a Blenheim from here, Bernard Beadle writes: 'I do agree with you and Squadron Leader Brandon, it was a very dispersed station. On my arrival, I had a two-and-a-half-mile walk with full kit from Marchmont Station to the "main entrance", ie the SP's hut and guard room. From there it was probably a mile and a half to my billet, a hut on No 5 Site.

'Because there was an abundance of wireless operators on the station, I spent my first few weeks on maintenance, working on "B" Flight dispersal — that little wood at the foot of your picture on page 66. It was a morning and evening walk of two and a half miles each way and lunch time meant not far short of two miles to and from the cookhouse. Can you wonder that almost my first action was to send home for my bicycle!

'I must query your opening paragraph; I wonder from whence came the details in your report on the death of Richard Hillary [His biography *Richard Hillary* by H. Lovat Dickson]. The landmark beacon was towed out every afternoon to one of four sites selected by Operations as appropriate to the runway in use. That night it was at Mount Pleasant (map reference NT 805497) and I was the duty wireless operator and, thus, duty observer on the crew. The other two members were the driver and electrician.

'I remember the occasion very clearly. Hillary's aircraft passed over us very low — low enough to bring one of my colleagues from inside the back of our lorry to see what was happening. Together we watched as it flew on in a roughly north-westerly direction and disappeared over a hill. Moments later there came a red glow in the sky, probably in the Lammermuir Hills beyond Duns.

'I reported to "Ops" at once and I suppose I can claim the somewhat doubtful honour of being the one who notified the station of the death of its notable student. Obviously, I am speaking 45 years after the event but for one reason especially I feel certain that the aircraft did not circle us. Such a manoeuvre was one for which I would have been on the look-out. An aircraft in trouble had to signal the two letters of the night on its downward identification light or

fire the two colours of the night with a Very pistol. On receiving either signal and recognising it as correct, we lit the landing "Tee", which we had previously laid out, and notified "ops" by telephone.

'But, and this is important, we had also to watch for an aircraft circling — it might not be able to correctly signal to us. In this case we notified "Ops" who could authorise us to light up the "Tee" nevertheless. I am certain that Hillary did not circle, but passed straight over our beacon, rather lower than was usual. At that time of year the night is long; it must have been nearly 11 o'clock in the morning before we had towed our beacon back to camp. When I went to SHQ Signals to sign off and to report the event of the night, I learned that the casualty telegrams had already been sent, and of course was told the identity of the pilot.'

The book *Mary and Richard*, published by Andre Deutsch in 1988, casts much light on Hillary's unhappy sojourn at Charterhall. Author Michael Burn observes: 'The name of the aerodrome to which Richard had been posted was Charterhall. It may stand for the deadest of all dead ends, the graveyard of all illusions, desolate, run-down, swept by freezing winds, abstract as a setting for a play by Samuel Beckett... "The forgotten man's last stop" Richard called it in a letter.'

Connel, Strathclyde

During 1940 it was noted that vital areas in western Scotland, including the naval ports at Loch Ewe and Kyle of Lochalsh, and the British Aluminium works at Fort William needed defence against air attack. Several new aerodromes in the Western Isles were suggested as sector stations and Tiree was the eventual choice.

A forward aerodrome was required on the mainland but a survey soon showed that the only possible site was the pre-war civil landing ground at Connel. It was considered barely acceptable because of the bad approaches from the north. Otherwise, the search for a fighter station site on the north-west coast of Scotland between Oban and Cape Wrath drew a blank.

It was, however, observed that land at Crinan and Corran, both in Argyllshire, might be developed as emergency landing grounds for fighters. No action was taken as it turned out, and it was recommended in April 1941 that Beaufighters or Bostons be stationed at Stornoway and Tiree for air defence, rather than short range fighters. Declining Luftwaffe activity made this unnecessary.

Left *The Bombing Teacher building on the old Instructional Site at Dumfries.* **Below left** *The Dome Trainer and Turret Trainer building at Dumfries, the latter clad in corrugated iron rather than the usual brick construction.* **Bottom** *Dumfries tower with Museum aircraft which include a Gannet and an ex-French Air Force Super Sabre.*

Dumfries, Dumfries and Galloway

The various Maintenance Unit sites are all in an excellent state of preservation, as is the control tower which is occupied by the Dumfries and Galloway Air Museum and surrounded by their collection of aircraft. The former Instructional Site still has its original synthetic training buildings. A row of three Bombing Trainers is derelict but some of the wartime fittings have survived, unlike those in most of these gutted buildings elsewhere.

Dunino, Fife

It was observed late in 1938 that Dunino should be nominated as Leuchars' satellite in order to ensure the continuity of North Sea patrols. The report commented: 'If Leuchars is rendered uninhabitable by bombing or useless on account of flooding, as has been the case this year for weeks on end, it will be necessary to move the squadrons imme-

A Firefly down in a potato patch at RNAS Eglinton (Roy Bonser Collection).

diately to a satellite. Dunino is, however, 11 miles away on high exposed ground far from any billeting area. Tentage at this place is likely to produce more casualties from pneumonia than from enemy action.'

Dyce, Grampian

Aberdeen Airport is currently served by British Airways, Air UK, Brymon Airways, Business Air, Dan-Air, Air France, Peregrine and SAS. Charter operators include Air Malta, Aviogenex, Partnair and Aviaco.

East Fortune, Lothian

Airfield Review, the magazine of the Airfield Research Group, reports that long-term planning is currently under discussion to convert part of the existing technical site into a representative Second World War aerodrome. At present, the tower in the centre of the airfield is owned by a local farmer but the locally-based Scottish Museum of Flight hopes to 'exchange' this for a suitable alternative storage building and rebuild the tower on the museum site. The hospital on the northern boundary of the aerodrome is due to close in the near future and the R34 memorial at the entrance will be moved to the technical site.

Eglinton, Londonderry

Derry City Council has recently upgraded Londonderry Airport's facilities to encourage scheduled services. A Manchester to Londonderry service was started by Loganair in March 1989.

Errol, Tayside

It is now known that Errol was planned as a fighter station, hence the 'T1' hangars which would have been adequate for the smaller types of aircraft expected to have operated from here.

On March 3 1943, the first Albemarle for Russia left Errol on a route which took it through the Skaggerak and over Sweden. Two more left on April 27 for Kalyazan but one was reported missing *en route*.

Mr B. Borland, who is involved with the everyday running of a sawmill at Errol, intends to open a museum relating to the airfield's history and has already collected some original relics and photographs. It is said that Preston Watson made the first powered flight from this site six months before the Wright Brothers. Unfortunately, it was not independently recorded and the

A T1 hangar at Errol.

claim remains unofficial. In view of its significance, it is strange that the event is veiled in obscurity.

Eshott, Northumberland

The aerodrome has now reopened for private flying, with three asphalt runways and a grass strip available.

Evanton, Highland

It is now uncertain whether the pillbox on the shore side of the aerodrome was roofed with corrugated iron to camouflage its true purpose or whether it was added after the war. Local people remember a now demolished structure known as the Botha Bridge, which enabled the Air Gunners School Bothas to cross a river to dispersal. In the event of an enemy invasion of northern Scotland, Evanton was designated a fall-back aerodrome for fighters based at Castletown.

Grangemouth, Central

John Walker of the Falkirk Local History Society has made a thorough investigation of this site and found much evidence of its former use. One of the two original hangars still bears the winged tiger's head emblem of Scottish Aviation Ltd and red obstruction lights are still fitted to roofs. Sections of runway, perimeter track and hardstandings can be found, along with two undisturbed dispersal pens. At no point does the BP refinery encroach on to the airfield site; it is all on the other side of the main Bo'ness road.

John writes: 'Scottish Aviation were looking for a site on the east coast of Scotland to form a reserve flying school and they originally intended to operate from the established airfield at Macmerry. For some reason, this site was unacceptable to the Air Ministry

Slingsby Cadet TS333 of 6 Gliding School being launched by winch from Grangemouth circa 1945 (via J. Walker).

KLM DC-3 PH-ASR *which arrived for the opening ceremony at Grangemouth on July 1 1939* (via J. Walker).

[too undulating? — DJS] and an alternative was urgently needed. The Grangemouth site was bought in late 1938 and on February 2 1939 clearance to proceed came from the Ministry. Planning permission was sought from the town council on February 3, was granted on February 6 and work started the following day! This has to be some kind of record.

'Operations did indeed commence on May 1 1939 but the official opening by Lord Trenchard did not take place until Saturday July 1. This was the social event of the year and most of the local dignitaries were invited. The guest list included Albert Plesman of KLM, who arrived in a brand-new DC-3, which caused something of a sensation.'

Greenock, Strathclyde

Mr J.A.S. Watson writes : 'I note with particular interest your description of RAF Greenock, Battery Park, where I served with Coastal Command 1943-44 and your reference to the sinking of Sunderland *DV978* at its moorings. I recall the incident and the wild weather conditions at the time and the valiant but fruitless effo.ts to bring the flying boat ashore.

'It had actually arrived about midday with a leaking float, hence the urgency to get it up the slipway. However, the weather worsened making the task impossible, so the Sunderland was secured to a buoy and sandbag ballast piled on the wing opposite to the leaking float. A watch was kept from the shore using Aldis lamps but eventually and sadly the flying boat heeled over and sank.

'There was more "fun" later when salvage began, the engines being dismantled from the wings and literally winched ashore. Gradually the remainder followed. Another amusing but potentially serious incident befell a Catalina undergoing routine daily inspection at its buoy in Cardwell Bay. Apparently the float motor was switched on by accident and of course the floats began to retract. The flying boat was set to heel over but fortunately there were enough mechanics around to get up on the mainplane and perform a balancing act until the floats were lowered by hand crank!'

Two T2 hangars were erected in 1944 to replace two canvas Bessonneaux which stood just inside the camp entrance.

Kinloss, Grampian

Kinloss is currently the home of three Nimrod squadrons, Nos 120, 201 and 206.

The watch tower at **Kinnell.**

Above *Miles Hawk* G-ACPC *(top) and Hawker Nimrod* K3656, *seen at* **Leuchars'** *Empire Air Day in 1938* (Dr A.A. Duncan).

Below *Short Seamews await disposal at Lossiemouth on June 23 1960, part of a small production batch for the Royal Navy* (S.G. Jones).

Lossiemouth, Grampian

The Jaguar Operational Conversion Unit remains here, along with two Buccaneer squadrons, 12 and 208, and the long-range search and rescue Sea Kings of 'D' Flight, 202 Squadron. Airborne Early Warning capability is provided by 8 Squadron's Shackletons. This important station is guarded by RAF Regiment-manned Rapier surface-to-air missile installations.

It is now known that the airfield incorporates the site of a pre-war Automobile Association landing ground, whose maximum run was 600 yards of grass, compared with today's 3,000-yard runway!

Macrihanish, Strathclyde

The airfield's current role is as a maritime patrol base but it is not normally provided with resident aircraft in peacetime. If necessary it will be used by our NATO allies, as well as the RAF, for detached aircraft. Harking back to an earlier era, a Pickett Hamilton retractable fort is still emplaced on the airfield.

Montrose, Tayside

Ron Day was a member of the RAF Regiment before being accepted for aircrew training in May 1943. For more than two years he was on ground defence duties at Montrose and remembers the pillbox illustrated on page 154. 'To me it is just as if it were yesterday that I was standing sentry on that pillbox instead of no less than 44 years since I last saw it for real. They were so dark and dingy inside and most of them just had a floor of sand or soil and were very dusty in hot weather. There was a field telephone in some around the airfield and one or two had emergency rations of hard biscuits, corned beef and tinned chocolate.

'Some of the pillboxes at Montrose were gun emplacements with 20 mm Hispano cannons on them. We, the Rifle Flight, used four of the pillboxes and the airfield always had an eerie feeling, especially on dark winter nights when you were alone in the darkness on the sand dune side of the airfield.'

The Montrose Museum Society was set up a few years ago to preserve material from the aerodrome's long history and Ron is an honorary member.

Nutt's Corner, Antrim

On June 19 1943, one officer and 22 enlisted men arrived on detachment from the USAAF's 69th Ferrying Squadron at Valley, Anglesey, to handle the onward delivery of transatlantic deliveries. Nutt's Corner was designated on September 29 as Station No 2, European Wing, Air Transport Command, with dispersal space for up to 70 four-engined aircraft or 90 twin-engined, or of course combinations of the two.

Between July 25 1943 and June 30 1944, the terminal handled 1,613 ferry aircraft, comprising 1,042 B-17s, 489 Liberators and 82 miscellaneous which included examples of the C-47, C-53, A-20, B-25 and PBY Canso. The record-breaking month was July 1944 when 372 transatlantic aircraft arrived, consisting of 246 B-17s, 90 B-24s, 12 B-26s and 24 C-47s. When Prestwick was temporarily filled to capacity with transit aircraft, Nutt's Corner became virtually the prime reception centre.

An indication of the domestic problems which this caused at Nutt's Corner was the arrival of 83 aircraft on April 24 1944. There were over 1,000 transient aircrew to feed and, it was recorded, 'Visiting personnel did not care to walk about the widely dispersed base and it was fully two weeks before the permanent personnel were able to straighten out the borrowed bicycle situation!'

The resident USAAF unit was the 1404th AAF Base Unit which disbanded on October 18 1944, except for a handful of men who were administered by Prestwick. In August 1943 the radio telephony code for the airfield was *Mousetrap*. *Coastal Ace*, the biography of Squadron Leader T.M. Bulloch, published by William Kimber in 1987, points out that the curious name of the airfield was derived from a bus stop outside a local farm. This book is recommended as a comprehensive account of anti-submarine operations from Northern Ireland.

Perth, Tayside

In January 1942 it was decided to reconstruct the airfield for use by Bomber, Fighter or Army Co-operation Commands in times of emergency. The plan was shelved, however, perhaps because priority was given in 1942 to use available labour to build airfields in East Anglia for the USAAF.

Peterhead, Grampian

Resident helicopters are housed in an original early-pattern Admiralty 'S' Shed

Above *The Kay Giroplane* G-ACVA, *built in Scotland before the war and seen here at Perth. It is now in the Glasgow Museum of Transport.*

Below *Early-pattern Admiralty 'S' Shed at Peterhead* (B. Warrender).

which dates back to use by the Fleet Air Arm during the mid-war period. Several mushroom pillboxes are still *in situ* around the aerodrome.

Mr F. Rawcliffe points out an error in my account of Peterhead: 'I was posted to Peterhead in July 1941 to form 132 Squadron (*not* 143 Squadron) with Spitfires and, as you rightly state, we were first billeted in the town, most of us in the Masonic Hall in the main street. When we finally moved to the dispersed sites, the conditions were still very spartan and we had to be transported by lorries to and fro!'

Prestwick, Strathclyde

Transatlantic Air Control was formed at Prestwick on August 15 1941, using Powbank Mill until October 20 when the more suitable Redbrae House was taken over. TAC's records contain many examples of interesting aircraft movements through Prestwick. On June 20 1942, King Peter II of Yugoslavia left for the USA via Reykjavik in a Boeing Stratoliner of Transcontinental and Western Air. The first B-26 Marauder to fly the Atlantic arrived from Newfoundland on September 4 1942 and the first C-54 Skymaster to be seen in Europe landed on October 10 1942. On October 21 1942, BOAC Liberator *G-ACGD* left Prestwick for Moscow on the first direct flight from the UK to the Russian capital.

TAC's day-to-day diary shows transatlantic aircraft straying all over Scotland after the ocean crossing and landing at the first available aerodrome. In this way Dyce, now Aberdeen Airport, received its first transatlantic visitor when a B-24 landed direct from Gander on November 11 1944. West Freugh hosted a TWA Stratoliner on August 8 1942 and a B-17 arrived at Evanton on January 13 1944. A B-24 went into Dumfries on February 3 1942 and another landed at Wigtown the same day.

The first Martin Mariner flying boat for

Top *C-54s, C-47 and B-17 seen from the control tower at Prestwick in 1944* (IWM EA18301).
Above *C-118A Liftmaster 53-3261 at Prestwick in 1964*. Below *Grumman Albatross 51-5287 of the resident 67th Air Rescue Squadron at Prestwick during July 1963* (S.G. Jones).

the RAF arrived at Largs on August 19 1943. Most of the transatlantic flying boat movements involved Catalinas but on September 14/15 1941 a US Navy Boeing XPB2Y made an experimental trip from Argentia in Newfoundland to Stranraer, returning on April 28/29.

As relations between the USA and Great Britain grew closer during the spring of 1941, surface transport became too slow and hazardous to cope with the volume of diplomatic mail and government officials. It was vitally important that they could move back and forth with the speed demanded by the course of events. The US Government set up a pioneer overseas transport service using modified Liberators which linked Washington DC with Scotland via Montreal and Gander. The first aircraft left Washington on July 1 1941 using RAF Ayr as the terminal but flights later switched to Prestwick when runways were constructed.

The British named the route 'The Arnold Line' as a tribute to General H.H. Arnold, Chief of the Army Air Forces. Operations were suspended for the winter but resumed in 1942, the Liberators being replaced by the purpose-built C-54 Skymasters operated by the North Atlantic Wing of Air Transport Command. They were flown by American civilian airline crews under contract to the US Government.

At Prestwick the priority passengers and cargo were flown to Hendon or Bovingdon to the north-west of London by C-47. This soon became a regular shuttle service administered by North Atlantic Wing. It was later expanded to serve the other Atlantic terminals at St Mawgan, Valley and Nutt's Corner. In March 1944 a typical C-47 shuttle left St Mawgan at 1000 hrs to arrive at London at 1130 hrs and connect with the Prestwick-bound flight. At 1430 hrs it left London to return to St Mawgan with onward passengers for the 1230 departure from Prestwick.

Prestwick's future remains uncertain in the face of competition from Glasgow Airport. It is currently served by Air Canada, Wardair and Northwest Airlines but the demise of the locally-based Highland Express and its transatlantic services was a severe blow. In 1988 the British Aerospace Flying College began operations from here, a short stretch of the 03/21 subsidiary runway being reopened on December 1 to provide more flexibility if cross-winds affected the main runway. The College also investigated the possibility of using the former RAF Turnberry as a relief landing ground but in the event chose Cumbernauld in Fife,

a purely postwar site whose facilities have been upgraded recently.

During the College's opening ceremony, it was observed: 'We have come full circle. On February 17 1936 the then Duke of Hamilton and Group Captain McIntyre opened Prestwick with the first course of student pilots at the Scottish College of Aviation. Over the next five years more than 1,300 pilots were trained for the RAF. British Aerospace is a direct descendent through Scottish Aviation of the company which trained them.'

All cadets spend 16 months at Prestwick on a full-time residential course designed to prepare young men and women with no previous flying experience for the initial job of second pilot on a modern jet airliner. Two hundred hours of flying instruction is provided on Warrior, Bravo and Seneca aircraft, along with intensive classroom work and simulator training. Graduates will be able to go straight to conversion courses on aircraft such as the Boeing 737 and will be fully qualified to be first officer on a passenger-carrying aircraft within two years of starting at Prestwick.

Renfrew, Strathclyde

Road names on the former airport site reflect the airliners which once operated through here. Examples include Britannia Way, Viscount Way and Vanguard Way.

Skeabrae, Orkney

In May 1938 the still unbuilt aerodrome was selected provisionally as a satellite for Wick.

Stornoway, Western Isles

Some new information has come to light on the airfield's use by the USAAF as an Atlantic Ferry staging post. It was designated Station No 5, European Wing, Air Transport Command and administered by the 1405th Army Air Force Base Unit. The principal transit aircraft were short-range types such as the A-20 Havoc which often stopped for fuel if headwinds were encountered on the way from Iceland to Prestwick. A radio range was installed to give navigational assistance to aircraft overflying to Prestwick.

At the beginning of May 1944, B-25 Mitchell 'weather ships' resumed the regular flights which had begun in the summer of 1943 and were suspended during the winter months. The aircraft were detached from the 30th Weather Reconnaissance Squadron, whose HQ was at Presque Isle, Maine. The Stornoway Weather Flight was part of the three-link chain across the North Atlantic: Goose Bay to Bluie West One in Greenland was code-named *Redbird*, BW1 to Meeks Field in Iceland was *Bluebird*, and Meeks Field to Stornoway *Blackbird*.

A diversionary attack on Iceland was considered a possibility in response to the planned Invasion of Europe, so the island's meagre fighter force was reinforced by 11 Thunderbolts which routed *via* Stornoway from the Air Depot at Burtonwood on May 6 1944. On June 24 1944, five A-20s landed but an expected Marauder strayed as far as Lossiemouth instead. Four other aircraft of unspecified type landed at Skitten in northeast Scotland, two of them overshooting. On June 12 a PBY-5A Canso amphibian staged through, followed two days later by four AT-23s, the training version of the B-26 Marauder.

By the summer of 1944, the few diversions could be handled by the existing RAF personnel so the 1405th BU was disbanded on October 18. The 1403rd BU at Prestwick became the parent unit for the small USAAF detachment which operated the radio navigation aids at Stornoway.

Over £40 million has been spent recently in improving Stornoway's facilities as a forward base for RAF and other NATO aircraft responsible for intercepting hostile aircraft in the UK-Faroes Gap. Work is also proceeding on up-grading the nearby radio communications station.

Sydenham, Co Down

Belfast's first air raid warning of the war was allegedly caused by a gentleman of my acquaintance who was gunner in a Hawker Demon from Sydenham which performed a loop over the city on September 3 1939. Unfortunately, a drum of ammunition fell out of the turret and landed in the market place!

Long before the airfield existed, a Handley Page 0/400 made a successful forced-landing on Harland and Wolff's wharf, which was only about 400 yards long and only slightly wider than the aircraft's wingspan. It was later flown out with only the pilot on board. The 0/400 belonged to the School of Aerial Navigation and Bomb Dropping at Andover and was engaged in a long-range navigation flight, landing at various points around the British Isles during April 1919. The crew were unable to locate Aldergrove in bad weather and with petrol

running low were obliged to land.

This story and many others can be found in Karl Hayes' book *A History of the RAF and US Naval Air Service in Ireland 1913-1923*, published by Irish Air Letter in 1988. Anyone interested in the history of the Irish airfields used by the RAF and the US Navy flying boat bases will find it indispensible.

For marketing purposes, the airport is now known as Belfast City to underline its favourable position compared with its bigger rival at Aldergrove. It is served by Jersey European, Loganair, Manx Airlines and Capital Airlines.

Tain, Highland

Euan C. Barbour investigated the Tain operations block and found a poignant notice which I missed on my 1981 visit. Painted over the entrance to the operations room, it reminds departing aircrew: 'Have you emptied your pockets?' In the near future the airfield site is likely to suffer further deterioration when some exploratory mineral drilling takes place.

Tiree, Strathclyde

Tiree was designated as a diversion airfield for wartime transatlantic aircraft, although Prestwick's weather record was so good that it was rarely used as such. One visitor was a rare US Navy PV-1 Ventura on September 11 1943 from Iceland and several C-54s landed on various occasions.

On April 1 1986, Tiree was one of the eight Scottish airports taken over by Highlands and Islands Airports Ltd, a wholly-owned subsidiary of the Civil Aviation Authority. The others were Inverness, Benbecula, Islay, Kirkwall, Stornoway, Sumburgh and Wick. The operation of these airports had previously been put out to tender but not surprisingly there were no takers. Few, if any, of the sites can ever hope to achieve commercial viability, but the Government recognises that they meet an important social need serving remote communities.

Turnhouse, Lothian

By November 1939, Turnhouse had two 800 by 50 yard concrete runways and was thus one of the first in the RAF to be so equipped. It is currently served by British Airways, British Midland, Air UK, Peregrine, Aer Lingus, Manx Airlines and Air France. In-

A Beech Expeditor of the Dutch Navy at Turnhouse in 1968.

clusive tour flights are operated by a variety of companies including Spantax, Cyprus Airways, Aviogenex, Britannia Airways and Dan-Air.

Twatt, Orkney

The old watch tower has been converted into a museum depicting the history of the aerodrome.

New construction at Twatt in 1945 (via M.J. Burrow).

Whitley Bay, Tyne and Wear

The Mad Major, the autobiography of Major Christopher Draper DSC, relates the haphazard way in which many of the early aerodrome sites were selected. 'Early in 1915, the Admiralty ordered me to find a more suitable field or fields on which to build a new Air Station. I was completely staggered at this, for there was nobody to whom I could go for help or advice on how to set about such a big undertaking, and I hadn't a clue. However, I soon chose a field just north of Whitley Bay.

'It was fairly easy to estimate the numbers

of hangars and huts that would be required and I placed orders for these with local contractors. All the furnishings, fittings and other equipment were also obtained locally, and must have cost thousands of pounds, but it was not until many years later that I found out that each of those local contractors had expected me to ask for a "rake-off". Such an idea never occurred to me, even after one of them, without a word to me, sent a very large and expensive-looking dinner service to my mother at Bebington. Right up to her death she thought I had bought it.'

Wigtown, Dumfries and Galloway

During 1988 the airfield was formally re-opened for flying by the Baldoon Flying Group. A 446 by 18 metre section of the wartime north-east/south-west runway is available for day use only and the site is known as Wigtown/Baldoon.

Index of units referred to in the text

Hinds of 83 Squadron lined up in front of the 'C' Type hangar at Turnhouse (A.K. Cook, via Chaz Bowyer).